Paul and the Apocalyptic Imagination

Paul and the Apocalyptic Imagination

Ben C. Blackwell, John K. Goodrich, and
Jason Maston, editors

Fortress Press
Minneapolis

PAUL AND THE APOCALYPTIC IMAGINATION

Cover design: Alisha Lofgren

Library of Congress Cataloging-in-Publication Data
Print ISBN: 978-1-4514-8208-9
eBook ISBN: 978-1-5064-0909-2

The paper used in this publication meets the minimum requirements of American
National Standard for Information Sciences — Permanence of Paper for Printed
Library Materials, ANSI Z329.48-1984.

Manufactured in the U.S.A.

This book was produced using Pressbooks.com, and PDF rendering was done by
PrinceXML.

Contents

Contributors

John M. G. Barclay (PhD, University of Cambridge) is Lightfoot Professor of Divinity at the University of Durham.

Ben C. Blackwell (PhD, University of Durham) is Assistant Professor of Christianity at Houston Baptist University.

Martinus C. de Boer (PhD, Union Theological Seminary) is Professor of New Testament at Vrije Universiteit Amsterdam.

Douglas A. Campbell (PhD, University of Toronto) is Professor of New Testament at Duke Divinity School.

J. P. Davies (PhD, University of St. Andrews) is Tutor of New Testament at Trinity College, University of Bristol.

Joseph R. Dodson (PhD, University of Aberdeen) is Assistant Professor of Biblical Studies at Ouachita Baptist University.

Beverly Roberts Gaventa (PhD, Union Theological Seminary) is Distinguished Professor of New Testament Interpretation at Baylor University.

John K. Goodrich (PhD, University of Durham) is Assistant Professor of Bible at Moody Bible Institute.

Michael J. Gorman (PhD, Princeton Theological Seminary) is Raymond E. Brown Chair in Biblical Studies and Theology at St. Mary's Seminary and University.

Edith M. Humphrey (PhD, McGill University) is William F. Orr Professor of New Testament at Pittsburgh Theological Seminary.

Jonathan A. Linebaugh (PhD, University of Durham) is Lecturer in New Testament at the University of Cambridge.

Jason Maston (PhD, University of Durham) is Assistant Professor of Theology and Chair of the Department of Theology at Houston Baptist University.

David A. Shaw (PhD candidate, University of Cambridge) is Tutor in New Testament and Greek at Oak Hill College.

Loren T. Stuckenbruck (PhD, Princeton Theological Seminary) is Professor of New Testament at Ludwig-Maximilians-Universität München.

N. T. Wright (DPhil, University of Oxford) is Professor of New Testament and Early Christianity at the University of St. Andrews.

Philip G. Ziegler (ThD, University of Toronto) is Senior Lecturer in Systematic Theology at the University of Aberdeen.

Preface

The debate about Paul and apocalyptic has experienced significant growth spurts in recent scholarship. One needs only to glance through the major Pauline theologies that have appeared in the past couple of decades to observe that so-called apocalyptic readings are not only in vogue, but that wrestling with the questions and themes raised by such readings (e.g., cosmology, eschatology, epistemology, agency) has become mandatory for any responsible treatment of Paul's worldview. It is equally apparent, however, that not all apocalyptic readings have adequately conversed with one another. This volume is an attempt to facilitate such a discussion between the major perspectives on Paul and apocalyptic, as well as to plot ways forward. The volume's contributors represent the two primary approaches on Paul's apocalyptic imagination, and our hope as editors is that the conversation will advance precisely because these different viewpoints have been placed alongside of and in conversation with one another.

Several of the chapters in this book were presented during a special session of the same name at the 2014 Society of Biblical Literature Annual Meeting in San Diego. We thank the authors for their contributions both to that event and to this volume. We really could not have asked for a better team—their enthusiasm for the project was evident from the start, and we are grateful to each contributor for carving out time in their busy schedule to participate in this stimulating dialogue. We especially wish to thank John Barclay, who provided invaluable guidance at the initial planning stages. Thanks are also due to Neil Elliott and the Fortress Press team for accepting the volume and seeing it through to publication. We are indebted as well to Joshua Bremerman for compiling the indexes. As always, we are enormously grateful to our respective families and academic institutions—without their unending support, this book would not have been possible.

We wish also to acknowledge our debt to two important scholars who, though not directly involved in the book, have shaped many of the ideas that appear between its pages. First, we wish to recognize John J. Collins, whose work on Jewish apocalyptic literature has been hugely formative for the framework of many who engage in apocalyptic readings of the NT in general—and of Paul, in particular. Astute readers will detect in the title of this book an allusion to Collins's seminal volume *The Apocalyptic Imagination* (Crossroads, 1987; 2nd ed., Eerdmans, 1998). Although he himself is not a Pauline scholar, Collins's impact on the current debate about Paul cannot be exaggerated, and our choice of title is a reflection of the widespread influence of his scholarship.

Finally, we (the editors on behalf of all the contributors) wish to acknowledge and give thanks to Richard B. Hays for his many significant publications on Paul (apocalyptic and otherwise) throughout his illustrious career. Hays's work has already influenced and inspired an entire generation of scholars, including all who have contributed to this particular project. Many of the important advances that have occurred in modern Pauline research would not have been possible without the penetrating and measured reflections of this distinguished scholar. It is, therefore, to him that we warmly dedicate this volume.

B. C. Blackwell, J. K. Goodrich, and J. Maston
Fall 2015

PART I

1

Paul and the Apocalyptic Imagination

An Introduction

Ben C. Blackwell, John K. Goodrich, and Jason Maston

Problematizing Apocalyptic in Pauline Scholarship

Over the course of the last century, the place of apocalyptic has grown increasingly prominent in Pauline studies. Following from Käsemann's now famous dictum that "apocalyptic was the mother of all Christian theology,"[1] it is now almost universally affirmed that Paul had an apocalyptic worldview. As Barry Matlock acknowledged (in fact, protested) some years ago, "'Apocalyptic' interpretation of Paul is, if not a consensus, then certainly a commonplace."[2] Beyond this basic affirmation, however, there is little consensus regarding what the label

---

1. Ernst Käsemann, "The Beginnings of Christian Theology," in *New Testament Questions of Today*, trans. W. J. Montague (Philadelphia: Fortress Press, 1969), 82–107, at 102.
2. R. Barry Matlock, *Unveiling the Apocalyptic Paul: Paul's Interpreters and the Rhetoric of Criticism*, JSNTSup 127 (Sheffield: Sheffield Academic, 1996), 11.

"apocalyptic" actually suggests about Paul's theological perspective. Indeed, lying conspicuously behind the employment of common language are many different definitions, and even competing interpretations of Paul's letters.[3] As N. T. Wright remarks, "this term has proved so slippery and many-sided in scholarly discourse that one is often tempted to declare a moratorium on it altogether."[4]

Since the term is unlikely to disappear from the scholarly vocabulary in the immediate future, what is needed now is a forum for clarifying the nature of apocalyptic language as it is currently being used in relation to Paul. Although a few past publications have sought to justify, clarify, or even discredit the application of "apocalyptic" in Pauline studies,[5] one problem in the rather recent surge of apocalyptic proposals is that Pauline theologians have often talked past one another. Instead of engaging in meaningful dialogue about the significance of apocalyptic language with the intent of moving toward unified employment, Pauline scholars of various stripes have simply recycled the specialized terminology of their respective theological predecessors, often leaving readers to themselves not only to decode such language, but also to differentiate between its parallel yet dissimilar usages.

In the light of the recent swell of studies on the so-called apocalyptic Paul, as well as the ambiguity that continues to accompany the "apocalyptic" label, this collection of essays aims to give voice to multiple perspectives and to place these alternative viewpoints side by side, so readers can see the similarities and differences firsthand. Moreover, we seek in this volume to further the discussion through additional exploration into the various contexts of apocalyptic discourse as well as through focused study on themes considered to be central to Paul's apocalyptic imagination.

Before progressing, however, to chapters that expound and explore

---

3. Ibid., 250: "No doubt everyone who needs the term has an understanding quite suited to his or her purpose."

4. N. T. Wright, *Paul: In Fresh Perspective* (Minneapolis: Fortress Press, 2005), 41.

5. See, e.g., the many contributions of Martinus de Boer (chapter 3, n. 1). See also Matlock, *Unveiling the Apocalyptic Paul*.

the various aspects of this debate, we seek in this introductory chapter to orient the reader to some of the issues involved by presenting a heuristic taxonomy of what we see as two current perspectives on apocalyptic in Paul, as well as some of the historical factors that have led to these paradigms. After sketching the history and key features of these groups, we summarize key questions in the debate and introduce the chapters in this volume.

Perspectives and Paradigms

Many rightly note that "apocalyptic" is a scholarly construct and a shorthand description of a concatenation of particular themes. It is the differing combinations of those themes, together with the nuances of their arrangement, that has led to the multiplicity of perspectives on the apocalyptic nature of Paul's worldview. But while apocalyptic touches upon a host of theological categories, it is important to pay special attention to three main axes, emphasized to varying degrees by recent contributors to the apocalyptic debate.

The first two are the space–time axes, highlighted in John J. Collins's important definition of "apocalypse." According to Collins, "'Apocalypse' is a genre of revelatory literature with a narrative framework, in which a revelation is mediated by an otherworldly being to a human recipient, disclosing a transcendent reality which is both *temporal*, insofar as it envisages eschatological salvation, and *spatial* insofar as it involves another, supernatural world."[6] Although some scholars incorporate additional aspects of Collins's definition into their study of Paul's apocalyptic theology, all viewpoints stress both *eschatology*—that is, Paul's two ages paradigm (temporal/horizontal axis)—and *revelation*—that is, the intersection of heavenly and earthly realms by way of God's redemptive activity and Paul's mystical experiences (spatial/vertical axis). Both these axes feature prominently within constructions of Paul's theology. However, the way they are understood shifts between the paradigms we note below.

---

6. John J. Collins, "Introduction: Towards the Morphology of a Genre," *Semeia* 14 (1979): 1–20, at 9 (emphasis added).

Beyond these two axes, scholars are also concerned with how God's revelatory activity affects Paul's *epistemology*. Apocalyptic, according to any account, involves cognition and enables a seer to understand previously hidden realities. But how has God's eschatological revelatory activity affected Paul's deep logic, causing him to view history differently, especially the human plight and the divine solution introduced through Christ and the Spirit? Does Paul view history *prospectively*, that is, does he understand God's redemptive work as the fulfillment of covenant promises made to Israel long ago? Or, does Paul view history *retrospectively*, that is, has God's revelation re-programmed the apostle's thinking such that he interprets the human plight in a radically new way, indeed as one disconnected from Israel's plight and promises and unanticipated in the Jewish Scriptures?

As in other debates, these themes are foregrounded or backgrounded in various ways by scholars as they expound their particular formation of ideas. While they do not always present simple binary options on this topic, scholars tend to adopt one of two general approaches as they describe how Paul's worldview is apocalyptic.[7] We refer to these approaches as *Eschatological Invasion* and *Unveiled Fulfillment*. For most readers, the first perspective will probably be the most familiar, since it is the one perhaps most often identified as "apocalyptic" in recent Pauline studies. However, the second paradigm also justifiably utilizes this terminology, yet in different ways, and therein lies the debate.

By offering this heuristic binary, we hope to clarify the basis for the distinctive approaches. The taxonomy does not imply that these are mutually exclusive or fixed categories, but the groupings are meant to help identify similar perspectives on Paul and his contemporaries. Also, the taxonomy is not comprehensive. Others, such as Troels Engberg-Pedersen, describe Paul as apocalyptic, but their various approaches fall outside of our primary discussion.[8] Several previous studies have ably detailed the social, intellectual, and conceptual

---

7. Cf. Edwin Chr. van Driel "Climax of the Covenant vs Apocalyptic Invasion: A Theological Analysis of a Contemporary Debate in Pauline Exegesis," *IJST* 17, no. 1 (2015): 6–25.

8. Troels Engberg-Pedersen, *Cosmology and Self in the Apostle Paul: The Material Spirit* (Oxford: Oxford

history of scholarship regarding apocalyptic within the field of NT studies, so we will not rehearse all those details here.[9] Rather, we will briefly note influential figures and explain how the two paradigms relate to our three key axes (*spatial*, *temporal*, and *epistemological*).

Eschatological Invasion

Although eschatology came on the stage strongly in the late nineteenth and early twentieth century with Johannes Weiss and Albert Schweitzer, the wider acceptance of Paul as an apocalyptic thinker is a fruit of Karl Barth's separate but parallel work. As the popularity of Barth's view of divine revelation breaking into human history through Christ began to take hold in wider theological circles, it became easier to see this "apocalyptic" perspective in Paul's letters as well.[10] While prominent NT scholars, such as Rudolf Bultmann, were influenced by Barth, it was Bultmann's student Ernst Käsemann who popularized this perspective. Bultmann's emphasis on existentialism (and therefore, anthropology) separated his reading from Käsemann's "apocalyptic" perspective in NT studies, which resisted Bultmann's demythologizing project and stressed the cosmological transformation wrought by God in Christ.[11] Käsemann primarily grounded his understanding of apocalyptic on God's act in Christ to establish his Lordship over the world and over the evil powers controlling it. The culmination of God's apocalyptic activity would arrive at Christ's imminent return as the kingdom of God was universalized and Christ's Lordship came to encompass the entire cosmos.[12]

University Press, 2011). However, Joseph Dodson's essay in this volume (chapter 8) does address this topic.

9. Some of the essays in this volume provide abridged discussions: Shaw (chapter 2), Wright (chapter 6), and Ziegler (chapter 10). For additional surveys, see esp. Richard E. Sturm, "Defining the Word 'Apocalyptic': A Problem for Biblical Criticism," in *Apocalyptic and the New Testament: Essays in Honor of J. Louis Martyn*, eds. J. Marcus and M. L. Soards (Sheffield: Sheffield Academic, 1989), 17–48; David Congdon, "Eschatologizing Apocalyptic: An Assessment of the Conversation on Pauline Apocalyptic," in *Apocalyptic and the Future of Theology: With and Beyond J. Louis Martyn*, eds. J. B. Davis and D. Harink (Eugene: Cascade, 2012), 118–36.

10. For the influence of Barth on the topic of Paul and apocalyptic, see Philip Zieglier's essay in chapter 10; and Douglas Harink, *Paul among the Postliberals: Pauline Theology Beyond Christendom and Modernity* (Grand Rapids: Brazos, 2003).

11. See Congdon, "Eschatologizing Apocalyptic," 119–27.

In the Anglo-American context, the influence of Käsemann's reading was mediated through (and modified by) J. Christiaan Beker and J. Louis Martyn.[13] Following Käsemann, Beker maintained a focus on the parousia as the key apocalyptic event, though Beker offered a threefold definition of apocalyptic: "(1) historical dualism; (2) universal cosmic expectation; and (3) the imminent end of the world."[14] Martyn, on the contrary, famously shifted the focus of apocalyptic from the second advent of Christ to the first, and particularly the cross, as the apocalyptic fulcrum for Paul's theology. Yet, in continuity with Käsemann (and Barth), the Christ-event serves as God's in-breaking to restore the world.[15]

Martinus de Boer, one of Martyn's students, has done as much as anybody to establish a *religionsgeschichtlich* foundation for understanding Paul as an apocalyptic theologian.[16] Having outlined two "tracks" of apocalyptic eschatology operative within early Judaism (cosmological-apocalyptic eschatology vs. forensic-apocalyptic eschatology), de Boer offers these as heuristic models with which to compare Paul's own view of apocalyptic eschatology. Paul's gospel, de Boer argues, consists mainly of the cosmological type of apocalyptic eschatology; in fact, the forensic brand is easily attributed to Paul's conversation partners and/or opponents.[17] A similar reading is attributable to Douglas Campbell, whose work seeks to demonstrate

---

12. David V. Way, *The Lordship of Christ: Ernst Käsemann's Interpretation of Paul's Theology*, Oxford Theological Monographs (Oxford: Clarendon, 1991), 119–76 (esp. 129).

13. For a longer (but still brief) survey, see N. T. Wright, "Paul in Current Anglophone Scholarship," *ExpT* 123, no. 8 (2012): 367–81, at 372–74. Other Pauline scholars influenced by Käsemann and Martyn who are not mentioned elsewhere in this section include Leander Keck, Beverly Gaventa, Alexandra Brown, and John Barclay.

14. J. Christiaan Beker, *Paul the Apostle: The Triumph of God in Life and Thought* (Philadelphia: Fortress Press, 1980), 136. Beker expanded this to a fourfold definition in his *Paul's Apocalyptic Gospel: The Coming Triumph of God* (Philadelphia: Fortress Press, 1982), 29–53: (a) God's self-vindication through faithfulness to his promises; (b) God's universal reign and redemption of the world; (c) the dualistic structures of time and the world; and (d) the imminent arrival of God's kingdom.

15. Martyn's *Galatians: A New Translation with Introduction and Commentary*, AB 33a (New York: Doubleday, 1997) is his defining work, and his four essays about "Apocalyptic Rectification" in *Theological Issues in the Letters of Paul* (Nashville: Abingdon, 1997), 85–156, summarize the heart of his argument.

16. See esp. de Boer's extensive bibliography in chapter 3 of this volume.

17. Martinus C. de Boer, *Galatians: A Commentary*, NTL (Louisville: Westminster John Knox, 2011), 31–35 (cf. 194). De Boer's scheme is crucial also for Martyn's view of Paul and the teachers in Galatia (Martyn, *Galatians*, 97–98n51).

that Paul's gospel consists exclusively of a liberative model of salvation, whereby justification is a non-contractual/unconditional declaration of freedom upon those who are in Christ.[18] Campbell is explicit about his indebtedness to Barth and Martyn, and he follows both quite closely in the second Eschatological Invasion programmatic essay of this volume as he extends a Barthian reading of Paul's "apocalyptic epistemology" (chapter 4).

With this historical overview in mind, we turn now to our three axes for analyzing this scholarly paradigm—the *spatial*, *temporal*, and *epistemological* axes. Our title "Eschatological Invasion" attempts to capture the spatial and temporal nature of God's work in Christ: "eschatological" describes the temporal shift marked out as the two ages, and "invasion" emphasizes the spatial activity of God in Christ (and the Spirit). Regarding the epistemological axis, this paradigm has a decidedly retrospective point of view, which is also conveyed by "invasion," denying, as it does, the notion of a straightforward progression.

Spatial Axis. With regard to the intersection of heaven and earth, those in the Eschatological Invasion group regularly frame the apocalyptic setting as a cosmological battle between evil powers that have usurped God's authority. God's invasive action in Christ (and the Spirit) to establish his control is the center of God's *revelation* (ἀποκάλυψις/ἀποκαλύπτω = "coming on the world scene"; cf. Gal. 3:23).[19] This christological act of God is often framed as unilateral, in the sense that God's agency is set against impotent humans under the subjection of these evil powers. Humans, thus, are part of the disputed territory of the cosmos, and, until Christ liberates them, they remain under the control of evil powers—Sin, Death, Flesh, and (sometimes) Law. The stress is most often on these personified, ontological powers, but at times, demonic beings—"rulers and authorities"—come into view. Ultimately, God transcends the heaven–earth duality through Christ and the Spirit and re-establishes his control of the entire cosmos.

18. Douglas A. Campbell, *The Deliverance of God: An Apocalyptic Rereading of Justification in Paul* (Grand Rapids: Eerdmans, 2009). See also his discussion in this volume in chapter 4.
19. De Boer, *Galatians*, 79–82.

Temporal Axis. While there has been a shift in the Eschatological Invasion group from a focus on Christ's second advent (Käsemann, Beker) to his first (Martyn, de Boer, Campbell), the Christ-event is seen as determinative for Paul's approach to history. That is, the advent of Christ marks the hinge between two ages, as God's action creates a new reality. In particular, the old age is marked by the control of Death and the Flesh, whereas the new age is marked by life and the Spirit, even as believers experience suffering in their participation in the death of the crucified messiah. As Käsemann explained:

> [T]he apostle does not understand history as a continuous evolutionary process but as the contrast of the two realms of Adam and Christ. Pauline theology unfolds this contrast extensively as the struggle between death and life, sin and salvation, law and gospel. The basis is the apocalyptic scheme of the two successive aeons which is transferred to the present. Apparently Paul viewed his own time as the hour of the Messiah's birth-pangs, in which the new creation emerges from the old world through the Christian proclamation. Spirits, powers and dominions part eschatologically at the crossroads of the gospel. We thus arrive at the dialectic of "once" and "now," which is absorbed into anthropology in the form of "already saved" and "still tempted." In the antithesis of spirit and flesh this dialectic determines the cosmos until the parousia of Christ.[20]

Though some others in this group would differ from Käsemann on where the fulcrum lies—the first, instead of the second advent—he captures the eschatological reserve that characterizes this perspective, even while they emphasize the radical newness inaugurated through Christ.

Epistemological Axis. According to the Eschatological Invasion model, Christ—as the true *revelation* (ἀποκάλυψις) of God—opens up new epistemic possibilities about everything: the world, the human plight, Israel, the law, and so on. Paul's new understanding extends especially to his view of history, which is fundamentally *retrospective*. That is, Paul's narrative logic develops in reverse: having experienced Christ as the divine *solution*, Paul is now able to look *back* and understand the *plight* previously misunderstood or even unknown to him. To be

---

20. Ernst Käsemann, "Justification and Salvation History in the Epistle to the Romans," in *Perspectives on Paul*, trans. M. Kohl (Philadelphia: Fortress Press, 1971), 60–78, at 67.

sure, Paul's understanding of the present is not determined by his understanding of the climax of a Jewish narrative within a larger story of the human plight. In fact, the reverse is true: Paul's understanding of the human plight, the Jewish narrative, and salvation history is only properly understood in light of Christ—indeed, "in Christ" (2 Cor. 5:16–17). The combination of the christological and pnuematological invasion, together with the radical newness established by Christ, reinforces this retrospective reading strategy. The effect is that discontinuity with the past is often highlighted.[21]

That said, this retrospective reading approach is not simply unidirectional. Within the Eschatological Invasion group exists a diversity of ways to approach the topic of continuity and discontinuity. While many in this group might be described as following a model of retrospective-discontinuity, Richard Hays presents a model of retrospective-continuity. That is, Paul does read backwards (i.e., retrospectively), but with an emphasis on narrative continuity, such that Paul presents God's eschatological activity in continuity with the story of Israel. Accordingly, Hays writes, "I contend that Paul's understanding of the new age in Christ leads him not to a rejection of Israel's sacred history but to a retrospective hermeneutical transformation of Israel's story in light of the story of God's startling redemptive actions. . . . [T]his requires a dramatic rereading of Israel's story, but what is required is precisely a rereading, not a repudiation."[22] Thus, Paul's theological vision is not fully captured by moving from Christ to Israel; rather, his vision begins with Christ but is two way, moving from Christ to Israel and then back to Christ again.[23]

Overall, the Eschatological Invasion model has strong affinities with Barthian theology. Indeed, God's revelation in the christological invasion, which thoroughly undercuts human pretense (found in

---

21. With the de-emphasis upon continuity with the past, scholars at times feel the need to defend themselves against a quasi-Marcionite interpretation of their position.
22. Richard B. Hays, "Apocalyptic *Poiēsis* in Galatians: Paternity, Passion, and Participation," in *Galatians and Christian Theology: Justification, the Gospel, and Ethics in Paul's Letter*, eds. M. W. Elliott et al. (Grand Rapids: Baker, 2014), 200–219, at 204.
23. We see a similar but inverted progression with N. T. Wright, for whom the movement is from plight to Christ and back to plight again (*Paul and the Faithfulness of God* [Minneapolis: Fortress Press, 2013], 750).

versions of natural theology), reflects several key elements in Barth's theological vision. These echoes may be due to the direct influence of Barth's own work, though not all these scholars explicitly acknowledge a connection to Barth or his hermeneutical approach; in some instances, then, Barth has perhaps been mediated through other authors. In any case, the Eschatological Invasion group, with this shared theological perspective, has, until recently, retained a more direct and widespread influence on Pauline scholarship than our second paradigm, the Unveiled Fulfillment group, to which we now turn.

Unveiled Fulfillment

If the Eschatological Invasion group has been influenced by Barth's theological perspective, the Unveiled Fulfillment group has been impacted—though perhaps to a lesser extent—by Christopher Rowland and the wider interest in reading Paul within a Jewish narrative. Among the many important studies of Jewish apocalyptic literature, Christopher Rowland's *The Open Heaven* has proven especially influential for the Unveiled Fulfillment group.[24] In fact, most of those whom we align with this group explicitly acknowledge indebtedness to Rowland's work.

One of Rowland's key arguments in *The Open Heaven* is that the *revelation* (ἀποκάλυψις) of divine mysteries is central to Jewish apocalyptic texts. Therefore, when Pauline interpreters make use of Rowland, they argue that the concept of apocalyptic has as much to do with the disclosure of knowledge about spiritual activity as it does with God's redemptive work itself. The significance of spiritual agents, then, concerns not only their participation in cosmic events (as emphasized in the Eschatological Invasion group), but also their mediation of heavenly knowledge. Thus, scholars in the Unveiled Fulfillment group tend to emphasize Pauline texts that highlight the revelation of Christ himself, Paul's mystical experiences, and the revelatory activity of

24. Christopher Rowland, *The Open Heaven: A Study of Apocalyptic in Judaism and Early Christianity* (New York: Crossroad, 1982 [Eugene: Wipf & Stock, 2002]).

spiritual agents—as seen in Galatians 1, and 2 Corinthians 3–4 and 12, as well as passages that highlight "mystery" language. However, as the influence of the group has grown, scholars such as N. T. Wright and Michael Gorman have expanded their discussions beyond these more traditional topics.

Arguably, those Pauline scholars who draw on this approach are not as numerous as the Eschatological Invasion group. In fact, many whom we identify with this group are not always considered to be partaking in a debate against the Eschatological Invasion perspective over the meaning and nature of apocalyptic in Pauline theology. Nevertheless, a number of studies—treating such topics as divine mysteries, heavenly visions, and mysticism—correspond to the methodology and perspectives of the Unveiled Fulfillment group, and thus form a foundation for the growing interest in this approach.[25]

The foremost early proponent of this view within Pauline circles was Alan Segal in his *Paul the Convert: The Apostolate and Apostasy of Saul the Pharisee*, who viewed texts such as 2 Corinthians 12 as important for understanding Paul's wider theological perspective.[26] Barry Matlock, with his *Unveiling the Apocalyptic Paul*, also stands out as an early advocate of the Unveiled Fulfillment approach among Pauline scholars. Focused more on critiquing the Eschatological Invasion perspective than providing a construction of his own, Matlock nonetheless leans heavily upon Rowland's *Open Heaven* approach, and thus proposes

---

25. See, e.g., Seyoon Kim, *The Origin of Paul's Gospel*, 2nd ed., WUNT 2/4 (Tübingen: J. C. B. Mohr, 1984); Carey Newman, *Paul's Glory-Christology: Tradition and Rhetoric*, NovTSup 69 (Leiden: Brill, 1992).

26. Alan F. Segal, *Paul the Convert: The Apostolate and Apostasy of Saul the Pharisee* (New Haven: Yale University Press, 1990). Before Segal's work, several studies were formative for this direction in Pauline scholarship: Markus N. A. Bockmuehl, *Revelation and Mystery in Ancient Judaism and Pauline Christianity*, WUNT 2/36 (Tübingen: Mohr Siebeck, 1990); James Tabor, *Things Unutterable: Paul's Ascent to Paradise in Its Greco-Roman, Judaic, and Early Christian Contexts* (Lanham: University Press of America, 1986); Andrew Lincoln, *Paradise Now and Not Yet: Studies in the Role of the Heavenly Dimension in Paul's Thought with Special Reference to his Eschatology*, SNTSMS 43 (Cambridge: Cambridge University Press, 1981). Various others have made use of the theme: e.g., J. M. Scott, "The Triumph of God in 2 Cor. 2.14: Additional Evidence of Merkabah Mysticism in Paul," NTS 42, no. 2 (1996): 260–81. More recently, Benjamin L. Gladd, *Revealing the Mysterion: The Use of Mystery in Daniel and Second Temple Judaism with Its Bearing on First Corinthians*, BZNW 160 (Berlin: de Gruyter, 2008); G. K. Beale and Benjamin L. Gladd, *Hidden but Now Revealed: A Biblical Theology of Divine Mystery* (Downers Grove: IVP Academic, 2014).

13

comparing Paul with individual apocalypses (and other texts) rather than a synthetic conception of "apocalyptic."[27]

In addition to Pauline specialists working directly on the topic of apocalyptic, there are also scholars primarily known for their work in Second Temple Judaism who have brought their expertise to bear on the issue of apocalyptic in the NT and in Paul. The collaborative project of Christopher Rowland and Christopher R. A. Morray-Jones, published as *The Mystery of God: Early Jewish Mysticism and the New Testament*, is a case in point.[28] This type of work is also captured by the SBL Early Jewish and Christian Mysticism Group and those who study Paul in the context of emerging Merkevah Mysticism. Recently, Loren Stuckenbruck has added his voice to matters Pauline, lending a perspective heavily informed by his extensive work on Second Temple texts. In particular, he has questioned the conceptualization of time and the "two ages" motif that characterizes much of the Eschatological Invasion perspective, arguing that early Jewish authors envisioned more continuity between the ages than is often assumed by Pauline specialists.[29]

In distinction to these studies more limited in scope, N. T. Wright has perhaps been the most influential champion of the Unveiled Fulfillment perspective, as he employs this reading strategy much more widely across the Pauline corpus than others associated with this paradigm. Concurring with a perspective like Rowland's, Wright argues that "apocalyptic characteristically speaks of the unveiling or revelation of mysteries, hidden secrets known in heaven but not before known on earth."[30] On the other hand, Wright is sympathetic to certain

---

27. Matlock, *Unveiling the Apocalyptic Paul*.

28. Christopher Rowland and Christopher R. A. Morray-Jones, *The Mystery of God: Early Jewish Mysticism and the New Testament*, CRINT 12 (Leiden: Brill, 2009). Cf. Christopher Rowland, "Apocalyptic, Mysticism and the New Testament," in *Geschichte-Tradition-Reflexion: Judentum*, ed. P. Schäfer (Tübingen: Mohr, 1996), 405–21.

29. Loren T. Stuckenbruck, "Overlapping Ages at Qumran and 'Apocalyptic' in Pauline Theology," in *The Dead Sea Scrolls and Pauline Literature*, ed. Jean-Sébastien Rey, STDJ 102 (Leiden: Brill, 2013), 309–26; idem, "Posturing 'Apocalyptic' in Pauline Theology: How Much Contrast with Jewish Tradition?," in *The Myth of Rebellious Angels: Studies in Second Temple Judaism and New Testament Texts*, WUNT 335 (Tübingen: Mohr Siebeck, 2014), 240–56.

30. Wright, *Paul: In Fresh Perspective*, 52. For this reason, in his recent assessment of the apocalyptic scheme developed by Martyn, de Boer, and Campbell, Wright protests, "How come it is so

aspects of Käsemann's understanding of apocalyptic in Paul (e.g., the shocking and invasive nature of God's redemptive work in Christ), though he insists that this notion converges with Paul's concept of "covenant" (i.e., "God's long and many-staged plan of salvation"[31]). As he explains, "In the messianic events of Jesus' death and resurrection Paul believes *both* that the covenant promises were at last fulfilled *and* that this constituted a massive irruption into the processes of world history unlike anything before or since."[32] For Wright, Christ is "the climax of the covenant" promises, such that "covenant and apocalyptic . . . are mutually reinforcing rather than antithetical."[33] Thus, "once we understand how 'apocalyptic' works, the convergence between it and what I have called 'covenantal' thinking becomes apparent. One of the things which is 'unveiled' is precisely *how the covenant plan has been worked out*"—namely, that through the covenant faithfulness of God expressed in the Messiah Jesus, Jews and gentiles have been brought together into one people of God.[34]

The majority of the Unveiled Fulfillment studies, to be sure, are topical in nature rather than attempts to frame the entirety of Paul's theology. Yet, these various scholars work from a generally similar paradigm when the three axes, *spatial, temporal,* and *epistemological,* are accounted for in Paul's letters. Our title, "Unveiled Fulfillment," attempts to capture these aspects: "unveiled" describes the spatial and epistemological axes as God acts to reveal the mystery of Christ in the world, and "fulfillment" emphasizes the temporal activity of Christ as the culmination of God's covenantal work, understood from a decidedly *prospective* point of view.

Spatial Axis. According to the Unveiled Fulfillment model, the thin separation between the heavenly and earthly domains means that God as well as other spiritual agents are frequently involved in this world.

---

different from what the leading analysts of first-century Jewish apocalyptic describe?" ("Paul in Current Anglophone Scholarship," 373).

31. Wright, *Paul: In Fresh Perspective,* 53.

32. Ibid., 54 (original emphasis).

33. Ibid., 42. See also Wright's *The Climax of the Covenant: Christ as the Law in Pauline Theology* (Minneapolis: Fortress Press, 1993).

34. Wright, *Paul: In Fresh Perspective,* 53 (original emphasis).

As the primary emphasis of Paul's theology, God's activity to solve the problem of evil plays out through the work of the Messiah Jesus, who defeats the powers of evil and introduces the age of the Holy Spirit. This serves as the climax to God's promises and the means by which God reveals his righteousness to the world. In addition, this group notes how other spiritual agents—both good and evil—infuse the language and worldview of Paul. In fact, rather than there existing a barrier between the earthly and heavenly domains, the interchange between these two spheres is quite porous—hence, Rowland's moniker "Open Heaven."

Temporal Axis. History, for the Unveiled Fulfillment group, is a progression. In a wider narrative of creation and renewed creation stands God's acts of covenant formation, restoration, and promise-making to the people of Israel, even in the midst of foreign oppression and the unfaithfulness of the covenant people. Jesus, as the Jewish messiah who inaugurates the age of the Spirit, stands as the climax of that covenant and the fulfillment of past promises. Yet, in contrast to a steady and evolutionary development, this fulfillment is sudden, unexpected, and difficult, which is like other Jewish apocalyptic texts that explain an arduous and surprising resolution to the problem of evil. Yet, behind this fulfillment is the expectation that God is already in control of history even when the righteous suffer at the hands of evil powers and their human accomplices (especially political enemies). Accordingly, current and future salvation is framed as standing in continuity with God's previous promises.

Epistemological Axis. Since, according to the Unveiled Fulfillment group, Paul views God's activity as a progression from and fulfillment of what was promised in the past, Paul's theology is grounded in a story that began before Christ, though it is fulfilled in him.[35] That is, the epistemological framework runs *prospectively* from Judaism to Christianity, from plight to solution (even if back to plight again),[36]

---

35. The Unveiled Fulfillment group agrees that Christ is the revelation of God in Paul's theology, yet we might say they also affirm that Paul and other Jews valued the other revelations that God had given before Christ.
36. Cf. N. T. Wright, *Paul and the Faithfulness of God*, chapter 9, esp. 750.

rather than retrospectively from Christ(ianity) back to Judaism, or from solution to plight.[37] The "prospective" point of view means that, in some way, the prior Jewish (apocalyptic) narrative, derived from the OT or Second Temple texts, is privileged and forms the interpretive grid for understanding Paul's theology. Accordingly, *continuity with Judaism* forms a structural foundation for this paradigm. This does not mean that these scholars see Judaism as monolithic or that Paul never disagrees with Jewish forms of thinking; indeed, foundational theological pillars of Judaism (e.g., monotheism, election, eschatology, to borrow Wright's threefold structure)[38] are transformed or "re-imagined" in the light of Christ and the Spirit. Nevertheless, Paul sees Christ as the "climax" of a distinctly *Jewish* narrative, and everything inaugurated in Christ is the goal or culmination of Israel's history. The prospective movement is no more a one-to-one fulfillment than it is a simple progression: the Christ-event was surprising and challenging, but a fulfillment nonetheless; it is for Paul, therefore, a prospective event. The surprising aspect of the Christ-event corresponds to the fact that many do not yet understand the nature of this divine mystery. Thus, in addition to the epistemology that undergirds Paul's theology as a whole, individuals—and, especially, Paul himself—have access to such wisdom and knowledge through revelation, that is, an unveiling of *mysteries* that have been hidden in the past, but which now make sense in view of the full breadth of the narrative.

Admittedly, this Unveiled Fulfillment group is less cohesive than the Eschatological Invasion group; however, the common reading strategies do form a common bond. One may, at times, find it difficult to see the ideological coherence between the different Unveiled Fulfillment studies since they tend to be focused on particular topics or passages rather than on Paul's larger theological vision and deep logic. This means that the group's boundaries and influences have remained less defined as well.

---

37. The comparison with Hays's reading approach (as discussed above) is informative. Though both Hays and Wright read the elements of the story as bidirectional and in continuity, their starting points are different.
38. Wright, *Paul: In Fresh Perspective*, chapters 5–7.

Summary of Key Questions

Of course, the binary taxonomy presented above does not include all the variations represented by the field of Pauline scholarship, but it does highlight the interpretive approaches that broadly unite these two groups. Importantly, we have seen that the distinctions explored here are not merely historical or exegetical, but hermeneutical in nature. The following, then, are some of the key questions that arise from the discussion in this volume:

1. With regard to the spatial axis, the two paradigms equally note that Christ plays a central place in God's activity on earth and that evil powers are active here as well. However, some diversity exists with respect to the nature and involvement of other mediating agents, such as angels. *Thus, to what extent do angels and other cosmic powers play a role in Paul's theology?*

2. With regard to the temporal axis, the two paradigms again agree on the pivotal role Christ plays in redemptive history. At the same time, the nature of how the Christ-event relates to God's previous acts in history is highly disputed between the two. *How, then, does Paul understand this (salvation-)historical relationship? Is it characterized more by continuity or discontinuity?*

3. With regard to the epistemological axis, both paradigms also agree that Christ and the Spirit are the ultimate solution to the problem of evil. However, between the two groups stands a fundamental disagreement about the direction of his narrative logic, and thus about how Paul frames the plight-solution relationship. *Does Paul's theology develop prospectively (from plight to solution) or retrospectively (from solution to plight)?*

Of course, these questions rarely elicit either/or answers, but the nature of the answers often lead scholars into one of our two paradigms. Having explained some of the key elements that exist within the groups, we will explain the direction of the chapters in this volume.

Progression of the Volume

The above survey has revealed not only a lack of clarity and consensus in scholarship about *why* Paul's theology should be considered apocalyptic; it has also shown that there remains disagreement about precisely *how* to approach Paul as an apocalyptic thinker. Beyond this, there remain outstanding debates over various individual themes considered to be central to Paul's apocalyptic worldview. This volume aims to help remedy some of these shortcomings.

Admittedly, our preliminary discussion here has merely scratched the surface. In order to orient the reader further, David Shaw in the next chapter ("'Then I proceeded to where things were chaotic' [*1 Enoch* 21.1]: Mapping the Apocalyptic Landscape") explores in more detail various questions and proposals on apocalyptic in Paul, as well as their developments in modern scholarship.

After having reviewed in Part 1 many of the significant discussions taking place in contemporary Pauline theology, we move to the heart of the book in the remaining three parts. Part 2 consists of four programmatic chapters by prominent scholars who have written extensively on Paul and apocalyptic. Two essays are devoted to each of the two paradigmatic views sketched above, one primarily on the space-time axes, and one primarily on the epistemological axis. The Eschatological Invasion perspective is represented by Martinus de Boer ("Apocalyptic as God's Eschatological Activity in Paul's Theology") and Douglas Campbell ("Apocalyptic Epistemology: The *sine qua non* of Valid Pauline Interpretation"); the Unveiled Fulfillment perspective is represented by Edith Humphrey ("Apocalyptic as Theoria in the Letters of St. Paul: A New Perspective on Apocalyptic as Mother of Theology") and N. T. Wright ("Apocalyptic and the Sudden Fulfillment of Divine Promise"). These chapters engage various texts—the Hebrew Bible, early Jewish and Christian literature, and especially the letters of Paul—in order to provide a synthetic overview of the topic as well as to demonstrate what is, in the views of the respective authors, essential for an apocalyptic reading of Paul.

Since the understanding and employment of the idea of apocalyptic is highly influenced by the setting in which it originated as well as that in which it is studied, Part 3 consists of contextual chapters that seek to show how knowledge of different historical and intellectual contexts helps us to approach and understand Paul's apocalyptic theology. Early Judaism is treated by Loren Stuckenbruck ("Some Reflections on Apocalyptic Thought and Time in Literature from the Second Temple Period"), Greco-Roman philosophy by Joseph Dodson ("The Transcendence of Death and Heavenly Ascent in the Apocalyptic Paul and the Stoics"), ancient Christian traditions by Ben Blackwell ("Second Century Perspectives on the Apocalyptic Paul: Reading the *Apocalypse of Paul* and the *Acts of Paul*"), and modern theology by Philip Ziegler ("Some Remarks on Apocalyptic in Modern Christian Theology").

Part 4 consists of chapters that seek to explain how apocalyptic perspectives are valuable for understanding specific Pauline texts and themes. In comparison to the essays in Part 2, these chapters are limited in scope. Rather than providing a synthetic overview of numerous texts and themes in Judaism and Paul's letters, these chapters focus on a smaller selection of texts and seek to demonstrate how apocalyptic (variously defined) informs Paul's theology. For simplicity's sake, these chapters have been arranged according to their canonical order and include discussions by Jonathan Linebaugh ("Righteousness Revealed: The Death of Christ as the Definition of the Righteousness of God in Romans 3:21–26"), Beverly Roberts Gaventa ("Thinking from Christ to Israel: Romans 9–11 in Apocalyptic Context"), John Barclay ("Apocalyptic Allegiance and Disinvestment in the World: A Reading of 1 Corinthians 7:25–35"), John Goodrich ("After Destroying Every Rule, Authority, and Power: Paul, Apocalyptic, and Politics in 1 Corinthians"), Jason Maston ("Plight and Solution in Paul's Apocalyptic Perspective: A Study of 2 Corinthians 5:18–21"), Michael Gorman ("The Apocalyptic New Covenant and the Shape of Life in the Spirit according to Galatians"), and Jamie P. Davies ("The Two Ages and

Salvation History in Paul's Apocalyptic Imagination: A Comparison of *4 Ezra* and Galatians").

By revisiting the question of "apocalyptic" in Paul in the following essays, this collection ultimately seeks to clarify how the word is being used and to demonstrate how the concepts it embodies remain serviceable in the explication of Paul's theology. Our hope is that this volume will move the discussion forward by bringing clarity to contested issues and offering fresh trajectories in the study of Paul's apocalyptic imagination.

2

"Then I Proceeded to Where Things Were Chaotic" (*1 Enoch* 21:1)

Mapping the Apocalyptic Landscape

David A. Shaw

Forasmuch as many have taken in hand to set forth in order a declaration of those things termed apocalyptic, it seems good to take one more swing at it. As we do so, it is well to recognize that, like the KJV from which those opening words are taken, the term "apocalyptic" has a remarkable power to command loyalty and divide opinion. Such divided opinions are regularly expressed in the works of those who have previously "taken in hand to set forth" the history and significance of apocalyptic readings of Paul—ranging from those who find the term powerfully evocative to those who feel the term is hopelessly ill-defined and as tangible as mist.[1] The task of this chapter,

---

1. For examples of the former, see e.g., Walter Lowe, "Why We Need Apocalyptic," *SJT* 63, no. 1 (2010): 41–53; Philip G. Ziegler, "Eschatological Dogmatics—To What End?," in *Eschatologie/Eschatology:* The Sixth Durham-Tübingen Research Symposium: Eschatology in Old Testament, Ancient Judaism and Early Christianity, eds. H.-J Eckstein, C. Landmesser, and H.

however, is neither to praise nor to bury the term, but simply to chart the current situation in the hope of orienting the reader to the apocalyptic landscape that stretches out in the chapters beyond this one. To that end, and by way of introduction, it will be helpful briefly to note two earlier surveys that highlight the major questions to be addressed.

The first is the 1989 essay, "Defining the Word 'Apocalyptic': A Problem in Biblical Criticism" by Richard E. Sturm, which opens a volume in honor of J. Louis Martyn.[2] A striking feature of this essay is that it outlines two distinct approaches to the question—one that defines apocalyptic as a literary genre, and another that defines it as a theological concept. In connection with the first, Sturm discusses the contributions of Emil Kautzsch, R. H. Charles, H. H. Rowley, D. S. Russell, Philipp Vielhauer, and John J. Collins; addressing the second, prominent names include Richard Kabisch, Albert Schweitzer, Rudolph Bultmann, Ernst Käsemann, Ulrich Wilckens, Wolfhart Pannenberg, J. C. Beker, Christopher Rowland, and J. Louis Martyn.

For Sturm's part, he believes the second approach is more significant because it allows Jesus and Paul to be discussed under the rubric of apocalyptic, even though "it remains uncertain how one can most adequately approach the problem of defining apocalyptic."[3] He has a proposal of his own to make, and we will come to that; for now, we simply note the major question that emerges, namely: how does

Lichtenberger (Tübingen: Mohr Siebeck, 2011), 348–59; Theodore W. Jennings Jr., "Apocalyptic and Contemporary Theology," *Quarterly Review* 4, no. 3 (1984): 54–68. For an example of the latter, see esp. Thomas Francis Glasson, "What Is Apocalyptic?," *NTS* 27, no. 1 (1980): 98–105, for whom apocalyptic "is a useless word which no one can define and which produces nothing but confusion and acres of verbiage" (105). In his review of Martyn's Galatians commentary, Graham Stanton calls for a moratorium on the use of the term "apocalyptic," bemoaning that it is "sprinkled like confetti over nearly every page" ("Review of Galatians by J. Louis Martyn," *JTS* 51, no. 1 [2000]: 264–70, at 268). See also, at greater length but with equal exasperation, R. Barry Matlock, *Unveiling the Apocalyptic Paul: Paul's Interpreters and the Rhetoric of Criticism*, JSNTSup 127 (Sheffield: JSOT, 1996).

2. Richard E. Sturm, "Defining the Word 'Apocalyptic': A Problem for Biblical Criticism," in *Apocalyptic and the New Testament: Essays in Honor of J. Louis Martyn*, eds. Joel Marcus and Marian L. Soards, JSNTSup 24 (Sheffield: JSOT, 1989), 17–48.

3. Ibid., 37. Matlock rightly wonders whether Sturm is less interested in defining apocalyptic than he is in attaching it to Paul. At least at this stage in the argument, Sturm is content to say that the theological approach to apocalyptic draws Paul into its orbit, and, for that reason, "this second approach to apocalyptic is invaluable."

apocalyptic, as a theological concept, relate to those literary texts known as apocalypses? Do those two sets of scholars ever talk to each other? And, more pointedly, to what extent ought the feet of those who speak of Paul as an apocalyptic theologian be held to the fire of the apocalypses? This is the first of our major issues.

The second is highlighted by a rather different survey, although it too appears in a volume honoring J. Louis Martyn. In a fascinating essay, David Congdon takes Sturm's category of apocalyptic as theological concept, focuses on its application to Paul, and detects two distinct streams.[4] The first, termed "Apocalyptic A," is represented by Käsemann and Beker; the second, "Apocalyptic B," by Martyn, Bultmann, and Barth. The arrangement of names in this configuration will perhaps be surprising to many, and to this too, we will return; the point for now is that it highlights the second major question for discussion, namely: how uniform is the apocalyptic reading of Paul?

This is a more significant question than has usually been recognized. In part, this is because so many theological concepts operate under the "apocalyptic" label, giving the appearance of uniformity, and partly because analysis or critique of the apocalyptic reading has often been a terminological one—questioning the nomenclature more than examining the content. Occasionally, the differences are acknowledged or new terminology is proposed, but for the most part and at least to the uninitiated, an impression of consistency has been given. For example, Martinus de Boer speaks of building "on the contributions of other interpreters of Paul, most notably, Albert Schweitzer, Käsemann, J. Louis Martyn and Beker."[5] Likewise, Douglas Harinck asserts, "the understanding of Paul as an apocalyptic theologian goes back as far as the work on Paul by Albert Schweitzer. It has been given vigorous revival by Ernst Käsemann, J. Christiaan Beker and J. Louis Martyn."[6] Of

---

4. David Congdon, "Eschatologizing Apocalyptic: An Assessment of the Conversation on Pauline Apocalyptic," in *Apocalyptic and the Future of Theology: With and Beyond J. Louis Martyn*, eds. Joshua B. Davis and Douglas Harinck (Eugene: Cascade, 2012), 118–36.

5. Martinus C. de Boer, *The Defeat of Death: Apocalyptic Eschatology in 1 Corinthians 15 and Romans 5*, JSNTSup 22 (Sheffield: JSOT, 1988), 7.

6. Douglas Harink, *Paul Among the Postliberals: Pauline Theology Beyond Christendom and Modernity* (Eugene: Wipf & Stock, 2003), 16.

course, neither de Boer nor Harinck are suggesting these figures hold a uniform understanding of Paul's theology or a uniform view of the relevance of apocalyptic to that theology, but the remarkable diversity among them is too little commented on. Hence, some exploration of those differences may be of help.

So, taking our cue from those two surveys, we will address these two questions, with an emphasis on the second—that is, on the theological significance ascribed to apocalyptic. Conceding that this is something of a simplification, and in recognition of the adjectival quality of "apocalyptic," we will group the theological proposals under four headings: *apocalyptic eschatology*, *apocalyptic cosmology*, *apocalyptic soteriology*, and *apocalyptic epistemology*.[7]

In each case, after outlining the various theological proposals under the heading, we will reflect on the historical and literary question, asking to what extent the apocalyptic reading of Paul relies upon reading the apocalypses. In relation to both questions, we have been offered a binary analysis (apocalyptic studied as genre/theological concept; Apocalyptic A/Apocalyptic B), but in both cases, we will find that a more complex picture emerges.

Apocalyptic Eschatology

Admittedly, not much clarity is achieved by attaching an ambiguous adjective to a disputed noun, but here, our focus falls on how apocalyptic relates to time and history.

On the one hand, apocalyptic has been used to assert the *futurity* of God's redemptive action. In this sense, Beker sets apocalyptic in polemical contrast to eschatology, concerned that the latter term has become "multivalent and chaotic" in the hands of modern theologians. More specifically, he is troubled by neo-orthodoxy (which has "collapsed eschatology into Christology"), C. H. Dodd's realized eschatology, and Bultmann's existentialism. Against this, Beker asserts

---

7. It is worth noting at the outset that many of these are sometimes identified as *the* apocalyptic characteristic, even though most proponents of an apocalyptic Paul will, in different proportions, draw from more than one of these, and some authors identify several aspects as definitive in different contexts.

"apocalyptic": "Paul's gospel is formulated within the basic components of apocalyptic. To be sure, Jewish apocalyptic undergoes a profound modification in Paul, but this does not affect the intensity of its expectation."[8] Those modifications involve the relative absence of literary motifs common in apocalypses and the softening of apocalyptic's historical dualism,[9] but for Beker, because the intense expectation remains, Paul's apocalyptic credentials are in order. In this respect, and self-consciously so, Beker follows Käsemann, who expressed similar misgivings about the multivalency of "eschatology" and hoped his use of the term apocalyptic "to denote the expectation of an imminent Parousia" would introduce clarity—not least to his dispute with Bultmann.[10]

On the other hand, there are those for whom apocalyptic eschatology looks back rather than forward. Martyn, for example, notes Käsemann and Beker's interest in the future and their consequent difficulty with Galatians, and so proposes to "begin with a certain amount of ignorance as to the definition of apocalyptic," preferring to allow Galatians to offer one.[11] What emerges for Martyn is an emphasis on the coming of Christ as "*the* cosmic apocalyptic event. There was a 'before,' and there is now an 'after.'"[12] We will have more to say about the significance of that event for Martyn later. Already, though, we can see that Congdon's bifurcation of apocalyptic readings holds where this temporal aspect is in view. When using the

---

8. J. Christiaan Beker, *Paul the Apostle: The Triumph of God in Life and Thought* (Edinburgh: T&T Clark, 1980), 145.

9. Beker speaks of the Christ-event as "proleptic," and embraces Cullman's D-Day/V-Day analogy approvingly. He also increasingly develops a sense that apocalyptic speaks to a salvation-historical tension: a "tragic tension between faithfulness to Torah and its apparent futility . . . fed by his faith in the faithfulness of the God of Israel and his ultimate self-vindication" (*Paul the Apostle*, 136.). As early as the preface to the paperback edition of *Paul the Apostle*, Beker argues that apocalyptic motifs of historical dualism, universal cosmic expectation, and the imminent end of the world "are actually anchored in the even-more-central motif of the faithfulness of God" (*Paul the Apostle: The Triumph of God in Life and Thought*, 1st paperback ed. [Philadelphia: Fortress Press, 1984], xv).

10. Ernst Käsemann, "On the Subject of Primitive Christian Apocalyptic," in *New Testament Questions of Today*, trans. W. J. Montague (London: SCM, 1969), 108–37, at 109n1.

11. J. Louis, Martyn, "Apocalyptic Antinomies," in *Theological Issues in the Letters of Paul* (Edinburgh: T&T Clark, 1997), 111–23, at 113.

12. Ibid., 121 (emphasis original). Or, in answer to the central question of Galatians: "What time is it?" Paul answers: "It is the time after the apocalypse of the faith of Christ (3:23–25), the time of things being set right by that faith" (ibid., 122).

term apocalyptic in relation to time, Käsemann and Beker think of the future; Martyn, like Bultmann and Barth, looks back.

In addition to the basic tense of apocalyptic (past, not future), we should note that, for Martyn, it is also a disruptive, punctiliar event. He shares with Käsemann (already the binary typologies are breaking down!) a deep suspicion of salvation-history, although he expresses himself more strongly: Galatians, for example, "can be read as revealing a conscious avoidance of—if not an attack on—the continuum of salvation history."[13] Indeed, an interest in salvation history is characteristic of Paul's *opponents*.[14]

As for the relation between these theological assertions and the apocalypses, we can note, first, that Beker's direct engagement with apocalyptic literature is scant, relying instead on the analyses of Koch and Vielhauer.[15] In response to criticism on that score, he believes those objections "could have been muted if I had frankly emphasized the polemical thrust of my usage as directed to the systematic theologians of our time."[16] That he can rely on Koch and Vielhauer for summaries of apocalyptic thought—which Beker further distils down to "(1) historical dualism; (2) universal cosmic expectation; and (3) the imminent end of the world"[17]—shows that even some of those whom Sturm lists as focusing on apocalyptic as a genre attempt to derive theological positions from literary forms. Of those who have, eschatology has long been considered integral to the theological vision, in part because apocalyptic was regularly thought to derive from prophecy and to be distinguished from it by an alternative and more pessimistic or radical eschatology.[18]

Like Beker, Martyn makes little appeal to the apocalypses

---

13. Idem, *Galatians*, AB (New York: Doubleday, 1997), 179.
14. Martyn represents a high-point of antipathy toward salvation-history. His successors are happier to affirm a degree of continuity, albeit within certain parameters.
15. Beker, *Paul the Apostle*, 135–36.
16. Beker, *Paul the Apostle* (paperback ed.), xiv.
17. Beker, *Paul the Apostle*, 136.
18. Note, for example, the place of eschatology in the influential definition offered by John J. Collins in "Towards the Morphology of a Genre," *Semeia* 14 (1979): 1–20, at 9; for a dissenting voice, see Christopher Rowland, *The Open Heaven: A Study of Apocalyptic in Judaism and Early Christianity* (London: SPCK, 1982), 23–48.

themselves, but, in part, this is because the view that apocalypses are fundamentally eschatological in character and hold to a radical doctrine of the two ages is such a commonplace one. With reference to the latter, we have already seen that Beker argues the division of the two ages is not as sharp in Paul as in the apocalypses, softened from both sides by a sense of God's fulfillment of ancient promises, on the one hand, and the inauguration of the eschatological age, on the other. Martyn will not allow at least the first of those in Paul, but both are agreed that the Jewish parallels exhibit a strong division of the ages. This is another point, however, where there is some noteworthy dissent: it might first be asked whether the two-age scheme is not a basic Jewish conviction rather than a distinctive of apocalyptic literature. Furthermore, some have questioned how sharply Jewish apocalyptic itself divides the ages, given its well-documented interest in historical sequences, and even some parallels to Paul's overlapping now and not-yet tension.[19]

Apocalyptic Cosmology

At least in the case of Käsemann, apocalyptic is theologically bi-vocational. It restrains an overly-inaugurated eschatology, but it also denies an overly-individualized soteriology, moving the locus of God's action away from the existential encounter of the individual to the cosmic battleground between the Creator and his creatures.[20] It is thus both "Nein" and "not yet." The effect is to insist that salvation is played out on a larger stage. The apocalyptic question is, "To whom does the

---

19. See, respectively, Carol Ann Newsom, "The Past as Revelation: History in Apocalyptic Literature," *Quarterly Review* 4, no. 3 (1984): 40–53; Loren T. Stuckenbruck, "Overlapping Ages at Qumran and in Pauline Theology," in *The Dead Sea Scrolls and Pauline Literature*, STDJ 102, ed. Jean-Sébastien Rey (Leiden: Brill, 2014), 309–26. N. T. Wright has also attempted to introduce some much-needed clarity to the whole discussion of "dualisms" in *The New Testament and the People of God*, Christian Origins and the Question of God vol. 1 (London: SPCK, 1992), 252–56.

20. Apocalyptic also serves an *historical* purpose in Käsemann, providing an alternative to a theory of Gnostic origins for Paul's theology. This multivalency exasperates many. See, i.e., David V. Way, *The Lordship of Christ: Ernst Käsemann's Interpretation of Paul's Theology*, Oxford Theological Monographs (Oxford: Clarendon, 1991), 175; Matlock, *Unveiling the Apocalyptic Paul*, 235. Moule complains of "the use of 'eschatological' and even 'apocalyptic' in such wide senses as to threaten to debase linguistic currency" ("Review of *Commentary on Romans* by Ernst Käsemann," *JTS* 32, no. 2 [1981]: 498–502, at 501).

world belong?,"[21] and God's righteousness relates to the reassertion of his creative rights. In Käsemann, a secondary effect is to place more actors upon this stage. Humanity's life "is from the beginning a stake in the confrontation between God and the principalities of this world."[22] This thought is left rather vague, however; the powers chiefly become a way of expressing the reality of evil at a supra-individual level, which is an understandable impulse, given his context. More fundamentally, for Käsemann, as for Bultmann, the drama revolves around the contest between God and his creatures: "The Judge always comes upon the scene in conflict with human illusion. Illusion is any state which attacks the lordship of the Creator by forgetting one's creatureliness."[23]

This is worth highlighting because many other apocalyptic readings of Paul make this expanded cosmological cast central to apocalyptic. Prior to Käsemann, Schweitzer had relished announcing that "the natural world is, in the eschatological view, characterised not only by its transience, but by the fact that demons and angels exercise power in it."[24] And Wrede had argued similarly before him, discussing the human plight with reference to "dark and evil powers. The chief of these are the 'flesh,' sin, the Law, and death," but in addition, "the picture is supplemented by a view taken from a particular standpoint. Paul believes that mankind is under the sway of mighty spirits, demons, and angelic powers."[25]

Beyond Käsemann, Beker takes up this theme: sin and death, along with divine wrath and the law, are "ontological powers" and "major apocalyptic forces."[26] For Martyn, the distinctive contrast between

---

21. Käsemann, "Primitive Christian Apocalyptic," 135, cf. idem, "On Paul's Anthropology," in *Perspectives on Paul*, trans. Margaret Kohl (London: SCM, 1971), 1–31, at 25.

22. Käsemann, "Primitive Christian Apocalyptic," 136. Idem, "On Paul's Anthropology," 26.

23. Idem, *Commentary on Romans*, trans. Geoffrey William Bromiley (Grand Rapids: Eerdmans, 1980), 58. Accordingly, God's righteousness represents "God's victory amid the opposition of the world. By it, all human self-righteousness and insubordination come to destruction" (*New Testament Questions of Today*, 181).

24. Albert Schweitzer, *The Mysticism of Paul the Apostle*, trans. William Montgomery (London: A&C Black, 1931), 57.

25. William Wrede, *Paul*, trans. Edward Lummis (London: P. Green, 1908), 92. Of course, Schweitzer and Wrede hardly spoke of apocalyptic, but they are cited regularly enough as forerunners.

26. Beker, *Paul the Apostle*, 145.

Paul and his opponents is that where they perceive a two-actor drama (God and human beings), Paul discerns three actors (God, human beings, and "supra-human powers other than God"), and this discernment constitutes Paul's apocalyptic insight.[27] More generally, Martyn argues that "Paul's view of wrong and right is thoroughly apocalyptic, in the sense that on the landscape of wrong and right there are, in addition to God and human beings, powerful actors that stand opposed to God and that enslave human beings."[28] We could go on, but in all likelihood, the centrality of cosmological powers to the apocalyptic readings is sufficiently well-known that we need not. Perhaps more helpful is to highlight a number of issues to which it is worth being alert. First, despite some appeal back to Wrede and Schweitzer, the demonological element has largely fallen away from these contemporary readings.[29] Second, it is frequently stated that the powers of sin, death, the law, and the flesh are "ontological powers," "quasi-beings," "ontological metaphors"—in some way, more-than-personifications. It is not always clear what that means. There is greater clarity, however, concerning their usefulness within Paul's theology conceived apocalyptically.

For example, in de Boer's view, Paul is engaged in a polemical mythologizing program, opposing a more optimistic account of anthropology and moral agency: "Paul's cosmological appraisal of death, and sin, functions to exclude the Law's observance as the source of justification, righteousness, or eternal life."[30] Likewise, for Beverley Gaventa, these *dramatis personae* are "attempts to convey what Paul sees as the deep captivity of human beings, their inability to free

---

27. J. Louis Martyn, "Epilogue: An Essay in Pauline Meta-Ethics," in *Divine and Human Agency in Paul and His Cultural Environment*, eds. John M. G. Barclay and Simon J. Gathercole, LNTS 335 (London: T&T Clark, 2006), 173–83, at 178. In the context of that essay, Martyn states that he "uses the term 'apocalyptic' for the most part to refer to this three-actor drama" (178n12).

28. J. Louis Martyn, "Apocalyptic Rectification," in *Theological Issues in the Letters of Paul* (Edinburgh: T&T Clark, 1997), 87–88, at 87.

29. Campbell, for example, considers Wrede's work on Paul to be an "astonishingly deft" and "exquisitely balanced" account of the same soteriological model he advances, but makes nothing is this aspect of Wrede's account (*The Deliverance of God: An Apocalyptic Rereading of Justification in Paul* [Grand Rapids: Eerdmans, 2009], 177–78; the discussion of Wrede covers 177–83).

30. *The Defeat of Death*, 179. Cf. "Paul's Mythologising Program in Romans 5–8," in *Apocalyptic Paul*, ed. Beverly Roberts Gaventa (Waco: Baylor University Press, 2013), 1–20.

themselves."[31] Thus, it appears that the apocalyptic reading is substantially a statement about moral agency, and this will be borne out when we outline what we will call apocalyptic soteriology.

Before we turn to that, however, we ought to note that on this point, there is far greater concern to engage with the apocalypses. In several studies, de Boer seeks to distinguish two streams of Jewish apocalyptic (another binary analysis!), namely, *forensic Jewish apocalyptic eschatology* (FJAE) and *cosmological Jewish apocalyptic eschatology* (CJAE).[32] In FJAE, characterized by *2 Baruch* and *4 Ezra*, the human plight is traced back to Adam and Eve, but the Torah is an adequate tool by which to subdue sin and inherit life in the age to come, whereas CJAE, found in "*relatively pure form*" in "The Book of the Watchers" (*1 Enoch* 1–36),[33] emphasizes human captivity to powers that requires divine intervention. For de Boer, Paul combines the perspectives, but is fundamentally attempting to help his churches identify with CJAE. When Martyn takes up de Boer's typology, however, he radicalizes it a little further—Paul is purely an exponent of CJAE, while his opponents belong to FJAE with their belief that "by one's own decision," one can receive salvation.[34]

Two results of de Boer's work are worth noting at this stage. First, in the eyes of several apocalyptic readers of Paul, he has offered an adequate response to accusations that "apocalyptic" has drifted too far away from the genre whose name it bears.[35] Second, the question of soteriological and moral agency is brought to the fore.

---

31. Beverly Roberts Gaventa, "The Rhetoric of Violence and the God of Peace in Paul's Letter to the Romans," in *Paul, John, and Apocalyptic Eschatology: Studies in Honour of Martinus C. de Boer*, NovTSup 149, eds. Jan Krans et al. (Leiden: Brill, 2013), 73.

32. For de Boer's analysis, see the summary in *The Defeat of Death*, 83–91. Similar accounts can be found in idem, "Paul and Jewish Apocalyptic Eschatology," in *Apocalyptic and the New Testament: Essays in Honor of J. Louis Martyn*, 172–80; idem, "Paul and Apocalyptic Eschatology," in *The Encyclopedia of Apocalypticism Volume 1: The Origins of Apocalypticism in Judaism and Christianity*, ed. John J. Collins (London: Continuum, 2000), 357–66.

33. de Boer, *The Defeat of Death*, 85 (original emphasis).

34. J. Louis Martyn, "Glossary," in *Theological Issues in the Letters of Paul* (Edinburgh: T&T Clark, 1997), 298–301, at 299. For some discussion of de Boer's typology, see David A. Shaw, "Apocalyptic and Covenant: Perspectives on Paul or Antinomies at War?," *JSNT* 36, no. 2 (2013): 155–71. See now also John Anthony Dunne, "Suffering and Covenantal Hope in Galatians: A Critique of the 'Apocalyptic Reading' and its Proponents," *SJT* 68, no. 1 (2015): 1–15.

35. See, e.g., Beverly Roberts Gaventa, *Our Mother Saint Paul* (Louisville: John Knox, 2007), 83.

Apocalyptic Soteriology

We begin by picking up a quotation from Martyn:

> Since humans are fundamentally slaves, the drama in which wrong is set right does not begin with action on their part. It begins with God's militant action against all the powers that hold human beings in bondage. Thus, that action of God, instead of consisting at its center of a call for the slaves to repent and seek forgiveness, proves to be the deed by which God frees human beings.[36]

Several themes emerge here. To continue with the question of agency first, Martyn is clear that Paul's account of the human situation demands that God makes the first move. Salvation is unconditional and this too can be identified as the heart of apocalyptic, as Douglas Campbell proposes: "the term 'apocalyptic' emphasizes the dramatic, reconstitutive and fundamentally unconditional nature of the acts of which these narratives speak."[37] In addition, we might add, as Campbell often does, apocalyptic comes to imply a participatory aspect to those acts of salvation. Indeed, his preferred alternate terminology to "apocalyptic" is *pneumatologically participatory martyrological eschatology* (PPME). While the adjectives proliferate, this is useful in that it signals the way Campbell has positioned "apocalyptic" within the interpretive tradition that descends from Deissmann and Schweitzer, via Sanders's "participatory eschatology."[38] He has also thereby positioned it over against "justification by faith," traditionally understood.

Third, and relatedly, there is, in Martyn's expression, an orientation away from categories of repentance and forgiveness toward the language of liberation, and this is a key feature of apocalyptic soteriology. To the mind of many apocalyptic interpreters, any forensic understanding of salvation implies a conditional soteriology—

---

36. Martyn, "Apocalyptic Rectification," 87. Cf. de Boer for whom "apocalyptic eschatology . . . has little to do with a decision human beings must make, but everything to do with a decision God has already made on their behalf" ("Paul, Theologian of God's Apocalypse," *Int.* 56, no. 1 [2002]: 21–33, at 33).

37. *The Deliverance of God*, 756.

38. Campbell explicitly highlights the connections in *The Quest for Paul's Gospel: A Suggested Strategy* (London: T&T Clark, 2005), 39.

an impossibility, once the apocalyptic depth of the human plight has been grasped. It also wrongly implies a soteriological system in which God's hostility must be overcome, rather than one in which God benevolently makes the first move. Wrede expresses the preferred thought well: "God does not appear before man as judge at all, he shows himself rather as giver."[39]

In all this, it is striking how many other theological concepts (*Christus Victor*, "interchange," "participation," etc.) are interwoven into the apocalyptic reading of Paul, and sometimes, baptized in its name. Whereas, in reference to our first two headings, the apocalyptic reading sets itself against salvation-historical enthusiasts and distinguishes itself by an interest in cosmological forces; on this question of soteriology, it often makes common cause against a Lutheran reading.[40]

In relation to the apocalypses, the main proposal is that Paul is adopting and adapting the motif of cosmic conflict that is found in those texts—a proposal that meets with widespread approval. N. T. Wright, for example, thinks that if a reference to a cosmic struggle with powers and principalities is how we define apocalyptic, then "Paul would be, in this sense, an irreducibly 'apocalyptic' figure."[41]

However, things are not quite so simple, given the way apocalyptic readers of Paul deploy the language of cosmic warfare and redefine those powers and principalities in such diverse ways. For example, the military character of God's intervention was there in Käsemann, and he is credited for recovering the motif by Martyn.[42] However, the theme

---

39. Wrede, *Paul*, 131. Given these emphases, one can see why Luther especially serves as a foil, and why Käsemann's apocalyptic status is disputed; for all of Käsemann's talk of apocalyptic powers, Campbell is right to highlight the enduring centrality of justification by faith and forensic categories in his thought, viewing him someone who "attempted to modify the JF [i.e., Justification by faith] model in an apocalyptic direction, rather than as someone who shifted to an entirely new paradigm" (*The Quest for Paul's Gospel*, 38n16).

40. This tendency has demanded and produced a fascinating range of arguments concerning the flow of Romans 1–8 as apocalyptic interpreters seek to push beyond Schweitzer's puzzlement at the relationship between chapters 1–4 and 5–8.

41. N. T. Wright, *Paul and the Faithfulness of God*, Christian Origins and the Question of God vol. 4 (London: SPCK, 2013), 1:451.

42. J. Louis Martyn, "A Personal Word about Ernst Käsemann," in *Apocalyptic and the Future of Theology: With and Beyond J. Louis Martyn*, eds. Joshua B. Davis and Douglas Harinck (Eugene: Cascade, 2012), xiii–xv, at xv.

is less prominent than many suppose, and in Käsemann's analysis, God is principally taking action against creaturely pretension, as we have seen. This is loosely connected to the apocalypses (remember: at least one of his apocalyptic questions treats the earth as a contested battle ground), but he makes little reference to the literary background. For de Boer, we recall, the solution to humanity's plight found in CJAE is the divine invasion to rout the hostile powers that hold humanity captive. Since Paul has, in some sense, relocated the plight away from demonic powers toward the forces of sin and death, they become the focus of God's intervention. The result for de Boer is that participation with Christ is the daughter of apocalyptic: "Crucifixion of the old Adam with Christ constitutes Paul's soteriological adaptation and application of the cosmological-apocalyptic motif of God's eschatological destruction of the cosmic powers that have come to reign over the world."[43] Martyn also makes much of warfare language, but largely to emphasize a disjunctive note (God invades from *outside*), which Wright, for one, would not countenance calling "apocalyptic."[44] The result is that one must ask what is the reality expressed in military metaphor before one can begin to decide whether Jewish apocalypses might lend their support.

Apocalyptic Epistemology

In the previous section, I argued that apocalyptic soteriology (despite some of these metaphorical flourishes) often boils down to a participatory account of Paul's gospel that is more widely subscribed to. With the question of apocalyptic epistemology, however, we return

---

43. *Defeat of Death*, 177. This has echoes of Schweitzer for whom mysticism is "nothing other than the eschatological concept of redemption looked at from within" (*Mysticism of Paul the Apostle*, 112). It might appear as though apocalyptic readers of Paul are the ones adapting apocalyptic language of conflict to describe what Paul speaks of in other, less militaristic language. On the contrary, Beverley Gaventa has forcefully argued that military language is more pervasive in Paul than commonly appreciated. See especially, "Neither Height nor Depth: Discerning the Cosmology of Romans," *SJT* 64, no. 3 (2011): 265–78, at 269–73.

44. For Wright, such views operate "within a tacitly Deist framework in which one believes (a) in an absent god and a closed space-time continuum or (b) in a normally absent god who occasionally intervenes and acts in discontinuity with that space-time continuum" (*The New Testament and the People of God*, 298).

to a clearly distinctive element, and one that is prominent in the work of Martyn and Campbell, especially. Indeed, this also can be treated as the kernel of the apocalyptic reading. Campbell again: "I would argue for an apocalyptic account of Paul's theology, defining that descriptor suitably (i.e., with fairly strict reference to the *theological epistemology* enunciated in relation to Paul by Martyn)."[45] What is common to both is the view that Christology is crucial for epistemology; this is exegetically grounded in 2 Cor. 5:16 and theologically required by the apocalyptic account of the human plight—the enslavement to powers precludes the possibility of rational thought or true perception.[46] This basic assumption is then developed in distinct ways that merit separate comment.

For Martyn, the epistemological reliance of Christology serves, in part, to underscore the point about agency. Epistemological and moral faculties are incapacitated outside the sphere of Christ and the Spirit, but with their arrival, the Christian community is newly addressable and reconstituted as a moral agent.[47]

Beyond that, Martyn's epistemology focuses more upon *what* the Christ event reveals. For Martyn, the human plight centers on the construction of an enslaving religious cosmos, the key moment for which is the arrival of the Sinaitic Law, introducing a "Law/Not Law" distinction and dividing the sacred from the profane: "the binary religious categorization of human beings is the fundamental identity of the curse pronounced by the Law."[48] The result is both social division

---

45. "Paul's Apocalyptic Politics," *ProEccl* 22, no. 2 (2013): 129–52, at 140 (my emphasis). The seminal piece is J. Louis Martyn, "Epistemology at the Turn of the Ages: 2 Corinthians 5:16," in *Christian History and Interpretation: Studies Presented to John Knox*, eds. W. R. Farmer, C. F. D. Moule, and R. R. Niebuhr (Cambridge: Cambridge University Press, 1967), 269–87; republished as idem, "Epistemology at the Turn of the Ages," in *Theological Issues in the Letters of Paul* (Edinburgh: T&T Clark, 1997), 89–110.

46. Ironically, then, apocalyptic (at least in this sense) has become one of the very things Beker sought to oppose with his own brand of apocalyptic—a form of Neo-orthodoxy in which eschatology "signifies the transcendent, ultimate character of the Christ-event as God's new self-revelation" (Beker, *Paul the Apostle*, 142).

47. Martyn's emphasis on the moral addressability of the Christian community is found especially in "Epilogue: An Essay in Pauline Meta-Ethics."

48. *Galatians*, 406n59. Martyn does trace the human plight back to Genesis 3 as well, but this much less prominent. For that theme, see J. Louis Martyn, "World Without End or Twice-Invaded World?," in *Shaking Heaven and Earth: Essays in Honor of Walter Brueggemann and Charles B. Cousar*, eds. Christine Roy Yoder et al. (Louisville: Westminster John Knox, 2005), 117–32.

and religious delusion—the "thought that, provided with a good religious foundation for a good religious ladder, the human being can ascend from the wrong to the right."[49] For Paul, salvation comes definitively from the other direction—it is God's invasive movement *into* the world and its unconditional character that shatters the religious cosmos, declaring its old antinomies defunct. Thus, "crucifixion with Christ means the death of the cosmos of religion, the cosmos in which all human beings live."[50] Likewise, Christian baptism signifies "the loss of the world of religious differentiation, the world, that is, that had as one of its fundamental elements the antinomy of the Law/the Not-Law."[51] Accordingly, salvation is accomplished less by participation in the death and resurrection of Christ, and more in the event of being confronted with the message of the cross, which generates an "epistemological crisis."[52]

For Campbell, the significance of apocalyptic (=Christocentric) epistemology lies chiefly in its methodological implications. This is revealed in the morphing acronym, which represents the view that Paul (and Campbell) opposes. In *The Quest for Paul's Gospel*, the target was JF, "Justification by Faith"; that became JT, "Justification Theory," in *The Deliverance of God* in order to allow for an apocalyptic re-reading of the phrase δικαιοσύνη θεοῦ and to focus energies on a contractual theory that misread Paul. This remains a burden of his work, but the latest acronym, FT,[53] has clarified the central target: *Forward Theory*, that is, a prospective, foundationalist, plight-to-solution hermeneutic rather than a retrospective and Christocentric approach.

Campbell also adapts Martyn's insight to begin speaking of

---

49. J. Louis Martyn, "Galatians, An Anti-Judaic Document?," in *Theological Issues in the Letters of Paul* (Edinburgh: T&T Clark, 1997), 77–84, at 82.

50. Martyn, "Apocalyptic Antinomies," 119.

51. By now, it is clear why Congdon links Martyn with Barth and why, understood in these terms, he has ambitions of bringing Bultmann into the apocalyptic fold. One wonders though why Käsemann is excluded from their circle, given that *homo religiosus* was, clearly and frequently, in his sights. Granted he does not invoke "apocalyptic" to address these concerns—his preferred pin to burst religious pretension was the slogan "the justification of the ungodly"—but nevertheless, Käsemann was a prolific burster of pious bubbles.

52. Martyn, *Galatians*, 104.

53. For which, see Douglas A. Campbell, "An Attempt to Be Understood: A Response to the Concerns of Matlock and Macaskill with the Deliverance of God," *JSNT* 34, no. 2 (2011): 162–208, at 180.

apocalyptic politics. Here, the nature of God's intervention in Christ—liberative, unconditional, non-retributive—proves generative, as does the thought that God has subverted and turned upside down the world's cherished values and institutions. Which is to say, a Lutheran insight, of all things, seems to be making a comeback—namely, the *theologia crucis*.[54]

On that bombshell, we conclude the survey of the theological emphases that trade under the name "apocalyptic." There is the undeniable feeling, in Louis MacNeice's phrase, of "the drunkenness of things being various," but I hope the above will facilitate a more nuanced and sober engagement with this multifaceted tradition.

It only remains to note that on this last point of apocalyptic epistemology, it might appear as though the apocalyptic reading of Paul has finally come home to the apocalyptic genre, given the fact that revelation has often been thought central to the latter. Indeed, this is Sturm's proposal for bringing together the literary and theological strands of research, for he sees a rapprochement brewing in Christopher Rowland's emphasis on the disclosure of secrets as a central motif in the apocalypses, on the one hand, and Martyn's emphasis on epistemology, on the other. Might it be as simple as noting that *apokalypsis* means "revelation"?

Well, it is certainly true that Rowland has been influential, drawing attention to the motif of the revelation of mysteries.[55] And it is

---

54. The emphasis upon the way in which God's victory is won through self-giving and his power demonstrated in weakness is also tempering enthusiasm for the military language. See, e.g., Susan Grove Eastman, "Apocalypse and Incarnation: The Participatory Logic of Paul's Gospel," in *Apocalyptic and the Future of Theology: With and Beyond J. Louis Martyn*, eds. Joshua B. Davis and Douglas Harinck (Eugene: Cascade, 2012), 165–82, at 171; Richard B. Hays, "Apocalyptic Poiēsis in Galatians: Paternity, Passion and Participation," in *Galatians and Christian Theology: Justification, the Gospel, and Ethics in Paul's Letter* (Grand Rapids: Baker Academic, 2014), 200–219, at 217n37. Campbell, of course, is not alone in finding the theological senses of apocalyptic catalogued above fruitful for ethical and political reflection, and as one might expect, the theological diversity can be developed in various political directions. For other reflection, see, i.e., Jennings Jr., "Apocalyptic and Contemporary Theology"; Nancy J. Duff, "The Significance of Pauline Apocalyptic for Theological Ethics," in *Apocalyptic and the New Testament: Essays in Honor of J. Louis Martyn* (Eugene: Cascade, 2012), 279–96. Research into the significance of Jewish apocalypses as works of political resistance is also being acknowledged and embraced in this connection, e.g., Anathea E. Portier-Young, *Apocalypse against Empire: Theologies of Resistance in Early Judaism* (Grand Rapids: Eerdmans, 2011).

55. Rowland, *The Open Heaven*, 14: "To speak of apocalyptic, therefore, is to concentrate on the theme

certainly a feature of the works of Martyn and de Boer that they draw attention to the use of ἀποκαλύπτω and its cognates in Galatians.[56] However, things are once again more complicated than they appear, and for a number of reasons. First, the extent to which the apocalypses can be held together around the theme of revelation is disputed. Collins, for example, grants that Rowland has brought a helpful corrective, but warns against essentialist definitions that focus on revelation or that exclude eschatology.[57]

Second, the closer one stays with the trope of the revealing of heavenly realities by angelic beings, the further one moves away from the usual Pauline apocalyptic texts (Galatians, Romans 5–8). For example, although Rowland makes reference to Gal. 1:12 and 1:16, the bulk of his discussion is taken up with 2 Cor. 12:2–4 and references to revealed mysteries (i.e., the use of μυστήριον language).[58] If, alternatively, one concentrates on Paul's language of revelation more generally, then the connection to the apocalyptic genre becomes more tenuous,[59] and texts such as Rom. 1:17–18 will loom larger than they usually do in apocalyptic accounts of Paul.[60]

Third, it is worth being aware that the language of revelation/apokalypsis is pressed into the service of very diverse readings of Paul. Wright, for example, expounds Rom. 1:17 in an attempt to defuse the antithesis between salvation-historical and apocalyptic readings of Paul, detecting a reference to the covenant faithfulness of God revealed and fulfilled in unexpected ways.[61] By

of the direct communication of the heavenly mysteries in all their diversity." He is singled out for rare praise in Matlock, *Unveiling the Apocalyptic Paul*, 282–88.

56. See, e.g., J. Louis Martyn, "Apocalyptic Antinomies in Paul's Letter to the Galatians," *NTS* 31, no. 3 (1985): 410–24, at 424n26: "We have noted above that in composing Galatians Paul employs at crucial points the noun ἀποκάλυψις and the verb ἀποκαλύπτω. It is strange that in the investigation of apocalyptic patterns in Paul's thought relatively little attention has been given to the Apostle's use of these vocables."

57. John J. Collins, *The Apocalyptic Imagination* (Grand Rapids: Eerdmans, 1998), 9–10.

58. Rowland, *The Open Heaven*, 374–86.

59. "Revelation" as a theme by itself can hardly be restricted to apocalyptic literature, nor can an interest in "mysteries," as Beale and Gladd's survey of Jewish literature reveals. G. K. Beale and Benjamin L. Gladd, *Hidden But Now Revealed* (Nottingham: IVP, 2014), 47–55.

60. See, e.g., the discussion in Bockmuehl, *Revelation and Mystery in Ancient Judaism and Pauline Christianity*, WUNT 2/36 (Tübingen: Mohr Siebeck, 1990), 138–41.

61. Seeking to express the element of continuity *and* discontinuity, Wright speaks of Paul's conviction

contrast, both Martyn and de Boer interpret Paul's use of *apokalypsis* language to speak of something more than a revelation of unseen realities and emphasize it to sharpen the apocalyptic edge. In Martyn's view, the term "emphasizes once again that God's good news is fundamentally apocalyptic in the sense of being the event of God's stepping powerfully on the scene from beyond."[62] De Boer's survey of *apokalypsis* language in Paul notes that it can refer to the Parousia and to "the disclosure of divine mysteries through the Spirit," but it also functions "as a reference to God's cataclysmic invasion of the world in Christ."[63] It seems, then, that the use of these terms in Paul is most often seized upon, not as opportunity to draw nearer to the apocalypses, but rather, to shore up a theological reading of Paul.

Indeed, in closing, there is decreasing interest in using the term "apocalyptic" to make any historical or literary claim; instead, it is being used to signal an autobiographical or theological lineage. For example, though she once expressed concern that the term "obscures at least as much as it clarifies" when applied to historical matters,[64] Beverley Gaventa now sees it as a matter of necessity to use it, but simply as a point of intellectual honesty, signaling a debt to Käsemann, Beker, and Martyn.[65] Campbell goes further, arguing that "the only use I can see for such a phrase is to communicate 'in-house' information within Pauline debates quickly—where one stands roughly in interpretive terms, and who one reads (and the use of the word 'apocalyptic' usually denotes a strong link with either Käsemann or Martyn)."[66] If this chapter has done its work, then perhaps we wonder how quickly and effectively that information is communicated, given

---

that "the one God had acted suddenly, shockingly and unexpectedly—just as he had always said he would" (*Paul and the Faithfulness of God*, 2:1411).

62. Martyn, *Galatians*, 158.

63. Martinus C. de Boer, *Galatians: A Commentary*, NTL (Louisville: Westminster John Knox, 2011), 81. For de Boer, Rom. 1:17–18 also speaks of this cataclysmic invasion.

64. Beverley R. Gaventa, "The Singularity of the Gospel: A Reading of Galatians," in *Pauline Theology Vol. 1: Thessalonians, Philippians, Galatians, and Philemon*, ed. Jouette M. Bassler (Minneapolis: Fortress Press, 1991), 147–59, at 158–59.

65. Gaventa, *Our Mother Saint Paul*, 82–83.

66. Campbell, *The Quest for Paul's Gospel*, 57n3.

the great many theological concepts in play; but perhaps at least the apocalyptic landscape seems a little less chaotic now.

PART II

3

Apocalyptic as God's Eschatological Activity in Paul's Theology

Martinus C. de Boer

Apocalyptic Eschatology as the Expectation of God's Definitive Intervention

In publications devoted to "apocalyptic Paul," I have consistently used the term "apocalyptic" as an adjective, modifying the noun "eschatology." The focus of my research has been Paul's "apocalyptic eschatology."[1] But I am not averse to using the term "apocalyptic" also

---

1. See M. C. de Boer, *The Defeat of Death: Apocalyptic Eschatology in 1 Corinthians 15 and Romans 5*, JSNTSup 22 (Sheffield: JSOT, 1988); "Paul and Jewish Apocalyptic Eschatology," in *Apocalyptic and the New Testament: Essays in Honor of J. Louis Martyn*, eds. J. Marcus and M. Soards, JSNTSup 24 (Sheffield: JSOT, 1989), 169–90; "Paul and Apocalyptic Eschatology," in *The Encyclopedia of Apocalypticism*, Vol. I, ed. J. J. Collins (New York: Continuum, 1998), 345–83; reprinted in *The Continuum History of Apocalypticism*, eds. B. McGinn, J. J. Collins, and S. J. Stein (New York: Continuum, 2003), 166–94; "Excursus 2: Galatians and Apocalyptic Eschatology," in *Galatians: A*

45

as a noun.[2] When I do, I employ it as convenient shorthand for this particular form of eschatology.[3]

In using the expression "apocalyptic eschatology," I have profited from a threefold distinction propounded by Paul D. Hanson in an article published in 1976.[4] He distinguishes "apocalyptic eschatology" from an "apocalypse," on the one hand, and "apocalypticism," on the other. John J. Collins has propounded a similar distinction.[5]

The term *apocalypse*, for Hanson, designates a literary genre. This has become the accepted and ubiquitous academic use of the term, mainly through the efforts of Collins.[6] The paradigm of the genre is the NT book of Revelation, also known as the Apocalypse. In fact,

---

Commentary, NTL (Louisville: Westminster John Knox, 2012), 31–35. This chapter takes these publications as a point of departure, as also the following articles: "Paul, Theologian of God's Apocalypse," *Int* 56, no. 1 (2002): 34–44; and "Paul's Mythologizing Program in Romans 5–8," in *Apocalyptic Paul: Cosmos and Anthropos in Romans 5–8*, ed. B. Roberts Gaventa (Waco: Baylor University Press, 2013), 1–20. I am also deeply indebted to the work of J. Louis Martyn, in particular his article, "Apocalyptic Antinomies in the Letter to the Galatians," *NTS* 31, no. 3 (1985): 410–24, and his magisterial commentary, *Galatians: A New Translation with Introduction and Commentary*, AB 33A (New York: Doubleday, 1997), esp. 97–105.

2. This usage has probably occurred under the influence of the German noun *Apokalyptik*. Since the 1980s, some scholars have found the nominal use of the English word "apocalyptic" deeply problematic, but the nominal use has become ingrained in biblical scholarship in English through the publication of such influential works as D. H. Russell, *The Method and Message of Jewish Apocalyptic: 200 BC–AD 100*, OTL (Philadelphia: Westminster, 1964) and C. C. Rowland, *The Open Heaven. A Study of Apocalyptic in Judaism and Christianity* (New York: Crossroad, 1982). This usage can no longer be undone, nor does it need to be as long as authors are clear about how they are using the term.

3. I here use the term "eschatology" to mean simply human expectations concerning "the (very) last things," that is, the final destiny of human beings and the world in which they live. Apocalyptic eschatology is a particular form of such expectation, to be further specified below.

4. "Apocalypticism," *The Interpreter's Dictionary of the Bible: Supplementary Volume* (Nashville: Abingdon, 1976), 28–34.

5. *The Apocalyptic Imagination: An Introduction to the Jewish Matrix of Christianity* (New York: Crossroad, 1984), 2–11. See also Collins, *Apocalypticism in the Dead Sea Scrolls* (London and New York: Routledge, 1997), 1–11. It is, I think, unfortunate that this threefold distinction is not maintained by F. J. Murphy, *Apocalypticism in the Bible and its World: A Comprehensive Introduction* (Grand Rapids: Baker Academic, 2012), 5.

6. See his influential and much quoted definition in Collins, ed., *Apocalypse: The Morphology of a Genre*, *Semeia* 14 (Missoula, MT: Scholars, 1979), 6: "a genre of revelatory literature with a narrative framework, in which a revelation is mediated to a human recipient, disclosing a transcendent reality which is both temporal, insofar as it envisages eschatological salvation, and spatial insofar as it involves another, supernatural world." In his "Introduction to Volume I" of *The Encyclopedia of Apocalypticism* (see note 1 above), Collins expanded this definition with words taken from A. Yarbro Collins, ed., *Early Christian Apocalypticism: Genre and Social Settings*, *Semeia* 36 (Missoula, MT: Scholars, 1986), 7 concerning the social and rhetorical function of such writings: they were "intended to interpret present, earthly circumstances in light of the supernatural world and of the future, and to influence both the understanding and behavior of the audience by means of divine authority" (xiii).

the genre designation is derived from this book whose first word is ἀποκάλυψις, "apocalypse/revelation."[7] It is not clear, however, whether the term here already functions as a genre designation[8] or simply as a description of the book's content(s): "An ἀποκάλυψις of Jesus Christ, which God gave him to show his servants what must soon take place; and he made it known by sending his angel to his servant John" (Rev. 1:1, RSV, 2nd ed.). The ἀποκάλυψις of Jesus Christ, it may be noted, concerns *events* that must soon occur.[9] As the rest of the book makes plain, these coming *events* are *eschatological*.[10]

Hanson uses the term *apocalypticism* to describe "the symbolic universe in which an apocalyptic movement codifies its identity and interpretation of reality." "This symbolic universe," he continues, "crystallizes around the perspective of apocalyptic eschatology which the movement adopts."[11] Since apocalyptic eschatology is evidently the defining characteristic of an apocalyptic movement's symbolic

---

7. Both the Greek noun ἀποκάλυψις and the English noun "revelation" (from the Latin *revelatio*) literally mean "unveiling" ("veil" in Greek is κάλυμμα, in Latin *velum*), just as the corresponding Greek verb ἀποκαλύπτω and the English verb "reveal" (from the Latin *revelare*) both literally mean "to unveil," and thus "to uncover (what was hidden)."

8. The book actually has the formal features of a (circular) letter to seven churches (cf. 1:4; 22:21).

9. Moreover, the value of the genre designation for books written before the second century CE is dubious, since, according to Collins, the "use of the Greek title *apokalypsis* (revelation) is not attested in the period before Christianity." Works written before Revelation, he notes, "had not yet attained the generic self-consciousness" evident in later works, and thus "have affinities to more than one genre" (*Apocalyptic Imagination*, 3). An "apocalypse" is thus to be regarded as "a generic framework" incorporating other literary genres (letter, testament, parable, hymn, prayer, etc.) and "is not constituted by one or more literary themes but by a distinctive combination of elements, all of which are found elsewhere" (*Apocalyptic Imagination*, 8–9). (Similar remarks are made by Hanson, "Apocalypticism"). Such observations make any clear definition of the genre whereby an apocalypse (as a self-contained book) can be usefully distinguished from other literary genres (other books) well-nigh impossible (see the confusion about the matter in Murphy, *Apocalypticism*, 4–8). Collins notes that the formal definition offered in *Morphology* (see note 6 above) actually applies only "to various sections" of such works as *1 Enoch, 4 Ezra* and *2 Baruch* (*Apocalyptic Imagination*, 4), but this has not prevented many scholars, including Collins himself, from referring to *1 Enoch, 4 Ezra, 2 Baruch,* etc. in their entirety as "apocalypses" (cf. Collins, *Apocalyptic Imagination*, 5–7). In *Defeat of Death* (197n4), I suggested that Collins's definition in *Morphology* amounts to a definition of a "vision" (more accurately, "a written report of a vision"), a genre designation not normally applied to whole books. The various parts of works such as Daniel, *1 Enoch* or *4 Ezra* are often labeled "visions." It may thus be better to think of an apocalypse as a smaller literary genre (*Form*) akin to prayer, parable or hymn, and not as a larger literary genre (*Gattung*) for a whole book such as letter, gospel, or history. By this definition, Mark 13 and 1 Thess. 4:13-18 are apocalypses (as generally recognized), but Mark and 1 Thessalonians, of course, are not. The same would apply, e.g., to Isaiah 24–27 ("the Isaiah Apocalypse") or *1 Enoch* 83–91 ("the Animal Apocalypse").

10. See note 3 above for a brief, working definition of "eschatology."

11. "Apocalypticism," 30.

universe and is also given separate treatment by Hanson, a more appropriate definition of "apocalypticism" would be: "a social movement adopting an apocalyptic perspective on reality,"[12] or "a group having recourse to apocalyptic eschatology as its symbolic universe."[13] It is important for our purposes to note that, for Hanson, apocalyptic eschatology is not confined to historical apocalyptic movements to the extent such can be traced; it can be embraced by different social groups in diverse circumstances.[14]

That brings us then to Hanson's understanding of *apocalyptic eschatology*. He defines it as "a religious perspective, a way of viewing divine plans in relation to mundane realities."[15] For understandable reasons, apocalyptic eschatology as a perspective or worldview has been closely associated with the book of Revelation—the Apocalypse—and other ancient literature sharing (at least some of) its generic features,[16] especially the so-called "historical apocalypses" found in such works as Daniel and *4 Ezra*.[17] The eschatology found in Revelation is itself strongly indebted to Jewish antecedents and traditions, even if it goes far beyond them in its use of imagery and symbolism and has a specifically Christian focus.[18] Apocalyptic eschatology, whether Christian or Jewish, is assumed to bear at least a "family resemblance" to the eschatology found in the book of Revelation.[19] For this reason, among others, it has been called *apocalyptic* eschatology instead of something else.[20] Hanson notes that this perspective, or worldview, is

---

12. Cf. Collins, *Apocalyptic Imagination*, 10 ("a historical movement"), though in *The Encyclopedia of Apocalypticism* (see note 2 above), Collins uses the term to designate "a worldview" ("Introduction to Volume 1," xiv), as does Murphy (*Apocalypticism*, 8).

13. Cf. E. Cuvillier, "Das apokalyptische Denken im Neuen Testament: Paulus und Johannes von Patmos als Beispiele," *ZNT* 22 (2008): 2–12. *Apokalyptik*, according to Cuvillier, concerns three things: a literary genre (*Gattung*), a social movement, and a worldview or ideology characterized by apocalyptic eschatology (p. 2).

14. See further Hanson, "Apocalypses and Apocalypticism (Genre, Introductory Overview)," in *ABD*, vol. 1 (New York: Doubleday, 1992), 279–82. See also de Boer, *Defeat of Death*, 41.

15. "Apocalypticism," 29. This perspective, says Hanson, is not to be confused with "a system of thought."

16. But see the discussion in note 9 above.

17. See Collins, *Apocalyptic Imagination*, 5.

18. See R. Bauckham, *The Theology of the Book of Revelation* (Cambridge: Cambridge University Press, 1988), 9–12.

19. The actual "touchstone" for any definition of apocalyptic eschatology, therefore, is not "the kind of eschatology found in the apocalypses" generally (Collins, *Apocalyptic Imagination*, 9) but the kind of eschatology found in the book of Revelation specifically.

not confined to Revelation nor to apocalypses generally, but that it can also find expression in or through other genres of literature (parables, hymns, letters, testaments). As a perspective, it is not genre-specific, it is not genre-bound.[21]

Hanson's definition of apocalyptic eschatology as "a religious perspective, a way of viewing divine plans in relation to mundane realities," is rather vague and needs elaboration. This Hanson, in fact, provides. He points out that as a religious perspective, *early* Jewish apocalyptic eschatology, which was Hanson's particular area of expertise,[22] concerns *God's* "final saving acts" and these final divine saving acts involve "deliverance out of the present order into a new transformed order" of reality. Hanson appeals in this connection to Isa. 65:17: "For behold, I [God] create new heavens and a new earth; and the former things shall not be remembered or come into mind" (RSV).[23] We may compare Rev. 21:1–2: "Then I [John] saw a new heaven and a new earth; for the first heaven and the first earth had passed away. . . . And I saw the holy city, new Jerusalem, coming down out of heaven from God" (RSV). The expected new order of reality will not be a rehabilitation or a reconfiguration of the present (social and political) order of reality ("this age"), as is generally the case in OT prophetic eschatology,[24] but its termination and *replacement* by something

---

20. It may go without saying that the expression "apocalyptic eschatology" is "a construct of scholars that purports to epitomize certain phenomena discernible in the sources" (de Boer, "Paul and Jewish Apocalyptic Eschatology," 172). Any definition of the term is partly a matter of scholarly tradition and convenience even though it is based, as it should be, upon the data of the available sources, primarily Revelation, but also such conceptually related works as (parts of) Daniel, *1 Enoch* and *4 Ezra*. There may be ancient apocalypses that contain no eschatology or an entirely different one, or that use the language of revelation outside the framework of apocalyptic eschatology, but that is of no consequence for the soundness of the definition since there is enough data to support it.

21. See Collins, *Apocalypticism in the Dead Sea Scrolls*, 8: "A worldview is not necessarily tied to one literary form, and the apocalyptic worldview could find expression in other genres besides apocalypses." On the problem of genre definition, see note 9 above. The nature of the relationship of apocalyptic to the literary genre apocalypse has bedeviled biblical scholarship since the pioneering work of F. Lücke in 1832. See R. Sturm, "Defining the Word 'Apocalyptic': A Problem in Biblical Criticism," in *Apocalyptic and the New Testament*, eds. J. Marcus and M. Soards, JSNTSup 24 (Sheffield: JSOT, 1989), 17–48.

22. Cf. *The Dawn of Apocalyptic. The Historical and Sociological Roots of Jewish Apocalyptic Eschatology*, 2nd ed. (Philadelphia: Fortress, 1979).

23. "Apocalypticism," 30.

24. On this issue, see Hanson, *Dawn* (note 22 above) and J. J. Collins, "From Prophecy to

completely new ("the age to come").[25] The new Jerusalem will replace the old Jerusalem.[26] The new order of reality will replace the old order of reality, and it will do so definitively, finally, and irrevocably, that is, eschatologically. This act of replacement will be initiated and brought about by God and God alone, which is to say that it cannot be initiated by human beings or effected by them.

The word "apocalyptic" in scholarly discussion—especially since the work of Johannes Weiss, and after him, Albert Schweitzer,[27] Ernst Käsemann,[28] and more recently, J. Louis Martyn,[29]—evokes this expectation of God's own eschatological activity of putting an end to the present order of reality ("this age") and replacing it with a new, transformed order of reality ("the age to come"). As Weiss wrote, in connection with Jesus' proclamation of the Kingdom of God: "By force and insurrection men might establish a Davidic monarch . . . but God will establish the Kingdom of God without human hands, horse or rider, with only his angels and celestial powers"; "God himself must come and make everything new"; "The actualization of the Kingdom of God is *not* a matter for human initiative, but entirely a matter of

---

Apocalypticism: The Expectation of the End," in *Encyclopedia of Apocalypticism*, I.129–61 (note 1 above).

25. Cf. Philipp Vielhauer, "'Einleitung' zu 'Apokalypsen und Verwandtes,'" *Neutestamentliche Apokryphen in deutscher Übersetzung, Band II* (eds. E. Hennecker and W. Schneemelcher; Tübingen: J. C. B. Mohr [Paul Siebeck], 1964), 407–42 (413), for whom the eschatological dualism of the two ages is *the* defining characteristic apocalyptic eschatology. The classic text is *4 Ezra* 7:50: "the Most High has not made one age, but two." There are scattered references to "this age" and/or "the age to come" in the relevant literature (cf. *1 Enoch* 71:15; *4 Ezra* 7:112, 119; *2 Baruch* 44:8, 15; 83:4, 9; in the Mishnah, see *Abot* 4:1; *Sanhedrin* 10:1; *Berakot* 9:5), including the NT (e.g., Eph. 1:21; Matt. 12:32; Luke 20:34–35). For Paul, see below. This dualism should probably not be called a doctrine (as D. S. Russell does in *Method and Message*, 269), as if it were some carefully worked out principle or teaching. It is better to think of it as the basic presupposition of an apocalyptic-eschatological worldview, whether that be Jewish or Christian and whether or not the specific terms are used. The dualism of the two ages can be given expression in a rich diversity of imagery, symbolism, and concepts, derived from a wide variety of sources. It is thus somewhat misleading and even futile to provide a list of "characteristics" of the apocalyptic worldview or of apocalyptic literature, as is often done. The "family resemblance" between apocalyptic texts in all their diversity lies in the eschatological dualism of the two ages.

26. The new age does not merely succeed the old age as on a timeline; it *replaces* this age with another age. For the two ages are not merely temporal epochs; they are also, perhaps even primarily, orbs or spheres (spaces) in which certain activities take place. The two ages are fundamentally distinct, mutually exclusive "orders of reality" (to use Hanson's terminology) or "worlds."

27. A. Schweitzer, *The Mysticism of Paul the Apostle* (London: A&C Black, 1931; German 1930).

28. E. Käsemann, "The Beginnings of Christian Theology" and "On the Subject of Primitive Christian Apocalyptic," in *New Testament Questions of Today* (Philadelphia: Fortress, 1969), 82–137.

29. Martyn, "Apocalyptic Antinomies"; idem, *Galatians* (see note 1).

God's initiative."[30] Weiss described such views as "eschatological-apocalyptic." They are not just apocalyptic (matters of divine revelation) and not just eschatological (expectations of events concerning "the last things"), but both—what I would call (reversing Weiss's word order) "apocalyptic-eschatological"! Apocalyptic (as I use the term) is a form of eschatology that expects God to come and establish a new order of reality for human beings.[31] That new order of reality will have a "heavenly" character because it will come from heaven, which is to say, from the realm of God (cf. Rev. 21:1-2, cited above). For that reason, this new world will be nothing like what has been seen before (cf. 1 Cor. 2:9: "what no eye has seen, nor ear heard, nor the heart of a human being conceived").

To adopt an apocalyptic perspective, then, is not "to concentrate on the theme of the direct communication of heavenly mysteries in all their diversity,"[32] but on the expectation of God's own visible eschatological activity, what we may, I think, call the Apocalypse of God[33]—where the term "apocalypse" obviously does not denote a literary genre, nor does the term signify only divine revelation or disclosure of previously hidden information, but also, visible divine movement and activity on a cosmic scale.

In the view of Paul (but also in that of John, the seer of Revelation), this Apocalypse of God occurs in the event of Jesus Christ. So, Paul writes: "When the fullness of time came, *God* . . . ." God did something. He "sent forth his Son . . . so that he might redeem those under the Law, so that we might receive adoption as sons" (Gal. 4:4-5; cf. Rom. 5:8; 8:3-4). As part of this same Apocalypse of God, "God sent forth

---

30. J. Weiss, *Jesus' Proclamation of the Kingdom of God*, eds. R. H. Hiers and D. L. Holland (Chico, CA: Scholars Press, 1971), 102, 108, and 132 (original emphasis), respectively, a translation of the first German edition of *Die Predigt Jesu vom Reiche Gottes* (Göttingen: Vandenhoeck & Ruprecht, 1892).

31. Let that serve as a concise definition of apocalyptic eschatology. See note 20 above.

32. Rowland, *Open Heaven*, 14. See my critique of Rowland's approach in "Paul, Theologian of God's Apocalypse."

33. De Boer, "Paul, Theologian of God's Apocalypse," 24, 33. It is true that neither Paul nor Revelation uses this expression, but both do use the expression "an apocalypse of Jesus Christ" (Gal. 1:12; Rev. 1:1) and for both, God is effectively present in the person and the work of Christ. The apocalypse of Jesus Christ, then, is for both tantamount to the Apocalypse of God (I capitalize the term here to indicate the finality of the event). See further below on Paul's use of the terms ἀποκάλυψις and ἀποκαλύπτω.

the Spirit of his Son into our hearts" (Gal. 4:6). As Martyn has written, "The advent of the Son and of his Spirit is thus *the* cosmic, apocalyptic event."[34] The difference here from ancient Jewish apocalyptic eschatology is the conviction that in the coming of Jesus Christ, God has inaugurated "the final saving acts" (to use Hanson's phrase) that mark the definitive end of the old order of reality ("this age") and its irrevocable replacement by the new order of reality ("the age to come," which for Paul and John of Revelation is no longer solely a future expectation).[35] It is therefore a mistake to limit apocalyptic eschatology in Paul (or in Revelation) to the future acts of God (or Christ), that is, to the Parousia (1 Thess. 4:15; 1 Cor. 15:23) or the End (1 Cor. 1:8; 15:24).[36] For Paul (as for John of Revelation), apocalyptic eschatology involves an "already" and a "still more."[37] The death and resurrection of Christ has inaugurated a unified apocalyptic drama that reaches its

---

34. J. L. Martyn, *Theological Issues in the Letters of Paul* (SNTW; Edinburgh: T&T Clark, 1997), 121 (emphasis original).

35. Paul refers specifically to "this age" (ὁ αἰὼν οὗτος) in several passages (Rom. 12:2; 1 Cor. 1:20; 2:6, 8; 3:18; 2 Cor. 4:4. He can also call it "this world" (ὁ κόσμος οὗτος) in 1 Cor. 3:19; 5:10; 7:31; cf. Eph. 2:2; 4 *Ezra* 4:2; 8:1). He does not use the expression "the age to come" (ὁ αἰὼν ὁ μέλλων/ὁ ἐρχόμενος) in his undisputed letters though it does occur in Eph. 1:21 as well as other NT texts (Matt. 12:32; Mark 10:30; Luke 18:30; cf. 1 Cor. 10:11; Eph. 2:7; Heb. 6:5). It would seem probable that such expressions as "the Kingdom of God" (Rom. 14:17; 1 Cor. 4:20; 6:9-10; 15:50; Gal. 5:17; cf. Eph. 5:5; Col. 1:13), "eternal life" (Rom. 2:7; 5:21; 6:22–23; Gal. 6:8), and "new creation" (2 Cor. 5:17; Gal. 6:15) in Paul (and elsewhere in the NT as well as in Jewish apocalyptic texts from the period) are often best understood as other ways of speaking about the age to come (looked at from different angles). The absence of the expression "the age to come" can also be explained by the fact that, for Paul, the new age had already begun to dawn in God's sending the Son and his Spirit.

36. In "Primitive Christian Apocalyptic," Käsemann observes that he speaks of "primitive Christian apocalyptic to denote the expectation of an imminent Parousia" (109n1). It is in this sense that "Apocalyptic was the mother of all Christian theology" ("Beginnings," 102). But Käsemann nuances this strict definition later in the former essay: "Christ is God's representative over a world which is not yet fully subject to God, although its eschatological subordination is in train since Easter and its end is in sight. No perspective could be more apocalyptic. . . . Paul is absolutely unable and unwilling to speak of any end to history which has already come to pass, but, he does, however, discern that the day of the End-time has *already* broken" (133; emphasis added). It is Martyn who has insisted that Paul's present eschatology must also be given the label "apocalyptic," not just his future eschatology, which remains equally important for Martyn's understanding of Paul as an apocalyptic theologian. Cf. Martyn, "Apocalyptic Antinomies in Galatians," 421: "Paul's perception of Jesus' death is, then, fully as apocalyptic as is his hope for Jesus' parousia (cf. 1 Cor. 2.8)."

37. For this formulation of the tension, see de Boer, *Galatians*, 34. This tension has often been formulated as an "already" and a "not yet," the latter reflecting "an eschatological reservation" formulated by Paul over against pneumatic enthusiasts in Corinth (Käsemann, "Primitive Christian Apocalyptic," 132). But for Paul himself and other believers, such as those in Thessalonica or Jerusalem, the (eager) expectation of an imminent Parousia was a matter of "still more."

conclusion at the Parousia/the End (1 Cor. 15:20–26).[38] The Apocalypse of God in Jesus Christ covers events from the initial sending of the Son and his Spirit into the world to the transfer of Christ's messianic sovereignty to God at the End (1 Cor. 15:23–28).[39]

God's Apocalypse and the Human Plight

But now, the question arises: What makes God's eschatological intervention necessary in ancient Jewish apocalyptic eschatology and in Paul's christologically informed adaptation?[40] Why, in other words, is it that human beings are not capable of putting an end to the old order of reality ("this age") and replacing it with a new one ("the age to come")?

The answer is that "this age" is characterized, above all else, by death.[41] The term "death" is applied not only to the physical demise of human beings (bodily death), but also (in a metaphorical extension) to sinful behavior (moral or spiritual death) and to damnation or

38. Jewish apocalyptic eschatology, it is sometimes asserted, has its own version of "already" and "still more" (or "not yet"). This was already noted by Käsemann, "'The Righteousness of God' in Paul," in *Perspectives on Paul* (Philadelphia: Fortress, 1971), 178. The point has received new emphasis in the work of L. Stuckenbruck, "Overlapping Ages and 'Apocalyptic' in Pauline Theology," *The Dead Sea Scrolls and Pauline Literature* (ed. J. B. Rey; Leiden: Brill, 2013), 309–26; idem, "Evil in Johannine and Apocalyptic Perspective: Petition for Protection in John 17," *John's Gospel and Intimations of Apocalyptic* (eds. C. H. Williams and C. Rowland; London: Bloomsbury, 2014), 220–32, esp. 229–32. However, the term "eschatology" in the expression "apocalyptic eschatology" involves finality and irrevocability, things that cannot be said of earlier divine interventions, also in the history of Israel. Furthermore, for Paul, previous divine interventions did not (in retrospect) deal with the problem (the human plight). Only Christ has done that. See Martyn, "Apocalyptic Antinomies," 121: "For the true war of liberation has been initiated not at Sinai, but rather in the apocalypse of the crucified one and in the coming of his Spirit." Until the coming of Christ, the promise to Abraham remained just that, a promise (cf. Gal. 3:6-29). See further note 47.

39. See de Boer, *Defeat of Death*, chapter 4. Cf. Martyn, *Galatians*, 105: Paul's "view has, in fact, three foci: Christ's future coming [his Parousia], Christ's past advent (his death and resurrection), and the present war against the powers of evil, inaugurated by his Spirit and taking place between these two events."

40. The revelation of the age to come simultaneously unmasks the present time and everything leading up to the new age as the old age that is doomed to pass away, usually very soon, when it will be replaced by the new age. Apocalyptic eschatology thus involves not only the expectation of the new age, but also, the assessment of the past (up to the present moment) as the order or realm of evil, as what Paul calls "the present evil age" in Gal. 1:4. Both ages, then, are matters of revelation.

41. This was a fundamental point of my book, *Defeat of Death*, where the relevant texts are scrutinized. The key texts in the letters of Paul are 1 Corinthians 15 (esp. vv. 20–28) and Romans 5 (esp. vv. 12–21).

perdition (eternal or eschatological death).[42] In all these usages, death signifies separation from God and from life, which is understood to involve being in the presence of God and there acting according to God's will. A presupposition of this picture is that human beings are incapable of doing anything about death. Death signifies the end of all human possibilities and hopes.[43] The understanding of "this age" as marked by death (irremediable separation or alienation from God) explains why there is no continuity between "this age" and "the age to come." It is only God who can bring life out of death, something out of nothing (cf. Rom. 4:17b), and for that reason, there is no remedy for the human plight apart from God's own intervention. It is also for this reason that the resurrection of the dead, however it may be conceived anthropologically and whatever its scope may be, is an apocalyptic event. It is in fact, soteriologically speaking, *the* apocalyptic event, for through it, God rectifies what has gone wrong with the human world, and does so once and for all. Without this divine intervention, physical and moral death are tantamount to eternal death.

There are two basic and competing explanations in the relevant sources for the human plight (death in its threefold form), and thus also for the solution to this situation. In the first explanation, represented especially by *1 Enoch* 1–36 (cf. also chs. 37–71), the human plight is attributable to evil angelic powers (Satan and his minions). These angelic powers are (ultimately) responsible for human sinfulness (idolatry in particular) and its primary consequence, the violent death of those who seek to acknowledge God's rightful sovereign claim on the world. In the second explanation, represented especially by *2 Baruch* (cf. also *4 Ezra*), human beings are themselves responsible for their plight (cosmological powers play no role). All human beings beginning with the first, Adam, have sinned, and thus deserve the death that overcomes each and every human being.

---

42. See de Boer, *Defeat of Death*, 83–84, 143–44.

43. Cf. 2 Sam. 14:14: "We must all die; we are like water spilled on the ground, which cannot be gathered up"; Job 7:9: "As the cloud fades and vanishes, so those who go down to Sheol do not come up." It is a characteristic of apocalyptic that (bodily) death is no longer regarded as a naturally necessary event or reality as it is in the OT. Death has become *the* indication that something has gone terribly wrong with the world.

The expected solution must address or correspond to the plight. For the first explanation of the human condition, therefore, the Last Judgment is expected to entail a victorious cosmic war against the evil cosmological powers,[44] at which time, God also vindicates their primary victims, the righteous few who have not allowed themselves to become complicit in the hegemony of the evil powers, often at the cost of persecution and death. God raises the righteous martyrs from the dead (a limited resurrection) and rewards them with eternal life (cf. Dan. 12:1-2). For the second explanation, the Last Judgment is expected to involve a cosmic courtroom before which all human beings appear before God for sentencing on the basis of their deeds.[45] To make this possible, all those who have already died are raised (a general resurrection) so that God can reward the righteous (a small number) with eternal life in the new age and condemn the wicked (a much larger group) to eternal death (perdition)—what Revelation calls "the second death" (Rev. 2:11; 20:6, 14; 21:8). For the former group, the sentence of death passed on Adam and his descendants is overturned; for the latter, it is confirmed and made eternal.[46]

In both of these distinguishable patterns of ancient Jewish apocalyptic eschatology, the Last Judgment is a cosmic event (involving all people from all times), in and through which the Creator God of Israel eschatologically (i.e., finally, definitively, and irrevocably) rectifies (puts right) the world God has created: "this evil age" ceases to exist and "the age to come," in which God reigns unopposed, takes its place. From a soteriological angle, the realm of life replaces the realm of death. In both patterns of ancient Jewish apocalyptic eschatology, furthermore, the righteous (or saints) are those who have

---

44. Cf. *1 Enoch* 1:3-9: "The God of the universe, the Holy Great One, will come forth from his dwelling. And from there he will march upon Mount Sinai and appear in his camp emerging from heaven with a mighty power. And everyone shall be afraid, and Watchers [fallen angels] shall quiver. . . . Behold, he will arrive with ten million of the holy ones in order to execute judgment upon all" (trans. E. Isaac, in J. H. Charlesworth, *Old Testament Pseudepigrapha*, vol. 1 [New York: Doubleday, 1983]).

45. Cf. *4 Ezra* 7:33-38; *2 Baruch* 49-52. According to *4 Ezra* 7:113, "the day of judgment will be the end of this age and the beginning of the immortal age to come."

46. The preceding paragraph is a brief summary of a complex set of data. For more detail and nuance, see de Boer, *Defeat of Death*, chapter 3. The same can be said for the paragraph that now follows.

acknowledged the sovereign claim of Israel's God (the First Commandment) and have done so by committing themselves to God's Law, which is God's standard for determining who is to be rewarded and punished at the Last Judgment.[47] The Law, then, is God's proffered remedy for death and its underlying cause, sin (the repudiation of God, which is the fundamental sin of Adam and each of his descendants). With the gift of the Law, God gives human beings a weapon to withstand evil powers (in the first explanation of the human plight) or a second chance to get it right (in the second explanation). In other words, when chosen and observed, the Law functions as a bridge for crossing the otherwise unbridgeable chasm—death—that separates human beings from God, and thus from life in the world to come.

There is, nevertheless, a fundamental difference between the two patterns, as indicated above: in the first or "cosmological" pattern, human beings are *victims of forces beyond their control*,[48] whereas in the second or "forensic" pattern, human beings are held to be *fully accountable moral agents*.[49] As a result, the Apocalypse of God is also differently conceived, either primarily as a cosmic war against evil cosmological powers which have usurped his sovereignty, or primarily as a cosmic courtroom in which all human beings are held accountable for what they have done or not done.[50]

---

47. For this reason, the righteous, in a sense, already proleptically experience and possess the eternal life that will be their reward at the Last Judgment.

48. This counts, though in different ways, both for those human beings (usually rulers) who are morally complicit in the hegemony of the evil powers and for those (the righteous) who resist the powers and are persecuted and even put to death as a result.

49. For the nomenclature "cosmological" and "forensic" to describe the two patterns or "tracks" of ancient Jewish apocalyptic eschatology, see de Boer, "Paul and Jewish Apocalyptic Eschatology." The "forensic" pattern is a weakened form of the "cosmological" pattern, that is to say, the former is a form of apocalyptic eschatology from which cosmological evil powers have disappeared, to be replaced by the notion of human guilt and responsibility. The cosmological pattern can have, and normally does, forensic elements (the evil powers or angels are judged as are the human beings who have been complicit in their hegemony; cf. *1 Enoch* 1), but the forensic pattern seeks to suppress or remove "cosmological" explanations for evil (see my discussion in "Paul and Jewish Apocalyptic Eschatology," 177–80).

50. At the Last Judgment, God can be expected to provide an effective remedy, usually the Spirit, in the new age for the strong human inclination to sin either by submitting themselves to the powers that be (in the cosmological pattern) or by making the wrong choice between life and death (in the forensic pattern). Cf. Ezek. 11:19–20; *Jub.* 1:23–24; 1QS 4:20. For Paul, see especially Gal. 3:1–5; 4:6, 16–25; Rom. 8:1–26, where the Spirit is God's powerful weapon against the works of the Flesh.

Paul adapts elements from both patterns of ancient Jewish apocalyptic eschatology.[51] As Albert Schweitzer pointed out eighty-five years ago, however, Paul's own perspective stands "closer"[52] to the apocalyptic eschatology of *1 Enoch* than to that of *2 Baruch* (or *4 Ezra*), which is to say, closer to the cosmological pattern of Jewish apocalyptic eschatology than to the forensic pattern. For Paul, according to Schweitzer, the present world-age is "characterized not only by its transience, but also by the fact that demons and angels exercise power in it," whereas the coming world-age "will put an end to this condition."[53] Salvation is "thus cosmologically conceived,"[54] that is, as the expurgation of evil demonic or angelic powers from the cosmos. This has also been the view of Käsemann and Martyn. I, in turn, have sought to show that in Romans, Paul appears to be in conversation with Jews, holding to a contemporary version of the forensic pattern, whereas in Galatians, he is seeking to rebut Christian Jews (preachers who have invaded the Galatian churches), holding to a modified ("Christianized") version of the very same pattern. In both letters, Paul does not reject or abandon the forensic categories, terms, and perspectives dear to his conversation partners,[55] but he does circumscribe or recontextualize them with notions that are fundamentally indebted to the cosmological pattern of Jewish apocalyptic eschatology. Sin and death, for example, are no longer simply matters of human behavior or experience, but are also conceptualized as evil cosmological powers that oppress, and thus *victimize* human beings—hence, Sin and Death (see esp. 1 Cor. 15:20–28, 54–56; Rom. 5:12–21). Paul sees all human history as a monolithic whole in which Sin and Death reign in tandem over the world, and have done so from Adam's transgression onward. In such an understanding of the human plight, the Law is not only too weak and ineffectual

---

51. The same is true of Revelation. Furthermore, the relevant Jewish texts also often exhibit elements from both patterns, especially the Dead Sea Scrolls.
52. Schweitzer, *Mysticism*, 57.
53. Ibid., 55.
54. Ibid., 54.
55. See de Boer, *Defeat of Death*; idem, "Justification in Paul: A Comparison of Galatians with Romans," available online at www.academia.edu.

for expurgating Sin, and thus also Death from the cosmos, it has also (ironically and lamentably) become a major tool in the hands of Sin for solidifying its Death-dealing hegemony over human beings.[56]

When God's Apocalypse is conceived of as the defeat and destruction of evil cosmological powers, God's intervention at the Last Judgment has the character of an invasion, a military metaphor Martyn has consistently used with respect to Paul.[57] With the coming of Christ and his Spirit, God has begun a war of liberation against and from evil powers that have ruined, distorted, despoiled, and perverted human life.[58] God's eschatological saving activity in Jesus Christ is, from beginning to end, apocalyptic in the sense that it entails a war of cosmic proportions against evil cosmological forces that have oppressed and victimized human beings.[59]

As indicated, the Law, for Paul, functions as a tool in the hands of Sin, solidifying its Death-dealing grip on the human world. Especially in Galatians, but also in Romans, Paul regards being "under the Law" as being tantamount to being "under Sin" (Gal. 3:22–23; cf. Rom. 3:9; 6:14–15). Christ's crucifixion is understood by Paul to be *the* event that announces and effects the end of the "world" (κόσμος) determined and given structure by the Law (Gal. 6:14–15).[60] For Paul, a world has been judged and destroyed in Christ's crucifixion, and that is what

---

56. See de Boer, "Paul's Mythologizing Program." The way in which the Law functions in the dual reign of Sin and Death shows that Israel does not constitute an exception any more than Abraham does. Abraham is placed among the ungodly (Rom. 4:5), and thus among the dead (4:17), as is Israel (11:15). There is, for Paul, "no distinction" with respect to either the plight or the solution (3:22; 10:12).

57. Martyn, *Galatians*, 105: "Specifically, both God's sending of Christ to suffer death in behalf of humanity (the cross) and Christ's future coming (the parousia) are *invasive* acts of God. And their being invasive acts—into a space that has temporarily fallen out of God's hands—points to the liberating war that is crucial to Paul's apocalyptic theology. It is this apocalyptic vision, then, that has given Paul his perception of the nature of the human plight. . . . The root trouble lies deeper than human guilt, and it is more sinister" (emphasis original). Cf. Käsemann, *Commentary on Romans* (Grand Rapids: Eerdmans, 1980), 134.

58. Cf. Martyn, "Antinomies," 122. See further, Beverly Roberts Gaventa, "The Rhetoric of Violence and the God of Peace in Paul's Letter to the Romans," in *Paul, John, and Apocalyptic Eschatology*, eds. J. Krans et al., NovTSup 149 (Leiden: Brill, 2013), 61–75.

59. As noted above, Paul does not abandon or reject forensic elements, such as a final judgment for deeds (cf. Rom. 14:10; 1 Cor. 5:10). It is this combination of elements that makes Paul a great and challenging thinker.

60. In 1 Corinthians 1–2, Paul uses the rhetoric of crucifixion to establish the end, that is, the destruction, of human "wisdom" for the believers in Corinth.

Paul wishes to emphasize in Galatians with his repeated references to Christ's cross and his crucifixion, instead of merely to his (atoning) death (cf. 2:19-20; 3:1, 13; 5:11, 24; 6:12, 14).[61] To be crucified is to be killed, to be violently put to death, and that is what happened to Paul—he was crucified with Christ (Gal. 2:19; 6:14)—of course, not in a literal, but in an extended sense: The "world" (Gal. 6:14) that he had known had been utterly destroyed, that world given structure and meaning and coherence and hope on the basis of the Law (cf. Rom. 6:6, 14). In short, the cross is understood to be an apocalyptic event which destroyed Paul's earlier conviction that by being Law-observant, and so, creating his own righteousness based on the Law (Phil. 3:9), he could bridge the gap of death that separates the present evil age from the Kingdom of God. He came to understand that the bridge from the one to the other can only be the righteousness that comes as a divine gift through the faith(fullness) of Christ (πίστις χριστοῦ: Gal. 2:16, 20–21; Rom. 3:21–26; Phil. 3:9)[62] and the Spirit that came into the world as a result (Gal. 3:1–5, 14; 4:6; 5:16–18, 22–23; Rom. 5:5; 8:1–26).

Paul's Apocalyptic Language and Faith

In contrast to the book of Revelation itself, Paul often uses the Greek noun ἀποκάλυψις "apocalyptically," that is, to signify God's eschatological activity in and through Christ, as he does the cognate verb ἀποκαλύπτω.[63] In 1 Corinthians 1:7, in particular, he refers to the Parousia as "the ἀποκάλυψις of our Lord Jesus Christ." In the next verse, he asserts that God "will strengthen" the Corinthian believers "to the End (τέλος)" (1:8; cf. 15:24) so that they "may be blameless on the day of

---

61. Cf. de Boer, *Defeat of Death*, 176–77.

62. Πίστις χριστοῦ can be translated either as "(human) faith *in* Christ" (the traditional rendering) or as "the faith(fulness) *of* Christ," which has received increasing support in recent years. See de Boer, *Galatians*, 148–50; and further below. My point would still stand if one were to adopt the traditional interpretation and translation.

63. Cf. Martyn, *Galatians*, 362: "On the whole . . . his [Paul's] apocalyptic language refers not to an *unveiling* of some *thing*, but to an *invasion* carried out by some *one* who has moved into the world from outside it" (emphasis original). I sought to provide a firmer basis for this claim, first in "Paul and Apocalyptic Eschatology," 354–57, and more expressly in "Paul, Theologian of God's Apocalypse," 25–29. This material was then incorporated into an excursus on "Paul's Language of Apocalyptic Revelation" in *Galatians*, 79–82. What follows is a brief summary of some relevant points.

our Lord Jesus Christ" (1:8). These two verses clearly point forward to chapter 15 where Paul refers explicitly to Christ's Parousia:

> all will be made alive in Christ. But each in his own order: Christ the first fruits, then at his παρουσία those who belong to Christ. Then is the End (τέλος), when he hands over the kingdom to God the Father, after he has destroyed every ruler and every authority and power. . . . The last enemy to be destroyed is Death. (1 Cor. 15:23b-24, 26)

The ἀποκάλυψις of Jesus Christ concerns, then, his visible eschatological appearance at his Parousia and this is clearly an apocalyptic *event*, whereby the cosmological principalities and powers of this evil age, especially Death, are finally and irrevocably brought to submission "so that God may be all in all" (cf. 1 Cor. 15:24–28). The ἀποκάλυψις referred to is no mere disclosure of previously hidden heavenly secrets, nor is it simply information about future events, but rather, concerns eschatological activity and movement, an invasion of the world below from heaven above, which is also, in a sense, an invasion of the present by the future.[64] According to 1 Thess. 4:15–16, where Paul uses the imagery of war, "the παρουσία of the Lord" means that Jesus "himself will descend from heaven with a cry of command, with the archangel's call, and with the sound of the trumpet of God" (cf. 2 Thess. 1:7).

Paul also uses this language in connection with the gospel he preaches. In Romans 1:16–17, he claims that in the gospel, "the righteousness of God *is being revealed* (ἀποκαλύπτεται) from faith for faith." This gospel is "the power of God (δύναμις θεοῦ) for salvation." Paul here relates the verb ἀποκαλύπτω directly to the notion of "the power of God." The righteousness of God becomes visible and powerful, or powerfully visible, in the gospel itself, and for that reason, within the sphere of faith (πίστις). Faith is elicited or created by the gospel of God's powerful righteousness and it is evidently, for Paul, a form of sharing in God's eschatological revelation, that is, in God's eschatological activity and movement.[65] Among other things, faith

---

64. Paul uses the terms ἀποκάλυψις and ἀποκαλύπτω in other passages (Rom. 2:5; 8:18; 1 Cor. 3:13) in a similar way, that is, in connection with a *future* apocalyptic-eschatological event.

signifies for Paul that a believer can truly see and perceive this action, this movement, of God *into* (and then, *in*) the world. The movement and presence of God are to be seen in the crucified and risen Christ and his Spirit. Furthermore, that this activity and movement of God involves judgment upon "this world" is evident in Rom. 1:18–32: The revelation of God's righteousness "through faith for faith" also means that "the wrath of God," normally associated with the Parousia (cf. Rom. 2:5; 5:9; 1 Thess. 1:10), "is [now also being powerfully] revealed (ἀποκαλύπτεται) from heaven upon all ungodliness and wickedness of those who by their wickedness suppress the truth" (Rom. 1:16–18). The creation of something eschatologically new in the world, faith, also entails God's judgment of a world marked by its absence before and apart from Christ.

That the terms ἀποκάλυψις and ἀποκαλύπτω are also being used "apocalyptically" in Galatians was suggested by Martyn: "it is precisely the Paul of Galatians who says with emphasis that the cosmos in which he previously lived met its end in God's apocalypse of Jesus Christ," with references to Gal. 1:12, 16; and 6:14. "It is this same Paul who identifies that apocalypse as the birth of his gospel-mission (1.16), and who speaks of the battles he has to wage for the truth of the gospel as events to be understood under the banner of apocalypse (2.2, 5, 14)."[66] The basis for these claims actually lies in Gal. 3:23: "Now before faith came (ἐλθεῖν) [into the world], we were confined under the Law, being shut up until faith should be revealed (ἀποκαλυφθῆναι)." The noun "faith" (πίστις) is the subject of the verb "came" as well as of the verb "revealed" (both infinitives in the Greek text). As Martyn points out, this parallelism indicates that that the latter verb must mean something more than simply "unveiling (of previous hidden information)" for Paul.[67] Paul is redefining the word in terms of God's eschatological *movement into* the world.

Furthermore, the context indicates that Paul here understands faith

---

65. This eschatological activity and movement are a sign and a confirmation of God's liberating love: cf. e.g., Rom. 5:8. Further, faith itself "works through love" (Gal. 5:6: cf. 1 Cor. 13).

66. "Apocalyptic Antinomies," 417 (emphasis removed).

67. Ibid., 417, 424n29.

to be a metonym for Christ himself (cf. 1:23). According to 3:24, the "Law was our custodian until Christ [came on the scene], so that we might be justified on the basis of faith [i.e., on the basis of Christ]. But now that faith has come [i.e., now that Christ has come on the scene], we are no longer subject to a custodian [that is to say, the Law]." The πίστις in view is, in the first place, that of Christ himself.[68] By identifying πίστις with Christ in this way, Paul makes clear that faith as a human activity (or "response") does not involve an innate or natural human possibility, but an apocalyptic-eschatological possibility, which becomes an anthropological reality when elicited (in effect, created) by the proclamation of Christ's faithful death "for our sins" or "for us" (cf. 1 Cor. 15:3; Gal. 1:4; 2:20-21; 3:13; Rom. 3:21-26; 2 Cor. 5:21). Faith is the visible mark of the "new creation" (Gal. 6:15),[69] an apocalyptic-eschatological *novum* inseparable from Christ as God's Apocalypse. Faith itself is a mark of the divine activity, of God's invasion of the cosmos with God's Son and the Spirit of that Son. Or, as Martyn puts it: "Paul envisions, then, a world that has been changed from without by God's incursion into it, and he perceives that incursion to be the event that has brought faith into existence."[70]

Paul's distinctively "apocalyptic" use of the noun ἀποκάλυψις and its cognate verb ἀποκαλύπτω may be indebted to two passages from Second Isaiah, a portion of Scripture Paul often cites from or alludes to in his letters, Galatians and Romans in particular.[71] According to Isa. 52:10, "the Lord shall reveal (ἀποκαλύψει) his holy arm (βραχίων) in the sight of all the nations (πάντα τὰ ἔθνη); and all the ends of the earth

---

68. The evidence of 3:23 is one of the reasons that the phrase πίστις χριστοῦ (see note 62 above) is probably to be construed as "the faith(fullness) *of* Christ," referring specifically to his death as the defining mark of that faithfulness (cf. Gal. 2:20-21; Rom. 3:21-26).

69. Note the parallel between Gal. 5:6 (faith working through love) and 6:15 (new creation).

70. Martyn, *Galatians*, 363. For Martyn, the epistemological implications of Christ's apocalypse are crucially important. About this, Stuckenbruck has perceptively written: "Martyn's approach to apocalyptic does not obligate the interpreter to find any essential continuity with comparable or contrasting Jewish paradigms. Once God has disclosed God's self in the Christ event as a new way of knowing, all that came before becomes functionally irrelevant, not only for Paul but even for Paul's interpreters" ("Overlapping Ages," 317).

71. The two terms are rather rare in secular sources; cf. A. Oepke, "ἀποκαλύπτω, ἀποκάλυψις," *TDNT*, vol. 3 (Grand Rapids: Eerdmans, 1965), 570-71. The noun occurs in the LXX only four times, with the meaning "disclosure" or "revelation" (1 Sam. 20:30; Ode 13:32; Sir. 11:27; 22:22), though the verb occurs much more frequently.

shall see the salvation that comes from our God" (cf. Rom. 1:5, 16–17; Gal. 3:8; LXX Ps. 97:1–2). And in Isa. 53:1, whose initial question Paul cites in Rom. 10:16, we read: "O Lord, who has believed our report? and to whom has the arm of the Lord been revealed (ἀπεκαλύφθη)?" The "revelation" of God's "arm" (a symbol of power and military might) is no mere disclosure of previously hidden information or of a heavenly mystery, but the visible coming of God to effect salvation in the world. Paul frequently uses the term in a very similar, though more "apocalyptic" way, to describe God's eschatological invasion (in and through Christ) of the human cosmos under the hegemony of cosmological powers destructive of human life and opposed to God's will and intention for the world (especially Sin, Death, and the Flesh).

Conclusion

In one longstanding tradition of scholarship of ancient Judaism and Christianity, apocalyptic concerns the (ancient Jewish) expectation of God's own eschatological activity, whereby God will put an end to the present evil order of reality ("this age") and replace it with a new, transformed order of reality ("the age to come"). Paul is an apocalyptic theologian in this sense, though it must also be noted that his apocalyptic theology: (a) is closer to the cosmological pattern exemplified by 1 Enoch 1–36 than to the forensic pattern exemplified by 2 Baruch, and (b) assumes (as does the book of Revelation) a christological modification to this expectation: The coming of Christ (or, if you will, of Jesus as the Messiah) represents God's apocalyptic-eschatological invasion of the human world, whereby God has begun to wage a war of cosmic proportions against evil cosmological forces that have oppressed and victimized all human beings and brought about their separation from God and from life; this war will end in God's sure triumph at Christ's Parousia.

4

———

Apocalyptic Epistemology

The Sine Qua Non of Valid Pauline Interpretation

Douglas A. Campbell

An apocalyptic explanation of Paul's epistemology is one of the most important positions that an interpreter of the apostle can adopt; indeed, I will argue here that it is the *sine qua non* of all further valid interpretation. But in my experience, Paul's modern interpreters do not always grasp what is at stake here very clearly. Linguistic and historical-critical training are not, one suspects, the best preparations for intense discussions of epistemological warrant. So, I will try to clarify in what follows just what is implicit in an apocalyptic approach to Paul's theological epistemology, and its importance. A classic essay on the subject can provide us with a useful way into these issues.

Epistemology in 2 Corinthians 5:16–17

J. Louis (Lou) Martyn's "Epistemology at the Turn of the Ages"[1] orbits around Paul's dramatic assertions in 2 Cor. 5:16–17:

[5:16] Ὥστε ἡμεῖς ἀπὸ τοῦ νῦν οὐδένα οἴδαμεν κατὰ σάρκα· εἰ καὶ ἐγνώκαμεν κατὰ σάρκα Χριστόν, ἀλλὰ νῦν οὐκέτι γινώσκομεν. [17] ὥστε εἴ τις ἐν Χριστῷ, καινὴ κτίσις· τὰ ἀρχαῖα παρῆλθεν, ἰδοὺ γέγονεν καινά.

[5:16] So then, we know no one from the present moment according to the flesh. Even if we knew Christ according to the flesh, we now no longer know [him in these fleshly terms].[2] [17] So then, if someone is in Christ, he[3] is a new creation: the old has departed; behold, he has become quite new. [My translation]

Paul is clarifying here—among other things—that humanity is no longer to be understood from a location in the "flesh," which almost certainly means, from a created and fallen location "in Adam" (see also Rom. 5:12-21; 1 Cor. 15:22, 48). Now, everyone is to be understood "in Christ," which, Paul elaborates immediately, denotes from the point of view of the "new creation" inaugurated by Christ. Hence here, his auditors almost certainly detected an eschatological claim bound up with Christ's resurrection and ascension. Furthermore, we can infer both implicitly, over against the phrase κατὰ σάρκα, and from the broader context (see esp. 4:13; 5:5), that this dramatic new location has been established by the divine Spirit.

Martyn goes on to describe Paul's broader assertions that the Corinthians are not reading their situation correctly—in the light of this revelation that is taking place in Christ that establishes a new creation. They are consequently not in touch with the truth of the situation, which is to say, with its reality. Admittedly, this reality is largely unseen, so Paul denotes it with the language of understanding

---

1. The full title of the essay is "Epistemology at the Turn of the Ages: 2 Corinthians 5.16," and it can now be accessed in Martyn's essay collection, *Theological Issues in the Letters of Paul* (Edinburgh/Nashville: T&T Clark/Abingdon, 1997 [1967]), 89–110.
2. The adverbial reading seems preferable to the famous but implausible adjectival construal. See, *inter alia*, W. D. Davies, *Paul and Rabbinic Judaism: Some Rabbinic Elements in Pauline Theology*, 4th ed. (Philadelphia: Fortress Press, 1980 [1948]), 195.
3. The gender of Paul's discussion is masculine, but the point is generic.

and believing versus sight and visibility,[4] and in terms even of inner versus outer.[5] But it is nevertheless quite real, and the Corinthians are overlooking it when they should be attending to it. They are, after all, caught up with it themselves.

However, with this very basic account of what Paul is saying in this text in place, his modern interpreters need to confront some important and difficult questions, and as much about themselves as about Paul. They must enquire about their own epistemology—which, in this case, must be theological since it involves God—and ask if what Paul is saying is true and how this can be known. And they must ask this question now, before doing any further analysis of the apostle.

Theological epistemology is concerned with the assessment of what theologians sometimes call "God-talk"—an activity that Paul is clearly involved with all the time and not just in 2 Cor. 5:16–17, although this text is an especially good example of it. The key question that must be placed to God-talk concerns, quite simply, the question of its truth. How do we know that the talk about God that we are hearing or reading—or perhaps even writing—is actually true? Or, more precisely: What is the status of the truth claims implicit in every statement that involves speech about God, a question raised by almost every sentence Paul wrote? Modern interpreters clearly need to address this question when they interpret Paul. But why do they need to place this question *first*, prior to all subsequent analysis of different questions in Paul?

The reasons are directly implicit in the dramatic statements of 2 Cor. 5:16–17. Indeed, this point is really quite obvious once one notices it, for our reconstruction of what is actually going on in and around Paul must change dramatically, depending on how we judge the truth or falsity of his assertions.

As we have just seen, Paul is claiming that he is involved with God—the God who has resurrected and located him, at least primarily,

---

4. See, *inter alia*, the use of belief/believing terms in 1:24; 4:13 [3x]; 5:7; 8:7; 10:15; and 13:5. In this relation, see also my essay "Participation and Faith in Paul," in *'In Christ' in Paul: Explorations in Paul's Theology of Union and Participation*, WUNT 2/384, eds. Kevin J. Vanhoozer, Constantine R. Campbell, and Michael J. Thate (Tübingen: Mohr Siebeck, 2015), 37–60.

5. See, *inter alia*, 4:10–18.

within a new creation. From this dramatic new vantage point, he now understands things correctly, whereas from other vantage points within the realm of the flesh, he could not. In Christ, therefore, Paul possesses the correct knowledge of humanity, and indeed, of Christ himself. From *this* location, he articulates various claims and recommendations—and hence, much of the rest of 2 Corinthians— largely if not completely reflecting this new starting point's accounts of God, of Christ, and of his own striking new existence. But it follows directly from this that the truth of almost all of Paul's statements is directly dependent on the truth of his initial programmatic claims concerning his new, revealed, participatory location "in Christ." If this location is, in fact, true, then his further claims might be true; if it is not, then his further claims are definitely *not* true. And the implications for further explication are immediate and far-reaching.

Paul's own account of his location *attributes its principal causality to divine action*. Moreover, he is claiming nothing less than that he is "in Christ," and consequently, is primarily and fundamentally, at the divine behest, "now" "a new creation." But if all this is true, any more extended account of the reality with which he is involved—and indeed, of history more broadly—must reflect this truth; God is at work in it, in and through Christ. So everything is not as it seems to the naked eye, and one must "believe" and "know" that this "veiled," "inner," and unseen dimension within reality is, in fact, the most important one within its dynamics, and analyze accordingly.

Conversely, if God is not at work through Christ, *we will have to supply a fundamentally different account of Paul's meaning—and motivations, and perhaps even of his sheer rationality—from the one he himself is supplying.* Our reconstruction of his history will differ radically, as well as our reconstruction of the history surrounding him more broadly. Moreover, it will most likely be a reductionist account from Paul's point of view. We will probably flatten the situation's causal dynamics into immanence. The key causes are all apparent to the naked eye. God is not involved with Paul. There is no veiled, inner, or unseen dimension driving events. Indeed, Paul's claim to be resurrected in some sense is fundamentally deluded, as are his corresponding assessments of the status of Jesus and of his own apostolic importance.

In short, then, fundamentally different accounts of the historical realities in play in and around Paul will be supplied, depending on our answer to the question of the truth of his God-talk. So, clearly, we need to confront this important question concerning the status of his God-talk, and do so immediately. However, further reflection suggests that the assessment of this situation cannot be undertaken independently of some consideration of *our* approach to this question. Modern interpreters themselves are immediately and inextricably caught up in assessments of the truth of God-talk.

One does not typically find this sort of consideration in a modern scholarly essay on Paul, but it should be clear by now that I have introduced it here for unavoidable reasons. Paul's modern interpreter must decide whether God is really at work in Christ reconciling the cosmos—and therefore, partly by way of Paul's life and letters—or is not. As we have just seen, the broader historical explanation of his activity will pivot dramatically around the answer that is supplied to this question—whether in terms of endorsement or reductionism, not to mention the conceptualization of history itself. And as we ask how we know whether God was at work in Paul or not—a question reaching out inevitably to include us—another interlocutor will be helpful, namely, Karl Barth.[6]

---

6. Barth devoted the mature period of his theological work, namely, the production of the *Church Dogmatics* (at the least), to the elucidation of just this dynamic—what is implicit in the claim that all true knowledge of God and humanity is located in Christ, who has been revealed to us (which is, it should be recalled, exactly Paul's concern in 2 Cor. 5:16–17), along with the implications of this for Christian thinking about other theological *loci* such as creation and Israel. But Barth also had strong opinions concerning the importance of clarity on these questions (as indeed Paul did, vis-à-vis Corinth)—opinions generated in large measure by the catastrophic failures of the European church in relation to two world wars, although it should not be forgotten that he was also significantly informed by the church's indifference to social and economic marginalization. His thought is usefully introduced by Eberhard Busch, *The Great Passion: An Introduction to Karl Barth's Theology*, trans. Geoffrey Bromiley (Grand Rapids: Eerdmans, 2004); and by Stanley Hauerwas, *With the Grain of the Universe: The Church's Witness and Natural Theology. Being the Gifford Lectures Delivered at the University of St. Andrews in 2001* (London: SCM, 2002), 141–204.

Barth's Recommendations in Relation
to the Assessment of God-Talk

Barth himself begins to answer this question by, in effect, endorsing the christologically enthusiastic side of "the divine identity" debate in Paul.[7] Indeed, he anticipated its key moves by some distance. *Part I, Volume 1* of the *Church Dogmatics* (hereafter *CD* I/1, etc.[8]) is a sustained reflection on the implications of the claim "Jesus is Lord," on the assumption that Jesus is being identified as God in this predication that uses terminology drawn from the Bible. So, clearly, Barth would encourage readers of Paul to take this claim in the apostle's writings with complete seriousness. However, Barth argues that this confession has several immediate and critical implications.

He observes that the realization and consequent conviction and confession that the human being, Jesus of Nazareth, was God present in God's fullness must be a disclosure or revelation. Nothing can prepare someone to assess the truth of this statement. So, for example, prior to the incarnation nobody, including Paul, knew that the human Jesus would be part of the divine identity, or vice versa. Barth argues then that this conviction rests on a revelation—or, as Paul sometimes said, an "apocalypse" (see esp. Gal. 1:15–16; 3:23)—that this is, in fact, the case. Put slightly differently, he is suggesting that this truth is self-authenticating. This truth is known because, at bottom, *the* truth *has made it known*. And at this moment, it becomes clear that this revelation really requires a revealer in addition to its revealed content, which Paul turns out to be quite explicit about as well.

The Holy Spirit discloses this deepest truth about God. Only God can reveal to persons such as Paul, located elsewhere from Jesus in time and space, that God is fully present in Jesus (cp. esp. 1 Cor. 2:10). So, as Barth articulated later on with more precision, the realization that Jesus is God has an implicitly Trinitarian structure (see esp. *CD* I/1; and I/2). We must therefore speak henceforth of God in terms of one

---

7. See esp. now Chris Tilling, *Paul's Divine Christology* (Grand Rapids: Eerdmans, 2015 [2012]).
8. *Church Dogmatics*, 4 vols. in 13 parts, eds. T. F. Torrance and G. W. Bromiley (Edinburgh: T&T Clark, 1956–96).

who sends, whom Paul calls "the Father"; one who is sent, Jesus; and one who comes to Paul's (or Barth's) location and discloses this truth, namely, the Spirit (again using here—at least primarily—terminology drawn from the Bible; see esp. 2 Cor. 13:13).[9]

In relation to our current question, then, Barth advises Christians that their recognition of the truth of the claim "Jesus is Lord" is a gift from the Lord to those so convinced, generating the knowledge that God is Father, Son, and Holy Spirit.[10] But this insight into the basis of the most fundamental Christian truths places modern interpreters in an intriguing relationship with Paul and his modern analysis.

Historical reconstruction might suggest that Paul himself attributed his critical realizations about God acting in Christ to a revelation or apocalypse in this sense too—as, in effect, an early Barthian. But it follows now both from the modern experience of revelation—assuming that this has been acknowledged—*and* from the historical reconstruction of Paul's revelation, that Paul's modern interpreters will *not* share his point of view that Jesus is revealed as Lord simply because they have reconstructed it in him, finding this view there using a historical method (and even if this takes place on the basis of an authoritative text). That would not be a revelation; that would be the discovery that *he* had had a revelation. We might know that Paul thought that Jesus was Lord because he had had a revelation; but we would not necessarily know for ourselves that Jesus is Lord, and therefore, know whether his God-talk was true. A reductionist account of his texts and life would still beckon. Moreover, Paul's attribution

---

9. On Paul's use of this important language, see my essay "The Narrative Dimension of Paul's Gospel, with special reference to Romans and Galatians," in *The Quest for Paul's Gospel: A Suggested Strategy* (London: T&T Clark, 2005), 69–94. My key claims here are that the language of "father," "son," "sonship," and "adoption" is informed by the patriarchal narratives concerning Abraham, Sarah, and Isaac, not to overlook, Hagar and Ishmael. As such, the filial and familiar categories are significant, although the *gendered* dimension within the stories is irrelevant. The OT intertexts structure the relations between the different characters in narrative and dramatic terms. God "the father" offers up Isaac like Abraham; God "the son" obediently is offered up, like Isaac. This suggests that Paul's use of this terminology has critical implications for personhood, but detaches those implications from gender.

10. Barth's position is summarized with incisive clarity by Alan J. Torrance in "The Trinity," in *The Cambridge Companion to Barth*, ed. John Webster (Cambridge: Cambridge University Press, 2000), 72–91; see also his "Jesus in Christian Doctrine," *The Cambridge Companion to Jesus*, ed. Markus Bockmuehl (Cambridge: Cambridge University Press, 2001), 200–219.

of this truth to revelation would stand over against our access to this truth by way of historical reconstruction as well. He himself would therefore dispute our approach to the assessment of this claim. It is, he would say, revealed and not reconstructed. So, Paul's later readers will only share his point of view if they too have first detected and responded to the same revelation in their *own* location(s). Consequently, the assessment of the truth of Paul's God-talk really challenges his modern interpreters to make this judgment first, in relation to themselves—a moment of self-reflection that is now unavoidable, somewhat ironically, in the interests of good historical reconstruction.

If this moment has taken place, however, and we assume—perhaps optimistically—what we might call a Pauline outcome, then this allows a moment of *recognition* during the historical reconstruction of Paul. The modern interpreter would be standing within a revelatory situation analogous to Paul's. In the light of the disclosure to this interpreter that "Jesus is Lord," she would presumably be comforted to find that, after appropriately sensitive historical reconstruction, the apostle Paul seemed to inhabit the same situation too. Paul's own account of christological revelation would consequently attest—or "witness to"—and thereby, additionally confirm, the modern interpreter's location. (This would not necessarily be the most important use of Scripture, but it would be a use of Scripture.) So, the situation for the modern interpreter in relation to revelation is, perhaps somewhat counter-intuitively, "backward." It proceeds from her to Paul, and not vice versa.

It follows directly from this, nevertheless, that any modern interpreter who shares Paul's apocalyptic location in the sense of his basic revelation concerning the nature of God in Christ—having responded to it personally and then recognized it in him—endorses, by direct implication, an essentially apocalyptic account of history,[11]

11. This point is nicely articulated by Nathan R. Kerr in a critique, from an apocalyptic point of view, of Ernst Troeltsch; see his "Ernst Troeltsch: The Triumph of Ideology and the Eclipse of Apocalyptic," in *Christ, History and Apocalyptic* (London: SCM, 2009), 23–62. The need for an alternative account of history is noted—of course—by Stanley Hauerwas, in *War and the American*

meaning by this the most basic claim of Jewish Apocalypses that visible history is not all that is. History is affected by unseen powers, and ultimately driven by God, so an accurate grasp of history is only possible as those powers and the divine action are grasped by revelation.[12] In that literature, revelation generally takes place through heavenly journeys or dreams. But the modern interpreter aligned with Paul must modify this antecedent view to center history on a fundamentally christological account of the divine nature and action. (A journey, we might say, has taken place in the opposite direction.[13]) Hence, any resulting account of Paul will proceed by affirming that he was indeed located in Christ, in some resurrected sense, and will strive to unravel exactly what that means more broadly in the rest of his life as attested by his letters, since this history—in which God is palpably at work, along with other powers—is now fraught with significance. Moreover, this will be a true account of him in historical terms, because it will be rooted in a correct view of history—a suitably open one—even if many modern historians might be a little nervous about it.

It should be clear by this point in our brief discussion, then, just why "apocalyptic" is so important as a description of Paul's theological epistemology. If Paul is described in these terms, then he attests to the basic structure of Christian truth, in terms of revelation. If he is not so described, then he does not.[14]

Difference: Theological Reflections on Violence and National Identity (Grand Rapids: Baker Academic, 2011), 44n16. He also notes appositely the work of Michel Foucault (*Society Must Be Defended: Lectures at the Collège de France, 1975–1976*, eds. Mauro Bertani and Alessandro Fontana, trans. David Macey [New York: Picador, 2003]); and Jonathan Schell (*The Unconquerable World: Power, Nonviolence, and the Will of the People* [New York: Henry Holt, 2003]) in this relation in *War*, 47–51. To these studies, we could add the perceptive essays of Brad S. Gregory, "The Other Confessional History: On Secular Bias in the Study of Religion," *History and Theory, Theme Issue* 45 (2006): 132–49; and "No Room for God? History, Science, Metaphysics, and the Study of Religion," *History and Theory* 47, no. 4 (2008): 495–519. (My thanks to John Stenhouse for these references.)

12. See Anathea Portier-Young's wonderful study, *Apocalypse against Empire: Theologies of Resistance in Early Judaism* (Grand Rapids: Eerdmans, 2011).

13. So, Paul's engagement with this tradition in 2 Cor. 12:1–10 is most instructive, along with what is effectively a reversal in Phil. 2:5–11. The motif of a heavenly journey or disclosure was the heart of a classic study of this tradition by Christopher Rowland, *The Open Heaven: A Study of Apocalyptic in Judaism and Early Christianity* (Eugene: Wipf & Stock, 2002 [1982]).

14. It is presumably still possible for Paul not to attest to the basic structure of Christian truth, as Christians such as Barth later came to explicate this. This is not *fatal*. The later articulation by theologians such as Barth would still be correct. But the loss of a key canonical witness to this approach would doubtless still hurt. As we have just seen, those modern interpreters located

With these critical primary or "first-order" realizations in place, it is time to turn and address some further key implications and related confusions. These unfold as we reflect in more detail on the way in which the revelation of the truth found in Christ takes place within a context—whether Paul's or ours.

The Apocalyptic Starting Point and Its Context

The focus on epistemology in our previous discussion—in the senses of knowledge, information, and disclosure—can artificially isolate one aspect of a broader, richer situation that is fundamentally interpersonal, and consequently, at least in some sense, ontological. It is worth emphasizing that Paul, in the text we noted at the outset of our discussion, does not isolate his claims about correct and incorrect knowing from a location that is deeply relational and bound up with what he now *is*. He is "in" Christ, through the indwelling work of the Spirit, living thereby, in some sense, in a resurrected location characterized by life beyond death, and hence, by the fullness of the presence of God. Those of his modern interpreters attuned to this dimension in his thinking tend to refer to this in terms of "participation" (see esp. 2 Cor. 13:13 again).[15] But let it suffice for now to say that any affirmation of an apocalyptic starting point for Paul's analysis in epistemological terms is simultaneously an affirmation that

revelationally will still need to give a more broadly apocalyptic account of Paul's history—an open account—since this is a true account whether Paul is viewed as oriented primarily by a revelation of Christ or not; God was—and is—at work in history. But one suspects that this will all unfold rather more smoothly if the interpreter of Paul can detect the apostle's apocalyptic orientation, and explicates his life accordingly. We could interpret apocalyptically with Paul rather than in spite of him.

15. In most recent Pauline discussion, the advocacy of this important motif would be associated most strongly with Michael Gorman; see esp. his *Inhabiting the Cruciform God: Kenosis, Justification, and Theosis in Paul's Narrative Soteriology* (Grand Rapids: Eerdmans, 2009). Robert C. Tannehill supplies a useful summary in "Participation in Christ: A Central Theme in Pauline Soteriology," in *The Shape of the Gospel: New Testament Essays* (Eugene: Cascade [Wipf & Stock], 2007), 223–37. The origin of an emphasis on the importance of this motif for Paul within the modern period is usually held to be G. Adolf Deissmann; see his *St. Paul: A Study in Social and Religious History*, 2nd ed., trans. L. R. M. Strachan (London: Hodder & Stoughton, 1912). Deissmann points out that the phrase "in Christ," or its close equivalent, occurs over 160 times in Paul's writings. While not all instances are of equal importance, some certainly are. Moreover, this number is impressive, along with the motif's distribution. That is, this data is good *prima facie* evidence that this motif and the broader notions it points to are critical for Paul. An important recent positional volume is Vanhoozer, Campbell, and Thate (ed.), *"In Christ" in Paul*; WUNT 2/384 (Tübingen: Mohr Siebeck, 2014).

Paul's actual "location" participates in a new reality; it has ontological correlates. Indeed, the latter is the basis for the former.[16] If we appreciate this, then we now need to think about how this ontology intervenes into a context.

There is, of course, a context for the revelation of Christ, whether to us or to Paul. At the very least, we have to speak of "us" or "Paul" at this moment although, clearly, a great many other things are involved! The revelation takes place to someone somewhere. So, this divine activity is clearly not *a*-contextual. But it now follows, given that revelation has taken place in a context, that we must engage immediately in further analysis of that context, ultimately in an act or process of discernment.

As the programmatic Pauline text for his inquiry states directly, there are true and false ways of knowing in play that detect the hidden but determinative realities of the context, or that fail to do so. Moreover, to fail to do so is to supply a defective account of a context. Only in the light of God revealed in Christ is any context known truly for what it is, since this will enable figures such as Paul, responding to revelation, to detect what is actually going on. We must think and act κατὰ πνεῦμα and ἐν Χριστῷ, and not κατὰ σάρκα. Moreover, as Paul's famous but cryptic text implies, this discernment will detect discontinuities and continuities with what precedes it contextually.

Discontinuities

Discernment will detect contextual discontinuities. As Paul freely confesses, he formerly knew both humanity and Christ from a "fleshly" point of view that has been revealed to be fundamentally false. These old perspectives were wrong. The truth is found in Christ, where humanity is primarily located. Moreover, Christ himself is now known truly—as Lord, and not, presumably, as some sad messianic pretender

---

16. Hence, Barth moves seamlessly between revelation and participation in *CD* I/1; see i.e., the statement—that also, most significantly, denotes the critical role in all this of the Holy Spirit: "The Spirit guarantees man what he cannot guarantee himself, his personal participation in revelation" (453). Later, briefly expounding Rom. 8:15 and the believer's cry of "Abba Father"—"a decisive passage"—he states: "Herein consists his participation in the atonement effected in Christ. This is what it means to have the Holy Spirit. To have the Holy Spirit is to be set with Christ in that transition from death to life" (458).

and/or demonic collaborator. But we should probably detect two different types of discontinuity here.

First, there are those aspects revealed within Paul's present location that are simply new as unanticipated pieces of information. As we noted already, prior to the coming of Jesus of Nazareth, neither Paul nor anyone else (perhaps excepting very special circumstances that need not hold us up here) could know that Jesus of Nazareth was God incarnate. This discontinuity with preceding history simply has to respect God's incarnation within history at a particular point in space and time. The incarnation necessarily entails the presence of information after this event that was not present to humanity before it. Moreover, it was probably new information too that God incarnate in Jesus was crucified. That God would be rejected, shamefully treated, and publicly tortured, was probably new information, prophetic anticipations notwithstanding.

But the revelation of God incarnate in Jesus Christ clearly disclosed to Paul ways in which his own previous life was sinful and misdirected—most obviously, his zeal. Paul's deep commitment to God prior to his call entailed, he thought, the deployment of violence against members of the early church—an activity revealed to be diametrically opposed to the intentions of God, and hence, necessarily informed by a fundamentally incorrect account of the nature of God, a God who desires to kill Christians (see esp. Gal. 1:13). Indeed, it is vital to appreciate here what I sometimes refer to as Paul's "Augustinian moment" (or ". . . dimension").[17]

The revelation of Christ clearly functioned to illuminate and to judge many aspects of Paul's location, revealing much of its content to be fundamentally sinful. Much that was previously thought to be good, and perhaps, even the height of piety, was revealed to be less central than was previously thought; not to mention, differently oriented (thinking here of the Torah), and even just plain wrong (thinking here of Paul's violence).[18]

---

17. An excellent point of access into some further implications of this realization that I will not pursue here is Stanley Hauerwas, "Seeing Darkness, Hearing Silence: Augustine's Account of Evil," in *Working with Words: On Learning to Speak Christian* (Eugene: Wipf & Stock, 2011), 8–32.

It is in this way and at this moment that the language of discontinuity can—and sometimes must—be deployed. As Paul's pre-Christian behavior suggests, fundamentally misguided accounts of God are often inextricably bound up with fundamentally misguided, and occasionally vicious actions. Indeed, God-talk that is uncontrolled by Christology has a horrific track record in church history, which is to say that God-talk, independent of Christ, frequently kills. So, when appropriately controlled by Christology, it is sometimes necessary to pronounce an unambiguous verdict of "no!" against such talk and its sinister accompaniments—the role that Barth's famous *Römerbrief* played after WWI, not to mention his rejoinder to Emil Brunner in 1934 as National Socialism was on the rise in Germany.[19]

Apocalyptic readers of Paul can sometimes overstep the mark here, but I take it that this legitimate and important dynamic is what is going on mostly when they deploy the language of discontinuity strongly. The God of Jesus Christ asks his[20] representatives at times to pronounce a negative verdict courageously and firmly against other God-talk that is corrupt; the God of Jesus Christ is simply not to be identified with such talk, and hence, is radically discontinuous with it.[21] Barth pronounced this anathema on the pretensions of modernist and essentially liberal theology in Europe, and especially, when it facilitated nationalism and nationalist aggression (and I am tempted to pronounce the same against Christian advocates of the death penalty in the U. S. A.).

It follows, then, from the intersection of christological revelation with Paul's context *that every aspect of that context must now be re-*

---

18. That is to say, an event of unconditional grace, in which salvation and its implicit knowledge are "sheer" gifts, implies simultaneously, necessarily, and intrinsically that the situation into which that grace has come is under complete judgment. It offers *nothing* to the knowledge of God.

19. This famous exchange between Barth and Brunner is available in their *Natural Theology: Comprising "Nature and Grace" by Professor Dr. Emil Brunner and the reply "No!" by Dr. Karl Barth* (Eugene: Wipf & Stock, 2002 [1946]). It is critical to grasp, however, that the articles collected—and partly revised and expanded—here first appeared in 1934.

20. As indicated earlier, I do not view the gendered language in Paul as denoting gender strictly in relation to divine personhood. English is notorious for causing difficulties here.

21. This is a *status confessionis*. Parts of the church in South Africa pronounced a similar anathema against apartheid. See esp. *The Kairos Document* written by "the Kairos Theologians" (Braamfontein: Skotaville, 1986). The second edition is available from Eerdmans.

evaluated and sifted under the ongoing impress of this revelation, while the level of distortion present previously within the analysis of that context *cannot be overestimated*. The revelation of Christ to Paul reveals that he is, as Calvin nicely put it somewhat later, *totally depraved*.[22] His very thinking—and by direct implication, all of humanity's—is shot through with corruption, and can only be decisively clarified by the work of God revealed in Christ and the Spirit (Rom. 12:1; Col. 1:21[23]). Fundamental discontinuities will almost certainly become apparent.

However, this is emphatically not to claim that Paul's context is totally depraved in the sense that it is absent of all goodness—which would lead us to Marcionism. It is simply to claim that his context is comprehensively contaminated; no aspect is free from distortion. Consequently, clear thinking about it will need to lean in the future on the clearest and most decisive illumination within it, who is Christ—a point worth reiterating.

It is not being claimed here that either Paul's or my context completely lacks either truth or goodness. However, these things are inextricably intertwined with corruption and evil. In order to discern what is what, then, we need desperately to rely on the clearest illumination of this entanglement that we possess, namely, the light of Christ. Without this, we cannot endorse or affirm elements within our previous contexts. But a further reason lies just to hand for operating steadfastly in a christologically-controlled and retrospective fashion. This will also allow Paul's modern interpreters to detect and to repudiate foundationalism, this being the deadly methodological heresy that slips into the Christian city like the Trojan horse, leading to its fall and destruction.

As we have already seen, it is implicit within the statement "Jesus is Lord" that its truth is self-authenticating. But it follows from this that its truth is a matter of obedience and not merely of recognition

22. Calvin's views were, of course, nuanced. They are analyzed crisply by David Steinmetz, in "Calvin and the Natural Knowledge of God," in *Calvin in Context* (New York: Oxford University Press, 1995), 23–39.
23. I know of no good arguments for excluding Colossians from Pauline authorship, a judgment applying also to Ephesians and 2 Thessalonians; see my *Framing Paul: An Epistolary Biography* (Grand Rapids: Eerdmans, 2014).

or affirmation. To fail to recognize its self-authentication in any way, perhaps by asking if this claim is true, is immediately to step outside of the lordship of God as revealed in Christ, and to assert the existence of a set of truth criteria independent of, and superior to, this location. And consequently, this is to deny the *lordship* of Christ, here at its most critical moment. It is to deny that the Lord *is* the truth and the Lord *of* the truth, and hence, *is* the Lord! And it is necessarily to assert the existence of *another* lord—a lord necessarily of one's own making. (It is not of God's.) Hence, as Barth elaborates, it is to replicate the primordial sin of Adam and Eve, who were expelled from the garden of Eden for, in effect, requesting an independent starting point for divine knowledge (albeit on the deceptive recommendation of the serpent; see esp. *CD* III/1). And it is to establish one's own truth criteria—by which to measure the nature and arrival of God!—and this is clearly an idolatrous and foolish move. Far better to rely on what God says about God. (One could add that this is an utterly artificial reconstruction for a Christian to undertake as well.)

Barth refuses, then, to step outside of God's self-authenticating self-disclosure that has taken place definitively in Christ, by the Spirit, and to embrace some alternative. This is and must remain his epistemological starting point. Only this steadfast refusal to wander keeps the interpreter located—obediently—within the truth. So all appropriate God-talk is done from within this location, after the fact, in response to this location. Hence, there must now be no *a priori* or antecedent epistemological task fundamentally preparatory to and for the truth.

This mistaken procedure, however it is undertaken, is usefully called "foundationalism," because it is an attempt by human beings to construct their own foundation for talk about God as against relying on the one God supplies; it is, in Alan Torrance's terms, "criterial immanentism."[24] But any such procedure is disobedient, unnecessary,

---

24. "*Auditus Fidei:* Where and How Does God Speak? Faith, Reason, and the Question of Criteria," in *Reason and the Reasons of Faith*, eds. Paul J. Griffiths and Reinhard Hütter (New York & London: T&T Clark [Continuum], 2005), 27–52. Edwin Chr. van Driel also identifies helpfully the flawed infralapsarian Christology at work here as against an appropriate supralapsarian account,

and inaccurate to boot. So Barth urges Christian thinkers in the strongest possible terms to eschew such an approach. (He had further, extremely important reasons for adopting his position in addition to mere theological and epistemological purity, namely, inevitable political and cultural compromises, but space precludes addressing them here as they deserve.)

Hence, there are good reasons for emphasizing the discontinuities present within the context of revelation. We must be open to aspects of the divine revelation that are genuinely new (i.e., to "us"—things such as the assumption of humanity in relation to Jesus from Nazareth); we must be open to the judgment of that revelation on elements of our context that we might previously have identified with the divine purposes but that turn out to be anything but; and we will, in this fashion, also maintain a constant vigilance against the fundamentally destructive methods of foundationalism. But with this appropriate level of vigilance in place—the recognition of the "no" that is spoken to a context—we *must also* turn toward and recognize the positive elements within our context to which God is saying "yes." To fail to do this would be to fall into a set of different but equally egregious errors.

Continuities

Christ is God arriving in his own "context," hence he is *per definitionem* its climactic moment (Rom. 9:5; 10:4). Moreover, he must also be *per definitionem* its inner rationale (1 Cor. 8:6; Col. 1:15-20). He therefore illuminates what creation *is*. What Christ reveals God to be in his incarnate revelation, we know God to be "antecedently," as the theologians later put it, in his creation, and even "prior" to this, in election (Rom. 8:28-30).[25] Hence, although this might be dramatically

---

especially appositely in relation to the work of J. Louis (Lou) Martyn and N. T. Wright; see his "Climax of the Covenant vs Apocalyptic Invasion: A Theological Analysis of a Contemporary Debate in Pauline Exegesis," *IJST* 17, no. 1 (2015): 6–25.

25. Strictly speaking, we cannot ask what God was and was doing before the invention of time, which is itself one of the key structuring components within creation. See, in this relation, esp. T. F. Torrance, *Space, Time, and Resurrection* (Edinburgh: Handsel, 1976). The claim that God is antecedently what is apparent in revelation is pursued by Barth in *CD* I/1. The importance of election is then explored in *CD* II/2—an account shaped significantly by Rom. 8:29–30 and Eph. 1:4.

new information for us, this is not a new initiative or development on the part of God. God has always been a communion of Father, Son, and Holy Spirit, and this is now revealed unambiguously to be the key to creation, as well as to redemption (and as Paul well knows; see i.e., Rom. 8:29–30). The early Fathers used the language of "mystery" or "[divine] secret," drawn largely from Paul, to describe this dynamic. Christ has always been the key to creation and to history, but this information was a divine secret, locked up in the hidden counsels of God, and only disclosed after the coming of Christ to his apostles and prophets, and through them to the church.[26] And much the same logic applies to history, and to God's special relationship within history with Israel.

Even as creation is now revealed to be the context that God has created for fellowship with humanity, redemption is now revealed to be the restoration of God's original creative purposes. Moreover, that restoration, made necessary by the intrusion of evil and the advent of sin (Rom. 5:12), is effected when God assumes a particular human body specifically located within Judaism (Rom. 9:1–5). And at this crucial moment, several things become apparent.

As Paul is well aware, in assuming a human body, God is effecting the salvation of humanity (so 2 Cor. 5:14b); the counter-point to Christ is consequently Adam (Rom. 5:12–21; Gal. 3:28). But God assumed a particular human body, within a specific time, place, and people—a *Jewish* body (Gal. 4:4–5). Moreover, a *Jewish* body was then resurrected, becoming the template for the new humanity (1 Cor. 15:22, 45). It follows from these realizations that Jesus is the climactic moment for Israel (Rom. 10:4), and that Israel was shaped primarily by its anticipation of this climactic moment. Hence, the basic structure of Israel prior to the incarnation is *promissory*. Paul therefore crafts a narrative of Israel oriented by this pinnacle, in the calling of Abraham and of the other patriarchs, which points ineluctably forward to the great moment when God gifts Israel with life (i.e., permanent

---

26. A critical elucidation of this dynamic is T. J. Lang, *Mystery and the Making of a Christian Historical Consciousness: From Paul to the Second Century*, BZNW 219 (Berlin: Walter de Gruyter, 2015).

resurrected life) in and through Christ (see esp. Gal. 3:15–29). This crafting is emphatically retrospective; it is clear as we look back from the answer to the question what the question was. But this is not a revised *historical* claim; it is an epistemological one. Israel was always determined by its anticipation of Christ, and hence, had a fundamentally anticipatory or promissory structure.[27] Paul—and perhaps even many of Israel's other earlier occupants—simply did not know this.

With these realizations in place, this is hopefully the right moment at which to attempt some brief clarifications in relation to the very difficult and important further questions clustering around this aspect of Paul's thinking (and not only Paul's, of course).

It is simply the case now that any form of Marcionism has been decisively repudiated and in the strongest possible fashion. The assumption by God of a body, that is to say, of a part of creation, and, moreover, of a Jewish body, effectively locks in an account of preceding reality in a fashion that perceives and affirms all the key continuities. God is revealed by this to be emphatically, unconditionally, and irrevocably committed to creation, to humanity, and to Israel. These continuities are revealed unambiguously, and hence, endorsed irrevocably by the apocalyptic moment in which Christ is revealed as both God *and human.*

In keeping with its nature, moreover, as an event of revelation proceeding from God to humanity, it needs to be appreciated that this event, in effect, commandeers language, among other things, to communicate. People will need to talk about this revelation and are

---

27. Hence, as I put this elsewhere a few years ago: "Israel was a light in a dark place; she pointed forward from her origins in Abraham to the dawning of the new creation in the Christ event, and her Scriptures attest to this and explain it. Indeed, given that Christ comes from within the heritage of Israel and also constitutes its crowning moment, there could hardly be a more important or positive heritage within human history (so [Rom.] 9:4–5). Anyone in Christ is 'grafted into' the historical lineage of Israel (see 11:17–24). Israel's history is the only Adamic history that really matters. Moreover, Jesus Christ the Jew, and now the Jewish King, is the template of the new, eschatological reality. So heavenly existence is Jewish, and in a way that is far more programmatic even than humanity's original Adamic existence! But of course everything depends here on the legitimacy of the Christ event itself, in the light of which these stunning continuities are perceived" (*The Deliverance of God: An Apocalyptic Rereading of Justification in Paul* [Grand Rapids: Eerdmans, 2009], 70).

indeed summoned to do so.[28] However, clearly, divine pressure is placed on linguistic categories so that they freight the truth in question accurately—that God has come in Jesus to creation and to Israel. Linguistic actions convey the truth of this event although they cannot and do not establish its truth; that truth is, as we have seen, internal to this event, and consequently, self-authenticating.

With these clarifications in place, however, we should now appreciate that the linguistic resources used by the first key witnesses to this event such as Paul were supplied primarily if not solely by the writings developed and preserved by Israel. The categories Paul uses in 2 Cor. 5:16–17 are drawn from the linguistic reservoir of late Second Temple Judaism. Hence, he makes claims in terms of the Christ or Messiah, the "flesh" (Greek σάρξ, rendering the Hebrew basar), the Spirit (i.e., of God), and the new creation, which is to say, a resurrected state. This is not necessarily to deny the phenomenon of translation, broadly speaking, whereby notions expressed originally in Jewish terms can be expressed in appropriately defined terms drawn from other cultures; indeed, this process might well be apparent in Paul's texts.[29] But it is merely to affirm that as a matter of fact, Paul's articulation of the Christ event was couched—at least primarily—in terms drawn from and semantically configured by the Jewish Scriptures.

For both the foregoing reasons, then—that Jesus, God incarnate, was a Jew, and that Paul, as a Jew, articulated this truth with language and conceptualities drawn from Judaism—we ought to repudiate strongly any Marcionite anti-Judaism within the apocalyptic account of Paul's gospel. But it is important to emphasize in the same breath that his interpretation of Scripture is in service to the revelation taking place definitively in Christ. That revelation is articulated linguistically under

---

28. See Hauerwas, "Speaking Christian," in *Working with Words*, 84–93.

29. A classic analysis of this dynamic is Lamin Sanneh, *Translating the Message: The Missionary Impact on Culture*, American Society of Missiology Series 42, 2nd rev. and exp. ed. (Maryknoll, NY: Orbis, 2009 [1989])—although Sanneh's views are not uncontested; see i.e., the concerns articulated by Willie James Jennings in *The Christian Imagination: Theology and the Origins of Race* (New Haven: Yale University Press, 2010). Closer to the Pauline data, see also John M. G. Barclay, *Paul and the Gift* (Grand Rapids: Eerdmans, 2015).

its own control, presumably as the Spirit enables its appropriate articulation. Consequently, the fundamental hermeneutic at work must be *christological* and *pneumatological*—something Paul seems well aware of (cf. esp. 2 Cor. 1:20; 3:14-18; see also 4:3-4). The Scriptures are utilized to speak of Christ, and of God and of other notions, as they orbit around this central truth, that is, furthermore, at work within this very articulation (1 Thess. 2:4, 13).[30]

Most importantly, we must also appreciate that, just as we can repudiate Marcionism in the strongest possible terms, we can also repudiate Gnosticism, although, again, it is important to appreciate just why this is the case.

Like Marcionism, Gnosticism impugns the goodness of creation in some radical sense, an action that leads to a host of subsequent difficulties and distortions.[31] But it is apparent in the incarnation that God is committed in the strongest possible terms to creation. In assuming it, albeit in its warped and fractured state, it is affirmed. Moreover, in rescuing and healing it with resurrection, it is doubly affirmed. So, Gnosticism ought to be repudiated as strongly as Marcionism by this understanding of Paul's gospel.

In sum, then, an apocalyptic approach to the analysis of Paul—and here, contrary to the way it is sometimes presented—provides the strongest possible warrant for the repudiation of both Marcionism and Gnosticism. These repudiations are necessary entailments of the apocalyptic construal that begins with the revelation to Paul of God's activity in Christ, and subsequent location of all valid Christian ontology and epistemology in the resurrected situation that Christ,

---

30. This dynamic is nicely articulated by John Webster in his essay "Resurrection and Scripture," in *Christology and Scripture: Interdisciplinary Perspectives*, eds. Andrew T. Lincoln and Angus Paddison (London: T&T Clark, 2008), 138–55. I am not sure his earlier and widely-read study *Holy Scripture: A Dogmatic Sketch* (Cambridge: Cambridge University Press, 2003) articulates this dynamic as clearly. A useful point of entry into the church's hermeneutic might be Henri de Lubac, *History and Spirit: The Understanding of Scripture According to Origen*, trans. Anne Englund Nash and Juvenal Merriel (San Francisco: Ignatius Press, 2007 [1950]).

31. Indeed, the tragic possibilities of this "gospel" are never more evident than in Charles Marsh's compelling account, "Douglas Hudgins: Theologian of the Closed Society," in *God's Long Summer: Stories of Faith and Civil Rights* (Princeton: Princeton University Press, 1997), 82–115. (My thanks to Curtis Freeman for this reference.) N. T. Wright grasps the ethical debilitations flowing from Gnosticism clearly; see his *Paul and the Faithfulness of God* (Minneapolis: Fortress, 2013), 2:1307.

in tandem with the Spirit, inaugurated. To grasp this location and think out of it is necessarily and immediately to set one's face against Marcion, Valentinus, and their like. Indeed, it is the *only* location from which to decisively repudiate these heresies because it is the only position that repudiates foundationalism. Unfortunately, foundationalism of any sort, even in opposition to significant heresies, inevitably collapses, taking any legitimate concerns down with it. But it is also to be thrust into a tempestuous analysis of context. Discontinuities and continuities are in play, while the deep sinfulness of the human mind and heart make the accurate detection of God's purposes extremely difficult. Much that was previously thought to be good and pious is revealed by the work of Christ to be its very opposite, at which moment it is clearer than ever that we must grasp the single great truth that has been revealed both to Paul and to us: that God was, in Christ, reconciling the world to himself. If we grasp this, even as we are grasped by it, then everything else is, at bottom, just commentary.

5

Apocalyptic as Theoria in the Letters of St. Paul

A New Perspective on Apocalyptic as Mother of Theology

Edith M. Humphrey

This chapter all began "because of the angels." To be more precise, its catalyst was Paul's throwaway comment, "because of the angels." The phrase, coming abruptly, and as the capstone to his argument concerning women in worship, has long tantalized me. Frequently, the rhetoric of 1 Cor. 11:1–16 is explained solely in terms of cultural norms, so that the little phrase "because of the angels" is handled merely as an aporia to be solved by appeals to the legends of fallen angels and the like—more cultural baggage that Paul was carrying. This has never seemed quite satisfactory to me! Instead, I have added the phrase to a mental list of other suggestive hints in the apostle's writing—many of these, it seems, indicative of his apocalyptic view of mysteries not seen by the unaided human eye, but revealed to those who are in Christ.

Of course, we inherit an entire legacy of Pauline scholarship that equates "apocalyptic" with "eschatological," playing out Käsemann's perceptive and enduring dictum concerning "apocalyptic"[1] as the "mother of Christian theology."[2] But for more than three decades, that synonymous use of "apocalyptic" has been questioned by those in our guild who have studied the genre of the apocalypse, beginning with the work of the SBL apocalypse seminar in *Semeia* 14 (1979)—a volume that traced the mysteries revealed in apocalypses along *two* axes, the vertical (or spatial) as well as the horizontal (or temporal). Yet, there remains a hangover of the old habits of speech, for example, when some have noted that "apocalyptic," in terms only of eschatological dimension, comes to the fore in the second half of Käsemann's career. This was, we are told, his way of balancing participation and justification in Paul's letters. As Käsemann puts it, "It is characteristic of the letters that the entire mission of Paul is determined by the expectation of the imminent end of the world."[3] However, even Käsemann harbored interest in the spatial dimension: "The eschatological happening consists precisely in this, that God has begun to reclaim for himself the world which belongs to him";[4] "As the world is determined by the conflict of forces, so there is laid on man as a corporeal being the necessity of having a lord, of being incorporated into a dominion, whether it is that of Adam as the representative of the cosmos or that of Christ as the representative of the world of the Resurrection."[5]

For Käsemann, then, Christ is not merely the eschatological Victor, but also the Cosmocrator over numerous realms.[6] This is true also of his

1. I had once hoped that the use of this adjective-qua-noun would come to an end in our guild, due to its infinite elasticity. I myself prefer to use the noun "apocalypse," in reference to the genre, and to use the adjective more precisely by attaching it to a particular noun, such as "eschatology," "structure," or "imagery."
2. Ernst Käsemann, "The Beginnings of Christian Theology," *JTC* 6 (1969): 17–46, at 40.
3. Ernst Käsemann, "Paul and Early Catholicism," in *New Testament Questions of Today*, trans. W. J. Montague (Minneapolis: Fortress Press, 1969), 238–51, at 241.
4. Ernst Käsemann, "Worship in Everyday Life: A Note on Romans 12," in *New Testament Questions of Today*, trans. W. J. Montague (Minneapolis: Fortress Press, 1969), 188–95, at 191.
5. Ernst Käsemann, "The Pauline Doctrine of the Lord's Supper," in *Essays on New Testament Themes*, trans. W. J. Montague (London: SCM, 1964), 108–35, at 133.
6. David V. Way, *The Lordship of Christ: Ernst Käsemann's Interpretation of Paul's Theology*, Oxford Theological Monographs (Oxford: Clarendon, 1991), 112.

contemporary Oscar Cullman, who wrote primarily of *Christ and Time*, but who also noted the vertical axis: "There is in the NT an invisible heaven and an invisible earth; invisible powers and authorities are at work."[7] Unfortunately (in my estimation), he goes on to qualify the importance of this dimension: "But this invisible course of events is itself completely subjected to the progress of time. The essential thing is not the spatial contrast."[8] What might Cullman have seen had he not made this decision? What if he had organized his book not in terms only of *oikonomia* and *ephapax,* but in terms of *mysteria* as well? No doubt, the slight intimations of the hidden yet revealed worlds that we see in part II and part IV[9] of his work would have come to the fore.

Some have made strides toward reclaiming this aspect of apocalyptic discourse in St. Paul's works, notably Andrew Lincoln, whose monograph *Paradise Now and Not Yet* has not received the attention it deserves. Lincoln goes so far as to conclude, "If there is no heavenly dimension, then Christ is not risen and your faith is in vain,"[10] yet even he insists that the cosmic dimension is qualified by the temporal one in the theology of Paul. Always, he speaks about "Paul's references to heaven in the context of realized eschatology,"[11] and thus he does not consider this axis concerning the mysterious realm in its own terms. Then, there are those dubbed "neo-apocalypticists," whose guiding narrative is friendly to the spatial dimension of the mysteries, but, it seems, at the expense of the human temporal dimension, or at least, at the expense of a continuous covenantal history. In this construal, God's crucial act in Christ is typed wholly as an invasion, rather than a fulfillment of what God has done in Israel prior to the cross,[12] and so,

---

7. Oscar Cullman, *Christ and Time: The Primitive Christian Conception of Time and History,* trans. F. V. Filson (Philadelphia: Westminster, 1950), 37.

8. Ibid.

9. In these sections, Cullman notes the "mystical" dimension in Paul's phrases "through whom are all things" and "Your life is hid with Christ." Perhaps, had he paid more attention to the cosmic dimension in Paul's thought, Cullman might have read these statement not merely in an individualist context of piety, but as demonstrating the interconnected spatial mysteries handled by the apostle.

10. Andrew T. Lincoln, *Paradise Now and Not Yet: Studies in the Role of the Heavenly Dimension in Paul's Thought with Special Reference to His Eschatology,* SNTSMS 43 (Cambridge: Cambridge University Press, 1981), 174.

11. Ibid.

12. See, for example, J. Louis Martyn, "Apocalyptic Antinomies," "God's Way of Making Things Right,"

the spatial dimension is understood only to make a punctiliar rather than a chronological impact upon the human domain. As we recognize the ongoing debate between those who stress covenant over against those who insist upon God's sovereign and specific act, we can scarcely neglect the timely admission of N. T. Wright in his recent massive study of Paul that "Paul is involved in a cosmic struggle, . . . an implicitly ongoing battle . . . [and] believes in the reality of unseen powers."[13] Wright goes on to comment, "If that is what we were to mean by 'apocalyptic,' Paul would be . . . an irreducibly 'apocalyptic' figure."[14]

Those of us who study apocalypse as a genre will respond that this is *precisely* how we must understand "apocalyptic"—as a revelation that unveils both the temporal fulfillment of the covenant, and that illumines the significance of other mysteries, including beings, realms, and objects that are normally not seen (plus possible journeys to behold such wonders). The *spatial* and *temporal* axes plotted by the SBL apocalypse group are helpful in reminding us of these aspects even in Paul, who does not construct an outright apocalypse.[15] To these two axes, I think it is helpful to add a third, three-dimensional element, cutting through the first two, because there is a particular apocalyptic approach to *identity* that emerges as a result of awareness of the other mysteries.[16] As Roetzel opines, "[E. P.] Sanders was completely correct in emphasizing that the mystical and eschatological conceptions are intimately related"[17] in Paul, and that this is key to his conception of reality and identity. In this chapter, I will stress the spatial axis, that is, Paul's appeal to hidden but revealed beings and realms. As we consider select references in Paul's undisputed letters,[18] we will

and "The Covenants of Hagar and Sarah: Two Covenants and Two Gentile Missions," in *Theological Issues in the Letters of Paul* (Nashville: Abingdon, 1997), 111–23, 141–56, 191–208 (respectively).

13. N. T. Wright, *Paul and the Faithfulness of God* (Minneapolis: Fortress Press, 2013), 451.

14. Ibid.

15. Though see the ironic construction of an "anti-apocalypse" in 2 Cor. 12:1–9, which contains all the formal or structural elements of the genre without actually disclosing a visual revelation. Clearly, the apostle knew the genre well enough to subvert it, as shall be suggested below.

16. For evidence of this third basic element (the identical) in actual apocalypses, see Edith M. Humphrey, *The Ladies and the Cities: Apocalyptic Identity and Transformation in Joseph and Aseneth, 4 Ezra, the Apocalypse and The Shepherd of Hermas*, JSPSup 17 (Sheffield: Sheffield Academic, 1995).

17. Calvin J. Roetzel, *Paul: The Man and the Myth* (Minneapolis: Fortress Press, 1999), 101.

18. Some will lament that I have capitulated to the historical-critical tradition at this point. Certainly, there is much material in Colossians and Ephesians that would support an emphasis upon the

note how these beings and realms make their mark on the apostle's pastoral counsel, theological arguments, and liturgical decisions or sensibilities. We will discover that such mysteries frequently appear in the course of an enthymeme, where the major premise is shared between Paul and his readers, but not articulated. This unexpounded use in itself indicates the fundamental nature of their presence in Paul's theological imagination: the ability to perceive such mystery is part and parcel of his self-understanding as an apostle and his presentation of Christian identity in general.

Mysterious Presence in Pastoral Counsel

Porneia, Judgment, and Humility

It is not surprising that our example of pastoral conversation is drawn from the first part of 1 Corinthians, along with the grab-bag of issues Paul addresses there. At the point where we glimpse apocalyptic matters (chapters 5 and 6), Paul is already in a warmly rhetorical mode, since he has addressed schism in the church and has concluded with a not-so-veiled threat (4:21). The warmth spills over into his next two topics concerning judgment in the church. The first topic is introduced at 5:1 with an exclamation ("Actually, it is reported . . . !") and the second at 6:1 with a rhetorical question ("Do you dare?"). He is concerned with pragmatics and gives advice, merged with deliberative argumentation. Yet, the discussion goes beyond mere pragmatics as he tackles attitude—first, pride ("you are puffed up!" 5:2), and then, self-centered behavior (6:8). In the discussion of the first topic, *porneia*, an unseen being appears as a central part of the argumentation, just after the case has been introduced (5:1–2), and before the apostle gives his

---

vertical axis. Not to deal with these two letters also makes it difficult for me to respond to the most recent challenge of Edwin van Driel that both the covenantal (cf. Wright) and apocalyptic (cf. Martyn) accounts of Paul's Christology miss the supralapsarian contours implicit in Pauline election (see Edwin Chr. van Driel, "Climax of the Covenant vs. Apocalyptic Invasion: A Theological Analysis of a Contemporary Debate in Pauline Exegesis," *IJST* 17, no. 1 [2015]: 6–25). However, in uncovering a neglected aspect of the apostle's thought, it is better to begin on common ground: unfortunately, there is no space here for an *apologia* defending the apt use of these ecclesially-oriented letters.

advice (5:5) with a closing exhortation to humility and purity (5:6–8). This unseen being is startlingly associated with Paul himself: his "spirit" is "present with the power of our Lord Jesus" (5:3–4) during the assembly of the Corinthians. In his handling of the second topic, judgment, unseen beings are adduced at the climax of a list of rhetorical questions: "do you dare to take these matters to pagan judges? Do you know not that saints will judge the world? Do you not know that we are to *judge angels*?" (6:1–3).

In both cases, Paul does not introduce the mysterious beings as though this were a new revelation to the community. *We* may be startled about his reminder that he is "present in spirit" in the *ekklesia*, but clearly, Paul did not expect the Corinthians to be puzzled. Rather, the presence of the unseen spirit of Paul is subsumed under the main actions, that is, his judging, and the gathered Corinthians handing over the man to judgment.[19] Moreover, Paul's mysterious presence with the church is not argued but assumed, and functions, rather, to add substance and authority to the prescribed action of judgment. Missing from his argument is any sort of explanation for the phenomenon, such as, "I am present with you in the spirit, *because* this is the unified and spiritual nature of the Church which is made up of all its members, present and not present in the flesh." Or, is it even possible that the argument might have run like this: "my spirit is gathered with you, *because* I have an angelic *Doppelgänger* who attends your gatherings when I cannot be with you in body"?[20] It has been customary, of course, to understand "present in the spirit" as a picturesque way of expressing solidarity, but this hardly fits the manner in which Paul insists, three times no less, that he is there with them. Indeed, many translations take the easy way out in supplying the second participial phrase ὡς παρών (1 Cor. 5:3) with the qualifier "as *if* present": an equally

---

19. The main clause is prefaced with the participial phrase concerning his presence, ἀπὼν τῷ σώματι παρὼν δὲ τῷ πνεύματι (1 Cor. 5:3); then the presence is introduced as the second part of a genitive absolute construction: συναχθέντων ὑμῶν καὶ τοῦ ἐμοῦ πνεύματος (5:4).

20. If this seems too far-fetched, consider the insistent assumption of those gathered in John Mark's mother's house that Rhoda was mistaken about the presence at their door, and that his "angel" was visiting them (Acts 12:15). Luke presents this detail concerning the opinion that "his spirit" may be at the door rather matter-of-factly, without registering any compulsion to correct the worldview, over against his critique of magic in Acts 8 or 19.

possible translation would be "as one who is present [in this way, i.e., in the spirit]," yielding the meaning "*because* I am present [in this way], I have already judged." Even if we cannot parse his exact meaning, Paul is appealing to a common or shared understanding concerning a mystical possibility: this is real presence, not a figure of speech![21]

The interconnection of the unseen world with the church re-emerges in chapter 6, where Paul argues that it is prerogative of the church to settle internal disputes. To many in the twenty-first century, the movement from a small legal matter, to judging the world, to judging angels at the *eschaton*, is hardly compelling. For Paul's audience, however, the crescendo up to the judgment of angels works as an effective shaming device, as is clear from the rhetorical negative questions employed here. Just as the apostle assumes that the Corinthians know that his spirit can be present with them when they are gathered, so he assumes that they share with him an understanding that there are angels who require discipline, and over which the church will ultimately have authority (1 Cor. 6:3). Here again, he introduces the argument enthymematically, suppressing major propositions such as, "*Because* you know that there are fallen angels, and *because* you know that the visitation of Christ has raised the faithful to a status above these beings, you know that you are destined to judge them."

Both chapters 5 and 6 work pastorally because the apostle can assume that the Corinthians share with him a common lore about the spirit world. It would seem that the same can be said about his ironic reference to the "angel of Satan" in 2 Corinthians 12, where, at the height of a vision report, the ideal reader would expect a reference to an "interpreting angel." Paul, however, coyly plays with such expectations, and provides an *inverse* interpreting figure, a messenger of Satan. He is not, of course, encouraging the adulation of mystical

---

21. A further example of Paul's appeal to unseen beings may be seen in the perspective that he offers in 1 Thess. 4:13–18, where, as Roetzel argues, Paul "bridged the great divide and drew the boundaries of the community broadly enough to include both the living and the departed saints" (*Paul*, 103). Though the apostle's explicit teaching here is eschatological, it is based upon a cosmic ecclesial picture that embraces the living and "those who are asleep." Those who are unseen (whether by geography or by "sleep") are still present to the church.

experiences, though he owns them for polemical purposes. As we reflect upon these three passages, we should note that only the apostle's critique concerning judgment before unbelievers (1 Corinthians 6) is connected in any direct way with eschatological teaching; in his instruction concerning *porneia* (1 Corinthians 5) and his reference to the third heaven (2 Corinthians 12), the apostle is concerned to demonstrate the *present* effect of the unseen upon the community and upon himself. Moreover, though the thought of eschatological judgment forms part of the argument in 1 Corinthians 6, the apostle's real concern is to encourage orderly and authoritative behavior in the present matter of judging. Further, he encourages his hearers to mimic him (rather than the super-apostles) in a common life of humility and dependence upon God (2 Cor. 11:30; 12:9, 19–20). In all three cases, that which is unseen is simply dropped into the discussion, as something that will be readily understood. Thus, the pastoral needs of the readers are addressed by reference to mystery—whether Paul's compelling "spirit," angels whom humans will judge, or the "angel" who forcibly demonstrates human weakness.

Abiding Angel in the Human Realm

There is another oddity to note. In apocalyptic literature, the proper domain for angels is usually the heavenly realms, where the visionary views them, or whence the angel comes briefly to carry a message, or where a specific interpreting luminary accompanies the visionary in order to be of help. This is alluded to in 2 Corinthians 12, where Paul visits the "third heaven" and "paradise," and where he claims to have seen undisclosed mysteries. However, here, he ironically discloses that God provided for him an "angel of Satan" to interpret the meaning of his experiences: this *angelus interpres* does not leave him at the end of the journey, but, it seems, stays with the apostle for the duration of his ministry, continually interpreting to him the true significance of his "apocalypses of the Lord." Many have noted the polemical nature of this passage, and typed it as an *apologia*; while this element is present, we should also note the apostle's own signaled intent not to engage in self-defense, but rather, in edification (2 Cor. 13:19).[22] Though he is partially concerned to mount a defense, his ultimate purpose is pastoral, that is, to provide himself as a model for those who are in danger of seduction by those who boast visionary prowess. Instead, those who have seen the Lord of glory are to imitate the apostle, bearing like him the marks of Christ in their bodies, and the scourge that makes for wholeness: "death is at work in us . . . so that the life of Jesus may be revealed in our mortal flesh" (2 Cor. 4:11). Though St. Paul appeals to his heavenly journey, his real concern is to communicate the continuing imprint of that journey—strength made perfect in weakness—as learned by means of the inverse ministering "angel" who accompanies him.

Though there are mysteries in the heavenlies, it is significant here that the location of the mystery has been (at least in part) transferred to the human realm. Käsemann, Cullman, and numerous others demonstrated how the eschatological dimension of Paul's theology lends it a sense of fulfillment yet to come. Attention to the unseen beings and their location in the world or the church balances their insight with the conviction that the great mystery is now present among us. The apostle has made three interventions, adducing the integrity of the church by means of Paul's present "spirit," the potential competence of the church to judge *now* based upon its future role in judging angels, and the turning of the enemy's ongoing strategies to a good end. His arguments intimate that the unseen world has already been transported to this world: something has changed. In the pastoral counsel, the immanence of spiritual beings is assumed, while the implications of this assumption are drawn out. We turn now from pastoral exhortation to theological argumentation.

---

22. For an argument that casts this speech in the deliberative mode, see Edith M. Humphrey, "Ambivalent Apocalypse: Apocalyptic Rhetoric and Intertextuality in 2 Corinthians," in *The Intertexture of Apocalyptic Discourse in the New Testament*, ed. Duane F. Watson (Atlanta: Society of Biblical Literature, 2002), 113–36.

Mysterious Beings and Realms in Theological Argument

Presence of Jesus

We do well to register, in the first place, Paul's constant reference to the unseen presence of Jesus, or sometimes, to the spirit of Jesus. This trope is cast apocalyptically in the course of his famous discussion of Israel and the law in Romans 9–11.[23] Though the intertexts for 10:5–6 ultimately go back to Deuteronomy, their nearest and clearest echoes are the rabbinic mysticism in the targumim and the apocalypses, since Paul hypothetically envisions the bringing of Christ down from the heavens and up from the abyss. What is implied is that such cosmic journeys are no longer necessary, because what the visionary would seek is in the midst of the community that proclaims the ῥῆμα τῆς πίστεως (10:8b) or the ῥῆμα Χριστοῦ (10:17). The ῥῆμα merges with the "name of the Lord" (10:13) and indeed, with Jesus himself. The word is present and the name is effective because this one is no longer too high nor too low, but "near" and among those who believe. What the mystics searched for in the hidden and exalted Torah is now present among those who believe—in a person who has been seen but now is known by his action, his ῥῆμα. At no point does Paul actually declare to the Roman Christians that Christ is present, for they share this understanding, and he has already assumed it in earlier conditional clauses: "If Christ is among you" (ἐν ὑμῖν, 8:10)—and you know he is, because the Spirit has been received (8:15)—then everything else follows, including the redundancy (even faithlessness?) of seeking him and fuller evidence of God's righteousness through otherworldly journeys. Chapter 10's argument depends upon the shared belief that the unseen Jesus is present among the community, because he has both entered and spoken into the human arena. For Paul and his hearers, this has changed everything: what was unseen may now be known, by

---

23. On the apocalyptic mode of Romans 10, see Edith M. Humphrey, "Why Bring the Word Down?: The Rhetoric of Demonstration and Disclosure in Romans 9:30—10:13," in *Romans and the People of God: Essays in Honor of Gordon D. Fee on the Occasion of His 65th Birthday*, eds. S. Soderlund and N. T. Wright (Grand Rapids: Eerdmans, 1999), 129–48.

Jew or gentile (10:17; 11:11), and what remains unseen cannot exert destructive influences upon God's faithful (8:38).

The Powers, Active and Watching

Indeed, this knowledge may be said to surpass the knowledge of unseen beings! We hear about this from the apostle only in passing, as he argues the centrality of the cross. Paul's pastoral concern in the opening chapters of 1 Corinthians is that of schism, but he develops a theological and argumentative excursus that goes beyond the practical needs. Yes, he is holding his weakness up as an example of humility for the church. But he also trains his eyes upon the mystery evident in the cross: "For I decided to know nothing among you except Jesus Christ and him crucified. . . . We sound forth the concealed Wisdom of God in a mystery, that Wisdom decided before all ages by God for our glory, which wisdom none of the archons of this aeon recognized, for if they had, they would not have crucified the Lord of glory!" (1 Cor. 2:7-8). Some, of course, will want to restrict Paul's meaning of *archontes* to human potentates, but this is very unlikely, considering Paul's description of them in 2:6 as bound for destruction, and his reference to them as finally "destroyed" in the dénouement of the cosmic plan (15:24-28). No, Paul here shares with his community a belief in "Powers" who are interconnected, no doubt, with human authorities, but who remain unseen, and who are ultimately responsible for the death of Jesus. What that act unleashed, though, was more than they anticipated. Jesus crucified, the quintessential Sign of weakness to the archons, has become the Source of all wisdom and power, he implies. This mystery supports the polemic against human wisdom that undergirds 1 Corinthians. To really *see* the mystery of weakness and strength is to put all other human arguments in perspective.

This same line of reasoning is echoed in Paul's reference to the shameful display of the apostles before the cosmos, before both angels and humans (1 Cor. 4:9). Here, as in chapter 2, Paul's unexplained assumptions concerning unseen participants—whether as actors or as spectators—play an important role in his argument. In chapter 2, the apparent wisdom of unseen spiritual agents, bearing down upon the human rulers of the world, is ranged against the surprising wisdom and power of the cross: what even supernatural beings could not fathom can now be taught in the church, as spiritual things are taught to those who have been incorporated into Christ. In chapter 4, the weakness of the apostles, witnessed to by both unseen and human spectators, itself participates in the unexpected strategy that Paul insists is at play: foolishness and weakness make eventually for wisdom and strength. This is the dynamic that is argued, directly in chapter 2 and ironically in chapter 4, while the role of unseen beings in this scenario adds to the substantive nature of the arguments. Not even the unseen *archontes* understand truly what and whom the apostles are proclaiming; not even their scorn can diminish what God has done and is about to do in the human realm! They will pass away, but God's power and wisdom will be established.

Galatians, Power, and Place

The most argumentative of Paul's letters is, by consensus, Galatians. At both the beginning and the ending of this letter, Paul "ups the ante" by associating himself with an angelic figure: first, as he speaks of the adulteration of the gospel, which they should reject, even if he "or an angel from heaven" (1:8) were to engage in it; then, when he recalls the reception the Galatians first gave him, as an "angel of God" (4:14) or even as though he were Christ himself! Both the hypothetical possibility of their being deceived (perhaps not so entirely hypothetical), and the memory of their actual reception of the gospel, serve to underscore the seriousness of his polemic. The reference to angels adds to the *pathos* and *ethos* here forged: curiously, in reverse order to the conventions of oratorical beginnings and endings! Then, within the center of Galatians's argument, we hear that the Torah was given through angels by a mediating hand (3:19), and that the Jewish people were, while in their infancy, placed under the στοιχεῖα τοῦ κόσμου (4:3), in parallel to the gentiles who also were enslaved to unseen powers that "are not gods by nature" (4:8–9). Though elsewhere Paul insists that the Torah itself is holy, whereas the gods of other nations are merely usurping demons, here, he grants these an equivalency for the sake of argument, dissuading the Galatian gentiles from heeding the Judaizers. The unseen powers provide strong ammunition for his case since, by appealing to them, he can diminish the importance of the Torah in the present state of affairs. It is consistent with the penultimate authority of the Torah to note that it did not, in fact, come directly from God's hand. Indeed, the full revelation of the gospel, which places Christ in the center, justifies his classification of those mediating στοιχεῖα with the more malicious powers that oppressed the gentile peoples for centuries. To turn away from Christ by supplementing the gospel with observance of Torah distinctives is, he implies, tantamount to relinquishing one's adult position in the household. It is a return to the authority of unseen mediators, and whether these powers are by nature benign or malevolent is beside the point, since the time of tutelage or imprisonment has passed.

Nor is it only a matter of era, a matter of the question, "What time is it?" Paul also concerns himself with the *source* and *identity* of God's people in his reference to the Jerusalem above. Here, again, we are hampered by the apostle's intimacy with his interlocutors. "Jerusalem above" (Gal. 4:26) is simply dropped into the discussion—and as part of a complex midrashic/typological/allegorical construction![24]—without warning or explanation. As Lincoln comments, "He could introduce the concept of a heavenly Jerusalem quite casually and presuppose knowledge of it, which suggests that traditions about a heavenly Jerusalem were fairly widespread."[25] (We see, it would seem, a very similar line of argument in the dramatic climax at Heb. 12:18–29, with its contrast between a hedged mountain and the heavenly Jerusalem). In his careful exposition of this passage, Lincoln ranges Paul's

---

24. Lincoln's description of Paul's method—he "serves up a [midrashic] cake, the basic ingredients of which are typological but which has some allegorical icing"— is comic though apt (*Paradise Now*, 14).
25. Ibid., 18.

conception of the heavenly Jerusalem less with the eschatological expectations of the prophets (cf. Isaiah 2; 54; 60–62; Ezekiel 40–48) than with the rabbinic material, which posited an actually present city in the heavenlies. However, Paul's *negative* typing of the "now [present] Jerusalem" differs from the procedure of the rabbis. Lincoln also argues that the apostle "does not appear to hold that there is an actual city in heaven, for in seeing this city as the mother of all believers he relieves the concept of its purely material and national connotations."[26] The first contrast with the rabbis is clear, but I am not so sure about his conclusions concerning the character of the city. Certainly, the Jerusalem above is not construed by the apostle in terms of Judaism alone, nor can he conceive of it as material in a naïve sense, given his category of those things understood *kata sarka*. However, this does not mean that there is no sense whatsoever of an actual Jerusalem above, and that the phrase is only a metaphorical way of speaking about the origin of believers, that is, their being begotten and conceived "from above." Perhaps we get a clue in the "mixed nature of the antithesis"[27]—that is, the first Jerusalem is described in temporal terms ("now") whereas the other is described in terms of space ("above"). By contrast, then, the first Jerusalem is the one "below," whereas the second Jerusalem is "then." But is "then" necessarily *future*, or might it also be seen as existent in an august *past* and in a "timeful" eternity?

Let us remember that the earthly Jerusalem was constructed according to a pattern revealed to Moses, and that this typological grammar is retained in Hebrews, relieved of Platonic stasis by reference to what has happened there. Hebrews traces the entrance of the anointed Hero beyond the veil and his stance as a present Priest among the holy things and among his saints (τῶν ἁγίων λειτουργός, Heb. 8:2), who thereby enables his own to enter among the holy things and among the saints (τῶν ἁγίων, 10:19) by the blood of Christ. Though there is an expectation of fuller residency "on that Day," in Galatians,

26. Ibid., 21.
27. Ibid.

as in Hebrews, the present tense dominates: "she *is* free"; "she *is* our mother"; "the children . . . *are* more numerous"; "you . . . *are* children"; "so it is also *now*." The "now" of the Jerusalem above differs from the limited and enslaved "now" of the Jerusalem associated with Hagar. Lou Martyn would seem correct in saying that Paul is referring "emphatically to the real present" in Gal. 4:29;[28] yet, there is also a parallel series of events taking place in Paul's "now," since it is those events (the actions of his blinded countryman and the Judaizers) in the "now Jerusalem" (4:24) that grieve the apostle. The timeful "now" of the Jerusalem above alone is remarkable for its permanence and solidity; the "for now" enslavement of that other city has no staying power. As an analogy to the situation that St. Paul (or Hebrews, for that matter!) has in mind, consider the fantasy of C. S. Lewis's *That Hideous Strength*, which makes use of the ancient tradition of Logres as a mysteriously ongoing and intensifying reality, in parallel to and over against decaying England.[29]

In some ways, perhaps, the "children" merge with the mother-City-mountain, but in other ways, they remain distinct. Just as John the seer envisions matters in Revelation 12, so here, St. Paul speaks of childbearing with effort, and of believers as children of the mother above. The heavenly City, in the understanding of first-century Christians, had not just recently come into being, but had a long and august history, in which St. Paul and the Galatians are now participating. There is continuity in God's provision for his people, a matrix into which they are called. Yet, here, there is also something new—a way has been prepared for *many*, and an unprecedented power and freedom. Even amidst trouble and persecution (Gal. 4:29), the mother is delighted to welcome children whom she did not expect (4:27)! As suggested in the visionary declaration of Rev. 12:10–12, the Galatian Christians are to see themselves as inhabiting two realms, both earth and heaven. Their life is attended by the "woe" that comes

---

28. Martyn, "The Covenants of Hagar and Sarah," 200.
29. C. S. Lewis, *That Hideous Strength*, The Cosmic Trilogy (London: Bodley Head, 1989).

for now on earth, but embraced also by the joy properly expressed by those whose home is newly opened to them (Gal. 4:29, 31 cf. Rev. 12:12).

In theological discourse, as in pastoral advice, Paul's unseen mysteries take their role, but without careful explication. These passages provide us not only with the raw material for debate concerning their exact meaning, but also with tantalizing expressions of the intricate relationship of the past, present, and future, including a contrast between the temporary "for now" over against the permanent "now." In dealing with the apostle's complex arguments, we must construe both his meaning and his view of Christian identity with care.

Mystery in Liturgical Instruction

Probably the most famous reference to unseen beings is in Paul's excursus on love, an excursus which interrupts his instruction on worship in 1 Corinthians 12 and 14. Here, the power of Paul's opening statement regarding human and *angelic* language (13:1) implies a common wisdom concerning mysterious worshipping beings. The flow of the opening sentence moves from the human to angelic, to the most sublime—"if I speak in the tongues of human beings *or even* of angels," but do not have love, it is insignificant.

Unseen Beings and Idolatry

A less frequently noted trope in the same letter suggests that when human beings offer a libation or partake of a common cup in their cult, they are sharing in the one who is being honored—either Christ, or a demon (10:21). Paul may adopt a "don't ask, don't tell" policy with regard to food that has been *previously* blessed and is for sale on the market, since there is only one God, and the God is a one who gives true freedom (8:6–13). God, after all, is the creator of all, and so, all food ultimately is his. The apostle's liberality, however, does not extend to the worship situation, presumably because he and the Corinthians envisage the presence of actual unseen beings in such a context. In 1 Corinthians 10, Paul carefully sets up the principle of participation in the true God by means of liturgical actions, by appealing typologically to the Old Testament (10:1–4), and by noting the unseen presence of Christ in the bizarrely "following Rock." He then asserts the cautionary function of Old Testament precedents, and gives a command against idolatry to those who recognize the unseen presence of Christ. Finally, he appeals to the table and its constituent parts, the cup and the bread, by which both the presence of Christ and the identity of the community are understood. He encourages the Corinthians to see how this reality is incompatible with participation in idolatry, not because idols have power, but because they represent some unseen power that seeks to usurp the place of Christ—but cannot, of course, do so.

Paul's argument is on a razor's edge at this point, for he wants to establish the rebellion of hostile powers without dignifying them or acknowledging their power. Even his rhetorical question at 10:19 concerning the substance of idols spills over, it seems, into the realm of rival gods: are the demons *themselves* (not simply their images) "not anything"? His return in chapter 10 to the previous discussion of chapter 8 (whether the food can be eaten by Christians) seems disorganized, but in fact it drives home his point that God alone is the creator who has given all food, not the rival gods, who have no being, nor even the demons, in whatever form they may be said to exist. Here, then, Paul uses doubt concerning the "being" of demons—which, of course, depends upon a shared understanding concerning these entities—in order to strengthen his case. The Christian's identity is certain, but the continued force of these other rival powers is another matter, despite their association with religious rites.

Unseen Beings and Worship

This assumption that unseen beings are, in some way, present during human worship underlies, also, the strange phrase with which we began this paper—the obscure argument concerning female deportment by reference to angels. In 1 Cor. 11:1–16, Paul appears (as in chapter 14) to be dealing with disruptions in worship that have sprung from the newfound freedom of women who misconstrued their new identity. He echoes the primeval Genesis account, but goes beyond it in interpretation when he speaks about woman created as the "glory" of man. He has, unfortunately, been misread by many on this score, including John Milton, who, in *Paradise Lost*, re-narrates his argument as a neatly graded scale of being, suggesting that woman is made in the *image* of man, who is made in the image of the Son, who is the image of the Father.

However, St. Paul never suggests that women are not also reflective of Christ's image, for indeed, these instructions concern actions a woman performs in the community because she is in Christ, the archetypal Prophet and Priest—she prophesies and prays! What the apostle does seem to assume is that woman has a *second* reflective purpose, expressing also the glory of man, and thus of humanity, whom Adam represents. (Is St. Paul meditating upon Adam rejoicing "This is bone of my bone"?) It is this reflective purpose that should not be the center of focus in worship, since worship is for glorifying God, not for the exaltation of humanity. In this context, Paul goes on to develop his argument, touching upon a more esoteric part of the tradition concerning cosmic worship in the little phrase, "because of the angels." We may assume that he does need to explain the connection between angels and liturgy to the Corinthians: perhaps they have received this in spades from those who are disturbing them, and whom he combats more strenuously in 2 Corinthians. In Isaiah 6, the angels cover their feet and sing the Thrice-Holy Hymn, while in Revelation 4–5, they orchestrate and choreograph cosmic and celestial worship, cuing the various parts of creation to adore the Lord in their peculiar way.[30] If God the Son acknowledges his head (1 Cor. 11:3), and the glorious seraphim cover themselves as they fly, then why should women be chagrined to cover their heads, acknowledging the diversity of creation and the wonder of God-with-us? In Isaiah 6, there is an antiphonal worship between angels, as "Holy, holy, holy is the LORD of Hosts" refers to his transcendence, while the reply "the whole earth

---

30. An implicit reminder of the angelic role in directing worship is consonant with the apostle's final word on worship to the congregation, that all things should be done with an eye to *taxis*, that is, "according to order" (1 Cor. 14:40).

is full of his glory" acknowledges his immanence. So too, it seems, in human worship, men and women "speak" antiphonally, one group declaring by its posture to the entire congregation (not just to the women!) the creaturely submission that is seemly before utter Holiness, the other declaring the marvelous freedom of the anointed children of God.

Despite its abrupt appearance, the phrase "because of the angels" appears not as an impermeable statement, nor as an item in a grab-bag argument for cultural norms that are incoherent with the apostle's teaching on freedom. Rather, it may be that the apostle's instructions on attire in worship here are doubly counter-cultural, as men are told to "uncover," perhaps in distinction to their Jewish counterparts,[31] whereas women are to "cover," over against the mystery cults of Corinth, where they loosened their tresses as a sign of ecstasy.[32] In any event, the reference to the angels comes as part of a carefully conceived cumulative argument that begins with a reference to Christology, anthropology, and theology (11:3), that moves on to describe the actions of worship (11:4–6), and that explains these in terms of the creation story (11:7–9). Following the reference to the angels (11:10), the apostle will remind the Corinthians of the interdependence of the created order (11:11–12), and appeals to their understanding of nature (11:13–15). Here, then, he encourages his readers to understand their identity not simply in terms of personal liberty, but in light of salvation history, cosmic reality, nature, and (as he book-ends the argument at 11:2 and 11:16), transmitted tradition. The traditions are not arbitrary, but bound up with a way of worship that does not obliterate the distinctions of nature, but naturalizes and transforms these in a larger sphere. Worshippers, whether male or female, are to be mindful that what they do in worship joins them to unseen hosts whose sole occupation is to glorify God. Many questions

---

31. Much is uncertain concerning what can be known about the origin of head-coverings in the Jewish synagogue, but it is clear that at least the priests covered their heads when serving in the Temple.
32. Paul's understanding of prophecy assumes that "the spirits of the prophets are subject to the prophets" (1 Cor. 14:32), and so, a woman, when she prophesies, does not yield to ecstatic abandon, but retains a sign of "authority" or "power" on her head.

remain. But what we can declare on the basis of Paul's recognition of unseen beings is that he believes that in worship, there is more than normally meets the eye—whether we are speaking of entities that may be conjured up by irregular worship (chapter 10) or angels that are present in the assembly of God (chapter 11).

Mysterious Identity In the Face of Jesus

It is this perception of what has heretofore been largely hidden that distinguishes the family of God from both the fallen creation, and from the earlier situation of that nation which God called. It is, of course, risky, to make a claim for *theoria* in the letters of the apostle, since he never uses the noun, and in fact, uses the verb related to it for various actions, not limited to God-inspired sight. Yet, the concept is in his letters just as surely as the divinity of our Lord Jesus is present (cf. 1 Cor. 8:6), though there is no statement of his co-essential being with the Father! We could show this aspect of special sight throughout the letters, but will fasten on the argument of 2 Corinthians 3–4, which brings together many of the themes of mystery that we have seen so far, and joins them with the question of apostolic and general Christian identity. Here, the apostle begins with what appears to be a defense of his own apostolic calling, but moves into a discussion of corporate transformation (3:18; 4:6), before concluding with a reference to the "outside" and "inside anthropos" (4:16) and an antinomy concerning the community's gaze upon eternal mysteries (4:17–18).

Throughout these two chapters, there is an emphasis upon sight: internal letters that can be seen by all (3:2–3); not seeing and seeing the glory (3:7, 15, 16); veils and unveiling (3:16–18); hiding and not hiding (3:2–3); blinded eyes and being given the gift of inner sight (4:4, 6); what is visible and hidden (4:7–11); what is inside and outside (4:16); and looking on what cannot be seen (4:18). It is not just a matter of what Israel could not see because of the era in which she was called (though this is part of the dynamic), since Paul speaks of a mystery that Moses saw at that same time; it is not just a matter of a resurrection life to come, but one that is to be perceived now by gazing at Christ and each other (3:18), by recognizing the character of the apostolic message (4:1–4), by perceiving the command given to the heart that we should see (4:6), by rejoicing in the deepening of worship among the people of God (4:14–15), and by seeing the true value of suffering in the light of Christ (4:16–18). To look slightly beyond our passage, St. Paul does not simply anticipate the future resurrection, but uses the present tense to describe Christian possessions: we *have* a dwelling in the heavens (5:1), and we have been given the gift of the Spirit as the outward (or inward) sign of this (5:5).

True sight, then, goes beyond mere theological understanding (with the mind) to something that is deeply internal, and that redirects the body, the attitude, the entire life of believers together. It involves symbiosis, give and take, sacrifice and reception (4:7–12), and it is described as a metamorphosis from glory to glory, together. Clearly, a major characteristic of the unveiled or apocalypsed life that Christians inhabit is that they *see*—perhaps not all the same thing or in the same way, but there is a communal sight that God has declared by a performative utterance concerning the new creation. "For God, that very one who said, 'Let light shine out of darkness' has shone in our hearts for the light of the knowledge of the glory of God in the face of Christ Jesus" (2 Cor. 4:6). This means that such sight is not simply a characteristic, but also a means by which the glory of God is seen ("*for the light*"). The proof of the pudding comes when the Corinthians see, with the apostle, that even the earthen vessel that hides the light or the body that is wasting away (4:16) becomes itself a means by which the light can be seen. When this happens, the community is reflecting Jesus, who sacrificed by means of the cross, but first, by the taking on of entire humanity in its dying and limited condition. So, then, the "seeing" involves recognizing the worth of the entire creation, and the continuity of God's action in it, throughout history, and in the entire apocalyptic coming of the Son—his life, his cross, his resurrection, and his exaltation. Material things that direct the newly-enlightened eyes to God are now everywhere, as the character and purpose of God are perceived not simply in the invasion of the cross, nor even only in covenantal history, but in the entire creation, made new.

The identity of God's people, then, is such that everything, and indeed, every event, communicate God's glory to them, including even (or especially) affliction, which is preparing a "weight of glory" that is unimaginable, yet even now presently glimpsed. There is, because of this, a paradoxical relinquishing and reaffirmation of the world that God has made—for it, like us, is being unmade and will be remade. Human sight being what it is, we can only conceive of one action at a time. And so, at times, the enlivened eyes will see the vanity and fleeting nature of this world, and fix instead upon the heavenlies, where Christ has been exalted. At other times, however, illumined eyes will see the power of God at work in earthen vessels, and the ongoing birth pangs of the cosmos, made clearer as God's people pray in the Spirit, and have confidence that the resurrection is already accomplished for them in Christ. Both the language of a present heaven, making its mark on our world, and a future resurrection, intimated in the Risen One, are appropriate: not the one without the other, but both together, as we have need either for ascesis and chastisement, or for comfort and assurance. Thus, the two axes, vertical and horizontal, are conjoined by the One whose identity we share, the Alpha and Omega, the One who has descended to the depths, and who has ascended above all things, but remains in company with us. As the Orthodox Troparion in the Paschal Hours exclaims, "In the tomb with the body and in Hades with the soul, in Paradise with the thief and on the throne with the Father and the Spirit, wast Thou, O boundless Christ, filling all things."

Conclusion

D. Francois Tolmie concludes an intriguing paper on unseen beings with this question and answer: "[D]oes Paul use angels as arguments? . . . Only rarely, but when he does, he does so in a variety of ways, which in some cases, are very complex."[33] I would concur with the complexity and nuance which he observes, but am not so sure that the envisioning of mysterious beings, along with the reality of mysterious realms, is so very rare in Paul. The mysteries, seen here in the letters to the Corinthians, Thessalonians, Galatians, and Romans, perhaps *seem* few and far between because they are summarily affirmed, and because Paul never *argues* for their reality nor dwells upon them in an esoteric or detailed discussion. Rather, the angels serve, to borrow the language of Hebrews, as merely "ministering spirits," furthering the apostle's advice, theological argument, or liturgical instructions. Angels are barely named, not ranked, and not given a history—though we may assume that some are fallen and that others are connected with the transmission of the Torah. Such omissions distinguish Paul from the pseudepigrapha and the gnostic writings that treat the angels as subjects in their own right. Instead, Paul assumes their existence, expecting that his readers share this perspective with him. As a result, unseen beings find a natural but unexpounded place in his writings.

Similarly, realms that are not normally seen are never presented by means of titillating travelogues in the letters of Paul, such as we observe in, for example, the pseudepigraphic exploits of Enoch. Instead, St. Paul both discourages such exploits (Rom. 10:6–8), and downplays them (2 Corinthians 12) by frustrating our expectations for visual details. After all, the apostle knows that he must prepare his readers to live in this world, though they may, at times, feel that it is better to "be with the Lord" in a more definitive way. Moreover, he sees that the Lord has sanctified this world and this era, coming at the climax of his work in creation, at just the right time, in order not only to correct the creation ("rectify," as Lou Martyn would have it), but also, to affirm, heal and re-instate it as (at least potentially!) very good. Where unseen realms are intimated, they are incorporated, almost entirely without explanation, within his pastoral counsel, as part of his argument with those who glory in such visions, and as a central part of his calling to worship the lord of both heaven and earth. This oblique

---

33. D. Francois Tolmie, "Angels as Arguments? The Rhetorical Function of References to Angels in the Main Letters of Paul," *Hervormde Teologiese Studies* 67, no. 1 (2011): 1–8, at 7.

approach means that full mastery of his argument is frequently elusive for the contemporary reader.

What we can determine is this: Paul considers not only that he is one of the apostolic "stewards of the mysteries of God" (1 Cor. 4:1), but also that he is fulfilling his ministry in full view not only of human beings, but also of the angels. Moreover, the life of the entire church is making its mark not only on earth, but also in heaven! (But to demonstrate this clearly, we would have to move beyond the undisputed letters, to, say, Colossians). What he proclaims not only includes the reality of mystery, putting this in its place, but also proceeds in the light of these revelations. So, then, both the spatial and temporal dimensions of apocalyptic are traced in Paul's letters, and are interconnected with how he construes his own identity, and the identity of his brothers and sisters. His ministry is envisaged as an episode in the story that is moving to an eschatological dénouement, but that also partakes, because of what Christ has done, in here-and-now mysteries. It is not simply that the *eschaton* has been brought into Paul's time through the resurrection of Christ, but that heaven has embraced earth. Apocalyptic, in her motherly conception of theology, employs many nurturing techniques, borrowed from the world of time and space, from those things seen and unseen, and also from the recognition of humankind's ambivalent identity in that world. Though not accentuated, the "apocalyptic principle" noted by Patrick Reardon is everywhere present in Paul's letters: "More is going on than appears to be going on."[34]

34. Patrick Reardon, *The Trial of Job* (Ben Lomond, CA: Conciliar, 2005), 24.

6

Apocalyptic and the Sudden Fulfillment of Divine Promise

N. T. Wright

The space is too constrained, and the current debates too many-sided and wide-ranging, to allow for detailed interaction with other views. There will, however, be many times when Mark's "apocalyptic" warning will be appropriate: "Let the reader understand."

Paul's Setting

Saul of Tarsus lived in a world of intense eschatological expectation, rooted in Israel's scriptures and heated to boiling point by political circumstances. Jewish life since the Babylonian exile was a story of hopes raised and then dashed. The hope was for Israel's ultimate rescue (after an "extended exile"), and the ultimate glorious return of Israel's

God. "O that you would tear open the heavens and come down"; "the glory of YHWH shall be revealed, and all flesh shall see it together"; "Then YHWH my God will come, and all his saints with him"; "the Lord whom you seek will suddenly come to his temple" (Isa. 64:1; 40.5; Zech. 14:5; Mal. 3:1). Israel's God would return in person to sort everything out—to put the world right, and particularly, to put Israel right, by dealing with pagan oppression and rescuing God's people from their grip. This powerful strand of Jewish thinking can be seen under the overall heading of "new Exodus." All this is massively documented and should be uncontroversial.[1] It constituted the "sudden fulfillment of divine promise." Saul of Tarsus came to believe that these promises had been fulfilled in the dramatic and unexpected events concerning Jesus and the Spirit.

Within this world, the literary form sometimes called "apocalypse" served a particular purpose. Hope deferred may have sickened the heart, but it sometimes inspired the mind; and one writer after another wrote—whether like Coleridge because of actual dreams or like Bunyan because of literary choice—in a form which declared that, though the coming ultimate revelation was still delayed, a word from beyond, a vision of the heavenly realm and its mysteries, might be given to select mortals to encourage them ahead of the final great day, perhaps even to stir them to new ways of looking at their present circumstances, understanding the dark nature of present oppression, and grasping the sure promise of eventual deliverance. If the longed-for glorious presence of the *Shekinah* was delayed, and if (in particular) the dark forces of the non-Jewish world seemed to be all-powerful, there might nonetheless be ways in which, through prayer and study, glimpses might be granted, even in the present time, of heavenly truths, heavenly purposes, and perhaps, also eventual divine victory. The literary genre we call "apocalypse" was one way of reflecting or embodying this belief, whether or not, in this or that case, it was intended as a transcript of actual visionary experience. Thus, both (what we call) "mysticism" and (what we call) "apocalyptic" can be

---

1. See, e.g., my *Paul and the Faithfulness of God* (London: SPCK, 2013) [=*PFG*], chapter 2.

credibly located, within the ancient Jewish world, within the puzzlement, persecution, and dogged hope of the Second Temple period.

The genre we have come to know as "apocalypse" is found in many cultures. But if we are to place Paul in relation to this kind of writing, or its supposedly specific content, we must focus on Jewish sources in particular: on the line from Ezekiel and Daniel through to *4 Ezra* and *2 Baruch*, and within early Christian writing from certain passages in the gospels through to the book of Revelation and second-century texts such as the *Shepherd of Hermas*. When we speak of "apocalyptic" in relation to a Jewish or early Christian text, we must at the very least indicate that we mean to bring it into this orbit. (How odd it is, in passing, that people discuss "Paul and apocalyptic" without reference to Revelation or the *Shepherd*! If we want to investigate early Christian apocalyptic, and Paul within it, they might be obvious places to begin.[2]) The point of introducing "apocalyptic" as an explanatory or organizing category in New Testament studies, at least since Käsemann, was to locate it within a credible history-of-religions, and perhaps also theological, setting. Whatever form the proposal now takes, it must make sense within that Second Temple Jewish world.

Marking out this *literary* territory does not, of itself, mean highlighting a distinct *theology*. Nor does the theology sometimes expressed in some "apocalyptic" writings need this particular genre. Most Jews of Paul's day, and on into the high Rabbinic period long after "apocalyptic" had fallen from favor, distinguished "the present age" from "the age to come." Most Jews, then and later, acknowledged the existence of non-human agencies, both good and evil. All ancient Jews for whom we have evidence believed that heaven and earth were neither identical nor separated by a vast unbridgeable gulf. Commerce between heaven and earth was thinkable, and the Jerusalem Temple symbolized, and might perhaps actualize, their ideal overlap. (Details of the Temple and its liturgical practices continued, of course, to be

2. See J. P. Davies, *Paul Among the Apocalypses? An Evaluation of the 'Apocalyptic Paul' in the Context of Jewish and Christian Apocalyptic Literature*, LNTS 562 (London: Bloomsbury T&T Clark, 2016).

discussed for centuries after its destruction.) None of these beliefs is specific either to the literary genre we call "apocalypse" or to any "movement" that might deserve the name "apocalypticism." The particular genre we know from Daniel, 4 *Ezra*, and the rest was one way among others in which these issues could be addressed. In other words, you did not have to write an "apocalypse" in order to talk about "the present age and the age to come," or about the baleful influence of hostile non-human powers. Equally, if you *were* writing an "apocalypse," you didn't have to talk about those themes. Two-age discourse and the narrative of cosmic warfare and victory were neither necessary nor sufficient conditions for the presence of something which can, with historical basis, be called "apocalyptic," and vice versa. Details about the promised future were naturally an important feature of such writings. But these works were concerned with many other things besides, as Christopher Rowland and others have demon-strated.[3]

Referring to any of these elements as "apocalyptic," therefore, simply begs the question. To refer (as some do) to suprahuman powers, believed by some to influence the course of this-worldly events, as "apocalyptic" powers is a combination of muddled thinking about the first century and subtle influence from our own (where the word "apocalyptic" is used as an arm-waving indicator of the enormous or terrible scale of, say, a natural disaster). Calling them "cosmic" powers may not be much better, since the word "cosmic" is itself used in a variety of ways, of which "non-spatio-temporal" or "suprahuman" is only one. Granted, we are here at the borders of language, and we may suspect that first-century Jews were as well. That is why they developed particular genres, to say in symbol and metaphor what ordinary language might struggle with.[4]

One particular problem with our descriptions of ancient Jewish

---

3. C. Rowland, *The Open Heaven* (SPCK, 1982); C. Rowland and C. R. A. Morray-Jones, *The Mystery of God: Early Jewish Mysticism and the New Testament* (Leiden: Brill, 2009). On all this see further Part II of N. T. Wright, *Paul and His Recent Interpreters* (London: SPCK, 2015).
4. See George B. Caird, *Language and Imagery of the Bible* (London: Duckworth, 1980). Cf. the defense of this point in *PFG* 163–75.

thought, and particularly with "apocalyptic," centers on the word "dualism." That word regularly misleads.[5] There is such a thing as radical ontological dualism, in which the present world of space, time, and matter is basically evil and in which another world—without space, time, and matter—is basically good. But that is not, so far as we can tell, how most ancient Jews characteristically saw things. There are indeed, within ancient Jewish writings, what may be called "dualities": between, for instance, "the present age" and "the age to come," which (as I noted a moment ago) was a distinction made as much by the Rabbis as by the writers of apocalypses. Paul himself, in Gal. 1:4, labels the "present age" as "evil." But to call that statement "dualistic" (or to regard a belief in the existence of hostile powers as "dualistic") can mislead us into forgetting that most Jews, Paul included, regarded the present world as, nonetheless, the good creation of the good Creator, and the present time as under the Creator's sovereign providence. Part of the point of many actual apocalypses is to affirm this very point, in the teeth of apparently contradictory evidence.[6] If we today find it difficult to believe in divine sovereignty at the same time as saying (with, for instance, 1 John 5:19) that the world is "under the power of the evil one" or of the delegated agents of that dark force, that is our problem. The early Jews, and the early Christians, managed, not perhaps without a struggle, to hold those things in dynamic tension (e.g., John 19:11).

Nor was the content of "apocalyptic" writing polarized over against other strands of Jewish culture.[7] People used to play off a supposed "apocalyptic" Jesus against a supposed "wisdom" Jesus (this was a favorite ploy of the "Jesus Seminar"), but this is a false antithesis. Insofar as we can isolate elements characteristic of "wisdom" or of "apocalyptic," we find them regularly intermingled, as in the Scrolls, the Wisdom of Solomon, the synoptic tradition, or the book of

---

5. N. T. Wright, *The New Testament and the People of God* (London: SPCK, 1992), chapter 10.
6. Among possible exceptions we might include *1 Enoch 42*.
7. This point was already made by J. C. Beker: e.g., his *Paul the Apostle: The Triumph of God in Life and Thought* (Philadelphia: Fortress Press, 1987), 137. See too W. Meeks, *The First Urban Christians* (New Haven: Yale University Press, 1983), 179–80.

Revelation. A good deal of ancient Jewish literature, in fact, warns us against confusing genre and content, at this or any other point.

Jewish "apocalyptic" literature, then, frequently affirms divine sovereignty over the history, not only of Israel, but of the wider world. Such writings often describe the long, dark, and puzzling purposes of the One God, purposes which can be mapped through devices such as the many-metaled statue in Daniel 2, the four beasts out of the sea in Daniel 7, or the sheep, the bull, and so on in *1 Enoch*. The authors of these writings did not envisage the ultimate deliverance, if it were to come, as emerging from a steady crescendo of "progressive revelation" or immanent development. Any suggestion of such a developmental eschatology, even if dignified with the slippery term "salvation history," is out of the question; though, as we shall see presently, there *is* something in the texts, both Jewish and Pauline, which can properly be named in that way, as Ernst Käsemann rightly saw. The strange, terrible, and often apparently chaotic events of history, into which deliverance would break as a fresh and cataclysmic act, were nonetheless under some kind of ultimate divine control, and the divine promises of ultimate deliverance, often coming at what seemed like the darkest moments, could be seen at least in retrospect as signs of that control, and of its covenantal focus (see below). Thus, "apocalyptic" texts regularly saw the present state of affairs, not as mere chaos, nor of course as constituting any kind of "progress" or "development," but as a nevertheless divinely ordered sequence of woes or wicked kingdoms, symbolized by metals, animals, or monsters. The coming event would be a dramatic reversal in which, suddenly, the long, dark sequence would be over and the ancient promises would be fulfilled. But the sequence itself, though not in any way about "progress," was all about *providence*. Articulating all this in a balanced way is, to be sure, quite difficult. That, no doubt, is why special literary forms were used for the purpose.

My basic point here concerns false antitheses. Within the literary genre "apocalypse," and within any putative movement labeled "apocalypticism," it was normal to *combine* a sense that the present age was evil, dominated by wicked suprahuman forces, with an equal sense that Israel's creator God was working his purpose out, not as a steady evolution, but with an inscrutable justice and timing, and that at the right moment, he would unveil, to an unready world, the shocking and sudden fulfillment of his ancient promises. The underlying doctrine of providence, so prominent in Josephus (to take an example from a quite different genre),[8] did not mean that one could read divine purposes out of observable historical events. When Josephus wanted to explain what God was really up to, he had to invoke his own supposed prophetic powers (e.g., *War* 3.405-7). Nor did belief in providence imply a steady crescendo leading to a *fortissimo* fulfillment. The apocalypses affirm a dogged trust that somewhere, somehow, even in the thick darkness, the one God was still in control, and would fulfill his seemingly impossible purposes at the proper time. But the phrase "at the proper time" was important. Once more, this had nothing to do with a *linear progress*, an evolution or development. On the contrary, it would seem that the night was getting darker. When the dawn came, it would not be heralded by a long, slow twilight, but would burst suddenly upon a slumbering, unready world. Here is the first false antithesis to avoid: the idea that because the divine action will come suddenly and unexpectedly, it bears no relation to the ancient promises, or to the ultimate divine overruling of the dark history that precedes it.

Nor do I find a major difference of theology between different putative types of apocalyptic, such that some might be "cosmic" and others "forensic." This is a second false antithesis. The introduction of this supposed distinction (by my fellow essayist Martinus de Boer in his original dissertation) was linked explicitly to the debate between Bultmann and Käsemann, thereby, in my view, foisting an ill-fitting mid-century German polarization on to the ancient material.[9] Quite

---

8. See the account of basic Jewish belief in e.g., E. P. Sanders, *Judaism: Practice and Belief 63 BCE-66 CE* (London: SCM, 1992), 247-51.

9. M. C. de Boer, *The Defeat of Death: Apocalyptic Eschatology in 1 Corinthians 15 and Romans 5*, JSNTSup (Sheffield: JSOT, 1988), 84-88, 182-83; Cf. M. C. de Boer, "Paul and Jewish Apocalyptic Eschatology," in *Apocalyptic and the New Testament*, eds. Joel Marcus, Marion L. Soards, and J. Louis Martyn (Sheffield: JSOT, 1989), 180-81; M. C. de Boer, *Galatians: A Commentary*, NTL (Louisville: Westminster John Knox, 2011), 31-35, 79-82. In his Hermeneia commentary on *1 Enoch*, George Nickelsburg also makes use of similar categories, but insists they are not antithetical (*1 Enoch 1*

apart from the slippery and anachronistic nature of both the terms in question, we cannot fail to notice that the texts hailed as "cosmological" (including *1 Enoch*) also foresaw a great final Assize (the "forensic" idea); while those hailed as "forensic" (including *4 Ezra*) also foresaw the coming showdown with the forces of evil. (Paul's letters as they stand, of course, include both.) It is not clear that any of the writers invoked on either side were addressing the question which de Boer puts to them—that is, whether the origin of evil lies with non-human evil powers (which must therefore be defeated) or with evil human deeds (which must therefore be atoned for), and hence, whether salvation comes through the defeat of evil powers or through the divine dealing with human sin and guilt. Even if there had been any merit in reading back into these ancient texts such a modern polarization (which looks suspiciously similar to that made by Gustav Aulén in his famous book *Christus Victor*),[10] the subsequent dichotomous use that has been made of de Boer's (initially heuristic) categories[11] has made matters much worse, as we shall see presently.

The third false antithesis which we must avoid—if, that is, we intend to talk about the actual history of belief and practice in the Jewish world of Paul's day, and so to provide a credible historical context—is that between "apocalyptic" and "covenant." The Jewish belief in divine "providence" went hand in hand with the persistent belief that the creator God was, more specifically, the God of Israel. The word "covenant" remains an accurate and convenient shorthand for this belief, held by most Second Temple Jews for whom we have evidence, and certainly, more importantly for our topic, by the authors of the actual apocalypses we possess. The "covenant" hope, allied to the underlying belief in providence, was brought into focus by the scriptural promises to Abraham, Moses, and David: the God who was

[Minneapolis: Fortress Press, 2002], 41). A similar point to mine is made by Meeks, *First Urban Christians*, 172: debates about "apocalyptic" have unfortunately focused on "the abstractions represented by the terms *anthropology* versus *cosmology*, both of which the discussants use in peculiar senses" (italics original).

10. G. Aulén, *Christus Victor: An Historical Study of the Three Main Types of the Idea of Atonement* (London: Macmillan, 1967).

11. De Boer, *Defeat of Death*, 85.

hailed as the world's creator, ultimate ruler, and final judge was *Israel's God*. The coming moment when the previously inscrutable providence would suddenly erupt in a fresh act of judgment and mercy would be like the Exodus: after long years of unrelieved darkness, God would remember his covenant, and deliverance would appear. Closely allied with all this is "salvation history," often attacked as radically incompatible with an "apocalyptic" reading of Paul in particular—though neither Käsemann himself, nor indeed de Boer, drew that conclusion from their more nuanced studies. The idea of "covenant," and the correlated idea of "salvation history," have been criticized by those who see them as encapsulating either a private soteriology (the "covenant" people distinct from the rest of the world) or an automatic or evolutionary revelation or salvation (a steady, linear development leading gradually to the goal). To those, I reply with Latin tags: *abusum non tollit usum*, and *corruptio optimi pessima*. The abuse does not remove the proper use; the worst is the corruption of the best. In fact, Käsemann, to whom appeal is often made in this connection, saw very clearly that there were indeed important strands of covenantal and salvation-historical thinking, both in Israel's scriptures and in Paul's retrieval of them. Whether his description of either, and his attempt to integrate them into his understanding of Paul, really worked is another matter.[12]

Thus, to invoke "covenant," as I have done in my writing on the Second Temple Jewish world, and on Paul in particular, is not to deny the presence or importance of "apocalyptic." It is, rather, to contextualize it historically and theologically. In the same way, to invoke "apocalyptic," as I am happy to do, is not to deny "covenant" or "history." It is, rather, to explain that, in the first century, the covenant hope had been so long deferred that it was natural to choose, for the continued expression of that hope, a genre ideal for expressing secret advance revelations of the divine presence and purpose. Though Paul refers to such revelations, he did not choose that genre to express

12. See my article "A New Perspective on Käsemann? Apocalyptic, Covenant, and the Righteousness of God," in *Studies in the Pauline Epistles: Essays in Honor of Douglas J. Moo*, eds. M. S. Harmon and J. E. Smith (Grand Rapids: Zondervan, 2014), 243–58.

them. As we shall see, that was at least partly because he believed the decisive unveiling of the long-awaited divine rescue operation had already taken place.

Was there, then, an actual "movement" which we could call "apocalypticism"? I doubt it. How many books in a particular genre does it take—spread over several centuries!—to make an "ism"? Did people think of themselves as belonging to such a body? Did other people speak of them in that way? Did anyone in the ancient world think in terms of different types of movement of which "apocalypticism" might be one? I am skeptical. When Josephus describes the four "philosophies" within the Jewish world, he makes no mention of this one (*Ant.* 18.12–25). The real roots of "apocalypticism," I suggest, lie in the same place as those of many other "isms": in the world of nineteenth-century idealism (that term being itself an example of its own blessed rage for categorization). But to probe further, we must turn from Paul's context to our own.

Our Own Setting

If we are to understand the resonances of the word "apocalyptic" in today's biblical scholarship, we need at least as much hermeneutical sophistication as when trying to understand the first century. I have written about this elsewhere, so here, need only summarize (risky though that is).[13] The relevant parts of the story begin in the German scholarship of the nineteenth century; I still find one of the most helpful accounts to be that of Klaus Koch in his book *The Rediscovery of Apocalyptic*. The original German title, *Ratlos vor der Apokalyptik* ("Clueless in the Face of Apocalyptic") made the point: for much late nineteenth-century German scholarship, "apocalyptic" was the dark, dangerous mindset at the heart of *Spätjudentum*. Compared with the supposedly earlier "prophetic" strands of Jewish religion, far more congenial to the optimistic liberal mindset of the day, "apocalyptic" appeared as a negative, world-denying religion, abandoning hope for

---

13. See Wright, *Interpreters*, Part II.

the present world and looking only for divine judgment on the wicked. Books such as Daniel and Revelation made little sense in a world which, drawing on Kant and Hegel, believed in social improvement (in some cases, in Social Darwinism), and had no historical sense of what the ancient "apocalyptic" writers were trying to do. Such writing represented, to them, a degenerate and sectarian retreat from the world. One can see a similar reaction in the so-called "Jesus Seminar" of the 1990s, who saw "apocalyptic" as the "bad" side of traditions about Jesus, representing a bombastic, judgmental attitude rather than the wise, savvy "wisdom" teaching characteristic (so they thought) of Jesus himself. No doubt, the bizarre and supposedly "apocalyptic" teachings in American fundamentalism made such a solution appear all the more attractive.[14] Thus, for some in late nineteenth-century Germany, and for some in late twentieth-century America, "apocalyptic" came to represent the wrong sort of religion, a religion so clearly visible as a separate entity that it could be dignified as an "ism." Thus, "apocalypticism" was born, a hypothetical movement with its own worldview and theology.

The mainstream tradition was therefore horrified at Albert Schweitzer's portrait of Jesus as a first-century apocalyptic Jew. Instead of the wise, loving teacher of "the fatherhood of God and the brotherhood of Man," Jesus suddenly became remote, unappealing, a first-century fanatic followed by other first-century fanatics, all of them believing that the world was about to end, and all (including Jesus) dying disappointed. Schweitzer represented a would-be Christian version of Nietzsche, warning the upbeat nineteenth century that its easygoing optimism was based on quicksand. Unsurprisingly, most Jesus-scholarship looked the other way, not only for "religious" reasons (who wanted a "Jesus" like that?), but for political reasons as well: "apocalyptic" sounded too much like Marxism for comfort.

But the horrific events of World War I sowed the seeds for the comeback of a post-Schweitzer "apocalyptic." Karl Barth's famous *Romans* commentary did not make "apocalyptic" as such a main theme,

---

14. On the "Jesus Seminar" see my *Jesus and the Victory of God* (London: SPCK, 1996), 29–35.

but its effect was the same: instead of the liberal belief in "progress," with humans advancing their own cause and improving their own lot, God had to step in, vertically from above, and denounce the whole plan, breaking in with a fresh Word of judgment and grace. (Barth, himself suspected of being a Marxist, was and remained a sort of Calvinist. Elements in that combination remain powerfully attractive to many.) With the hindsight of nearly a century, we can see that Schweitzer and Barth were saying something similar, however different their details. Both were protesting in favor of a better understanding of Israel's Scriptures. Both were envisaging the gospel as God's sovereign intervention ("invasion"?) into a rebellious and unready world.

By the middle of the twentieth century, the earlier sneers against "apocalyptic" had given way to a despairing re-embracing. Walter Benjamin, often cited at this point, had developed his own brand of messianic Marxism, a secular version of his native Jewish hope. If there was no divinity, no outside agency to bring the necessary upheaval, revolution would have to emerge instead from the immanent processes of history. But when that hope was thwarted, and with it, the parallel (and equally Hegelian and Darwinian) hopes of National Socialism, Benjamin rejected the possibility that "history" might lead anywhere except wreckage.[15] What Benjamin and others were rejecting, however, as in Käsemann's famous angry response to Stendahl, was the kind of secularized *Heilsgeschichte* which many had embraced, on both sides of the political divide, in the 1930s.[16] There is no sign that either the embracers or the rejecters knew much about the ancient Jewish apocalypses.

Käsemann invoked the category "apocalyptic" to provide a history-of-religions context for early Christianity, replacing Bultmann's proposal of "Gnosticism." He did this partly for historical reasons: he had seen that the gnostic sources did not support the hypothesis. But he also had theological, social, and political reasons: Käsemann, like Barth in some ways and Benjamin in others, had seen that immanent

---

15. For this whole subject, see *PFG* 1473–84.
16. On the debate between Käsemann and Stendahl, see N. T. Wright, *Pauline Perspectives: Essays on Paul* (London: SPCK, 2013), chapter 1.

historical processes would produce, not utopia, but nightmares. Something quite different had to happen. But what?

Käsemann's placing of "apocalyptic" as "the mother of Christian theology," meaning by that, that the first Christianity focused on "imminent expectation," was a proposal not only about theology, but about history. The proposal stands or falls by whether or not it can produce a historically credible reconstruction and understanding of first-century Jewish "apocalyptic"; most specialists would say that, by that test, it falls. Käsemann's view of "apocalyptic" was still far too colored by the older German ideas. That, indeed, was why it appealed: the first half of the twentieth century had demonstrated the dismal failure of the old liberal dream, including Bultmann's version. The features which had previously made "apocalypticism" unattractive were the very things Käsemann wanted to find. But Käsemann, a serious historical critic, was not simply spinning ideas. He was proposing a history-of-religions setting. We can, of course, use words how we like, but we cannot invent a non-historical movement called "apocalypticism" and expect it to provide a firm historical basis for theories about early Christianity.

That does not mean, of course, that Käsemann was completely wrong, or that we should return (as some now want to do!) to non-Jewish sources as the primary matrix for understanding early Christianity.[17] We need to do history better. But this has been made more difficult by the fact that, in the post-Käsemann flurry of "apocalyptic" studies, there are almost as many meanings for the word as there are exegetes using it. For Käsemann, it meant simply the imminent Parousia-expectation.[18] For Martyn, despite his homage to Käsemann, it means something very different: a divine "invasion" of the world that has *already* taken place in Jesus' crucifixion.[19] For de Boer, on whose work Martyn claimed to rest, the original proposal was

---

17. See the discussion of G. van Kooten, O. Wischmeyer, and N. T. Wright, "How Greek was Paul's Eschatology?," *NTS* 61, no. 2 (2015): 239–53.
18. I have in my possession a letter from Käsemann in which he says that, for him, "apocalyptic" simply means "Naherwartung."
19. J. L. Martyn, *Galatians: A New Translation with Introduction and Commentary*, AB 33a (New York: Doubleday, 1997); J. Louis Martyn, *Theological Issues in the Letters of Paul* (Nashville: Abingdon, 1997).

a hypothesis about possible tendencies ("cosmic" or "forensic") *within* Jewish "apocalyptic eschatology." De Boer was careful to note that the distinction was not absolute; that many texts contained elements of both; and that both were, in their own way, species of "apocalyptic."[20] This fine-grained proposal has been oversimplified and distorted in subsequent discussions, and it has been assumed that an "apocalyptic" reading of Paul stands over against "forensic justification," on the one hand, and "salvation history" or "covenant," on the other hand.[21] This, as we saw, is strange, considering that the writers of actual Jewish apocalypses generally believed in the coming great Assize, and also in the providential ordering of history by the God whose covenant with Israel continued to give them grounds for hope. (It also gave them grounds for difficult questions, as with *4 Ezra*; but the questions raised in that work are themselves signs of a strongly implicit covenant theology.) In particular, Douglas Campbell has absolutized the distinction between "apocalyptic," on the one hand, and Paul's "forensic" doctrine of justification, on the other. This would have horrified Käsemann, for whom Paul's forensic justification was central.[22]

It is not always easy to keep one's bearings in this many-sided discussion. The eagerness with which some have heralded and promoted Martyn's version of "apocalyptic" is an interesting phenomenon in itself. Martyn's polarization of the main alternatives in Pauline interpretation looks remarkably like the either/or proposed, in relation to theories of Atonement, by Gustav Aulén, leading one to speculate about hidden but powerful faultlines within Western Protestantism.[23] These are indeed important questions; but invoking "apocalyptic" in favor of an Aulén-like reading of Paul will not help. Sometimes, this approach merely collapses into a newer, and supposedly historically rooted, version of the debates between

---

20. See, e.g., de Boer, *Defeat of Death*, 85; de Boer, *Galatians*, 32.
21. E.g., the dichotomous analyses of Gal. 1:4 offered de Boer himself (*Galatians*, 30) and by Martyn (*Galatians*, 90).
22. D. A. Campbell, *The Deliverance of God: An Apocalyptic Rereading of Justification in Paul* (Grand Rapids: Eerdmans, 2009). See the discussion in Wright, *Interpreters*, chapter 9.
23. See Aulén, *Christus Victor*.

Augustine and Pelagius, or between the Reformers and the Arminians (or, even, between Calvin and Luther). Sometimes, the main thing at stake seems to be grace itself, with "apocalyptic" being invoked as the instrument of that grace (the sovereign divine "invasion"): at this point, the word "apocalyptic" can seem, for some at least, to mean merely "Barthian."[24] Not for the first time, a supposed technical term can become a blank check which those playing theological Monopoly can use as they please. This is precisely why we need history, and historical exegesis: to prevent the whole thing descending into a chaos where the real issues, theological, political, or whatever, are hidden behind the outward appearance of historical exegesis. All of which brings us, at last, to Paul.

Paul the Apocalyptist?

If "apocalyptic" is primarily a literary genre, then Paul is not primarily an "apocalyptist." None of his letters looks remotely like Daniel, Revelation, or *4 Ezra*. Granted, he sometimes employs imagery which reminds us of some of the Jewish "apocalyptic" works, as in the description of the Parousia in 1 Thessalonians 4, of the final judgment in 2 Thessalonians 1 and 2, the victory of the Messiah over all hostile powers in 1 Corinthians 15, or the renewal of all creation in Romans 8. Granted, too, that Paul speaks in 2 Corinthians 12 of being caught up into the third heaven; that he describes his Damascus Road experience in terms of the *apokalypsis* of God's son; that he speaks of the gospel as the means whereby God's "righteousness" is "revealed" (ἀποκαλύπτεται); that he sees the "rulers of this age" being thwarted through their own crucifying of the Lord of glory; and that he writes of "new creation" as the key not only to Christian ontology, but also to Christian epistemology (2 Cor. 5:16–17). Does this make him an "apocalyptic" thinker? Does it make him a representative of something called "apocalypticism"?

No. It simply makes him *Jewish*. Granted that there were many

---

24. This was readily admitted by Douglas Campbell in a recent panel discussion at Duke University, and again, at the SBL session at which the present collection of essays were first presented.

varieties of Jewish thought, life, and hope in the period, most Jewish writing of the period might comfortably include most of this list. To categorize such material as "apocalyptic" *over against* other hypothetical categories is to revert to nineteenth-century constructs, setting "apocalyptic" against "legalism" or prophetic insight, or, more recently, against "wisdom" or "forensic" categories, or against "covenant" or "salvation history." Just as in Isaiah, Ezekiel, Daniel, or the Psalms (all, of course, highly influential in early Christian writing), we find all these things together, not played off against one another. As with the earlier attempts to polarize constructs such as "Jewish Christianity," "gentile Christianity," "early Catholicism," and "enthusiasm," we should resist such blatant anachronisms, and the projection of modern Western antitheses on to ancient texts, as much as we should avoid perpetuating the older, misleading understandings of "apocalyptic" (even if, now, such views were seen as positive rather than negative!). Jewish thought and life was many-sided. Paul exactly reflects that pluriformity.

However, we must readily acknowledge that much Pauline exegesis has long screened out the supposedly "apocalyptic" elements in his thought altogether, and that it is important to put them back, and indeed, to give them a central place. For that, we must be grateful to Käsemann, Beker, Martyn, de Boer, and others. But the challenge of producing a fully rounded account of Paul's thinking and writing, highlighting elements sometimes forgotten, ought not to involve the heavy *Sachkritik* which privileges one "strand" and relativizes, or even rejects, others that supposedly conflict with the favored one. The question ought rather to be: How can we give an account of Paul in which previously forgotten themes and emphases, not least those highlighted with the modern label "apocalyptic," are given their proper place?

Part of the answer to this, which strangely has not featured in the school of supposedly "apocalyptic" interpretation which draws centrally upon the work of J. L. Martyn, is to recapture the *ancient political* dimension of "apocalyptic." Most ancient Jewish apocalypses were decidedly political, offering symbolic narratives about the divine plan which gave coded encouragement to the oppressed, enabling them to see apparently chaotic and horrifying events within a different framework, and predicting the downfall not just of "cosmic" powers (in the sense of "suprahuman" entities), but of the actual pagan empires and their rulers. This is so well-known in relation (for instance) to the book of Revelation that it is surprising that the study of "apocalyptic Paul" and the equally vibrant contemporary study of "political Paul" have not made common cause. Attempts to separate out these two, for instance, by suggesting that Paul's real target was non-human powers and that therefore he was uninterested in earthly ones, have not, in my view, proved successful.[25] Recent major studies of actual Jewish apocalypses, as opposed to hypothetical "apocalypticism," strongly confirm this.[26]

So, to the texts. Obviously, there is no room for detailed exegesis. I simply offer a sketch.

If I had to sum up Galatians in three passages, I would choose the beginning, the end, and the middle. Chapter 1, verses 1–5, states that, in fulfillment of the divine purpose, Jesus "gave himself for our sins to rescue us from the present evil age."[27] We cannot de-emphasize the "giving himself for our sins," or suggest that this is a mere concession on Paul's part to a view he does not completely share, since when Paul reaches the climax of the first two chapters (2:19–20), he makes this central ("the son of God . . . loved me and gave himself for me"). But nor may the "giving up for sins" obscure the larger purpose—the rescue "from the present evil age." For Paul the events concerning Jesus, particularly his death "for our sins," have launched the long-awaited age to come. These two cannot be played off against one another, as (to be fair) much older Pauline exegesis has done in one direction, and the recent "apocalyptic" interpretation has done in the other.

25. See *PFG*, chapter 12. See now C. Heilig, *Hidden Criticism? The Methodology and Plausibility of the Search for a Counter-Imperial Subtext in Paul*, WUNT 2/392 (Tübingen: Mohr Siebeck, 2015).
26. A. Portier-Young, *Apocalypse Against Empire: Theologies of Resistance in Early Judaism* (Grand Rapids: Eerdmans, 2011).
27. Quotations from the NT are taken from my own translation, N. T. Wright, *The Kingdom New Testament* (San Francisco: HarperOne, 2011).

The end of the letter makes the same conjunction. "Circumcision . . . is nothing; neither is uncircumcision" because "what matters is new creation" (6:15). This means what it means because of 6:14, which highlights the Messiah's cross, through which "the world has been crucified to me and I to the world." The cross and the new creation go hand in glove; and the latter inaugurates the "new age," which supplants "the present evil age."

The purpose of new creation, of being rescued by the cross from the present evil age to share in God's new world, is unveiled in the middle of the letter (4:1–11) as the meaning of the Exodus-shaped covenantal rescue. Once we were slaves, says Paul, but God acted to redeem us, to make us his children and heirs, so that now, we have a new sort of knowledge, generated by God's knowledge of us, in which we recognize the enslaving powers for what they are ("now that you've come to know God, or, better, to be known by God," how can you turn back to the *stoicheia*?). How, in other words, could you think of going back to "Egypt"? This (like Romans 8) is an Exodus narrative. At its heart, echoing Gen. 15:16 (from the chapter expounded at length in Galatians 3), Paul says that the redeeming action came "when the fullness of time arrived" (ὅτε δὲ ἦλθεν τὸ πλήρωμα τοῦ χρόνου). We note that Paul uses χρόνος, not καιρός. He has in mind a *temporal sequence*, previously invisible. This again, of course, has nothing to do with immanent development or evolution, but rather, as in 1:4–5, with the divine purpose. Thus, as new-Exodus people, believers are to understand themselves as *Abraham's family, heirs according to promise* (3:29).

When, therefore, in chapter 1, Paul describes his conversion in terms of God's "apocalypse" of his son (1:12, 16), this does not mean that we must abandon the ideas of divine promise, of the covenant with Abraham concerning his family and his inheritance. We should not mistake Paul's use of a first-century Greek word for an allusion to a nineteenth-century theory. *The covenant promises have been suddenly and shockingly fulfilled.* Paul believes that this is the way in which the ancient Israelite vision of new creation itself is to come about, and with it, new knowledge, a new mode of knowledge. The Messiah's apocalypse unveils the covenant purpose. Isaiah, frequently echoed in Galatians, says as much. Paul's thinking remains Jewish to the core, however much his beliefs about Israel's crucified Messiah have caused radical revisions.

If this is true of Galatians, what of the Corinthian epistles? The whole of 1 Corinthians can be seen in the light of chapter 15, where the thoroughly "apocalyptic" doctrine of resurrection is expounded at length. In 15:20-28, Paul describes the *inauguration* of the Messiah's rule over all opposing powers: he is *already* reigning, but *not yet* over death itself, the final enemy. This is the stuff of what some today call "apocalyptic," and Paul expounds it through a complex interwoven exegesis of Psalms 2, 8, and 110: apocalypse, in other words, in service of messianic, and hence covenantal, theology. This produces a new-creational reading of Genesis 1, 2, and 3. The last Adam, the second Man, undoes the fault of the first, and so inaugurates, with his own risen body, the new creation itself. The resurrection of Jesus, symbolizing and embodying the new creation, was not detached from the ancient messianic promises. It was rather to be seen as their fulfillment, however shocking this may have been to Jews who demanded signs and Greeks who sought wisdom.

That, of course, is the point of 1 Corinthians 1–3, one of Paul's central statements of the new mode of knowing brought about by the Messianic revelation. God's foolishness and weakness overthrow human wisdom and power, generating a new wisdom. For the ancient philosophers (to speak very broadly), *how* you knew things was a function of *what there was*; that is, *logic* correlated with *physics*.[28] Because Paul believed that in the resurrection God's new world had been launched, there was now *a new mode of knowing*: "we speak God's hidden wisdom in a mystery . . . the wisdom God prepared ahead of time, before the world began, for our glory" (2:7). The "rulers of this present age" did not, of course, know about it; otherwise, they wouldn't have crucified the Lord of glory. A new kind of wisdom had been let loose in the world, in sudden fulfillment of God's ancient purposes.

---

28. For this, and what follows, see esp. *PFG* chapter 14.

That is why Paul could speak later of the new knowing which was called forth by the divine "knowing," and which took the form of love (8:2-3, closely parallel to Gal. 4:9; 13:8-13). This knowledge is still "partial," because the eschatology is inaugurated, not complete. But it looks on to the completion as the fulfillment of what is already begun.

All this points to the classic passage in 2 Corinthians 5 and 6, where Paul explains the nature of his apostolic ministry. He understands this ministry, as in Galatians, in terms of the "servant" passage in Isa. 49:8, quoted here at 6:2. When he says "the right time is now! The day of salvation is here!," he is interpreting Isaiah: this has been the sudden fulfillment of divine promise. This is the context within which we should understand the statement of new epistemology in 5:16-17: "From this moment on, we don't regard anybody from a merely human point of view. Even if we once regarded the Messiah that way, we don't do so any longer. Thus if anyone is in the Messiah, there is a new creation! Old things have gone, and look—everything has become new!" One could, of course, take this out of context, as an irruptive invasion of epistemological reflection, without any prior promise. But the wider passage forbids this. The new creation, and with it, the new mode of knowing, have come about—Paul says it four times—through the Messiah's death, which has reconciled people to God by dealing with their sins (5:14, 18, 19, 21). Exactly as in the compressed formula of Gal. 1:4, the Messiah's sin-bearing death brings about new creation. Paul holds together what later traditions divide.

The new creation in 2 Corinthians 5 is, for Paul, directly dependent upon the new covenant expounded in 2 Corinthians 3. Some suppose that Paul only discussed Moses and the Exodus because his opponents had done so first. But the use of related themes elsewhere makes this unlikely. It is better to see the transformation in chapter 3, where the Spirit renews the covenant, as supplying the theological energy for chapter 5, since here (5:5), as in 1:22, the Spirit is the "first installment and guarantee" of what is to come. The new creation, already launched in the Messiah, will be complete when all appear before the Messiah's judgment seat (5:10). This produces the scandalous message and ministry which remain opaque to the wider world, but which Paul believes to be the appropriate vehicle for (what we might call) the apocalyptic gospel of new creation.

If, then, by "apocalyptic," we mean the unveiling of things previously hidden, for Paul the gospel was indeed "apocalyptic." As we said, he did not express it in the apocalyptic genre; 2 Corinthians 12 hints that he could have gone that route, but chose not to. His message remains that of the crucified and risen Messiah. And that message makes sense, not because of a dualistic "invasion" of creation, but because of the sudden, shocking fulfillment of ancient covenantal promises.

All of which leads to Romans. It is ironic that, in Douglas Campbell's now famous treatment, Romans 1–4 is relativized in the light, supposedly, of the "apocalyptic" message of chapters 5–8.[29] But it is in Rom. 1:16—2:16 that we find one of the most obviously "apocalyptic" passages in the whole letter. And the central thing revealed there is *the righteousness of God*, the covenant plan promised ages ago, discussed with such anguish in a genuine "apocalypse" by Paul's near-contemporary *4 Ezra*. For Paul the "apocalypse," the decisive divine revelation, *had* taken place in the gospel events, both in themselves and in their apostolic proclamation, and *would be completed* in the final denouement (2:16). The one God had unveiled his age-old purposes in a sudden fulfillment, which was only visible as such in retrospect. The gospel was, in this sense, "apocalyptic," not because it represented an invasion without prior warning, but because it was the ultimate revelation to which earlier writings (Torah, Psalms, Prophets) had all looked forward. For Paul the identity and achievement of Jesus was the revelation in action of Israel's returning God. The form and function of Second Temple Jewish apocalypses reflected the belief that God had promised to return in judgment and mercy, but had delayed. The

---

29. Campbell, *Deliverance*. I say "supposedly" because, though Campbell bases his argument on the "apocalyptic" theology he claims to find in chapters 5–8, he nowhere in this book expounds those chapters or that theology. In his contribution (113–43) to M. Bird, ed., *Four Views on the Apostle Paul* (Grand Rapids: Zondervan, 2012), Campbell promises a detailed engagement with Rom. 5–8, but fails to provide it, as one of his responders in that volume points out (L. T. Johnson, at 149–52).

form and function of Paul's letters, and supremely Romans, reflect the belief that God had indeed returned to judge and to save, but in a way hitherto unsuspected, and that this work would be fulfilled in the events yet to come (8:18–25; 13:11–12).

At the heart of Romans, as with Galatians, there lies the new Exodus-narrative: the slaves are set free by coming through the water (chapter 6), the law does its strange God-intended work of allowing sin to grow to its full height (chapter 7), so that Sin (with a capital S) is condemned in the flesh of the Messiah, whereupon the Spirit leads the people through the wilderness to their inheritance—which is, of course, the renewed creation. This is the larger narrative matrix which holds together "apocalyptic" and other elements such as "covenant" and atonement. New Exodus leads directly to new creation. The cross, at its heart, is for Paul both penal in force and cosmic in scope: "There is no condemnation for those in the Messiah, Jesus," because "God sent his son . . . and, right there in the flesh, he condemned sin." This is solidly *forensic* language within a larger *apocalyptic* and "cosmic" setting: no power in earth or heaven can undermine God's Messiah-shaped love (8:31–39), because this "love" is the *covenant* love spoken of in passages such as Deuteronomy 7 or Jeremiah 31, through which sins have been dealt with. This entire sequence, again, is an expansion of Gal. 1:4. In Rom. 8:31–39, themes rush together which both theology and exegesis have held apart: the victory of God over the powers, the forensic dealing with sin, the new creation which follows when death itself is defeated. This is the ultimate horizon of Paul's thought. If it deserves the name "apocalyptic," despite not belonging to the literary genre, such a label does not rule out, but rather insists upon, (a) the covenantal context of ancient scriptural promises, and (b) the dealing with human sin, which has prevented humans taking their intended place within the created order. Of course, there is more to be said; much more. But no less.

Conclusion

I have barely scratched the surface of a vital and fascinating topic. Let me, in conclusion, name two related issues.

First, if we are serious about the "apocalyptic Paul," there is no excuse for not bringing 2 Thessalonians and even Ephesians in from the cold. Ephesians is explicit about the divine plan hidden for ages but now revealed, and about ongoing warfare with the "powers."[30] Second Thessalonians, of course, clearly draws on some of the normal apocalyptic tropes. One of the main reasons for its demotion in early scholarship was the anxiety about allowing "Paul" to be quite so explicitly "apocalyptic": now that that has changed, why not welcome it on board?

The final point, again very briefly, concerns the Temple. For the devout Second Temple Jew, heaven and earth met in the Temple. That was where one might expect, as with Isaiah, the sudden revelation of things previously hidden. If Paul really had an "apocalyptic" strand in his theology, as I have argued he did (albeit reworked through the inaugurated eschatology of the crucified and risen Messiah and the gift of the Spirit), one might expect his frequent Temple-language to reflect this line of thought. In fact, it does: the Spirit who indwells God's people means that, corporately and personally, they are seen in terms of the Temple.[31]

It is, therefore, no surprise that for Paul the sudden fulfillment of divine promise which has come about through the gospel of Jesus has generated a community which discovers new knowledge, a new *mode* of knowledge. The renewal of the covenant leads directly to the renewal of creation, by the shocking, yet promise-fulfilling, route of cross and resurrection. That is Paul's apocalyptic gospel. It belongs historically on the map of Second Temple Jewish thought, reconceived around Jesus and the Spirit. It belongs theologically as an integrated whole, not

---

30. Meeks, *First Urban Christians*, 90 and 107, stresses the cosmic vision of both Ephesians and Colossians. It is not clear (as in his further comment at 184) that this goes beyond what is both stated and implied in e.g., Rom. 8:18–39, 1 Cor. 10:20; 15:26; or indeed, Gal. 4:1–11.
31. See, e.g., 1 Cor. 3:16–17; 6:19; 2 Cor. 6:16; and, in the light of these, Rom. 8:9–11; Col. 2:9–10.

to be split up into different component strands. If we find ourselves wanting to pry apart what Paul held together, that is our problem. We should not suppose it was his as well.

I am reminded of the lines which T. S. Eliot puts into the mouth of Thomas à Becket as he realizes his assassins have arrived at last:

> However certain our expectation
> The moment foreseen may be unexpected
> When it arrives. It comes when we are
> Engrossed with matters of other urgency.[32]

---

32. T. S. Eliot, *Murder in the Cathedral*, Part II, in *The Complete Poems and Plays of T. S. Eliot* (London and Boston: Faber and Faber, 1969), 266.

PART III

7

—————

Some Reflections on Apocalyptic Thought and Time in Literature from the Second Temple Period

Loren T. Stuckenbruck

Introduction and the Question

The term "apocalyptic" has been widely used in biblical scholarship, especially since World War II. Since its antecedent was "eschatology," the term has frequently been associated with notions of time, especially in relation to the ultimate conclusion of things at the end of history from a faith perspective. The simple equation of "apocalyptic" with "eschatology," however, has rightly been questioned, primarily on two fronts.

First, as Martin de Boer has emphasized since the appearance in 1988 of his monograph on *The Defeat of Death: Apocalyptic Eschatology in 1 Corinthians 15 and Romans 5*,[1] the term not only relates to time, but also to cosmology; hence, there may be the need to distinguish "apocalyptic eschatology" from "apocalyptic cosmology," although these dimensions frequently overlap in Second Temple Jewish literature and cannot be held so clearly apart. Second, since Christopher Rowland's influential work, originally published in 1982 and entitled *The Open Heaven: A Study of Apocalyptic in Early Judaism and Christianity*,[2] the term "wisdom" has come into play as a way to describe a "revealed" knowledge conveyed in texts conventionally designated as apocalyptic.

While both strains have had some impact on the interpretation of the New Testament and will continue to weigh in on reconstructions of "the historical Jesus" or of Pauline theology, the ultimate focus of scholars on the distinctive character of emerging Christian thought during the first century CE has sometimes short-circuited what can be said about *apocalyptic* thought, based on a remarkably diverse selection of Jewish literature composed in different areas of the eastern Levant over some 400 years between the third century BCE and the early part of the second century CE. What follows below can hardly provide a survey of the literature. Nevertheless, I hope to draw attention to some aspects thereof that, for a variety of reasons, have either been marginally noted or altogether overlooked.

Broadly, there is wide agreement that "apocalyptic" thought during the Second Temple period relates to the end of history or to the structure of the created order or both. This understanding, when put in such terms, goes back to the much quoted definition of "apocalypse" as a literary genre initially offered by John J. Collins in 1979[3]:

1. Martinus C. de Boer, *The Defeat of Death: Apocalyptic Eschatology in 1 Corinthians 15 and Romans 5*, JSNTSup 22 (Sheffield: JSOT, 1988).
2. Christopher Rowland, *The Open Heaven: A Study of Apocalyptic in Judaism and Early Christianity* (New York: Crossroad, 1982 [Eugene: Wipf & Stock, 2002]).
3. See John J. Collins, "Introduction: Towards the Morphology of a Genre," *Semeia* 14 (1979): 1–20, at 9; cf. idem, *The Apocalyptic Imagination: An Introduction to Jewish Apocalyptic Literature*, 2nd ed. (Grand Rapids: Eerdmans, 1998), 1–42 (esp. 9–11), for further refinement in light of criticisms and alternative definitions.

> ...revelatory literature with a narrative framework, in which a revelation is mediated by an otherworldly being to a human recipient, disclosing a transcendental reality which is both temporal, insofar as it envisages eschatological salvation, and spatial, insofar as it involves another, supernatural world.

While the German *Apokalyptik* had multiple connotations that would carry over into a vague English use of "apocalyptic" as a noun, it became necessary to introduce distinctions. "Apocalypse" would denote a literary genre that became the focus of Collins's definition, and "apocalypticism" could be understood as a socially rooted ideology. "Apocalyptic," then, would be used as an adjective (with the German equivalent "apokalyptisch") that refers to a worldview. These expressions have proved useful. While in relation to Second Temple Jewish tradition, "apocalypticism" draws attention to the ideologies that, in some Jewish groups, gave rise to the composition of apocalypses, the adjective "apocalyptic" not only serves as a label for the worldview of such groups and their literature, but also more broadly for such a worldview whenever and where it was held.

Thus, the presence of "apocalyptic" ideas is not limited to a certain kind of literature, nor can it be reduced to a well-defined sociological profile.[4] For example, among Second Temple writings, many compositions preserved in the Dead Sea Scrolls can arguably be designated "apocalyptic" in worldview, without technically being apocalypses themselves,[5] even if their relation to a broader social

---

4. It must be emphasized that the profile behind the early production and reception of Jewish apocalyptic literature was not static. If at any point, a socio-religious or political crisis gave rise to the need to appeal to a specially revealed form of otherworldly knowledge, one cannot assume that the same circumstances were existent each time the form was adapted and received again. While the production of such a genre might have been generated by crisis, one cannot infer the same circumstances behind the genre without close readings of a text. See further, Loren T. Stuckenbruck, *Angel Veneration and Christology: A Study in Early Judaism and in the Christology of the Apocalypse of John*, WUNT 2/70 (Tübingen: Mohr Siebeck, 1995), 39–40.

5. To illustrate the point, it helps to mention several writings, which do not formally share the features of Collins's definition, while few would argue that they do not, at the same time, reflect an "apocalyptic" worldview. (a) *Epistle of Enoch* (which, though part of the much larger collection of Enochic materials in *1 Enoch*, largely consists of prophetic denunciations of the wicked and exhortations to the righteous, focusing on eschatological judgment at the time of their fulfillment); (b) *Book of Jubilees* (though a narrative mediated through an angel to a human recipient—Moses—it is the angel of the presence who speaks and, significantly, the form of the work retells sacred tradition found in Genesis and Exodus with a focus on calendrical and halakhic matters that are supported by eschatological and cosmological or spatial dimensions); and (c) *War*

movement cannot be clearly ascertained. However, the greater degree of fluidity surrounding the use of the adjective has sometimes led to such casual application that its real connection to particular Second Temple writings can for the most part only be discerned on a profound level.[6] While such broad notions of the adjective "apocalyptic" have their place and can even be theologically constructive, a usage that is unhinged from a Jewish literary-historical context is at risk of engaging with an imprecise or even arbitrary range of ideas. Although one commonly speaks of modifications of Jewish apocalyptic thought in Paul, such adaptations have become so significant in characterizing the distinguishing emphases of the apostle that one wonders whether one is, in effect, dealing with two understandings of "apocalyptic" thought (in Judaism and Christianity, respectively), rather than one that allows adequate room for continuity.

Now, in what sense is the adjective "apocalyptic" meaningful if we attempt to describe *specific* characteristics of a shared worldview? In this connection, it makes sense to return to the connection between the term and the verb ἀποκαλύπτω, and take it as a point of departure. The verb, of course, means "to reveal" or "to uncover," a notion that in itself is far too nebulous to describe what emerges in the Second Temple period as opposed to, for example, a number of writings in the Hebrew Bible. Taking Collins's definition above into account—and therefore, having literary texts in view—we can propose that it signifies *an outlook* shaped by mediated knowledge of a hidden reality, whether spatial or temporal in character or both, that is ultimately attributed to God as the source.[7] As such, the expression serves to

---

Scroll (the narrative is orientated to the eschaton, but does not present itself as mediated through an otherworldly being). As is well-known, it is this distinction between worldview and genre that makes it possible to speak of Paul as an apocalyptic thinker.

6. This seems to be the case in the work of J. Louis Martyn, for whom, in taking Paul's thought as the point of departure, "apocalyptic" refers to "the conviction that God has now given to the elect true perception both of present developments (the real world) and of a wondrous transformation in the near future," and thus involves "a new way of knowing both present and future" ("Apocalyptic Antinomies in the Letter to the Galatians," in *Theological Issues in the Letters of Paul* [Edinburgh: T&T Clark, 1997], 111–23, at 123). See further, *Galatians: A New Translation and Commentary*, AB 33A (New Haven: Yale University Press, 2010 [1997]), 97–105. However, what Martyn, in my view, rightly regards as apocalyptic in relation to Paul is arguably not far removed from a perspective that can likewise be attributed to many Second Temple texts.

7. Thus, despite the imprecision associated with the term, I am not at present an advocate for

address the lack of parity between circumstances and piety, between what is seen and unseen, with a view to explaining *why things are in fact not as they might seem or even should be.*[8]

Applied to Second Temple Judaism, it would refer to a complex, multidimensional worldview found in sources such as *1 Enoch, Jubilees, Daniel, 4 Ezra, 2 Baruch*, and many texts among the Dead Sea Scrolls, in which socio-religious tensions and non-sequiturs were negotiated by appealing to a larger, yet apparently elusive reality, whether conceived in terms of the actual structure of the created order or to an eschatological reckoning at the final judgment. Applied to writings in the New Testament, it can refer meaningfully to how the purposes of the God of Israel can be thought to have been unveiled in the crucifixion of Jesus and its aftermath ("the Christ event"), through which time, space, and social relationships are reconfigured. To some extent, what is, in principle, claimed of the one (unveiling of an elusive reality or a reconfiguration thereof) can be applied to the other. The christological focus of New Testament texts, for example, does not at all dispense with eschatological judgment.

But what may be thought to distinguish New Testament perspectives, or more specifically, Paul, from Jewish apocalyptic tradition? While not wishing to uncouple emerging early Christian thought entirely from Jewish tradition, some have invested Pauline theology with a notion of apocalyptic that, by implication, looks disparagingly at its non-Christian Jewish equivalent or accords it a certain functional irrelevance.[9] To some extent, this view proceeds

---

dispensing with it entirely. After his thorough review of twentieth-century scholarship on Paul, R. Barry Matlock joins a chorus of those who question the casual use of "apocalyptic" and counsels, where possible, against the use of the term at all; so Matlock, *Unveiling the Apocalyptic Paul: Paul's Interpreters and the Rhetoric of Criticism*, JSNTSup 127 (Sheffield: Sheffield Academic, 1996), 247–316. See also Philip R. Davies, "The Social World of the Apocalyptic Writings," in *The World of Ancient Israel: Sociological, Anthropological, and Political Perspectives*, ed. Ronald E. Clements (Cambridge: Cambridge University Press, 1989), 251–71. This critique, however justified, challenges us to focus more specifically on literature and texts that contain terms which, whether as verbs or substantives, claim to offer divine mediated "disclosure" or "revelation" of otherworldly reality to humanity.

8. This point does not necessarily require an "apocalyptic" outlook to be a theological reflex of a crisis situation.

9. Douglas A. Campbell, *The Deliverance of God: An Apocalyptic Rereading of Justification in Paul* (Grand Rapids: Eerdmans, 2013).

straightforwardly from Paul's own polemical statements directed at Jewish and Jewish Christian interlocutors in 2 Corinthians (11:5; 12:11), Philippians (3:2–11), Galatians (1:6–9; 2:4–5, 12–13: 3:1–5; 5:12), and Romans (2:17–29; 3:8; 9:1–5). However, what Paul was doing theologically to make room for his gospel is one thing, while it is another, though a related matter, to discern whether this remained within or broke away from notions of apocalyptic thought preserved for us from the Second Temple period.

Some contributions have been and are being made in understanding Paul's thought by taking into account sapiential and cosmological features of Jewish apocalyptic tradition. When it comes to Pauline theology, most comparisons involving apocalyptic thought have focused on or related to eschatology in some way.[10] Paul's thought is seen to be both continuous with and distinct from Jewish "apocalyptic eschatology," that is, as a way of construing history as it is coming to an end through a series of events that culminate in a final judgment and in the inauguration of an endless age of justice in a new created order.[11] Seen in this way, apocalyptic thought is, at its core, a conceptual way to resolve the problem of persistent, and indeed, overwhelming evil despite religious faithfulness. It is not surprising, then, that an understanding of *time* occupies a central place in such a scheme,

---

10. See, e.g., Franzjosef Froitzheim, *Christologie und Eschatologie bei Paulus*, FB 35 (Würzburg: Echter, 1979); Andrew T. Lincoln, *Paradise Now and Not Yet: Studies in the Role of the Heavenly Dimension in Paul's Thought with Special Reference to His Eschatology*, SNTSMS 43 (Cambridge/New York: Cambridge University Press, 1981); Larry Kreitzer, *Jesus and God in Paul's Eschatology*, JSNTSup 19 (Sheffield: JSOT, 1987); C. Marvin Pate, *The End of the Age Has Come: The Theology of Paul* (Grand Rapids: Zondervan, 1995); Allan J. McNicol, *Jesus' Directions for the Future: A Source and Redaction-History Study of the Use of the Eschatological Traditions in Paul and in the Synoptic Accounts of Jesus' Last Eschatological Discourse* (Macon: Mercer, 1996); Robert S. Smith, *Justification and Eschatology: A Dialogue with "the New Perspective on Paul,"* RTRSup 1 (Doncaster, Australia: Reformed Theological Review, 2001); Joseph Plevnik, *What are They Saying about Paul and the End Time?*, Rev. ed. (New York: Paulist, 2009 [1986]). The study of de Boer, *The Defeat of Death*, offered a welcome attempt to recognize Paul as one who was negotiating in his correspondence between the idioms of "apocalyptic" cosmology and eschatology found in Second Temple literature, though they are, in fact, far more integrated than is generally recognized.

11. Collins (*The Apocalyptic Imagination*, 11) has pointed out that the post-mortem judgment of individuals in compositions such as *3 Baruch* and *Apocalypse of Zephaniah* is not accompanied by an account about the end of history *per se*. Nevertheless, it should be noted that these writings do not belong to earlier examples of apocalypses and may, given their influence by the latter, offer a selective presentation that presupposes awareness of a broader range of interrelated ideas.

especially as the ultimate resolution to evil is anticipated in a divine act in the future.

Under this umbrella, Paul, though retaining a thought structure that once regards the present world as an "evil age" (Gal. 1:6), is seen to depart from Jewish apocalyptic thought in the claim that in the Christ event—that is, Jesus' death and resurrection—the eschaton has, in an unprecedented way, already begun. One encounters this not infrequently in caricatures of Jewish apocalyptic schemes of the end time as "speculative" and absorbed by details surrounding the end of history,[12] whereas the best of the "Christian" message—whether it is Jesus proclaiming the nearness or dawn of God's rule or Paul claiming that God has set something definitive in motion through Jesus' death and resurrection—essentially leaves this behind. Such comparisons are dominated by a construction of apocalyptic thought in Judaism that is oriented around the future; by contrast, Pauline thought, though retaining the notion of eschatology from the Jewish tradition with which he was familiar, introduced something of a decisive act of God in the *past*, the recent past, through it offering hope that makes it possible for people to experience God's salvific activity in the present.

There is something to the claim that in the New Testament, convictions about Jesus bring a new dimension to contemporary schemes of apocalyptic thought, in which, for example, the notion of a messianic figure's future coming could often, though not in all the literature, shape eschatological expectation. Does the claim, however, that the messiah has already come rearrange the way Jewish tradition could structure time in relation to the overcoming of evil? In order to address this question, it remains here to sketch out something of the complexity and theological possibilities opened up by a fresh look at

---

12. This is often done when contrasting the "prophetic" character of Jesus' ministry with "apocalyptic" notions of time among Jesus' Jewish contemporaries. Examples of this, which push the distinction too far, can be found in Werner Georg Kümmel, *Promise and Fulfillment*, trans. Dorothea M. Barton (Naperville: Alec R. Allenson, 1957), 105–40; George Eldon Ladd, *Jesus and the Kingdom: The Eschatology of Biblical Realism* (London: SPCK, 1966), 48–55 and 91–213; Leonhard Goppelt, *Theology of the New Testament, Volume One: The Ministry of Jesus in Its Theological Significance*, trans. John E. Alsup (Grand Rapids: Eerdmans, 1981), 51–55; Gerd Theissen and Annette Merz, *Der historische Jesus*, 2nd ed. (Göttingen: Vandenhoeck & Ruprecht, 1997), 221–55 (esp. the comparative table on p. 229).

selected Second Temple materials. As we shall see, if we focus on: (a) temporality in literature associated with apocalyptic thought, and on: (b) the *function* thereof among early recipients, there is reason to give a negative answer to the question just posed.

Relativizing Temporal Dualism in Apocalyptic Thought

A focus on time, especially eschatology, has dominated much of scholarship on apocalyptic literature during the nineteenth and twentieth centuries. The future was understood as the end of history when God's purposes for the faithful would come to fruition and the evils of the present age would be eradicated. In support of this view of history, works such as Daniel, the Apocalypse of John, *4 Ezra*, and *2 Baruch* were given a privileged role. Salvific activity on the part of Israel's God was largely a matter for the future; and, while there could be a smaller group of faithful in the present, the world order essentially remains in a state of hopelessness. In such an outlook, the function of the past in the literature was either overlooked, was seen to have helped writers in formulating a theological problem (as in *4 Ezra* 3:4–36; 5:23–30; 6:38–59; 7:62–74, 116–131; 9:26–37), or received limited attention (see below). Such a portrait, which distinguished "apocalyptic" from "prophetic" eschatology,[13] served New Testament scholarship as a way to describe Jewish tradition, from which the Synoptic Gospels' presentation of Jesus and Paul's thought departed.[14] Thus, a largely static temporal dualism attributed to Jewish literature is thought to have been modified by Paul, for whom the death and resurrection of Jesus in the past has become the main event that separates the "old age" (Rom. 12:2; 1 Cor. 1:20; 2:6; cf. 1 Cor. 10:11; Gal. 1:4) from "the coming age" (cf. the early reception of Paul in Eph. 1:21).

Scholarship has observed the shortcomings of a one-dimensional

13. This distinction was underscored during the twentieth century by H. H. Rowley, *The Relevance of Apocalyptic: A Study of Jewish and Christian Apocalypses from Daniel to the Revelation*, 3rd ed. (New York: Association, 1963) and D. S. Russell, *Apocalyptic: Ancient and Modern* (Philadelphia: Fortress Press, 1978). See the informative and critical discussion of Martinus de Boer, "Paul and Apocalyptic Eschatology," in *The Encyclopedia of Apocalypticism, Volume 1: The Origins of Apocalypticism in Judaism and Christianity*, ed. John J. Collins (London: Continuum, 2000), 345–83.

14. See note 12, above.

future orientation of Jewish apocalyptic thought. It is noted, for example, that the earliest recoverable apocalypses were not simply interested in eschatology; in some documents, interest is also, perhaps even primarily, directed toward an interest in the disclosure of knowledge, and with it, of the world order (1 Enoch 2–4, 21–36, and 72–82).[15] Understood along the lines of a disclosure of hidden reality not readily apparent, such a worldview could make certain sense for Paul when interpreting the advent of Jesus, including his death (cf., e.g., Rom. 3:21–26; 1 Cor. 1:18–2:16; Gal. 1:16; 2:19–21). Cosmology was not, however, unhinged from the notion of time: seen from a divine perspective, the cosmos—the way things are in the created order—was unveiled in relation to how it was originally created, how it shapes socio-religious life in the present, and what it is to become in the future (cf. 1 En. 72:1; 80:1–8).

To be sure, sapiential and cosmological aspects in apocalyptic writings have enriched the way some have reflected theologically on the significance of the Christ-event. Due to the casual contrasts drawn between present and future reality, however, the function of temporality has not always been appreciated. I would like, therefore, to underscore the way apocalyptic literature considers the past, not so much to think of the past as remote, but of what the past as interpreted by a visionary or sage could mean for the present.

In many ways, the importance of past events has been recognized. Obviously, the past would be re-presented in the "historical apocalypses," such as the *Apocalypse of Weeks* and *Animal Vision* of *1 Enoch* (respectively, 93:1–10 91:11–17 and 85:1–90:42; cf. also *4 Ezra* 14), which find therein patterns of divine activity that not only shaped the unfolding story of Israel, but also have implications for interpreting the present and future. A look at the past, both remote and recent, identifies "open wounds" that have an impact on the present; indeed,

---

15. The critique by Christopher Rowland of the one-dimensional eschatological reading of Jewish apocalyptic literature, even if somewhat one-sided, remains valuable; see Rowland, *The Open Heaven*, 9–72. The disclosure of esoteric wisdom as emphasized by Rowland has not gone lost, for example, on de Boer, "Paul and Apocalyptic Eschatology," 352–54 (with several points of critique), and Matlock, *Unveiling the Apocalyptic Paul*, esp. 258–62 and 282–87.

certain problems that have loomed in the past and re-emerge in the present remain unresolved.[16]

Another, even more influential way of understanding the temporal dimension of apocalyptic thought has been to recognize the correspondence found in some of the writings between primordial time (*Urzeit*) and final time at the end of history (*Endzeit*). This framework is placed in service of eschatology, which in turn, reflects a temporal dualism.[17] Here, various ideological snapshots of the primordial past furnish images, symbols, and motifs that helped apocalyptic writers and their audiences to imagine what the future age will be like. For example, a paradisiacal existence, once lost, will be restored (Rev. 2:7); a messianic "white bull" concludes a story that began with an Adamic "white bull" (Animal Apocalypse, *1 En.* 85:3, 90:37; cf. Rom. 5:12–21); eschatological judgment draws on imagery from the Great Flood and, with it, Noah's rescue from the cataclysm prefigures the salvation of God's people (*1 Enoch* 10; 84; 91; 106–7).

Now, these scholarly construals of time in apocalyptic texts may reflect on the past and future. But other than seeing that they offer hope and furnish the imagination with details on what to expect, they do not sufficiently come to terms with what some texts imply about the present. Within the framework of temporality, especially the sacred past, another emphasis has been neglected, not only by New Testament scholars, but even also by specialists in ancient Jewish apocalyptic literature.[18] In addition to helping to describe worsening conditions in

---

16. A known proponent of this perspective is N. T. Wright (e.g., *The Climax of the Covenant: Christ and the Law in Pauline Theology* [Edinburgh: T&T Clark, 1991]), for whom the Sin-Exile-Return framework enables a reading that regards Paul's gospel as formulated to exhort Israel to return from a present state of being in "spiritual exile." Wright handles Jesus tradition similarly in *Jesus and the Victory of God* (London: SPCK, 1996), e.g., 193–97, 226–29.

17. The most important third- and second-century BCE documents which draw on such a correspondence between beginning and end include the Enochic *Book of Watchers* (*1 Enoch* 1–36), the *Dream Visions* (*1 Enoch* 83–84 and 85–90), *Apocalypse of Weeks* (*1 En.* 93:1–10 and 91:1117), *Exhortation* (*1 En.* 91:1–10, 18–19), *Birth of Noah* (*1 Enoch* 106–107), *Book of Parables* (*1 Enoch* 37–71), *Book of Giants*, and *Jubilees*. Except for the *Book of Parables*, the impact of the perspectives upheld by these works in Second Temple literature (including writings among the Dead Sea Scrolls and Jewish literature composed in Greek) was significant.

18. For all its excellence in reviewing recent scholarship on Jewish "apocalyptic" thought and literature and its implications for New Testament scholarship, the overview by Jörg Frey ("Die Apokalyptik als Herausforderung der neutestamentlichen Wissenschaft. Zum Problem: Jesus und die Apokalyptik," in *Apokalyptik als Herausforderung neutestamentlicher Theologie*, eds. Michael

the world and how God will someday bring about a new age, language that retold events from primordial time also provided audiences a basis for being confident about such an outcome in the present. Put in other words, God's definitive activity is not only a matter for the future and the distant past. Rather, it connects the past to the future through the present: God's invasive presence to defeat evil *in the past* (e.g., at the time of the Great Flood[19]), which can be manifested *in the present* through measures for curbing evil given to God's people, guarantees its annihilation *in the future* (*1 En.* 10:16-22; 15:3-16:4; 91:5-10; 106:13-107:1; *Jub.* 5:1-10:11; cf. *Book of Giants* at 4Q530 2 ii 6-7 8-12, lines 4-20).

As is well-known, for example, the Nephilim and mighty men in Gen. 6:4 were interpreted in several influential Jewish apocalyptic works as giant-sized offspring of disobedient angels and daughters of humanity, whose destructive activities led to a crisis in which God intervened to destroy their bodies, punish the angels, and ensure the survival of humans, who are integral to the created order.[20] Texts that pick up this tradition, among others, were not simply attempting to retell the sacred past in order to reflect on the future; they re-cast and interpreted revered traditions so that they could be revealed anew for their impact on the present. From the third century BCE until the beginning of the Common Era, they communicated to Jewish contemporaries that evil—in whatever form and however dominant of life as it is experienced—is essentially a defeated power whose time is marked. God's triumphs in the past, known in biblical tradition, are now revealed and interpreted in a particular way, and could be understood as the outworking of God's royal power (*1 En.* 84:2-6; *Book of Giants* at 4Q203 9 and 10; cf. *1 En.* 9:4). Since God's authority has

---

Becker and Markus Öhler, WUNT 2/214 [Tübingen: Mohr Siebeck, 2006], 23–94) does not press toward the emphasis of the discussion.

19. The Flood is a poignant example, given the cosmic dimensions of the evil and divine activity against it. The Red Sea episode or even the return from exile could be mentioned here as well, though these storylines do not play as prominent a role in the early apocalypses.

20. Cf. Archie T. Wright, *The Origin of Evil Spirits: The Reception of Genesis 6:1-4 in Early Jewish Literature*, rev. ed. (Minneapolis: Fortress Press, 2015); Loren T. Stuckenbruck, *The Myth of Rebellious Angels: Studies in Second Temple Judaism and New Testament Texts*, WUNT 335 (Tübingen: Mohr Siebeck, 2014), 1–57 and 78–102.

already asserted itself in the cosmos on a global scale (e.g., through the Great Flood) and on behalf of God's people Israel (cf. the Song of the Red Sea in Exod. 15, which celebrates the Israelites's rescue from inimical destruction), in principle, it cannot glibly be thought to have disappeared or to have withdrawn into the heavenly sphere, as one might be tempted to imagine.[21] The "present era" can be seen in a new light. The pious, with or without a messianic figure, can thus proceed with a measure of confidence as they deal with the effects, for example, of demonic power; though suffering attributed to the demonic world, whether in the individual or the socio-political order, cannot be completely eliminated before the ultimate end of things, it remains possible to curtail or manage its effects, or at least, to put it into perspective.

This way of looking at the past and at the imminent future was not ultimately a matter of charting or speculating about the end time or how time works, nor was it an escapist attempt to seek refuge from harsh reality. It was more a way of reclaiming a robust religious identity, that is, it was a way to recover what it visibly means to be God's people in the present. In addition, the possibility of combating evil with some measure of success in the present could be represented by an understanding of the faithful as those who, through participation in the covenant, share in the divine triumph over evil while negotiating the uncertainties of life that relentlessly confront them.[22]

In its influential retelling of the story from creation until the Israelites's freedom from bondage in Egypt, the *Book of Jubilees*, composed around the middle of the second century BCE, describes the condition of humankind after their rescue from the Great Flood. At this time (so *Jub.* 5:12), God is said to have given human beings a new and righteous nature, in order that with their whole being, they will never again sin, but will live righteously. This categorical new beginning

---

21. The complaint raised by the souls of humans who have been killed in *1 En.* 8:4–9:3 may give voice to a concern that in the midst of cultural and political upheaval, God seems to have withdrawn; however, the apparent lack of injustice is met by a decisive defeat *in the past* of powers (10:1–16), a defeat that now conditions and informs the perspective of those who receive the text.

22. Cf. further Stuckenbruck, *The Myth of Rebellious Angels*, 161–86.

does not, of course, resolve all problems.[23] Thus, the long remaining narrative of the book confirms, time and again, that missteps among Jews (halakhic and otherwise) continue to take place and that forces of evil continue to be effective among God's people. However, both this new nature and the defeated condition of demonic powers (cf. *Jub.* 10:1–11) also persist in the story. They anticipate the destruction of all evil, and with it, the fulfillment of God's plan for those who remain faithful. They can do so because means of dealing with the demonic were revealed to Noah and can also be invoked to do so in the present.

In other words, the "already" of evil's defeat in principle and the "not yet" of its manifest destruction was an existing framework that presentations of Paul's thought in the New Testament could take for granted. Paul's insistence that, in Christ, believers have become a "new creation" (2 Cor. 5:17; Gal. 6:16) does not introduce unprecedented terms of reference, but rather, adopts a different starting point out of which they become a reality. Moreover, analogous to *Jubilees*, Paul's declaration of the believers' status does not erase problems among them, but rather, lends them perspective. Furthermore, though in the case of Paul, the overlap between the present and future age is occasioned by a recent breakthrough in history, we would not be mistaken to think, by analogy, that there were pious Jews who understood themselves as living in an eschatological tension, inspired by confidence of concrete moments of divine activity in the past. It would therefore be misguided to infer, without qualification, that such religiosity is merely the domain of Pauline theology in a way that departs from contemporary apocalyptic thought.

I have alluded briefly above to one storyline that guaranteed the establishment of God's eschatological rule in the cosmos. The socio-rhetorical function of retelling sacred stories for recipients can be appreciated by readings of apocalyptically oriented texts by looking for clues in the text as to how they were to be received.[24] Without

---

23. The claim of this text goes well beyond that of its intertext in Gen. 9:1–17, according to which the establishment of a covenant between God and Noah and his offspring is not accompanied by a change of human nature.
24. A more obvious example for this is Noah's prayer in *Jub.* 10:3–6 that God not allow evil spirits

retelling the traditional storyline of the Flood, some texts presuppose its effective relevance for present maneuvers that the righteous can undertake to counteract evil.

Motifs clearly traceable to the Great Flood are discernible, for example, in references to the "bastard" spirits in the Dead Sea materials (so the *Songs of the Maskil* in 4Q510 1, 4–8 par. 4Q511 10, 1–6); these *mamzerim*, spirits that Enochic and other writers thought emanated from the giants whose physical bodies had been destroyed in the Flood (cf. *1 En.* 10:9), are powers of the present age. Having listed the "spirits of the bastards" among other demonic beings, *Songs of the Maskil* invokes the following temporal framework:

> . . . a time of the dominion [of] wickedness and in the eras of the humiliation of the sons of lig[ht] in the guilt of the times of those plagued by iniquities, not for an eternal destruction, [but] for the era of the humiliation of transgression (4Q510 1.6b-7 par. 4Q511 10.4-5, my translation).

By declaring God's radiant splendor and by celebrating God's power, the text holds that activities attributable to the catalogue of malevolent forces can be curbed. The powers are associated with the present order of things (called "the dominion [of] wickedness"). Two things in tension with one another are at once maintained: the text can speak of the righteous, "the sons of light," while, at the same time, acknowledging that they are subject to "humiliation" that characterizes the time. The righteous are not left without effective hope. The Maskil's song about God, addressed to them, presents itself an expedient measure that neutralizes threats associated with demonic power until the present age of wickedness comes to an end. One may infer that the song's confidence is based on the firm conviction that the malevolent beings have already been defeated.

This is, of course, not the only way powers in the present age are

---

to rule over his children and "over the children of righteousness now and forever" (10:6) is presented as a petition whose force extends to the recipients of the work. In order to recover the perspectives of ancient readers to texts such as *Jubilees* and *1 Enoch*, further audience-orientated work is needed; for a beginning in this direction, see Rodney A. Werline, "Ritual, Order and the Construction of an Audience in *1 Enoch* 1-36," *DSD* 22, no.3 (2015), forthcoming.

dealt with. In some of the more explicitly community-orientated and *Yaḥad* texts, liturgical curses are pronounced again against a chief angel (cf. *4QBerakot* at 4Q286 7 II, 3, 7) and Belial (*Serekh ha-Yaḥad* at 1QS I, 1–III, 11; cf. *Serekh ha-Milḥamah* at 1QM XIV, 9–10 par. 4Q491=4QMa 8–10 I, 6–7 and *4QCatena A* at 4Q177 III, 8). The pronouncements against and denunciations of Belial and his lot bring together and merge several evolving features that, in their specificity, are partly lost, yet whose conceptual framework is preserved within a new form. The eschatological framework found in earlier Enochic pronouncements of doom against the fallen angels, exorcisms (11Q11 V and 4Q560), and hymns of protection (*Songs of the Maskil*) is retained in the way the community deals with a chief demonic figure. In the *Serekh ha-Yaḥad*, curses against Belial adapt language from the Aaronic blessing (Num. 6:24–27) and should be understood in relation to the larger context of covenant blessings and curses found in Deuteronomy (cf. Deut. 28–30). If we may read the liturgy near the beginning of 1QS columns II–III in tandem with the hymn at the end at (columns X–XI), the way of dealing with Belial presupposes the community's present communion with "the sons of heaven" (cf. 11Q XI, 6–8); already in "the council of the flesh," God has granted them a participation in an eternal possession. Countermaneuvers against demonic power is less a matter of desperate measures than of calling into effect what the community's privileged status represents.

Traditions that are pivotal in receiving Enochic tradition and paving the way for the *Yaḥad* way of dealing with Belial may be seen not only in the *Songs of the Maskil*, but also in *Jubilees*, to which I have referred above. The *Book of Jubilees* presents demonic activity as coming under the leadership of a certain Mastema, an ordering of evil powers that is held to be characteristic of this age until the final judgment (10:7–13; cf. 10:8—*qedma kwennaneya*, "until my judgment"). Thus, in *Jubilees*, not only do angels reveal remedies to Noah (and his progeny) for the warding off or neutralizing the effects of evil spirits (*Jub.* 10:10–13), but also, the patriarchs—Moses (1:19–20), Noah (10:1–6), and Abraham (12:19–20). These patriarchs, in turn, are made in the text to utter prayers of deliverance against malevolent spirits, so that those receiving the text can know themselves to be covered by them.[25] Recast in this way, tradition associated with the patriarchal narratives from the Torah guides a Jewish community along paths of faithful obedience in anticipation of an end, the outcome of which is already assured. The present is shaped by both an eschatological past and a future that loops back as an *inclusio* to bring God's activity in history to its proper end.

Conclusion

The revealed worldview varied from text to text among Jewish apocalyptic writings. Though the notion of a final judgment is prominent in much of the literature, it does not proceed from a myopic hope that *only in the future*, in the transition from this world to the world to come, God will defeat evil. To a significant extent, eschatological hope is anchored in stories of past events, re-revealed out of tradition in a way that puts present evils, whether sin or suffering, into perspective. Whatever their circumstances, many Jews seeking to be faithful could receive stories about the past that have been re-interpreted for them by apocalyptic writers; those events have implications for life in the present. God's people, whom the text regards as righteous, are covered by a prior defeat of evil powers that God once put into place. The texts leave audiences confident that this defeat will manifest itself, time and again, in anticipation of and proleptic to eschatological reality.

The re-telling, even proclamation, of the past may be thought to have *done something* for at least some apocalyptic circles. Recipients of both the widespread and influential traditions found in *1 Enoch* and *Jubilees*, as well as in many of the Dead Sea documents, would have been confident that they themselves have been covered by the interpreted biblical traditions, as well as by the authority of and prayers against evil uttered by patriarchs on their behalf. They would have regarded demonic attack and danger—whether manifest through misdeeds,

---

25. For fuller discussion, see Stuckenbruck, *The Myth of Rebellious Angels*, 206–11.

multiple forms of affliction, or sociopolitical oppression—as threats that cannot be expected to vanish entirely in the present, but that nevertheless can already be curbed or put into perspective by various means. Conditions associated with the eschaton, even if only provisionally, can already be put into effect.

I do not wish to deny that something extraordinarily new on the scene was introduced in early Christian tradition. Drawing on and interpreting traditions about Jesus, Paul was convinced that in the Christ-event, a new age had dawned. By contrast, when Jewish apocalyptic texts enter into discourse about a messianic figure, that figure is invariably one whose coming is anticipated in the future. However, in a number of prominent and influential apocalyptic writings, the presence of an agent of God at the conclusion of history is conspicuously absent. Accordingly, the definitive activity of God to defeat evil is not simply a matter for the future. If, for Paul, a new age had begun because the messiah had already come, in some Jewish apocalyptic traditions, conditions anticipating the new age have been inaugurated through the defeat of evil in the sacred past without requiring a messianic figure to do it.

Like the perspectives of many others during the Second Temple period, early Christian ideas represented criticisms of and departures from what other Jews were advocating as a way of responding to their contemporary world. Departures—they can be arguably seen, for example, in exclusivist claims regarding Jesus and a filtered understanding of God's activity through Jesus' death and resurrection, and the de-emphasis of Torah—should, however, not be confused with a flight from the whole, taking with it fundamental categories and structures of thought, such as that regarding time. Rather than introducing an "already" versus "not yet" tension that modified a doctrine of the two ages,[26] Paul, for example, is actually better thought

---

26. This modification of Jewish apocalyptic thought has been and is held by a significant number of New Testament scholars; cf., e.g., Ernst Käsemann, "The Beginnings of Christian Theology," in *New Testament Questions of Today*, trans. W. J. Montague (Philadelphia: Fortress Press, 1969), 82–107; James D. G. Dunn, *The Theology of Paul the Apostle* (Grand Rapids: Eerdmans, 1998), e.g., 464–65, 475; David E. Aune, "Understanding Jewish and Christian Apocalyptic," in *Apocalypticism, Prophecy, and Magic in Early Christianity*, WUNT 199 (Tübingen: Mohr Siebeck, 2006), 1–12, at 9.

to have taken such a framework from the Jewish apocalyptic world for granted. The proleptic defeat of evil makes a new, revealed way of thinking and acting possible, whether this has to do with the re-visioning of past events or claims that relate to the most recent past (as with Paul's theology and some apocalyptic texts e.g., *Animal Apocalypse* of *1 En.* 90:6–16; 1QpHab cols. ii and vii; 1QM xiv 9–10). Paul's interpretation of the Christ-event as significant for how believers may live their lives grew out of the soil of an apocalyptic understanding of how God's determinative activity on behalf of humanity and Israel in the past has a continuing impact on strategies for coping with evil in the present.

Although this chapter concludes with a point that proposes a corrective to a religious-historical question, more can be said that is subject to further argument. If there is any analogy between the structuring of time in Paul's thought and those of apocalyptic Judaism described above, what is the significance of this continuity? In relation to evil, the most important point to make is that in the New Testament, no less so than in contemporary Jewish apocalyptic, the christological solution to the problem of sin and suffering, though presented as definitive, nevertheless remains provisional. No matter how central the Christ-event is to God's plan for the world, as Paul's thought abundantly claims, evil persists in all its forms, manifesting itself even within communities that strive to be faithful. Thus, categorical claims regarding God's activity in the ministry of Jesus or through his death and resurrection may, in comparison to Jewish apocalyptic tradition, have intensified the conviction that evil's destruction is certain, but they offer no basis to think that faith in itself can make any of it altogether disappear.

The reconsideration of time in apocalyptic thought that I have presented requires far more space than can be claimed here. In order to elicit the hermeneutical implications of the religious-historical comparison offered above, I close with two questions for reflection. Should the claim that God has uniquely acted through Jesus be necessarily bound up with a theological judgment that considers

Christian tradition as a *better* or *more effective* approach than that of non-Christian Second Temple religiosity to the vicissitudes of human experience? To what extent should Christian exegesis, when reflecting on the meaning of "apocalyptic" in Paul, deny Jewish tradition an efficaciousness that Christian tradition affirms?

A lot is gained when considering Pauline theology through the lens of apocalyptic. If in the process of interpreting Paul's understanding of time, the Jewish matrix with which it may be compared is ignored or neglected, we are bereft of a perspective that lends a certain realism to claims about Christ, not only in Paul's thought, but also in the New Testament as a whole.

8

The Transcendence of Death and Heavenly Ascent in the Apocalyptic Paul and the Stoics

Joseph R. Dodson

T. S. Eliot wrote, "All cases are unique, and very similar to others."[1] And so it is with Paul's apocalyptic eschatology.[2] Despite the "unique" outlook of the apostle's worldview,[3] many of its features are not without parallel, even beyond early Judaism. There were numerous works from various Mediterranean traditions in and around the first

1. T. S. Eliot, *Collected Plays* (London: Faber and Faber, 1962), 174.
2. Once scholars use this term in relation to Paul's letters, they are using it in an extended sense. See John J. Collins, *The Apocalyptic Imagination*, 2nd ed. (Grand Rapids: Eerdmans, 1998); Alan F. Segal, *Paul the Convert* (New Haven: Yale University Press, 1990), 34–71. On the relationship between *apocalyptic* and *eschatology*, see Christopher Rowland, *The Open Heaven* (New York: Crossroad, 1982), 70–72; Adela Yarbro Collins, *Cosmology and Eschatology in Jewish and Christian Apocalypticism*, JSJSup 50 (Leiden: Brill, 1996), 6.
3. Jonathan Z. Smith, *Drudgery Divine* (Chicago: University of Chicago Press, 1990), 36–53.

century containing accounts of revelatory experiences, disclosing visions of a transcendent world, and proclaiming eschatological doctrine.[4] Many of these parallels with Jewish-Christian apocalypses have been noted by biblical scholars. Harold Attridge, for instance, surveys a number of such Greek and Latin sources originating from the Hellenistic and early Roman periods and discovers that, among other elements, these works feature personal eschatology, journeys through the heavens, and end-time prophecies.[5] Furthermore, F. Gerald Downing traces the widespread first-century belief in cosmic eschatologies, and Stanley Porter surveys the strong tradition of the soul's destiny in the afterlife, identifying examples of resurrection and post-mortem judgment from early Greek religions.[6] Additionally, in their respective works, James Tabor and Alan Segal highlight the similarities and differences in ancient accounts of heavenly ascents.[7]

Of all the Greco-Roman works and traditions surveyed by these scholars, however, Stoicism is the perspective especially deserving of comparison with Paul's apocalyptic worldview. Stoic philosophy captivated a sizeable audience in the Mediterranean world from the third century BCE to the second century CE. Although by no means all-pervasive, more people during this time held "a more or less Stoic

4. See J. Gwyn Griffiths, "Apocalyptic in the Hellenistic Era," Walter Burkert, "Apokalyptik im frühen Griechentum: Impulse und Transformationen," and Morton Smith, "On the History of APOKALUPTW and APOKALUYIS," each in *Apocalypticism in the Mediterranean World and the Near East*, ed. David Hellholm (Tübingen: Mohr Siebeck, 1983), 15–17, 235–54, 273–93 (respectively); James Buchanan Wallace, *Snatched into Paradise (2 Cor. 12:1-10): Paul's Heavenly Journey in the Context of Early Christian Experience*, BZNW 179 (Berlin: de Gruyter, 2011).

5. Harold W. Attridge, "Greek and Latin Apocalypses," *Semeia* 14 (1979): 159–86.

6. F. Gerald Downing, "Cosmic Eschatology in the First Century," *L'Antiquité Classique* 64 (1995): 99–109; idem, "Common Strands in Pagan, Jewish and Christian Eschatologies in the First Century," *TZ* 51, no. 3 (1995): 196–211; Stanley, E. Porter, "Resurrection, the Greeks and the New Testament," in *Resurrection*, ed. Stanley E. Porter, Michael A. Hayes, and David Tombs (Sheffield: Sheffield Academic Press, 1999), 52–81.

7. James D. Tabor, *Things Unutterable* (Latham, MD: University Press of America, 1986); Alan F. Segal, "Heavenly Ascent in Hellenistic Judaism, Early Christianity and their Environment," in *ANRW II* 23.2, ed. Wolfgang Haase (Berlin: de Gruyter, 1980), 1334–88.

conception of the world than any other,"[8] so that even Stoicism's "methods and technical terms became common coin."[9]

Despite the ubiquity of Stoic thought, few modern studies have offered a comprehensive comparison of Paul's apocalyptic eschatology with the worldview of Stoicism. Troels Engberg-Pedersen's work is the most recent and recognized exception. In *Cosmology and Self in the Apostle Paul*, Engberg-Pedersen seeks to demonstrate that Paul's conceptions of spirit and body can only be fully understood in light of both a Jewish apocalyptic worldview and Stoic cosmology. In the volume, Engberg-Pedersen pinpoints striking Stoic parallels that many scholars have neglected. He attempts to show how using material from Stoic texts helps to provide "a more precise meaning to Paul's statements."[10] He concludes that—like the Stoics—the apostle understood the spirit "as a through and through material, bodily phenomenon."[11] Consequently, he argues that Paul's conception of the transformation of individuals into "pneumatic bodies should be understood on the model of the Stoic idea of the transformation of the whole world into (pneuma and) God at the conflagration."[12]

Engberg-Pedersen's work, however, has been met with significant resistance from various Pauline scholars. For instance, John Barclay criticizes Engberg-Pedersen for misinterpreting resonances between Stoic and Pauline literature "as signals of a common 'underlying' worldview."[13] Barclay insists that Pauline theology, on the whole, is

---

8. David E. Hahm, *The Origins of Stoic Cosmology* (Columbus: Ohio State University Press, 1977), xiii. See also A. A. Long, *Hellenistic Philosophy* (New York: Charles Scribner's Sons, 1974), 107, 232; J. Albert Harrill, "Stoic Physics, The Universal Eschatological Destruction of the 'Ignorant and Unstable' in 2 Peter," in *Stoicism and Early Christianity*, ed. Tuomas Rasimus, Troels Engberg-Pedersen, and Ismo Dunderberg (Grand Rapids: Baker, 2010), 115–40.

9. N. T. Wright, *Paul and the Faithfulness of God* (Minneapolis: Fortress Press, 2013), 1:218, 2:1384. See also David A. deSilva, "Paul and the Stoa: A Comparison," *JETS* 38, no. 4 (1995): 549–64; J. N. Sevenster, *Paul and Seneca* (Leiden: Brill, 1961), 240.

10. Troels Engberg-Pedersen, *Cosmology and Self in the Apostle Paul* (Oxford: Oxford University Press, 2010), 9. See also *Paul and the Stoics* (Edinburgh: T&T Clark, 2000), though here, Engberg-Pedersen fails to consider Paul's indebtedness to Jewish apocalyptic.

11. Ibid., *Cosmology and Self*, 3.

12. Ibid., 34.

13. John M. G. Barclay, "Stoic Physics and the Christ-event: A Review of Troels Engberg-Pedersen, *Cosmology and Self in the Apostle Paul: The Material Spirit*," *JSNT* 33, no. 4 (2011): 406–14. Cf. Joseph R. Dodson, "A Review of Troels Engberg-Pedersen, *Cosmology and Self in the Apostle Paul: The Material Spirit*," *BBR* 21, no. 3 (2011): 426–27.

"fundamentally incompatible" with Stoicism because—unlike Stoic philosophy—it is centered on a narrative of the Jewish messiah "that is shaped, in both thought and life, around a distinctive event with its own resulting logic."[14] Indeed, the new configuration of the community that results from this narrative "was far more at odds with the cosmos than Stoics could consider decent, natural or philosophically correct."[15] Similarly, N. T. Wright expresses astonishment that Engberg-Pedersen fails to address the differences in Paul's "creational monotheism" and the flexible pantheism of Stoicism, as well as in their respective symbolic worlds and characteristic narratives.[16]

Nevertheless, both Barclay and Wright find value in Engberg-Pedersen's work. For example, Barclay considers the book's discussion on powers in Paul and the Stoics "particularly illuminating,"[17] while Wright concludes that Engberg-Pedersen's comparison between Epictetus and Paul is a successful analysis that "should be factored in to subsequent studies."[18] In other words, the potential for abuse should not discount the heuristic benefit of comparing Pauline apocalyptic with Stoic cosmology. Rather, as Wright states on the heels of his critique of Engberg-Pedersen, "Tracking, plotting and assessing the many lines and levels of [Paul's] complex non-Jewish world is a task awaiting further attention."[19] Indeed, there remains value in setting out the apostle's "hypothetical and perhaps actual engagement" with the Stoics.[20] It is essential to stress, then, that Barclay and Wright's criticisms should not be taken as attempts to dissuade scholars from a fool's errand, but as reminders of the risks involved in navigating between the Scylla of neglecting Stoic parallels and the Charybdis of exaggerating their relevance.[21]

---

14. Barclay, "Stoic Physics," 413.
15. Ibid., 414.
16. Wright, *Faithfulness*, 2:1397–98, 1404.
17. Barclay, "Stoic Physics," 413n11.
18. Wright, *Faithfulness*, 2:1391.
19. Ibid., 1407.
20. Ibid., 1406.
21. Regarding the latter, *parallelomania* results any time a scholar marginalizes the point that no matter how "Stoic" Paul may sound, the apostle never abandons his Jewish-Christian convictions that set him apart from the Stoics. See Samuel Sandmel, "Parallelomania," *JBL* 81, no. 1 (1962):

In view of these challenges, in this chapter, I will seek to heed the warnings of Barclay and Wright while following Engberg-Pedersen's example of setting up a fresh comparison that elucidates the similar and dissimilar patterns of thought in Paul's letters and in literature representative of the Stoics. Rather than arguing for borrowing, a common parlance, or an exact match between the two, I will seek to highlight how the parallels between these traditions expose real differences that thereby confirm the "uniqueness" of Paul's apocalyptic eschatology.

The Transcendence of Death and Heavenly Ascent in Stoicism

Stoic writings contain elements that are often featured in apocalyptic literature, such as warnings of a universal destruction[22] and promises of a cosmic renewal[23] in which creation's *Endzeit* will correspond to its *Urzeit*.[24] Each of these makes a stimulating case study in its own right. In the interest of space, however, I will concentrate on references in Stoic literature to heavenly ascents used to demonstrate the transcendence of death—"the attainment of a higher, angelic form of life."[25] The following study will be different from those by Attridge, Downing, Stanley, Tabor, and Segal in that—rather than offering a cursory glance of a large number of texts from a wide swath of writings from various

1–13; Timothy A. Brookins, *Corinthian Wisdom, Stoic Philosophy, and the Ancient Economy*, SNTSMS 159 (Cambridge: Cambridge University Press, 2014), 64–65.

22. E.g. see Seneca, *Nat.* 3.27–30; Alexander Lycopolis 19.2–4; *Stoicorum veterum fragmenta* (henceforth: SVF) 1.107, 510–12; 2.526–620; Nemesius, SVF 2.625. Regarding the role of this theme in Greek literature, see Burkert, "Apokalyptik," 240–43.

23. See Bardo Maria Gauly, *Senecas "Naturales Quaestiones:" Naturphilosophie für die römische Kaiserzeit*, Zetemata 122 (München: C. H. Beck, 2004), 239; Edward Adams, *Constructing the World*, SNTW (Edinburgh: T&T Clark, 2000), 106; idem, *The Stars Will Fall From Heaven* (London: T&T Clark, 2007), 122–23; Christopher Rowland, "Paul as an Apocalyptist," in *A Companion to Jewish Apocalyptic Thought and the New Testament*, ed. Benjamin E. Reynolds and Loren T. Stuckenbruck (Minneapolis: Fortress Press, forthcoming); A. A. Long, "The Stoics on World-Conflagration and Everlasting Recurrence," *The Southern Journal of Philosophy* 28, no. 1 (1985): 13–37.

24. Cf. Hermann Gunkel in *Schöpfung und Chaos in Urzeit und Endzeit* (Göttingen: Vandenhoeck & Ruprecht, 1895); Jaap Mansfeld, "Resurrection Added: The Interpretation Christiana of a Stoic Doctrine" *VC* 37, no. 3 (1983), 218–33; Collins, *Seers*, 329; Loren T. Stuckenbruck, "Posturing 'Apocalyptic' in Pauline Theology," in *The Myth of Rebellious Angels: Studies in Second Temple Judaism and New Testament Texts*, WUNT 335 (Tübingen: Mohr Siebeck, 2014).

25. See John J. Collins, "Apocalyptic Eschatology as the Transcendence of Death" *CBQ* 36, no. 1 (1974), 21–43; Martha Himmelfarb, *Ascent to Heaven in Jewish and Christian Apocalypses* (Oxford: Oxford University Press, 1993), 4–46.

traditions—I will examine three passages representative of Stoicism: the dream of Scipio, the ascension of Metilius, and the apotheosis of Hercules. Even though there was variety of thought among the Stoics,[26] these three stories appealed to heavenly ascents to support the belief that virtuous souls continue to survive after being separated from the body.[27]

The Dream of Scipio

Cicero crowns his *Republic* with the Dream of Scipio, who was an esteemed paragon of Stoic virtue.[28] Although Cicero's entire work "shows a strong Stoic influence,"[29] his use of Scipio's dream especially associates a widely held eschatology and cosmology with Stoic themes such as the conflagration (*ekpyrosis*).[30] Therefore, as Marcia Colish demonstrates, Cicero's analyses and allusions here take him beyond the Hellenistic commonplaces into "a firmament where these elements revolve around an axis of Stoic doctrine."[31] Moreover, according to Pheme Perkins, Cicero uses the dream's eschatological vision of the future to respond to the political crises of the first century BCE. Fearing his class would flee public life due to the "new politics" of the Imperial age, Cicero employs Scipio's revelation to sustain "the view that only those who benefit the city have hope of immortality."[32]

Before Scipio recounts his own heavenly vision, he references the story of Er's return from the dead in Plato's *Republic* to explain the secrets of the afterlife. As Scipio's audience will recall from the myth, the judges gather Er together with the departed souls and appoint

26. See, e.g., SVF 2.809; Seneca, *Ep.* 36.10; Lactantius, SVF 2.623; Simplicius, SVF 2.627; Origen, *Against Celsus* 4.68, 5.20; Alexander, *On Aristotle's Prior analytics* 180.33-36; 181.25-31; Nemesius, 309.5-311.2.
27. Since no complete work from Early and Middle Stoicism survives, it is difficult to reconstruct the philosophy of any respective Stoic from these periods or ascertain any particular innovation. See Long, *Hellenistic Philosophy*, 114; René Brouwer, *The Stoic Sage* (Cambridge: Cambridge University Press, 2014), 3-4.
28. On the dating and purpose of the *Somnium Sciopionis*, see J. G. F. Powell, *Cicero* (Warminster, UK: Aris & Phillips, 1990), 119-35.
29. Georg Luck, "On Cicero's 'Dream of Scipio' and its Place in Graeco-Roman Philosophy," *HTR* 49, no. 4 (1956), 207-18.
30. Marcia L. Colish, *The Stoic Tradition From Antiquity to the Early Middle Ages* (Leiden: Brill, 1985), 95. See also Burkert, "Apokalyptik," 243; Powell, *Cicero*, 128, 158.
31. Colish, *The Stoic Tradition*, 95. Cf. Luck, "On Cicero's 'Dream of Scipio,'" 207-18.
32. Pheme Perkins, *Resurrection* (New York: Doubleday, 1984), 57.

him to be a messenger to humanity. They command him to listen and behold all that happens and even assign him an interpreter to ensure that he understands the experience enough to return and report it (Plato, *Resp.* 10.614d–619b). Er then watches as the judges separate the just souls from the wicked ones. While the righteous souls ascend into the heavens for a thousand years to experience indescribable beauty and bliss, the wicked souls are forced to descend under the earth to suffer until they repay their wrongdoings tenfold (*Resp.* 10.615a–616a). When Er comes back to life, he details these things in the hopes that people would constantly practice justice so that they may reap rewards—both while living in the body and in the thousand-year intervals in between (*Resp.* 10.619e; 621c–d).

Having referred to Er's rapture, Scipio now describes his own experience to demonstrate how the doctrines of heaven and the soul's immortality are sensible conjectures to be considered rather than fantastic fictions to be mocked (Cicero, *Resp.* 6.2.2).[33] Scipio begins by telling how he shuddered in terror when the deceased hero, Africanus, appeared to him in a dream.[34] In response to Scipio's fright, Africanus exhorts him to banish his fears. Then Africanus, who possesses "posthumous immortality among the stars,"[35] prophesizes about Scipio's future victories on the Earth.[36] He goes on to tell Scipio about the special place prepared for just souls in heaven, where the blessed enjoy everlasting life. Those considered dead are really still alive—so alive that, in comparison, life in the mortal body is death (*Resp.* 6.14).

To prove this, Africanus invites Scipio's father, Aemilius Paulus, to join them. At the sight of Paulus, Scipio lets out a spate of tears, and Paulus responds by embracing his son and forbidding him to weep (*Resp.* 6.15). Scipio then begs Paulus to let him depart from his so-called life on Earth to join his father in heaven. Paulus explains, however, that the soul must remain in the custody of the body to fulfill its obligations until God sees fit to release it. Therefore, rather than having his son

---

33. Cf. Tabor, *Things Unutterable*, 95.
34. On the motif of fear in heavenly ascent stories, see Gooder, *Third Heaven*, 155.
35. Powell, *Cicero*, 150.
36. Africanus also hints at the cause of Scipio's death. See Perkins, *Resurrection*, 57.

dodge his civic commitment,[37] Paulus calls Scipio to imitate him in cultivating justice (*Resp.* 6.16). If Scipio does so, one day he too will be able to live with the righteous forever.

"Like the heavenly journey's in the Enoch tradition, this vision includes a brief course in astronomical wisdom."[38] Scipio begins to describe cosmographical details. He says he is able to see heaven blazing brightly as a circle of light. Everywhere he looked, he beheld wonderful beauty. Filled with awe at the immensity of the universe, Scipio looks down and fixes his mind on how small the Earth is compared to the Milky Way (*Resp.* 6.16).[39] Africanus, however, redirects Scipio's gaze to the nine celestial spheres: the last of which is the heaven of the Supreme God (*Resp.* 6.17).[40] Africanus proceeds to explain to Scipio how foolish it is for a person to pursue fame when the coming conflagrations and floods will prevent anyone from gaining long-lasting glory: much less everlasting fame. The measurement of earthly years by the circuit of a single star pales in comparison to the Great Year when all the stars return to their original configuration (*Resp.* 6.23–24).

Therefore, rather than seeking vain and evanescent glory, Scipio should seek the celestial things (*Resp.* 6.20) and set his heart upon heaven where he will find his reward (*Resp.* 6.25). If Scipio will only look on high to contemplate this everlasting resting place, he would ignore the vulgar herd around him and allow virtue to lead him to true glory (*Resp.* 6.25). If his spirit remains committed to the best pursuits and detaches itself from bodily pleasures, soon enough, he will fly to the soul's proper home and permanent abode (*Resp.* 6.29). In light of this hope, Scipio promises to redouble his efforts to serve his country (*Resp.* 6.26).

Scipio's dream ends, however, with what will happen if he does not. The dreadful alternative is to suffer punishment and purgation with those enslaved to sensual desires.[41] When the wretched die, rather than

---

37. Cf. Powell, *Cicero*, 153–54.
38. Perkins, *Resurrection*, 58.
39. Ibid., 156.
40. Ibid., 158.

ascend to heaven: they fly close to the Earth. They who broke the laws of gods and men will be tortured for many ages (*Resp.* 6.29).

The Ascension of Metilius

With respect to how noble persons transcend death, Seneca's *Ad Marciam de Consolatione*[42] corresponds to (if not draws from) the Myth of Er and the Dream of Scipio.[43] According to this essay, when Marcia's son Metilius died, he tarried above his corpse just long enough to be rid of its blemish.[44] Once cleansed,[45] his soul burst its bounds to roam throughout the universe and traverse the limitless spaces of eternity.[46] Now, Metilius lives in an abiding place where "all noble souls are akin to one another," from which nothing can drive him. Having attained an everlasting peace,[47] he stands beyond the stings of lust, the reach of envy, and the range of scorn. He is no longer racked by anger or smitten by disease (*Marc.* 19.6).

When Metilius arrives in the heavens to dwell with blessed souls (*Marc.* 25.1), he is welcomed by the assembly of saints. His grandfather, Cremutius Cordus, steps forth from this company to initiate his grandson into nature's secrets (*arcana naturae*).[48] With true and intimate knowledge, Cordus reveals to Metilius the causes of celestial things, inducts him into newfound light, and guides him into the *arcana* (*Marc.* 25.1–26.1). For a moment, however, Cordus pauses from initiating Metilius into these mysteries to speak to his daughter, Marcia, from on high. He comforts her by informing her about the

41. See Perkins, *Resurrection*, 59.
42. This essay was written during 37–41 CE. See Jochen Sauer, "Consolatio Ad Marciam," in *Brill's Companion to Seneca*, ed. Gregor Damschen and Andreas Heil (Leiden: Brill, 2014), 135–39; James Romm, *Dying Every Day* (New York: Knopf, 2014), 13–16.
43. On the importance of Seneca in Stoicism, see John Sellars, *Stoicism* (Berkeley: University of California, 2006), 12; Brad Inwood, *Reading Seneca* (Oxford: Oxford University Press, 2008), 23–30.
44. On Seneca's uncertainty toward the afterlife, see Sevenster, *Paul and Seneca*, 224; Hoven, *Stoïcism*, 110–15; James Ware, "The Salvation of Creation: Seneca and Paul on the Future of Humanity and of the Cosmos," in *Essays on Paul and Seneca*, ed. Joseph R. Dodson and David E. Briones (Leiden: Brill, forthcoming).
45. Seneca only mentions what happens to the wise souls, see Hoven, *Stoïcism*, 113.
46. With respect to this idea of the purification of the soul, *"Nous n'en avons pas d'autre tmoignage,"* within the Stoics—at least not clear ones, ibid., 110–15.
47. On the Stoic's meaning of eternal, see ibid., 120–23.
48. On the motif of famous figures in ascent stories, see Gooder, *Third Heaven*, 152.

scope of Metilius's revelations (*Marc.* 26.4). From his celestial perspective, Metilius now knows the details concerning the rise and fall of future empires and the particulars of the conflagration—when all life will be extinguished and all matter will blaze in *ekpyrosis* (*Marc.* 26.6).[49] At that time, the blessed souls who had partaken of eternity will be transformed again into their former elements (*Marc.* 26.7). Therefore, Seneca concludes the essay by consoling Marcia. She should stop crying futile tears. Her son is in a better place, where he now knows all these secrets!

The Apotheosis of Hercules

As Cicero did with the Myth of Er, the author of *Hercules Oetaeus* adapts the legend of Hercules to a Stoic framework in order to demonstrate how righteous humans can attain to divinity through *virtus*.[50] The play's genre is different from Greek tragedy in that, as an example of *drama à thèse*, it is meant to expound a philosophical idea.[51] In this case, the author extends the original story to include how "Hercules burns away his mortal part and becomes a god."[52] Because of his virtue, even the flames could not defeat this wise representative of Stoicism. Consequently, Hercules's earlier claim of having mastered the world is fulfilled at his departure, when through death, he vanquishes the only enemy he had not yet overcome (*Herc. Ot.* 1610–1620). Now, as a result: "Everything has been conquered!" (*en domita omnia*).

Rather than shrinking from the fire, Hercules prays for Jupiter to let the flames prove he is God's son, who is worthy to dwell among stars (*Herc. Ot.* 1710–1714). In response, instead of God abandoning his son to death's infernal realm, Hercules hears Jupiter calling:

---

49. Cf. Seneca, *Ben.* 6.22.
50. The authorship of this play is uncertain; however, there are many arguments against Senecan authorship. See C. A. J. Littlewood, "Hercules Oetaeus," in *Brill's Companion to Seneca*, ed. Gregor Damschen and Andreas Heil (Leiden: Brill, 2014), 515–20.
51. Christine M. King, "Seneca's Hercules Oetaeus: A Stoic Interpretation of the Greek Myth," *Greece and Rome* 18, no. 2 (1971), 215–22.
52. Littlewood, "Hercules," 516.

Behold! Now my father opens up heaven
and summons me.
Father, here I come. (*Herc. Ot.* 1725; my translation)

Then, to the surprise of the bystanders, Hercules transcends death. While the mourners were lamenting over him, he appears to them from above and speaks to them from the skies (*Herc. Ot.* 1940). Hercules lets his loved ones know that he has not remained with the shades as they presumed. Rather, he conquered the grave and triumphed over hell. They should no longer weep for him because his virtue has borne him to the gods. Deathless and divine, the mighty conqueror and bringer of peace made a triumphal entrance into heaven (*Herc. Ot.* 1980–1990).

Summary

This section has summarized the themes of the transcendence of death and heavenly ascent in three stories representative of Stoicism. As demonstrated above, the authors drew upon the legends of Hercules, Scipio, and Er to show that "biological life is not the highest form of experience for which human beings can hope."[53] Rather, the pious will go to heaven when they die. Whereas Metilius and Hercules give an example of a celestial ascent after death, Scipio's rapture is the anticipation of that ascent.[54] Despite these differences, the composite is that virtuous souls ascend to heaven when they die, where the saints guide them into the mysteries of the universe, which include the particulars about the future all the way up to the conflagration. Wicked souls, on the contrary, will be dreadfully punished.

Paul's Apocalyptic Eschatology in Light of the Stoics

In this section, my aim is to show how the key features of Stoic apocalyptic surveyed above relate to elements in Paul's letters. No

---

53. John J. Collins, *Seers, Sibyls and Sages in Hellenistic-Roman Judaism* (Leiden: Brill, 2001), 92. Cf. Perkins, *Resurrection*, 62.
54. William Bousset, "Die Himmelsreise der Seele," *Archiv für Religionswissenschaft* 4 (1901): 136–69, at 136.

preformed definition of "Pauline apocalyptic" is adopted in this essay; rather, the Stoic sources have the primary control here in defining apocalyptic. The hope is that by letting the Stoic texts drive the discussion, light can be shed on the content of apocalyptic and how those Stoic concepts relate to Paul's theology, including where their respective worldviews overlap and contrast. I will focus on the following themes: (A) heavenly ascents, (B) hidden mysteries, (C) temporary sufferings, (D) life after death, (E) intermediate states, and (F) post-mortem judgment and reward.

Heavenly Ascent

Similar to the aforementioned authors' references to Er, Scipio, Metilius, and Hercules, Paul recounts the story of a "man in Christ"[55] who was caught up to heaven (2 Cor. 12:1–4).[56] Along the lines of the experiences of Scipio and Er, the heavenly ascent of this man provides a mere foretaste of the heavenly world[57] and stands over against those of Metilius and Hercules, who never returned from heaven.[58] Moreover, whereas Scipio gazed upon the nine spheres of heaven—the last of which was the abode of God (Cicero, *Resp.* 6.17)—Paul's man was raptured to the third heaven[59] and experienced a revelation in Paradise.[60] In response to Paul's ascent story, the Stoics might have wondered if Paradise referred to a location in the third heaven,[61] or if it

---

55. Most scholars agree that, despite his use of the third person, Paul himself is the "man in Christ." See Tabor, *Things Unutterable*, 114; Gooder, *Third Heaven*, 152. For a survey of the reasons scholars give for Paul speaking in the third person, see Margaret E. Thrall, *The Second Epistle to the Corinthians*, vol. 2, ICC (London: T&T Clark, 2004), 778–83.

56. On the timing of this vision, see Thomas D. Stegman, SJ, *Second Corinthians* (Grand Rapids: Baker, 2009), 267.

57. See Hans Bietenhard, *Die himmlische Welt im Urchristentum und Spätjudentum*, WUNT 2 (Tübingen: Mohr Siebeck, 1951), 161–86. For the different types of heavenly ascents according to Tabor, *Things Unutterable*, 69–97.

58. On the relationship between 2 Cor. 12:1–5 and Gal. 1:11–17, see William Baird, "Visions, Revelation, and Ministry," *JBL* 104, no. 4 (1985): 651–62.

59. On the tradition of three heavens in Jewish thought, see Mark A. Seifrid, *The Second to the Corinthians*, PNTC (Grand Rapids: Eerdmans, 2014), 439–40; Gooder, *Third Heaven*, 11–12; Baird, "Visions," 655. Cf. Himmelfarb, *Ascent to Heaven*, 39.

60. On Paradise, see Seifrid, *Corinthians*, 441–42; Tabor, *Things Unutterable*, 116–19; Rowland, *The Open Heaven*, 382–84; Victor Paul Furnish, *II Corinthians* AB (New York: Doubleday, 1984), 526.

61. Cf. *Slav. Enoch* 8; *Apoc. Moses* 37.5. See Murray J. Harris, *The Second Epistle to the Corinthians* NIGTC (Grand Rapids: Eerdmans, 2005), 844–45; Wallace, *Snatched*, 255; Collins, *Cosmology*, 32.

was similar to the highest heaven that Scipio saw.[62] If the former, why did the man in Christ fail to go all the way?[63] In contrast to Hercules's triumphant entry into heaven, did the man trip up somehow? Even if he did stumble, was the man in Christ—like Scipio—at least able to gaze upon the heaven of the Supreme God from a distance?

Moreover, since Paul is unsure whether or not the experience was in the body,[64] the Stoics might question if the man in Christ's revelation was more like Scipio's dream,[65] or more akin to Er's "near-death" experience.[66] If the latter, perhaps this man's rapture was a result of one of the "many deaths" mentioned in 2 Cor. 11:23.[67] Paul is certain about one thing, however. The man in Christ cannot repeat what he heard while he was in Paradise.[68] Over against the purpose of Scipio's vision, then, Paul's revelation reveals nothing.[69] The Stoics would likely have expressed frustration with the apostle's oxymoronic "inexpressible words" (ἄρρητα ῥήματα),[70] as well as with his lack of details.[71] For, while their ascent stories sought to satisfy people's spiritual hunger for eschatological and astronomical secrets,[72] Paul's account merely whets the appetite.[73]

Further, whereas Scipio and Metilius both had celestial guides to help them, Paul makes no mention of such a figure.[74] Is it because there

---

62. See Rowland, *Open Heaven*, 381–86.
63. See also Gooder, *Third Heaven*, 211–15; Rowland, "Paul as an Apocalyptist," forthcoming.
64. On Paul's confusion here, see H. Windisch, *Der zweite Korintherbrief*, KEK (Göttingen: Vandenhoek & Ruprecht, 1924), 374–76; Segal, *Paul the Convert*, 39; Segal, "Heavenly Ascent," 1349; Tabor, *Things Unutterable*, 57; Gooder, *Third Heaven*, 154; Wallace, *Snatched*, 259.
65. Cf. Engberg-Pedersen, *Cosmology and Self*, 89.
66. According to Wright, Er did not really die (N. T. Wright, *The Resurrection of the Son of God* [London: SPCK; Minneapolis: Fortress, 2003], 65).
67. See Seifrid, *Corinthians*, 441.
68. Scholars generally agree that Paul describes only one experience in 2 Cor. 12:1–10. See Furnish, *II Corinthians*, 542; Frank J. Matera, *II Corinthians*, NTL (Louisville: Westminster John Knox, 2003), 278.
69. Cf. Furnish, *II Corinthians*, 544; Baird, "Visions," 661; Rowland, *Open Heaven*, 380.
70. Cf. Rom. 8:26 and 1 Cor. 14:1–33. See Harris, *Corinthians*, 844; Jerome Murphy-O'Connor, *Paul, A Critical Life* (New York: Oxford University Press, 1996), 320; Paul Barnett, *The Second Epistle to the Corinthians*, NICNT (Grand Rapids: Eerdmans, 1997), 556.
71. This is assuming the Stoics would not consider this a parody, as Betz interprets it, Hans Dieter Betz, *Der Apostel Paulus und die sokratische Tradition*, BZHT 45 (Tübingen: Mohr Siebeck, 1972), 72–95. In response to why Betz's interpretation is unlikely, see Thrall, *Corinthians*, 776–77; Gooder, *Third Heaven*, 192–95.
72. Cf. Rowland, *Open Heaven*, 22.
73. Gooder, *Third Heaven*, 1.
74. This is assuming the apostle did not mean κυρίου as a genitive of agency. As for how to interpret the genitive in ἀποκαλύψεις κυρίου, see Harris, *Corinthians*, 833; Wallace, *Snatched*, 252–53; Thrall,

was no one to interpret the experience for him that the man in Christ cannot divulge the details? Or perhaps there was an unmentioned helper there who forbade the man in Christ to share what he heard.[75] Either way, the Stoics would likely assume in light of their own sources that Paul's vision related information about cosmography, the future events of kingdoms, the end of the world, and instructions regarding how to obtain everlasting life.[76]

Of course, in the context of 2 Corinthians, Paul uses the ascent story to counter his Jewish-Christian opponents who appealed to their own revelations to validate their apostolic authority. Paul therefore downplays the rapture in order to establish the true nature of apostleship.[77] The super-apostles pursued ecstatic experiences for personal validation, and the Stoics appealed to heavenly ascents to argue for the transcendence of death.[78] *But Paul did not need his ascent story for that either!* In the face of the super-apostles and over against the Stoic philosophers, the legitimacy of Paul's ministry and the promise of immortality were found *not* in the man in Christ's ascension, but in Christ's resurrection—through which, according to the apostle, the hidden wisdom of God had already been disclosed (1 Cor. 2:7).

Hidden Mysteries

Both Paul and the Stoics consider the saints as understanding cosmic mysteries. The Stoics, however, reserve the understanding of the divine plans for those who had already journeyed to heaven (cf. 1 Cor. 13:12). Paul, on the contrary, proclaims to all believers God's mysteries decreed before the ages (1 Cor. 2:6–7). Over against the wise philosophers, the apostle's churches already understand these mysteries because they have the Spirit of God and the mind of Christ

---

Second Corinthians, 774–75; Furnish, *II Corinthians*, 524; Baird, "Visions, Revelation, and Ministry," 659; Barnett, *Corinthians*, 558.

75. On whether to interpret this phrase as referring to inability or lack of permission, see Wallace, *Snatched*, 260–61; Tabor, *Things Unutterable*, 122–23; Gooder, *Third Heaven*, 201.

76. Cf. Rowland, *Open Heaven*, 10, 26.

77. Gooder, *Third Heaven*, 192–95, 213.

78. Cf. Segal, "Heavenly Ascent," 1352.

(1 Cor. 1:18–23; 2:6–16).[79] In contrast to the Stoics, for Paul, the secret concerns how the risen Christ conquered Satan, sin, and death.[80]

Nevertheless, the Stoics would likely see the commonalities of the death, victory, and ascension of God's Son with their own understanding of Hercules, Jupiter's virtuous offspring. Similar to Jesus, Hercules—"the mighty conqueror" and "bringer of peace"—did not shrink at death, but defeated the grave by rising triumphantly to join his Father in heaven. In contrast to Hercules's incorporeal ascent, however, Jesus' bodily resurrection inaugurated the new age. The Stoics, of course, have nothing strictly comparable to this. In fact, with respect to Christ's initiation of the coming age, the Stoics would agree with the apostle that to the "wise" his revelations seem quite absurd—absolute μωρία (1 Cor. 1:18–30).

Temporary Sufferings

Like the Stoics who were constrained to their bodies, believers are beleaguered with afflictions. In fact, Paul's churches will share in Christ's sufferings until Christ returns (Rom. 8:15–16). Nevertheless, similar to Africanus's assessment that life on Earth is death compared to the glorious life in heaven, Paul proclaims that the church's momentary afflictions lead to everlasting glory (2 Cor. 4:17). Moreover, like Seneca's promise of Metilius's post-mortem relief from sin and pain, Paul ensures believers that their present sufferings are not worth comparing to the glory about to be revealed (Rom. 8:18). This research underscores one critical difference: while the Stoics looked forward to their reward at the moment of their death, the believers' hope centered more on the day of their resurrection. This insight leads us to the next point of comparison.

Life After Death

Both Paul and the Stoics endorse a transcendence of death where

---

79. Cf. Wright, *Faithfulness*, 1366–67.
80. On a comparison between Paul's understanding of demons and Satan with the Stoic worldview, see Engberg-Pedersen, *Cosmology and Self*, 93–101.

righteous people attain a higher form of life after they die.[81] Further, both base this belief on an ascent story. The Stoics draw their understandings of the soul's afterlife from the myth of Er, the dream of Scipio, and the apotheosis of Hercules. Paul, on the contrary, bases his belief in the future resurrection of believers on the resurrection of Christ (1 Cor. 15:20).[82] Since believers have been buried with Christ by baptism into his death (Rom. 6:1–11), they have the certainty that they will be united with him in resurrection.

Similar to the hopes of Scipio and Metilius, soon enough, the believers will see their departed loved ones again (1 Thess. 4:14). At the *parousia*, the dead in Christ will rise from the grave and dash to the sky (1 Thess. 4:13–14).[83] Then, the remaining believers will follow them to meet the Messiah in the air (1 Thess. 4:17). Paul later explains that the Spirit will give life to believers' mortal bodies (Rom. 8:11), which will be transformed in the twinkling of an eye (1 Cor. 15:51–52). Therefore, over against the Stoics' portrayals of apotheoses of individuals at their deaths, Paul depicts an imminent mass "theosis" at the final resurrection.[84] This highlights how—in contrast to the Stoics—Paul's concern for the individual is "indissolubly linked with the history of salvation as a whole."[85]

Intermediate States

Similar to Scipio's desire to depart to be with his father in heaven, Paul confesses that he would rather be away from the body so that he could be with the Lord. Whereas Scipio resolves to stay for the sake of the Republic,[86] the apostle realizes that it is necessary for him to

---

81. "While resurrection and ascension must be viewed as different phenomena in the strict sense, they are so closely associated by Paul that one virtually implies the other" Segal, "Heavenly Ascent," 1374.

82. On the apocalyptic eschatology of 1 Corinthians, see Matthew Goff, "The Mystery of God's Wisdom, the *Parousia* of a Messiah, and Visions of Heavenly Paradise," in *A Companion to Jewish Apocalyptic Thought and the New Testament*, ed. Benjamin E. Reynolds and Loren T. Stuckenbruck (Minneapolis: Fortress Press, forthcoming).

83. For more on the Stoic reaction to this passage, see Engberg-Pedersen, *Cosmology and Self*, 11.

84. See Tabor, *Things Unutterable*, 9.

85. Sevenster, *Paul and Seneca*, 217.

86. See Powell, *Cicero*, 124.

remain in his body for the benefit of the church (Phil. 1:23). While the Stoics provide particulars regarding the state of righteous souls leading up to the *ekpyrosis*, the apostle never goes into detail regarding the condition of deceased believers leading up to the *parousia*.[87] Paul does say, however, that to die is gain and to depart from life is to be with Christ (Phil. 1:21–23). Furthermore, as long as a believer is at home in the body, she is away from the Lord (2 Cor. 5:6).[88]

Since Stoics went into detail concerning the blissful state of souls in heaven, they might want to know more about what Paul means when he says to be absent of the body is to be present with the Lord. For example, once Paul dies, will he—like Hercules—enter victoriously into heaven once for all? Like Scipio, will he be present with his loved ones who died before him? Like Metilius, will he see the events of the future and uncover all the secrets of the cosmos?

Post-mortem Judgment and Reward

For both the Stoics and Paul, "present experience and future hope were intrinsically connected and mutually interdependent."[89] As with Scipio and Er, Paul seeks to live virtuously because he believes everyone will give an account for their actions done in the body (Rom. 14:10–12; 2 Cor. 5:9–10). According to Paul, the Messiah will bring to light what is hidden in darkness, expose the motives of human hearts (1 Cor. 4:5), and judge people's secret thoughts (Rom. 2:16).[90]

Like the Stoics, Paul reserves the heavenly rewards for the righteous and warns of post-mortem judgment for the impious. As we saw above, however, the Stoics had accounts of the intermediate state of the wicked: unjust souls would be tormented until they were purified or perpetually tortured until the next conflagration. Conversely, Paul does not mention a double resurrection,[91] or give specifics with respect

---

87. See ibid., 238.
88. See Engberg-Pedersen, *Cosmology and Self*, 49.
89. Collins, *Seers*, 97.
90. On the apocalyptic eschatology in Romans, see Karina Martin Hogan, "The Apocalyptic Eschatology of Romans," in *A Companion to Jewish Apocalyptic Thought and the New Testament*, ed. Benjamin E. Reynolds and Loren T. Stuckenbruck (Minneapolis: Fortress Press, forthcoming).
91. Cf. *1 Enoch* 46–48; *4 Ezra* 7; *2 Baruch* 50–51.

to the depraved souls who have deceased. To be sure, he declares that the wicked will not inherit the kingdom, that God's wrath is already being revealed from heaven upon the ungodly, and that divine ruin will soon sweep them away (1 Cor. 6:9–11; Rom. 1:17–18; 1 Thess. 5:3). But what about the wicked who had already departed? Did Paul come closer to considering them as incarcerated in the abyss for a thousand years like in the Myth of Er? Or, as in Scipio's dream, does Paul believe that the unrighteous are being constrained to the Earth and tormented for many ages? On the contrary, perhaps the apostle considered the wicked souls as mere shades dwelling in the infernal realm as mentioned in *Hercules Oetaeus*.[92]

Summary

In this comparison, I have highlighted parallels in the writings of the Stoics and Paul to accentuate the differences with respect to heavenly ascents, hidden mysteries, temporary sufferings, life after death, intermediate states, and post-mortem judgment and reward. One overall distinction revealed is how scant of detail Paul's apocalyptic eschatology is compared to the lavish particulars found in the heavenly visions, journeys, and revelations of the Stoics. Therefore, Paul is not only bereft of details in comparison to other Jewish works, as others note, but also, in comparison with those represented in Stoic writings. Furthermore, many of the apocalyptic eschatological components spelled out in other Jewish ascent stories—such as the motif of fear, warnings of universal destruction, and details about celestial guides—appear in Stoic texts, *but not in Paul*. This is all the more remarkable if one considers apocalyptic eschatology as "the mother of all [Pauline] theology."[93]

---

92. Perhaps Paul even reckoned that they were simply annihilated as some Stoics assumed. See Sevenster, *Paul and Seneca*, 224; Hoven, *Stoïcism*, 110–15; Engberg-Pedersen, *Cosmology and Self*, 101.
93. Ernst Käsemann, "The Beginnings of Christian Theology," in *New Testament Questions of Today*, trans. W. J. Montague (Philadelphia: Fortress Press, 1969), 102; Engberg-Pedersen, *Cosmology and Self*, 9.

Conclusion

This chapter has been an attempt to join Engberg-Pedersen in going beyond the Judaism/Hellenism divide in the area of apocalyptic eschatology. Since many of those who heard Paul preach and participated in his churches would have been quite familiar with Stoic cosmology, I have explored the motifs of the transcendence of death and heavenly ascent in three writings representative of this dominant first-century philosophy. By surveying Scipio's dream, Metilius's ascent, and Hercules's apotheosis and comparing them with various themes found in Paul's letters, I sought to show that Paul's apocalyptic eschatology has many features in common with Stoicism. In fact, in view of the parallels and widespread popularity of Stoicism, one might imagine how an undiscerning first-century bystander could *prima facie* mistake the two worldviews.[94]

Yet, our comparison has revealed not only striking similarities between Paul and the Stoics, but critical differences as well.[95] Unsurprisingly, many of the features that make Paul's worldview different from Stoicism are quite at home in Judaism.[96] This might make it tempting for scholars to bypass the Stoic parallels in order to concentrate on more commensurate texts from Jewish traditions, as the majority of scholarship has done. Nonetheless, scholars should continue to push beyond the Judaism/Hellenism divide so as not to focus on one background to the exclusion of others. As David Aune notes, Paul's theology is "a creative combination of Jewish and Hellenistic traditions transformed into a *tertium quid*"—which, although related to these two traditions, transcends them both.[97]

---

94. Cf. Perkins, *Resurrection*, 56; Günter Wagner, *Pauline Baptism and the Pagan Mysteries*, trans. J. P. Smith (Edinburgh: Oliver & Boyd, 1967), 268.

95. See Sevenster, *Paul and Seneca*, 240.

96. Regarding the relation to the apocalyptic dimensions of Pauline theology with Jewish tradition, see C. R. A. Morray-Jones, "Paradise Revisited (2 Cor. 12:1–12): The Jewish Mystical Background of Paul's Apostolate. Part 2: Paul's Heavenly Ascent and its Significance," HTR 86, no. 2 (1993): 265–92; Loren T. Stuckenbruck, "Posturing 'Apocalyptic' in Pauline Theology," in *The Myth of Rebellious Angels: Studies in Second Temple Judaism and New Testament Texts*, WUNT 335 (Tübingen: Mohr Siebeck, 2014).

97. David E. Aune, *The New Testament in its Literary Environment* (Philadelphia: Westminster John Knox, 1987), 12.

This study also raises, as a byproduct, important questions about how and why the writings of a Jewish apostle resonate so deeply with Stoic philosophy. As a man of many worlds, Paul was, of course, as Timothy Brookins explains, "capable of shifting between them as the rhetorical situation demanded."[98] But do the influences run deeper than rhetorical pragmatism? Indeed, how many of the resonances occur due to Paul's tendency to employ rhetorical forms used in Stoic authors as well as his occasional penchant to express "his message in figures common among the Stoics"?[99] How many of them ensue from genuine agreements with the conceptual world of the Stoics?[100] And how many appear due to Stoic influence on Jewish thought?[101] Whatever the case, these questions invite more comparisons between Paul and Stoicism as well as explorations into the origin of the apostle's thought world.

---

98. Brookins, *Corinthian Wisdom*, 228.
99. deSilva, "Paul and the Stoa," 563. Cf. Sevenster, *Paul and Seneca*, 240.
100. Ibid., 563–64.
101. E.g., the use of Stoic ideas and terminology in the *Wisdom of Solomon*. See Collins, *Seers*, 93 and 329.

9

Second-Century Perspectives on the Apocalyptic Paul

Reading the Apocalypse of Paul and the Acts of Paul

Ben C. Blackwell

Introduction

As scholars debate how Paul is an apocalyptic theologian, the evidence they most often utilize, outside of Paul's letters themselves, is Jewish apocalyptic material, and rightly so. However, other material can provide a lens on this question because our contemporary debates over the nature and extent of Paul's apocalyptic theology are not new in the history of the reception of his letters. Indeed, some of Paul's earliest exponents faced similar interpretive challenges and opportunities, and it is this reception history that will be our focus here. Rather than walking through nearly two thousand years of reception history to assess contemporary discussions, I will focus on the second century.[1]

---

1. A number of good works have treated this topic recently. See, e.g., Michael F. Bird and Joseph R.

Paul was not the only authoritative figure for the second century church, but he held a special position in the early church across the theological spectrum, and many drew from his life and letters. His interpreters found a rich diversity of ways for exploring and developing his theology through their own writings.[2] To be sure, none merely repeat Paul, and yet, we should not fault them for this, as they all were answering questions from their different contexts. Rather than being anachronistic distractions from the real meaning of Paul's writings, studying the reception of these texts by later interpreters opens windows of meaning and approaches that we, as modern readers, might at times underestimate.[3]

No commentaries on Paul's letters exist from this period, but other genres better reveal how various Christian traditions during this time re-appropriated his letters and theology for their own context. Within the wider Christian exploration of apocalyptic themes in the second century,[4] two key narratives that appropriate Paul's memory stand out. An almost self-evident option is the gnostic *Apocalypse of Paul*, which recounts a heavenly journey by Paul.[5] In fact, with this original Coptic title—ⲦⲀⲠⲞⲔⲀⲖⲨⲮⲓⲥ ⲘⲠⲀⲨⲖⲟⲥ—this text likely represents the first explicit description of Paul as an "apocalyptic" figure by one of his

Dodson, eds., *Paul and the Second Century: The Legacy of Paul's Life, Letters, and Teaching*, LNTS 412 (London: T&T Clark, 2011).

2. Klaus Koschorke's conclusions about the reception of Paul in the Nag Hammadi texts apply more widely: "Paulus in den Nag-Hammadi-Texten: Ein Beitrag zur Geschichte der Paulusrezeption im frühen Christentum," *ZTK* 78, no. 2 (1981): 177–205, at 200–205.

3. See, e.g., my "Two Early Perspectives on Participation in Paul: Irenaeus and Clement of Alexandria," in *'In Christ' in Paul: Explorations in Paul's Theology of Union and Participation*, eds. Michael J. Thate, et al., WUNT 2/384 (Tübingen: Mohr Siebeck, 2014), 331–55. The recent work by Benjamin White also helpfully explores this need for more charity for the various interpretations we encounter in reception histories: *Remembering Paul: Ancient and Modern Contests over the Image of the Apostle* (Oxford: Oxford University Press, 2014), esp. 170–81. However, White's attempt to prove that his definite reading of 1 Corinthians stands against the readings of 3 Corinthians and Irenaeus seems to mitigate the effect of his own methodological plea.

4. Adela Yarbro Collins ("The Early Christian Apocalypses," *Semeia* 14 [1979]: 61–121) details Christian apocalypses with putative origins in the first three centuries, including ones found in the NT but excluding Gnostic works. Of these works, three are thought to have originated in the second century: the apocryphal *Apocalypse of Peter*, *Shepherd of Hermas*, and *Ascension of Isaiah* 6–11. In the same volume, Francis Fallon ("The Gnostic Apocalypses," *Semeia* 14 [1979]: 123–58) explores the rich variety of Gnostic apocalypses that span a wider time frame.

5. There may be a literary relationship with a later Latin text, the *Visio Pauli*, which at times is called the *Apocalypse of Paul* and which proved influential for Medieval heavenly journey accounts such as that of Dante. I am focusing here just on the earlier gnostic text.

interpreters. Another text equally focused on Paul (though here, from a proto-orthodox perspective) and infused with forms of apocalyptic thinking is the *Acts of Paul*, which is an apocryphal narrative of Paul's ministry and martyrdom. Together, these two narratives give us a window on some of the diverse approaches to Paul and his apocalyptic theology in the second century.

In our study, we will see that both are permeated with traditional apocalyptic themes: the agency of God and that of other spiritual beings, revelatory experiences, individual eschatology, and political re-assessment. Though similar themes are utilized, the nature of the discussion and the combination of these themes are quite distinct. After a separate assessment of both texts, we will then reflect upon issues related to contemporary debates.

The Apocalypse of Paul

A late second-century gnostic text, the *Apocalypse of Paul* is a relatively short work of just a few pages that describes a journey by Paul to the tenth heaven.[6] In the *Apocalypse*, Paul meets a small child, later revealed to be the Spirit, and is led from the fictive mountain of Jericho to the heavenly Jerusalem to meet the twelve apostles. Going directly to the third heaven, he progresses up to the tenth heaven. However, the third through the seventh heavens are under the control of "an old man in white clothing" (the demiurge) and his angelic minions, who attempt to prevent souls from ascending to the higher heavens. Indeed, in the fourth heaven, the narrator presents an extended scene where a soul is charged and punished by these angels. Through the help of the Spirit, however, Paul is ultimately able to ascend to tenth heaven. No detail is given about the higher heavens—the eighth, ninth,

---

6. Among the Nag Hammadi collection, the *Apocalypse of Paul* is found in Codex V, a fourth-century codex in which other apocalypses are found—the *Apocalypse of Adam* and two *Apocalypses of James*. For the critical edition and translation of the text, see "The Apocalypse of Paul: V,2: 17,19–24,9," in *Nag Hammadi Codices: V,2–5 and VI*, Coptic Gnostic Library, ed. Douglas M. Parrot (Leiden: Brill, 1979), 50–63. See Michael Williams for a discussion on the arrangement of Codex V in the context of the other codices: "Interpreting the Nag Hammadi Library as 'Collection(s)' in the History of 'Gnosticism(s),'" in *Les Textes de Nag Hammadi et le Problème de Leur Classification*, eds. L. Painchaud and Ann Pasquier (Louvain: Peters, 1995), 3–47, at 32–33.

and tenth heavens—aside from Paul meeting there with the twelve apostles, his fellow spirits.

As a Christian apocalypse, we should not be surprised to find that the *Apocalypse of Paul* has numerous affinities with the Jewish apocalypses and Jewish apocalyptic traditions. These traditions influenced many early Christian writings, especially the apocalypse genre.[7] According to Collins, Jewish apocalypses are generally placed in two categories: those with otherworldly journeys and those that are "historical" accounts.[8] The *Apocalypse of Paul* matches the otherworldly journey genre, and to the extent it alludes to Jewish apocalypses, it draws from those that also highlight otherworldly journeys. In particular, we see several intertextual connections to Jewish texts: judgment scenes in the *Testament of Abraham* 10.7–10 and the *Apocalypse of Zephaniah* 6.8–11, as well as the old, shining man from Dan. 7:13 and *1 Enoch (Similitudes)* 46–47.[9] Although the *Apocalypse of Paul* shows direct dependence upon Jewish apocalyptic traditions, the transposition of the God of Israel to a lower status, the mention of the Ogdoad, and bodily imprisonment betray the gnostic propensities of this text.[10] Thus, we see a performance of the apocalyptic Paul with stage lights that have the hue of Jewish and gnostic apocalyptic themes. With this background in mind, we can address the apocalyptic elements in the *Apocalypse*.

---

7. We should remember that the Jewish apocalypses that we have access to (e.g., *1 Enoch*) are primarily mediated to us through Christian communities and not Jewish ones. That is, whether they contain Christian accretions or not, these *Jewish* texts were of interest to *Christians* (even when not to Rabbinic Jews), so they also give us an indirect view on Christian perspectives.

8. John J. Collins, *The Apocalyptic Imagination: An Introduction to Jewish Apocalyptic Literature*, 2nd ed. (Grand Rapids: Eerdmans, 1998), 2–9.

9. In his extensive discussion of the *Apocalypse*, Michael Kaler notes in detail how our text conforms to the wider genre of apocalypses in late antiquity: *Flora Tells a Story: The Apocalypse of Paul and Its Contexts*, ESCJ 19 (Waterloo, ON: Wilfred Laurier, 2008), 98–189. Cf. George MacRae, "The Judgement Scene in the Coptic Apocalypse of Paul," in *Studies on the Testament of Abraham*, SBLSCS 6, ed. G. Nickelsburg (Missoula: Scholars, 1976), 285–300, at 285–86; Jean-Marc Rosenstiehl and Michael Kaler, *L'Apocalypse de Paul (NH V,2)*, Bibliothèque copte de Nag Hammadi, Section "Textes" 31 (Québec/Louvain: Presses de l'Université/Peeters, 2005), 238–39; Madeleine Scopello, "The Revelation of Paul," in *The Nag Hammadi Scriptures*, ed. Marvin Meyer (New York: HarperOne, 2007), 315.

10. Kaler, *Flora Tells a Story*, 182.

Paul as an Apocalyptic Character in the *Apocalypse of Paul*

Given the relatively short length of the *Apocalypse*, we have the opportunity to focus on the use of specific Pauline passages as well as wider apocalyptic themes. The most obvious Pauline text that comes to mind when reading the *Apocalypse* is Paul's ascent to the third heaven in 2 Cor. 12:1-5, yet key themes are also drawn from Galatians 1–2 (esp. 1:15-19) and Eph. 4:8-10. To evaluate the representation of Paul as an apocalyptic character, we will focus on the themes of revelatory experience and hidden knowledge, divine and spiritual agency, and individual eschatology.

Revelatory Experience and Hidden Knowledge

The otherworldly journey surely is the basis for the text bearing the title of an "Apocalypse," a revelation. Though this heavenly experience is different from that described by Paul in his letters (2 Corinthians 12; Galatians 1–2), this journey serves to confirm a common image with the letters: Paul is one who has experienced divine revelation, and therefore, he is to be considered as possessing equal authority with the other apostles. The revelation accounts in Galatians and 2 Corinthians serve to establish his apostolic authority vis-à-vis other apostolic leaders, with direct or indirect conflict in view. In the *Apocalypse*, however, there is no hint of conflict. Paul is on the mountain of Jericho and will be ascending to Jerusalem (an allusion to Gal. 1:17-18), where he will meet the twelve apostles. The ascent to Jerusalem is, therefore, re-interpreted as an ascent of the soul to the highest heavens, which is exactly what the rest of the *Apocalypse* entails.[11] Even though he sees the apostles bodily in creation (20.1-4), Paul also sees them ascending with him from the fourth to the fifth (21.28-30), and to the sixth (22.14-16) heavens. They are not mentioned in the seventh heaven, but he again encounters the apostles, his fellow spirits, in the eighth (24.1-3), ninth (24.4-6), and

---

11. Importantly, the "revelation" is not of (the most high) God or Christ, who are both absent from the whole of this text. Rather, it is a revelation of cosmological realities.

tenth heavens (24.7–8). He does not, in fact, meet anyone else—no other divine figures or mediators—in the highest heavens except for the apostles. Thus, in the *Apocalypse*, Paul's status as a spiritual authority is confirmed by his ability to ascend to this highest level. However, rather than situating his authority in contrast or distinction to the others, Paul cooperatively ascends to the highest level along with the apostles.

Like other apocalypses there is a tension between revealing hidden knowledge from the revelatory journey and keeping the mysteries secret. Paul is called to "Let your mind awaken . . . so that you may know the hidden things in those that are visible" (19.10–14). Paul is the model of the soul who learns this hidden knowledge about *himself* and about *the creator God*: 1) Concerning himself, Paul learns of his true spiritual nature and tells the old man "I am going to the place from which I came" (23.9–10), which is presumably the tenth heaven. 2) Concerning the creator God, he is one who governs the world of the dead as well as the lower heavens, and he tries to hold back the souls that attempt to ascend to the highest heavens. In several other apocalypses, the one on the celestial journey often receives a commission to share (if only partially) the details of the heavenly realities. Likewise, Paul has an implicit commission to share this knowledge, though his ministry is described esoterically as taking captive the captivity. This ministry, which subverts the demonic powers, brings us to the topic of divine and spiritual agency.

Divine and Spiritual Agency

Spiritual agency infuses the narrative of the *Apocalypse*. The activity of the Spirit vis-à-vis the judging and detaining demiurgic old man and his angels, who control the fourth through the seventh heavens, sets the context for the power dynamic within which Paul's ministry will take place. The function of the (demonic) angels, these principalities and authorities (ⲛⲁⲣⲭⲏ ⲙⲛ̄ ⲛⲉⲉⲓⲉⲝⲟⲩⲥⲓⲁ), is important to the whole narrative. Near the beginning of the entire account, the Spirit tells Paul to awaken his mind because of the agency of "principalities and authorities and archangels and powers and the whole race of demons" (19.3–5). As the story progresses, these evil powers serve as the main antagonists (besides the old man who controls them)—20.6–10; 22.2–10; 23.18–22, 28.[12] Accordingly, the main plight described in the narrative is the activity of these heavenly beings who torment, judge, and hinder the ascent of souls.

One of the key intertextual engagements with the Pauline letters relates to this demonic agency. In the seventh heaven, while Paul is being detained by the demiurgic old man, the old man asks, "Where are you from?" (23.11). Instead of his origin, Paul shares his destination: "I am going down to the world of the dead in order to lead captive the captivity that was led captive in the captivity of Babylon" (quoting Eph. 4:8–10). A distinct shift occurs from Ephesians 4 where Christ gives leaders to the church as a gift. Rather than Christ as the divine agent who takes the captives, it is Paul who will take the captives. However, when Paul returns to the world of the dead in the *Apocalypse*, this would serve a role not unlike those gifted leaders in Ephesians 4.

In contrast to the judging and imprisoning work of these demonic powers, the positive divine agent is the Holy Spirit. Indeed, Paul is led and empowered by the Holy Spirit throughout. The one who comes to Paul in the form of a little child (18.6, 13) is later identified as the Spirit (18.21), and this Holy Spirit is the one who guides Paul through each of the heavenly levels, often by speaking with him. It is important that we have not noted the agency of Christ in this work.[13] There is no mention of Christ in this text; only the Spirit leads, empowers, and enlightens Paul.[14] This coheres with Paul's distinctly *spiritual* eschatological experience, which we will address now.

---

12. Cf. Michael Kaler, "Pauline 'Powers and Authorities' at Nag Hammadi," *Archaeus* XI–XII (2007–2008): 37–59.
13. Though the child figure could be interpreted as Christ, as in other Gnostic texts and traditions (e.g., see *Apocryphon of John* 2.1–15; Hippolytus, *Elenchos* 6.42.2), the interpretation of the child as the Spirit in the text itself makes this unlikely.
14. Kaler, *Flora Tells a Story*, 192.

Individual Eschatology

The narrative is implicitly about the experience of life by ascent away from the world "of the dead" (20.9-10, 18-20; 23.13-14). However, the problem is not merely individual and anthropological; it involves the demonic agents who rule over the world of the dead. For example, the soul that is punished in the fourth heaven is charged on the basis of the testimony of three angels, but the angels were the very ones who led the soul into sin.[15] As the sins were committed "[in] the body" ([ⲉⲓϩ̄] ⲡⲥⲱⲙⲁ, 20.23, 29), the punishment for the soul is a return to a(nother) "body which had been prepared for it" (21.19-21). A body–spirit dualism is evident here, where the body is viewed as part of the punishment for sin. The anthropological problem of sin and imprisonment in the body are correlated and intertwined with the cosmic punishment carried out by the evil powers.

In distinction to bodily punishment enforced by these angels, the *Apocalypse* presents a spiritual ascent as the goal for believers. The souls that are able, such as Paul and the apostles, ascend to the highest heavens as spirits. While this eschatology presumes a separation from the body, the spiritual ascent to the heavens appears to be one that can be (partially) experienced in the present. Since there is no mention of Christ, the experience of death and life is only framed around a body–spirit dualism rather than an embodiment of Christ's death and resurrection, which is a primary focus in Paul's letters.

Now that we have explored the employment of particular Pauline texts and themes, we can analyze how the *Apocalypse* presents Pauline theology in an apocalyptic framework.

Preliminary Conclusions

After considering these apocalyptic elements—revelatory experience and hidden knowledge, divine and spiritual agency, and individual

---

15. When John Collins (*Apocalyptic Imagination*, 7) describes the elements that occur in Jewish apocalyptic texts, judgment or destruction of the wicked is the only element that occurs in all the texts he mentions.

eschatology—we have a basis to present a categorization of this text. Though the *Apocalypse* does not specifically use the OT, it has a decidedly retrospective point of view with regard to Jewish themes. That is, the theology presented here entails a radically new interpretation of the old, rather than a prospective view where the new is a fulfillment of previous promises. The creator God of Israel is (allusively) presented as the old man, the demiurge, who hinders souls rather than helps them. In fact, Kaler interprets this gnostic turn as a means of ironic transposition of the apocalyptic genre. Drawing from a similar critique by Pheme Perkins related to the *Apocalypse of Adam*,[16] Kaler argues that this is really an anti-apocalypse.[17] While the *Apocalypse of Paul* uses a variety of "apocalyptic clichés," the text also subverts the perspectives offered by more traditional Jewish texts: an angel is not his guide, but is actually a potentially subversive figure; the trial scene is a "mockery of divine justice"; and finally, Paul's experience of the creator God shows him to be a "threatening but ultimately ineffectual old man."[18] Kaler is responding to the decidedly retrospective paradigm in the text, where the new stands in strong discontinuity with the old, in contrast to Jewish apocalypses that work more from a prospective model. We will be able to assess this more fully once we incorporate the evidence from our second text. Accordingly, we now turn to explore the *Acts of Paul*.

The Acts of Paul

Rather than focusing on one narrative episode, as the *Apocalypse of Paul* does, the *Acts of Paul* is a collection of stories that narrate Paul's ministry and eventual martyrdom over the course of fourteen chapters.[19] Emphasizing continence and the resurrection, it includes

16. Pheme Perkins, "Apocalypse of Adam: The Genre and Function of a Gnostic Apocalypse," *CBQ* 39, no. 3 (1977): 382–95.
17. Kaler, *Flora Tells a Story*, 150–63.
18. Ibid., 155–56, cf. 170.
19. See the "Key to the Numeration of the *Acts of Paul*" provided by Jeremy Barrier, *The Acts of Paul and Thecla: A Critical Introduction and Commentary*, WUNT 2/270 (Tübingen: Mohr Siebeck, 2009), xvii–xx. Schneemelcher's translation, which I follow, only has 11 chapters because the other three chapters are fragmentary: Wilhelm Schneemelcher, "The Acts of Paul," *New Testament Apocrypha*,

numerous miracles (some fantastic, such as the baptism of a lion) and several run-ins with civic authorities as Paul travels on one single journey from Damascus to Rome with various stops along the way. The textual tradition, as we have it, includes subsections, such as the well-known *Acts of Paul and Thecla*, *3 Corinthians*, and the *Martyrdom of Paul*. These sections later circulated independently (and possibly before, especially *3 Corinthians*), but our earliest manuscripts contain all the major sections together, so I will treat the work as a whole here.[20]

The *Acts of Paul* stands with a handful of other apocryphal acts—*Acts of John, Peter, Andrew, Thomas,* and *Philip*—written in the second and third centuries.[21] There has been a question of genre regarding these acts: are they filling in the gaps of the canonical Acts, or something else? An increasingly popular opinion is that the acts are modeled more on the gospels than on Luke's Acts, in that they focus on the miraculous life of one protagonist and then (except for *Acts of John*) record his martyrdom.[22] (In fact, given the lack of continuity with Luke's Acts, there is a question of whether the author of the *Acts of Paul* even knew of the canonical work.) Accordingly, the very structure of the *Acts of Paul* demonstrates an affinity between the main character (Paul) and Christ.

With this general framework in mind, we can now address the *Acts of Paul* directly with our question of how it presents Paul as an apocalyptic theologian.

Paul as an Apocalyptic Character in the *Acts of Paul*

The *Acts of Paul* (APaul) is much longer than the *Apocalypse*, so our treatment of themes and topics will be more synthetic. That said, the discussion of how Paul is presented as an apocalyptic theologian is

---

Rev. ed., Wilhelm Schneemelcher, ed.; trans. Robert McL. Wilson (Philadelphia: Westminster John Knox, 2003 [1992]), 2:237–65.

20. Schneemelcher, "The Acts of Paul," 2:216, 230–31.
21. There is debate about the date of composition, but based upon external witnesses and the manuscripts the proposed date of editing/writing is mid-to-late second century.
22. See Andrew Gregory, "The *Acts of Paul* and the Legacy of Paul," in *Paul and the Second Century: The Legacy of Paul's Life, Letters, and Teaching*, eds. M. Bird and J. Dodson; LNTS 412 (London: T&T Clark, 2011), 169–89, at 172–74.

based on a selection of relevant texts from throughout the narrative. We will address the following apocalyptic elements: divine and spiritual agency, resurrection hope and apocalyptic ethics, and political engagement.

Divine and Spiritual Agency

One primary element in apocalyptic writings is the activity of God in rectifying the problem of evil in the world, which is often perpetrated by cosmic powers. In *APaul*, God's past action through Christ's death and resurrection is evident, and God remains active throughout the narrative. It is infused with the miraculous, namely, numerous healings (*APaul* 2, 5) and people are even raised from the dead (*APaul* 5, 14). In addition to divine agency, the influence of angelic beings is also important, such as Satanic opposition and the appearances of angels (e.g., 3.6; 5; 9.2–3; 9.19).

God's action to save Christians from persecution is especially noteworthy (3.22; 6; 9.22–27). For example, Paul and Thecla have a variety of visionary experiences of Christ himself in persecution settings, which attest to his continued active role in the world. In one instance, Thecla sees a vision of Christ (3.21), and after being saved from her second death sentence, she prays, "My God, . . . Christ Jesus the Son of God, my helper in prison, my helper before governors, my helper in the fire, my helper among the beasts, you are God and to you be glory forever" (4.17). With this direct and unambiguous affirmation of the deity of Christ, the shape of God's activity in the narrative is shown to be distinctly christological in nature.

After one encounter where an angel appears to Paul and speaks in tongues about Paul's upcoming persecution at Pentecost (9.2–3), Paul explains that he cannot be sad because "the Spirit which fell <upon me> from the Father is he who preached to me the Gospel of his Son, that I might live in him. Indeed, there is no life except life which is in Christ" (9.5). Paul then recounts his first "revelation of Christ" in Damascus (9.6). Thus, his initial revelation of Christ through the Spirit enables him to reframe his later experience of suffering in a christological manner, and these sufferings allow him to experience new life.

In fact, this christological framing of Paul's experience is evident in a subsequent vision of Christ. As Paul heads to Rome by boat, Christ appears to him walking upon the sea (*APaul* 13). Christ looks downcast, and Paul is disturbed and enquires why. The Lord responds, "Paul, I am about to be crucified afresh" (13.2). Misunderstanding this as a literal, second crucifixion, Paul objects. In response, Christ reiterates the call for Paul to go up to Rome, a call the Spirit had already revealed to him and others earlier (12.2–5). Rather than Christ literally being crucified again, Paul's death will serve as an embodiment of Christ's crucifixion. Thus, we again see how the christological perspective reframes the meaning of Paul's experience and presents God as still active even in the midst of evil events.

Though the larger plot is framed around Paul embodying the experience of *Christ* in his missionary journey, the narrative is also permeated with the leading and revealing work of the *Spirit*. Likely in response to the disjunctive readings of the OT by gnostic opponents, as is evident in the concerns of 3 *Corinthians* (10.1–2), the narrator highlights the Spirit's inspiration of the OT prophets (10.4.9–10; 13.5–6). This same Spirit is the one who inaugurates the incarnation of Christ (10.4.5–6; 10.4.12–14; 13.7) and who leads and empowers Paul and other Christian prophets (9.7–9; 12.2). Thus, God's economic activity is presented through the lens of proto-Trinitarian theology.

In contrast to the work of God himself through Christ and the Spirit, the work of demonic powers against God and his economy is evident. Besides general demonic oppression (cf. *APaul* 7), the emphasis is more directly on the devil. There are ascriptions to the "adversary" (*APaul* 6), "the lawless one" (10.2), "the evil one" (10.4.2; 14.3), and the "devil" (14.1). Accordingly, the nature of salvation through the incarnate Christ is a defeat of this evil one, as 3 *Corinthians* 10.4.14–16 explains: Mary "received the Holy Spirit in her womb that Jesus might enter into the world, in order that the evil one might be conquered through the same flesh by which he held sway. . . . For by his own body Jesus

Christ saved all flesh <and brought it to eternal life through faith>." Thus, in congruity with Jewish and Christian apocalypses, the *Acts of Paul* frames the human drama as one in which cosmic players—God and other spiritual agents—are in opposition. God has overcome the evil one through Christ, but his kingdom will not fully appear until later (14.2). This already/not yet assessment of time leads to a reassessment of the world's values in light of the impending resurrection, as we will see now.

Resurrection Hope and Apocalyptic Ethics

The focus on the resurrection is prominent throughout the entire narrative.[23] The first two chapters are quite fragmentary, but the first full section we have is the well-known *Acts of Paul and Thecla* (*APaul* 3–4). In chapter 3, the emphasis on the resurrection of Christ establishes the importance of this theme for the rest of the narrative (3.1, 6, 15–18, 25, 30). In fact, the hope of a future resurrection in the pattern of Christ (e.g., 3.39) grounds the eschatological reevaluation of the traditional social and economic values.

The nature of the resurrection hope in *APaul* is most evident in the *3 Corinthians* exchange (10.1–5). The letter refutes a number of generic gnostic claims: issues related to resurrection, Jesus not coming in the flesh, and the world being created by angels rather than God (10.2). In response, Paul defends the bodily life and resurrection of Christ and then gives a variety of defenses for the resurrection of the "flesh" (σάρξ), such as the seed metaphor, the example of Jonah, and the corpse rising when it touched Elisha's bones (10.5.24–32). This text stands as a materialist perspective on the resurrection in opposition to gnostic immaterialist conceptions of eschatology.[24] In the letter,

---

23. See P. Lalleman, "The Resurrection in the Acts of Paul," in *The Apocryphal Acts of Paul and Thecla*, ed. J. Bremmer (Kampen: Pharos, 1996), 126–41.

24. White (*Remembering Paul*, 121–34) critiques *3 Corinthians* for rejecting Paul's real meaning in 1 Corinthians 15. Besides the incongruity with White's overall proposal to get beyond "who got Paul right," one could argue that *3 Corinthians* is likely closer to Paul's meaning than the gnostic opponents. Even if we concede that Paul intended the resurrection to be understood in a pneuma-material way (so White), one could argue that the sarx-material reading of *3 Corinthians* would still be closer to Paul's theology than a gnostic immaterialist reading which *3 Corinthians* is opposing.

Paul then correlates the hope of resurrection to his willingness to suffer, and he holds out that same assurance to others who believe and remain faithful even in hardships (10.6.34–36). In contrast, there is punishment for those who turn away from Christ (10.6.37–38). This distinct emphasis on resurrection of the body allows for an eschatological reframing of life.

Indeed, this hope of a *future* resurrection is the foundation for a *present* apocalyptic ethic. In fact, the only theme more prominent than the resurrection of the flesh in the entire narrative is the call to renounce the passions of the flesh, as the emphasis on chastity and fasting throughout make clear. Yet, these topics are not unrelated. For example, the narrator summarizes Paul's message in the Thecla section in this manner: Paul gave "the word of God concerning continence and resurrection" (3.5). In the subsequent rendition of the beatitudes, Paul preaches, "blessed are the bodies of virgins . . . for the word of the Father shall be for them a work of salvation in the day of his Son" (3.6). The eschatological return of Christ leads women (and men) to reevaluate the world's sexual standards. And yet, the commands are just as pointed to those who are married: "Blessed are they who have wives as if they did not, for they shall be heirs to God" (3.5). This draws directly from 1 Cor. 7:29, where one of the Pauline letters also advocates for an apocalyptically informed ethic. This encratic preaching sets up the following narrative where, in obedience to Paul and disobedience to her parents, Thecla's refusal of her betrothed destabilizes familial and wider social structures, as evidenced by the involvement of the magistrates.[25] An eschatological perspective is thus the basis for this reevaluation of traditional values which undergird the culture. Indeed, those in opposition to Paul describe his basic message as this: "There is no resurrection for you, except that you remain chaste and do not defile the flesh, but keep it pure" (3.12). The reiteration of eschatological aspirations—the hope of "resurrection," of "salvation in the day of [God's] Son," and of inheritance ("they shall

---

25. See John Barclay's essay in this volume (chapter 15). In particular, Barclay is right that the challenge of singleness is not merely the renunciation of pleasure, but also destabilizes the fabric of society that is built upon children who will provide a form of immortality and economic output.

be heirs of God")—repeatedly serves to ground this reevaluation of social values and the resulting ethic of renunciation.

Just as the positive ends of discipleship motivate obedience, negative outcomes of rebellion are the basis for turning away from disobedience. In Paul's later sermons and speeches, he recounts the impending judgment on those who do not follow Christ (e.g., 9.13; 10.6.37–38). Not only is there eschatological punishment for disobedience, Paul advocates detachment due to the ephemeral nature of this world. Speaking to the wife of a governor, Paul reminds her that the things of this life—gold, riches, clothing, beauty, great cities, even the world itself—will ultimately wear away, but God alone remains and those in his family (9.17). Though framed with a different argument, the perspective is the same: when viewed in the light of eschatological hopes, Christians must detach themselves from traditional objects of value—whether sexual pleasure and social stability through children, or wealth that secures a comfortable lifestyle. Rather, they must invest in abiding goods, grounded in the one who abides eternally.

In addition to a willingness to renounce family and wealth, *APaul* equally presents a willingness to suffer for obedience to Christ. Paul and others suffer, not only due to their willingness to count eschatological goods of greater value than temporal ones, but also due to popular (and even political) rejection of the gospel (*APaul* 2, 9, 11, 12, 14). As noted earlier, a prominent theme is that God protects in the midst of the experiences of suffering (*APaul* 3–4, 11) and, in the end, through resurrection (*APaul* 3, 10). Thecla, for example, is condemned to die twice by political authorities for her devotion to continence (3.18–22; 4.1–38). As God saves her from the second punishment, she has the opportunity to testify about her motivation for persevering: God "alone is the goal of salvation and the foundation of the immortal life. To the storm-tossed, he is a refuge; to the oppressed, relief; to the despairing, shelter; in a word, whoever does not believe in him shall not live but die forever" (4.12). The eschatological telos of life or death, resulting respectively from salvation from God or rejection of God, is the basis for her willingness to reevaluate the ephemeral suffering in this world.

A leitmotif in the narrative is that family members and civic leaders—Roman magistrates and even the Emperor himself—will often respond to this radical obedience with hostility, even deadly opposition. Accordingly, we will conclude where the *Acts of Paul* concludes, the topic of politics.

Apocalypse Against Empire

Throughout the narrative the main characters are imprisoned and punished by civic authorities for their faith (*APaul* 3–4, 6, 9, 10, 14).[26] In the earlier sections of *APaul,* civic opposition primarily arises due to Paul's message of continence, whereas in Paul's *Martyrdom* (*APaul* 14) Nero's anger is provoked because of the decidedly political and martial language: 1) Christ is the "king" (βασιλεύς) who will destroy all other "kingdoms" (βασιλεῖαι), and 2) believers are "soldiers" (στρατιῶται) who serve in his army. Having addressed the social ramifications of continence above, we will focus here on the issue of Christ's kingdom.

The root βασιλε- occurs 13 times in chapter 14, showing its distinct importance. All the main Christian characters in the story affirm Jesus Christ as "King"—Patroclus (14.2), Barsabas Justus, Urion, Festus (14.2), and Paul (14.3, 4). In particular, Jesus is described as "the King of the Ages" (ὁ βασιλεὺς τῶν αἰώνων, 14.2) and "the great king" (ὁ μέγας βασιλεύς). In the interchange between Nero and his slave Patroclus, Nero asks if Jesus "will destroy all [other] kingdoms" (14.2). Patroclus responds affirmatively: "He alone shall be forever [τῶν αἰώνων], and there shall be no kingdom which shall escape him." A significant part of this kingdom is God's action to judge the world through Christ. Paul tells Nero that "in one day he [Christ] will destroy the world with fire" (14.3) and that the "Lord Christ Jesus . . . is coming to judge the world"

---

26. Ann Graham Brock's comparison with the *Acts of Peter* shows the distinctly subversive stance of the *Acts of Paul* toward social convention, and especially, civic accommodation: "Political Authority and Cultural Accommodation: Social Diversity in the *Acts of Paul* and the *Acts of Peter,*" in *The Apocryphal Acts of the Apostles,* F. Bovon, A. G. Brock, and C. Matthews, eds. (Cambridge: Harvard University, 1999), 145–69.

(14.4). God's kingdom will be established by purifying the world by fire, and those who are the members of the kingdom will be saved through resurrection.

This eschatological and heavenly kingdom challenges not only Rome's identity, but also the work of the evil one, whose role in the *Martyrdom* is clear (14.2–3). Paul does not actively subvert the political structure of the empire. Yet, the Christian ethic and devotion to an alternate kingdom is viewed as subversive by civic authorities, which is why Paul and his companions are repeatedly arrested and punished. To halt the perceived insurrection in Rome, Paul is beheaded (14.4–5), and yet, the narrator shows that Paul triumphs over death because he reappears to Nero and proclaims, "I am not dead, but alive in my God" (14.6). The local and ephemeral empire of Nero is shown to be a mere passing shadow in light of the universal and eternal kingdom of Christ. Christians thus grounded their ethic of sociopolitical identity in Christ and his kingdom, with the result that they embodied his narrative rather than a Roman one.[27]

With these apocalyptic themes in mind, we can now assess the image of Pauline theology presented here.

Preliminary Conclusions

After considering these apocalyptic elements—divine and spiritual agency, resurrection hope and apocalyptic ethics, and politics—we have a basis to present a categorization of this text. In distinction to the *Apocalypse*, the *Acts of Paul* presents a higher degree of continuity with the OT and Judaism, particularly with the description of the Spirit's work in prophecy, which would correspond to a prospective interpretive strategy. However, the primary image presented here is one of renunciation of the things of this world in light of the eschatological reevaluation of the world's goods. Christians are not

---

27. Accordingly, *APaul* functions as what Portier-Young calls *discursive* resistance, asserting God's supremacy over Nero (and, by extension, the Roman empire) by asserting the success of Christ's kingdom over against all kingdoms and by foretelling Nero's future judgment for his abuse of power. Anathea Portier-Young, *Apocalypse against Empire: Theologies of Resistance in Early Judaism* (Grand Rapids: Eerdmans, 2011). See also, John Goodrich's essay in this volume (chapter 16).

actively trying to dismantle the social, economic, and political structures, but their non-participation or radically re-oriented participation in these structures presents a real critique and subversion of those systems. At the same time, by highlighting the resurrection of the flesh, the creational order is not fully rejected. Accordingly, the text has prospective and retrospective elements, but the strong eschatological critique presents more of a retrospective point of view. That is, it reinterprets what has come before in light of the Christ-event, rather than vice versa. In this case, it is not so much Judaism that is reevaluated, but cultural norms. This retrospective approach is nuanced, in that it maintains continuity with key OT elements such as a physical creation and the work of the Spirit in the prophets.[28]

Now that we have assessed the *Apocalypse of Paul* and the *Acts of Paul* separately, we can now draw together our conclusions on the question of Paul and apocalyptic from the lens of second-century texts.

Ancient and Contemporary Views on the Apocalyptic Paul

With these two second-century texts, we see that the debate about how to understand Paul as an apocalyptic theologian is not new; it dates back to the earliest reception of his letters as they conveyed the nature of God's action in the world to resolve the problem of evil. Both of these texts represent attempts to understand Paul and to communicate their own theology in light of Paul's life. Neither merely parrots Paul or simply "got Paul right" (or wrong); in fact, none would be able to do that because interpretive contexts constantly change. Koschorke is therefore correct when he states, "Denn der Streit dürfte je länger je mehr nicht darum gegangen sein, *ob* Paulus, sondern *welcher* Paulus Gültigkeit beanspruchen könne."[29] With this diversity in mind, we can evaluate and compare the way early readers of Paul utilized his

---

28. In that way, the *APaul* follows a reading strategy similar to that of Richard Hays, which is retrospective but framed in continuity with the past. See the Introduction essay in this volume.
29. Koschorke, "Paulus in den Nag-Hammadi-Texten," 203.

memory and how this can help contemporary discussions of Paul as an apocalyptic theologian.

These two texts, the *Apocalypse of Paul* and the *Acts of Paul*, give us direct windows into how second-century writers/editors appropriated Paul's letters and his story through different apocalyptic frameworks. Though they drew on different Pauline material and presented it different ways, both texts portray Paul in an apocalyptic key. For example, they both highlight divine and spiritual agency as well as individual eschatology. They also present retrospective readings, though of different sorts: the *Apocalypse*'s reading is more strongly critical of a Jewish narrative, whereas the Jewish prophetic narrative in the *Acts of Paul* is treated positively, to the extent that it is mentioned. However, both consider the new revelation as a means radically to reinterpret the prior—Jewish or cultural—narratives.

The distinction, however, between the two texts is most evident when we consider how they present the issue of divine agency. With its sole focus on the Spirit, the *Apocalypse* obviously brackets out a significant aspect of the christological theology of Paul's letters. Like the letters, the *Acts of Paul* is more balanced in this regard with a strongly *christological* focus combined with an emphasis on the agency of the Spirit. Although I prefer the distinction of "better" and "worse" readings rather than "right" and "wrong" readings, the absence of Christ in the *Apocalypse* narrative undercuts the foundation on which all of Paul's theology stands. This is an aspect where the *Apocalypse* clearly got Paul wrong. And I suspect—in line with Paul's defense of his revealed-from-God, centered-on-Christ gospel—he would say to the writer of the *Apocalypse*, "If any angel (or Spirit) from heaven should proclaim to you another Gospel [than that of Christ], let him be accursed!"[30] This issue notwithstanding, the *Apocalypse of Paul*, like the *Acts of Paul*, is still helpful for highlighting ways of reading and understanding Paul.[31]

---

30. Cf. Gal. 1:8–9.
31. While noting the differences, Harrison perhaps makes the distinction between Paul and the *Apocalypse* too strong: James R. Harrison, "In the Quest of the Third Heaven: Paul and His Apocalyptic Imitators," *VC* 58, no. 1 (2004): 24–55.

When we bring these perspectives into conversation with our contemporary debate, we see that their frameworks do not always fit our patterns. For instance, the discussion in this volume is centered on two primary paradigms: retrospective and prospective.[32] The *Apocalypse* has a distinctly retrospective critique of the creator God. On the other hand, the *Acts of Paul* accepts certain creational values, such as the fleshly body, while also renouncing others like marriage. Even with this nuance, the reading strategy appears to be more retrospective. Of course, Paul's letters provide additional prospectively oriented fodder not addressed in these texts, which makes the interpretive decisions difficult. Nevertheless, these two witnesses give a glimpse of the variety of ways that Paul's theology and letters could be appropriated and (re)interpreted in different contexts.[33]

Our own interpretive contexts have unique influences and give rise to different questions, though some do engage these prior readings in this contemporary debate. In contrast to the narrative of the *Acts of Paul*, the type of reading the *Apocalypse* offers will be more familiar to most NT scholars who are more aware of gnosticism, and particularly, Marcionism—a cousin of gnostic thought represented in the *Apocalypse*. To the extent that they mention it, those in the contemporary Eschatological Invasion group (as described in this volume's Introduction) explicitly repudiate affinities with Marcionite retrospective readings. The fact that Martyn feels constrained to

---

32. Regarding the retrospective–prospective distinction, we should note that, in some sense, all Christian texts will likely have some element of a retrospective point of view. That is, if they were fully prospective, they would be indistinguishable from other Jewish texts. Also, given the nature of the Christ-event as arising through the surprising means of death and resurrection and as causing a new form of reality (even if it is in continuity with what has been promised before). Accordingly, the revelation of God in Christ cannot help but create some form of a new perspective on the nature of prior narratives and expectations. At the same time, no story is fully retrospective in the sense that issues of plight were absolutely restated, as if people did not understand or even know of death and evil powers before. By speaking of prospective and retrospective we are working with a spectrum, in which both terms contain elements of continuity and discontinuity.

33. Some would definitely question Irenaeus's credentials as an apocalyptic theologian, but if he were considered a witness in this debate, he would definitely represent a *prospective* (seeing Christ as a climax of OT promises) reading. See, e.g., my "The Covenant of Promise: Abraham in Irenaeus," in *Irenaeus and Paul*, eds. T. Still and D. Willhite (London: Bloomsbury, forthcoming). For a discussion of other apocalyptic elements, such as visionary experiences, see my "Paul and Irenaeus," in *Paul and the Second Century: The Legacy of Paul's Life, Letters, and Teaching*, eds. M. Bird and J. Dodson, LNTS 412 (London: T&T Clark, 2011), 190–206, at 194–95.

defend himself against resurrecting a form of Marcionism shows that more than one has seen the similarities between his reading strategy and theirs:[34] The radical newness in Christ has little continuity with what has gone before, what precedes Christ is only from the god of this world, and the law is mediated by (evil?) angels.[35] Martyn rightly defends himself by arguing that the temporal dualism in Paul cannot be confused for the ontological dualism in (some forms of) gnosticism that separates the physical from the spiritual and the creator from the most high God.[36]

Just as the American, two-party political system does not capture the diversity of contemporary political perspectives, neither does the retrospective and prospective taxonomy simply limit things. The diversity of ways apocalyptic texts employ biblical themes and texts shows they can expound, subvert, and transpose these themes when reframed for a new context. This complex of similarities and differences with Paul should not just be regarded according to a polarity of good or bad projections of Paul. Rather, the reception of his letters and life provides us with an interesting lens on Paul himself that leads us back yet again to the complexities we see in his own letters.

34. See J. Louis Martyn, *Galatians: A New Translation with Introduction and Commentary*, AB 33A (New York and London: Doubleday, 1997), 34. See also Douglas Campbell's essay in this volume (chapter 4).
35. E.g., Martyn, *Galatians*, 356.
36. Martyn, *Galatians*, 34.

10

Some Remarks on Apocalyptic in Modern Christian Theology

Philip G. Ziegler

"The end is beginning, signifies the apocalyptic tone."[1]

"We are living in apocalyptic times without an apocalyptic faith and theology."[2]

Introduction—Apocalyptic as Theological Problem and Prospect

When the intractable presence of New Testament apocalyptic was rediscovered around the start of the twentieth century, it was

---

1. Jacques Derrida, "Of an Apocalyptic Tone Recently Adopted in Philosophy," *Oxford Literary Review* 6, no. 2 (1984): 3–37, at 24.
2. Carl Braaten, "The Recovery of Apocalyptic Imagination," in *The Last Things: Biblical and Theological Perspectives on Eschatology*, eds. B. Braaten and R. Jenson (Grand Rapids: Eerdmans, 2002), 14–32, at 26.

acknowledged to be at once an historical fact and a theological impossibility. The parousiac Jesus and his adventist Kingdom of God, the agonistic dualism of "the ages" and its imminent catastrophic final resolution, the mythic cosmic imaginings and martial metaphysics of salvation—while all of this was, no doubt, the very stuff of primitive Christian faith and witness, it was also now, as Feuerbach had earlier said of Christianity as such, "nothing more than a *fixed idea,* in flagrant contradiction with our fire and life assurance companies, our railroads and steam-carriages, our picture and sculpture galleries, our military and industrial schools, our theatres and scientific museums."[3] Contemporary theology found itself simply *at a loss* as regards biblical apocalyptic: such ancient forms of thought—being "an excrescence . . . rank and wild" properly "left behind in the gothic nursery of the human imagination"[4]—are simply uninhabitable by us moderns; their concepts and idioms are a thoroughly devalued currency with no purchase in or upon the present.[5] "Eschatology in the strict sense, with all its apocalyptic features," it was agreed, "has long ago passed out of our view of the world."[6] For these reasons, original eschatological density and contemporary dogmatic credibility stood in strictly inverse proportion to one another.[7]

The start of our own twenty-first century has brought with it the suggestion that the relation between the original eschatological density of the New Testament witness and contemporary credibility of

3. Ludwig Feuerbach, from the preface to the second edition of *The Essence of Christianity,* trans. G. Eliot (London: J. Chapman, 1854).

4. William Sanday, "The Apocalyptic Element in the Gospels," *The Hibbert Journal* 10 (October 1911): 83–109, at 104; Theodore W. Jennings, Jr. "Apocalyptic and Contemporary Theology," *Quarterly Review* 4, no. 3 (1984): 54–68, at 54.

5. The German title of Klaus Koch's book, *The Rediscovery of Apocalyptic,* translated by M. Kohl (London: SCM, 1972), expresses this clearly: modern theology finds itself *Ratlos vor der Apokalyptik.* The currency metaphor is Johannes Weiss's own; see *Jesus' Proclamation of the Kingdom of God* (Philadelphia: Fortress Press, 1971). For a concise and critical assessment of this trope and its significance, see Christopher Morse, "'If Johannes Weiss is Right . . .': A Brief Retrospective on Apocalyptic Theology," in *Apocalyptic and the Future of Theology: With and Beyond J. Louis Martyn,* eds. J. B. Davis and D. Harink (Eugene: Cascade, 2012), 137–53.

6. So Walter Lowrie in his "Introduction" to Albert Schweitzer, *The Mystery of the Kingdom of God,* trans. W. Lowrie (New York: Dodd, Mead & Co., 1914), 40.

7. So thought Weiss, Schweitzer, Troeltsch, et al. "If the Kingdom of God is an eschatological matter, then it is a useless concept as far as dogmatics is concerned"—Julius Kaftan as reported by Rudolf Bultmann, "Introduction" to Johannes Weiss, *Jesus Proclamation of the Kingdom of God,* trans. R. H. Hiers and D. L. Holland (Philadelphia: Fortress Press, 1971), xi.

Christian dogmatics can and must be fundamentally reset. In view is a new kind of "apocalyptic theology" that overturns the high modern view of apocalyptic as a merely antiquarian curiosity while, at the same time, repudiating the weaponized eschatologies of soothsaying doomsday calendarists, often popularly associated with "apocalypticism."

So it is that convocating mainline seminarians may now be instructed that they must appropriate an apocalyptic "attitude" and "movement of mind," because their ministry and the churches they will serve "can never make do or be legitimate . . . without the themes of the radical sovereignty of God and the exercise of that sovereignty through the cross and resurrection of [God's] royal agent, Jesus Christ."[8] And academic theologians are openly advised that they "should press forward to a robust recovery of apocalyptic teaching and preaching" precisely because such is "pressed upon us by the character of the New Testament witnesses themselves" in texts that deliver a gospel that is "apocalyptic to the core."[9] Indeed, it has been suggested that we *need* apocalyptic as a "pertinent, perhaps essential" contemporary discourse if we are to rise to meet the theological challenges of the present day.[10] Over the course of a century, something decisive has shifted in our discernment of the proper relation between biblical apocalyptic and contemporary Christian dogmatics.

Essential to any telling of the story of this reversal of sensibility is the emerging conviction that the apocalyptic idiom of the New Testament is itself an indispensable *theological* vocabulary and is recognizable as such for all its strangeness.[11] This is to say that it

---

8. Thomas W. Gillespie, "Studying Theology in Apocalyptic Times," *Princeton Seminary Bulletin* 23, no. 1 (2002): 1–10, at 7.

9. Richard B. Hays, "'Why do stand looking up toward heaven?' New Testament Eschatology at the Turn of the Millennium," *Modern Theology* 16, no. 1 (2000): 115–35, at 133.

10. Walter Lowe, "Why We Need Apocalyptic," *SJT* 63, no. 1 (2010): 41–53, at 41.

11. For various tellings of the story, see Jennings, "Apocalyptic and Contemporary Theology"; Joshua B. Davis, "The Challenge of Apocalyptic to Modern Theology," in *Apocalyptic and the Future of Theology: With and Beyond J. Louis Martyn*, eds. J. B. Davis and D. Harink (Eugene: Cascade, 2012), 1–50; and from a different perspective, Cyril O'Regan, *Theology and the Spaces of Apocalyptic* (Milwaukee: Marquette University Press, 2009).

represents an originary theological discourse with which Christians described the world—and we in it—with relentless formative reference to the sovereign God of the gospel of salvation in Jesus Christ. The recovery of apocalyptic in theology begins when we discern that this disquieting evangelical idiom is not merely an historic fixture of early Christian witness, but also, something that can and must, in some sense, be recovered as a permanent feature of Christian faith and theology so long as we are about the business of the gospel. The force of Käsemann's famous dictum about apocalyptic being the "mother of Christian theology" is at least to suggest that "apocalyptic narrative and apocalyptic expectation are integral to the logic of the gospel" itself, and so, indispensable to any theological reflection keyed to it.[12] One might say that in Easter's wake, among the tongues that came upon an early church in receipt of the Spirit was the language of Christian apocalyptic, and that it is a tongue theologians may still learn to speak and to interpret.

From among the many things that can and should be done to further elucidate these claims and to fill out the wider theological context within which the "apocalyptic turn" in contemporary theology might be understood, in what follows, I undertake only two. First, I address the question of the place of the figure of Karl Barth, paying particular attention to the important, yet somewhat ambivalent, role played by his work in recent apocalyptic theological reflection. Second, and in a different mode, I present a series of six tersely annotated dogmatic theses. The aim of these theses is to signal concisely why apocalyptic might be considered both essential and relevant for the doing of contemporary theology, as well as something of what might be at stake in the ongoing business of appropriating New Testament—and in particular Pauline—apocalyptic impulses.

---

12. Käsemann's original paper, "The Beginnings of Christian Theology," is collected together with a range of responses in the *Journal of Theology and Church*, volume 6 *Apocalypticism*, edited by R. W. Funk (New York: Herder & Herder, 1969). The quoted words are from Richard B. Hays, "'Why do you stand looking up toward heaven?,'" 116.

Karl Barth—Pioneering Pauline Apocalyptic?

"Paul is the proper name for a ferment in the history of Christianity."[13]

The emerging apocalyptic sensibility in theology with which we are concerned is one inspired by a fresh hearing of the evangelical witness of Paul. Perhaps unsurprisingly, then, the name of Karl Barth is often encountered in the work of its advocates. For Barth's early theology, as crystallized around the second edition of the *Romans* commentary, was marked by a volatile conspiracy of themes, which together fill out the meaning of the *Krisis* that Paul's gospel represents: the radical *priority* of divine agency in salvation, the uncompromisingly "vertical" or transcendent nature of God's action, the real evangelical *power* of God—a theme taken up from the Blumhardts—the inviolate *particularity* of the incarnation, and the sharp *contrast* between the old upon which God's grace and Spirit fall, and the new thing brought into being thereby.[14] Barth swept all these themes up into the meaning of the term "eschatology" as it appears in his famous declaration that "if Christianity be not altogether eschatology, there remains in it no relationship whatever with Christ."[15] It often pointed out that the dialectical logic of Barth's early eschatology is more Platonic than not, exercising a merely negative relation between a timeless eternity and temporal reality.[16] Yet, it is also true that under the formative weight of Paul's own concepts, categories, and arguments, Barth was steadily driven to recast his eschatology in the form of a christological objectivism that offered an arguably "apocalyptic supplement" to received Protestant accounts of the gospel of salvation.[17]

---

13. Simon Critchley, *The Faith of the Faithless: Experiments in Political Theology* (London: Verso, 2012), 156.
14. A concise and direct treatment of these motifs is offered by Geoff Thompson, "From Invisible Redemption to Invisible Hopeful Action in Karl Barth," in *Messianism, Apocalypse and Redemption in 20th Century German Thought*, eds. W. Cristaudo and W. Baker (Adelaide: ATF, 2006), 49–62, at 50–54. On the influence of the Blumhardts for Barth's developing theology, see Christian T. Collins Winn, *"Jesus is Victor!" The Significance of the Blumhardts for the Theology of Karl Barth* (Eugene: Pickwick, 2009), esp. 155–207 (chapter 4).
15. Karl Barth, *The Epistle to the Romans*, trans. E. Hoskyns (Oxford: Oxford University Press, 1933), 314.
16. For exemplary criticism of Barth's "transcendent eschatology" in this vein, see Jürgen Moltmann, *The Theology of Hope*, trans. J. W. Leitch (London: SCM, 1967), 50–58. Cf. J. Christiaan Beker, *Paul the Apostle: The Triumph of God in Life and Thought* (Philadelphia: Fortress Press, 1984), 142–43, where Barth is treated summarily as an instance of a "neo-orthodoxy" that evacuates future eschatology into one at once over-realized in Christology and utterly tangential to historical reality.

In taking inspiration, in particular, from the Pauline scholarship of Ernst Käsemann and J. Louis Martyn, contemporary apocalyptic theology draws upon two thinkers who themselves admit Barth's notable influence. Käsemann did not need Barth to introduce him to Paul's apocalyptic gospel of course. Yet, by his own admission, the German exegete devoured Barth's writings "ravenously" during a formative period.[18] As David Way explains, Barth's hermeneutical program announced in the prefaces to his *Romans* were "of the greatest importance for the formation of Käsemann's views of the task of interpretation," cementing his conviction that Paul be read in light of his controlling subject matter—namely, God in his coming.[19] Käsemann did draw upon Barth at various individual points in his reading of Paul's letter; but Barth's influence was most significant in relation to two comprehensive concerns central to Käsemann's exegetical theology—namely, the Lordship of Christ and the "theological appropriation of Paul's eschatology."[20] Like Barth's, Käsemann's reading of Paul is funded by an acknowledgement that the Apostle, his vocation, his communities, and his witness to the gospel, all "exist from the very first within the eschatological parameter"—a parameter which is identical with Christ's salutary reign unto God.[21]

17. On this, see Bruce L. McCormack, "Can We Still Speak of 'Justification by Faith'? An In-house Debate with Apocalyptic Readings of Paul," in *Galatians and Christian Theology: Justification, the Gospel, and Ethics in Paul's Letter*, eds. M. Elliott et al. (Grand Rapids: Baker Academic, 2014), 177–83, and more extensively, Bruce L. McCormack, "Longing for a New World: On Socialism, Eschatology and Apocalyptic in Barth's Early Dialectical Theology," in *Theologie im Umbruch der Moderne: Karl Barths frühe Dialektische Theologie*, eds. G. Pfleiderer and H. Matern (Zürich: TVZ, 2014), 135–49. Cf. Shannon Nicole Smythe, "Karl Barth in Conversation with Pauline Apocalypticism," in *Karl Barth in Conversation*, eds. W. T. McMacken and D. Congdon (Eugene: Wipf & Stock, 2014), 195–210, for reflections on the broad congruence of aspects of Barth's theology with key features of the apocalyptic reading of Paul.

18. Ernst Käsemann, "A Theological Review," in *On Being a Disciple of the Crucified Nazarene*, trans. by R. A. Harrisville (Grand Rapids: Eerdmans, 2010), xv.

19. David V. Way, *The Lordship of Christ: Ernst Käsemann's Interpretation of Paul's Theology*, Oxford Theological Monographs (Oxford: Clarendon, 1991), 40.

20. Ibid., 41–42. Beverly Gaventa has observed in a recent essay that "what is most disturbing about Galatians has less to do with Marcion than with Barmen," explaining that Paul's singular announcement of the lordship of Christ which "knows no boundaries and permits no limits"—taken up by Barth as the theme of the second article of the Barmen Theological Declaration—represents the sharp edge of the gospel in Paul, a theme relentlessly emphasized by Käsemann as well. See "The Singularity of the Gospel Revisited," in *Galatians and Christian Theology: Justification, the Gospel, and Ethics in Paul's Letter*, eds. M. Elliott et al. (Grand Rapids: Baker Academic, 2014), 187–99, at 199.

21. Ernst Käsemann, *Commentary on Romans*, trans. G. W. Bromiley (London: SCM, 1980), 3. The

Influenced in turn by Käsemann, Martyn's path-breaking Pauline scholarship also manifests what Bruce McCormack has styled "a self-conscious affinity" with the theological vision Barth displays in the second edition of his *Romans* commentary.[22] McCormack goes on to argue that for Martyn and his "school"—"those who read Paul as an 'apocalyptic theologian' these days"—Barth's commentary is "regarded not as a (largely) defensible piece of exegesis but as opening up an approach for understanding Paul which they too embrace."[23] There is little enough direct discussion of Barth in Martyn's own writing, though he does comment to readers of his *Galatians* commentary that we do well to remember that "Barth was an exegete as well as a systematic theologian" who consistently argued—rightly in Martyn's judgment—that Paul's soteriology only conceives of its "problem" retrospectively, considering "Adam in the light of Christ, sin in the light of grace, and so on."[24] It is also possible, I would suggest, that Martyn discerned a true echo of Paul's radical gospel of the turning of the ages in the work of his Union Theological Seminary colleague, Paul Lehmann, who recommended Barth be embraced as a "theologian of permanent revolution"—a practitioner not of culturally reactive but rather "*Archimedean theology*"—for whom the gospel persistently unsettles all received truths of our present age, being ever "a hinge" and never "a door."[25] Certainly, Barth's vigorous registration of the

---

ubiquity of invocation of hope and the present transformative pressure of the *futurum resurrectionis* in Barth's *Romans*—especially in his exegesis of chapter 6—hold out the place of the future even in his early eschatology.

22. Bruce L. McCormack, "Can We Still Speak of 'Justification By Faith'?," 162.

23. Bruce L. McCormack, "Longing for a New World," 144. He later suggests that if we look to understand the present popularity of Barth's theology in the English-speaking world, to begin with, his current positive reception precisely among apocalyptic readers of Paul "would not be a bad place to start," (149).

24. J. Louis Martyn, "God's Way of Making Right What is Wrong," in *Theological Issues in the Letters of Paul* (Edinburgh: T&T Clark, 1997), 144n8; Martyn reiterates this remark in his *Galatians* (New York: Doubleday, 1997), 95, 163. Cf. Karl Barth, *Christ and Adam: Man and Humanity in Romans 5*, trans. T. A. Smail (New York: Harper & Bros., 1956).

25. Paul L. Lehmann, "Karl Barth, Theologian of Permanent Revolution," *Union Seminary Quarterly Review* 28, no. 1 (1972): 67–81, at 77 and 72, where Lehmann is citing Barth's *Römerbrief* (Munich: Chr. Kaiser Verlag, 1922), 11 in his own translation. Cf. Matthew Rose, *Ethics With Barth: God, Metaphysics and Morals* (Farnham: Ashgate, 2010), 8–9 where he provides a catena of readings of Barth, which associate him with the kind of radical repudiation of the theological significance of the stabilities of the created order which one associates with the radical logic of apocalyptic disjuncture. Rose is citing these readings—including Lehmann's—in order to refute their validity.

"menace and the promise of the Kingdom of God" comports with Martyn's reading of the disruptive advent of a reconciliation that is also, at once, God's own self-revelation.[26] Be that as it may, McCormack's considered view is that Martyn's vision of a pattern of "cosmological apocalyptic eschatology" (in Martin de Boer's phrase) captures and characterizes Barth's early reading of Paul very well; however, he also argues that Barth's later, decidedly *forensic* account of salvation rendered in the fourth volume of the *Church Dogmatics*, corrects his early reading and amounts to a better reading of Paul. Implied is a judgment that apocalyptic readings of Paul of the sort advanced by Martyn might share certain theological weaknesses ingredient in Barth's 1922 presentation of the Apostle, and in fact, fare much better as interpretations *of Barth on Paul*, than they do as renderings of Paul as such.[27]

But what of the invocation of Barth in the work of those who are continuing to develop "apocalyptic theology" at present? Walter Lowe's programmatic essays look to Barth as a uniquely generative source. Lowe argues that Barth's *Römerbrief*—a work that "throbs with an apocalyptic urgency," alert to the perpetual crises of the age—instantiates a distinctively Christian postmodern turn, communicating a vision of "apocalyptic postmodernism" whose prospects have not yet been fully explored, let alone realized.[28] This vision conceives of history with decisive reference to God's gracious and sovereign delimiting, overreaching and determining of all things in and by the scandalous particularity of his eschatological coming in Christ. Christian theology begins from a recognition of this divine seizure of reality, and it must register in its tasks, tone, and tempo that the God of the gospel is "*closing in.*"[29] In this, it resists the quintessential

26. The phrase is Barth's from his commentary on Philippians, cited in Timothy Gorringe, *Karl Barth: Against Hegemony* (Oxford: Oxford University Press, 1999), 94.
27. Bruce L. McCormack, "Longing for a New World," 146–48; "Can We Still Speak of 'Justification By Faith'?," 179. For a very concise presentation of the matter, see Martin de Boer, "Paul and Apocalyptic Eschatology," in *The Continuum History of Apocalypticism*, eds. B. McGinn et al. (New York: Continuum, 2003), 166–94.
28. Walter Lowe, "Prospects for a Postmodern Christian Theology: Apocalyptic Without Reserve," *Modern Theology* 15, no. 1 (1999): 17–24, at 19.
29. Ibid., 20, emphasis original.

move of modern rationality to contextualize, historicize, and so, relativize and domesticate all things, the apocalyptic gospel included. Lowe suggests that pursuit of an "unqualified apocalyptic" posture in theology turns the tables on modernity:

> Christian theology proceeds upon the quite different premise that we ourselves have been contextualized; and not just conceptually, but actually. It is we who have been inscribed. It may be that, whatever else it does, apocalyptic stands as a primary means by which scripture effects or announces such inscription.[30]

To the question, "Why we need apocalyptic?," Lowe replies that a Christian theology fit for purpose needs, first and foremost, to recover precisely this recognition of being contextualized by a comprehending divine reality that "presses in upon us"; apocalyptic is a scriptural idiom uniquely qualified to deliver this, to impress that we are at once utterly chastened and kept "appropriately off balance" by the gospel while also entrusted to the fact that we are "suspended within the event of Jesus Christ" and that *that* is enough.[31] As he explicates this vision, Lowe not only looks to Barth's *Römerbrief,* but also, to his *Church Dogmatics,* finding there a developed "eschatological realism" which sees nothing less than the fullness of God himself apocalypsed upon the world in Jesus Christ, the full "secondary objectivity . . . of God's ownmost reality—without loss, without diminution."[32]

Nate Kerr's widely discussed study, *Christ, History and Apocalyptic,* also opens its engagement with Barth with a reading of the second edition of his Romans commentary.[33] Barth's theology emerges here as an anti-ideological project, set firmly and expressly against theology's historicist captivity and funded by a recovery of the radical apocalyptic crisis which the gospel *is.* Kerr goes on to argue that Barth deploys the grammar of apocalyptic discourse—emphasizing as it does the

---

30. Ibid., 23. Cf. Walter Lowe, "Why We Need Apocalyptic," *SJT* 63, no. 1 (2010): 41–53, at 48–50.
31. Ibid., 51–52.
32. Ibid., 53. The phrase "eschatological realism" is drawn over from Ingolf U. Dalferth, "Karl Barth's Eschatological Realism," in *Karl Barth: Centenary Essays,* ed. S. Sykes (Cambridge: Cambridge University Press, 1989), 14–45, a text to which Lowe himself appeals as an ally.
33. Nathan R. Kerr, *Christ, History and Apocalyptic: The Politics of Christian Mission* (London: SCM Press, 2009).

interruptive, alien, extrinsic, miraculous, unconditioned, and *negative* character of divine activity upon the world—in the service of species of "metaphysical idealism" whose necessary counterpart is a "nihilistic description of bare 'historicity' such as we find it in Troeltsch" that evacuates the very reality of history as such.[34] Kerr's contention is that the historicity of Jesus of Nazareth himself falls victim to this project, leaving Barth bereft of any means for imagining how divine revelation can actually reach and transform us *"in our historicity."*[35]

Yet this critical assessment of Barth's early apocalyptic theology gives way to a somewhat more positive evaluation of his later treatment of history within the christological doctrine of the *Church Dogmatics*. Following Harink and Mangina, Kerr lifts out the "still-discernible apocalyptic 'logic'" of Barth's later theology in which the particular historicity of Jesus Christ comes to serve as a critical ingredient in specifying the mode of God's eschatological action.[36] The transcendence of the interruptive Word of God is now specified in terms of its gracious priority and *singularity*: revelation is never a predicate of history, but history is made a predicate of revelation—as Barth puts it—precisely where and when the lordship of Christ is effectively realized in the midst of the creation and for its sake. Yet, Kerr remains convinced that the metaphysical investments which structure and shape Barth's mature (at this point) thinking still ultimately efface the genuine contingency Christ's history, and thus abstract his person and work from "the hard core of real history, the tragic contradictions and intricate complexities of history's broken pathways." Kerr's own project presses beyond Barth, looking to repair this shortcoming in pursuit of what he calls an "apocalyptic *historicism*" ambitious to do better justice to the claim that "Christ is made to be Lord precisely *in* the flux and contingency of history, and that

---

34. Ibid., 64–73.
35. Ibid., 73, emphasis original.
36. Ibid., 74–79. Kerr appeals in this regard to Douglas Harink, *Paul Among the Postliberals* (Grand Rapids: Brazos, 2003), 45–56, and Joseph Mangina, *Karl Barth: Theologian of Christian Witness* (Louisville: WJK, 2004), 124–29.

it is *through* such flux and contingency that we are made to be 'contemporaneous' with him."[37]

As with Lowe, so with Kerr's account, Barth figures as a theologian who crucially inaugurates an apocalyptic "turn" in Christian theology, and then, significantly develops its contours. But Kerr, in particular, adjudges Barth's work in this regard to be incomplete, tethered to certain defining features of the intellectual milieu in which it was forged as well as categories and forms inherited from the longer theological tradition which serve to frustrate its fuller advance. In both readings, however, Barth stands as a critical pivot, pathbreaker, and pioneer of apocalyptic theology, discerning and displaying—even if not fully realizing—the revolutionary theological promise of a fresh hearing of Paul's eschatological gospel. Barth's tempestuous early work has pride of place in both these accounts; nevertheless, they also espy important developments of the apocalyptic sensibility in Barth's later dogmatic theology. Indeed, as Doug Harink summarizes,

> Perhaps the most remarkable imprint of Pauline logic on Barth's theology . . . is surely to be discerned in the very structure of the *Church Dogmatics*. The entire project begins with the "apocalypse," that is, with the doctrine of revelation which is determined from beginning to end by the world-dissolving and world-constituting event of God's advent in the cross and resurrection of Jesus Christ. This apocalypse epistemologically precedes and in turn determines everything that Barth will go on to say about the knowledge of God, the reality of God, the election of God, and the command of God. . . . [And he] will not treat the doctrine of creation and humanity apart from God's apocalypse in Jesus Christ, for we do not finally know their true shape and destiny apart from that revelation.[38]

Robert Jenson has suggested that "modernity's great theological project was to suppress apocalyptic, and to make messianism into guru-worship."[39] Barth's comprehensive and bracing recollection that the "Gospel is the power of God . . . the 'miraculous warfare' (Luther)" which God wages so that the old world might be "dissolved and

---

37. Kerr, *Christ, History and Apocalyptic*, 91–92.

38. Harink, *Paul Among the Postliberals*, 54.

39. Robert Jenson, "Apocalypticism and Messianism in Twentieth Century German Theology," in *Messianism, Apocalypse and Redemption in 20th Century German Thought*, eds. W. Cristaudo and W. Baker (Adelaide: ATF, 2006), 3–12, at 12.

overthrown by the victory of Christ," repudiated precisely *this* ambition of modern theology.[40] In so doing, it seeded a century of theology in which eschatology moved from the obscure margins in toward the center of the theological endeavor. We have good reason to see contemporary efforts to win through to a form of Christian theology, that is, particularly alert to and shaped by Paul's apocalyptic gospel as a late fruit of that particular sowing.

Some Theses on Apocalyptic in Contemporary Theology

I now turn to set out a series of dogmatic theses concerning apocalyptic and contemporary theology. My aim is to suggest that the focus, form, and substance of Christian theology itself are all at issue in the effort to re-appropriate the fundamental impulses of Pauline apocalyptic into the heart of our practice of theology.

(1) A Christian theology funded by a fresh hearing of New Testament apocalyptic will discern in that distinctive and difficult idiom a discourse uniquely adequate both to announce the full scope, depth, and radicality of the Gospel of God, as well as to bespeak the actual and manifest contradictions of that Gospel by the times in which we live.

To hear the apocalyptic gospel is to be confronted with the claim that the work of salvation is the work of remaking the world *as such*, a work of cosmic scope, metaphysical depth, and universal human concern. It is a work performed *by God* himself in acts of sovereign and adventitious grace that "tear down and build up," which "kill and make alive." The apocalyptic idiom strains to articulate the gratuity of divine sovereignty and the sovereignty of divine grace. Where and when God so acts—as manifest in singular concentration in the life and death of Jesus Christ—the invasion of sovereign love and mercy is met with open and covert opposition whose outworking threatens to belie the

---

40. The citations are from remarks on Romans 5:12–21, Karl Barth, *The Epistle to the Romans*, 166.

gospel itself. And lived faith knows all too well the experience of the manifold contradiction of the gospel. An "apocalyptic theology" keyed to the paradox of the divine victory on the cross furnishes categories "that match the realities of the present" by which faith may grasp and endure this *agonistic* "time between the times."[41] Thinking in this way leads, as Barth says, "straight to the place where light and darkness are locked in a grueling but victorious struggle . . . into the kingdom of grace, into Christ, where life in its entirely becomes complicated and gets call into question, but is, nonetheless, filled with promise."[42]

(2) A Christian theology funded by a fresh hearing of New Testament apocalyptic will turn upon a vigorous account of divine revelation in Jesus Christ as the unsurpassable eschatological act of redemption; its talk of God will be thus be marked by an intense Christological concentration.

To hear the apocalyptic gospel is to have one's attention riveted to the events of incarnation, crucifixion, and resurrection as the hinge upon which the "ages turn." The concrete outworking of the vocation of the Son sent "in the fullness of time," these events are confessed to be the very *parousia* of God come low to save. Created, arrested, and summoned by sovereign grace, faith acknowledges, and so, knows God in and through this salutary "apocalypse of the Son" (Gal 1:16). In Christ, we are met by a revelation that acquaints us with the "*dunamis*, the meaning and power of the living God who is creating a new world."[43] The concrete form, specific intention, and particular ends of this effective self-disclosure of God in Christ provide apocalyptic theology with a positive "pleromatic space" of knowledge and substantive ethical orientation.[44] This is because "the situation

41. Cark Braaten, *Christ and Counter-Christ: Apocalyptic Themes in Theology and Culture* (Philadelphia: Fortress Press, 1972), 16.
42. Karl Barth, "The Christian in Society (1919)," in *The Word of God and Theology*, trans. A. Marga (London: T&T Clark, 2011), 60–61.
43. Ibid., 40.
44. Cyril O'Regan, *Theology and the Spaces of Apocalyptic* (St Louis: Marquette University Press, 2009), 29 *et passim*.

between God and the world has been altered in such a fundamental and absolute way that our being in Christ radically governs the attitude we take toward life."[45]

(3) A Christian theology funded by a fresh hearing of New Testament apocalyptic will acknowledge and stress the unexpected, new, and disjunctive character of the divine work of salvation that comes upon the world of sin in and through Christ. As a consequence, in its account of the Christian life, faith, and hope, it will make much of the ensuing evangelical "dualisms."

To hear the apocalyptic gospel is to register the advent of a salvation accomplished at "the end of the law" and "apart from the law," a salvation consisting in a "*new* covenant" which overreaches the distinction between pagan and Jew, a salvation whose outworking by way of juridical murder in the flesh of a marginal Jewish criminal can, by any previous measure, be only a scandalous folly. An apocalyptic theology will hold Christian faith and thought hard by such claims, demanding that it register the unexpected and disjunctive newness of the good news, i.e., the newness of the new creation; the newness of the new and second Adam; the newness of the new covenant. It also demands that Christian faith and thought own the radical character of salvation expressed in the apocalyptic tropes of death and resurrection, the ending of the old age and the onset of the new, of the defeat of the "god of this age" by the God who is God, of a new and second creation, of a world "turned upside down" in which all things are to be "made new"—these are not images of mere repair, development, or incremental improvement within a broadly continuous situation. The content of Jesus' teaching, as much as Paul's testimony, bespeaks a salvation whose advent involves an unanticipated divine action that marks a radical break with what has gone before, its overturning, its revolution, its displacement. As Carl Braaten observes, "the apocalyptic God approaches history with

---

45. Barth, "The Christian in Society (1919)," 53.

oppositional power, in order that through crisis and conflict the existing reality may give way to a counter-reality" such that theology must reckon with "the eschatological otherness of a God who makes himself manifest first of all as the power of contradiction, of criticism, in crisis on the cross, and not in smooth continuity as the consummator and converging center of a continuing creation."[46] Correspondingly, an apocalyptic theology will insist on the standing importance of the new "dualisms"—e.g., Flesh and Spirit—that the gospel enjoins as "militant antinomies born of apocalypse."[47]

(4) A Christian theology funded by a fresh hearing of New Testament apocalyptic will be lead to account for salvation as a "three agent drama" of divine redemption in which human beings are rescued from captivity to the anti-God powers of sin, death, and the devil. To do so is, it will wager, a discerning realist gesture of notable explanatory power.

To hear the apocalyptic gospel is to be driven to an account of salvation whose fundamental form is "creative negation" of the present age, whose consequence is deliverance and whose substance is an exchange of lordships. Such redemption from Sin represents a comprehensive account of salvation able to encompass other soteriological motifs such as atonement, guilt, and forgiveness of sins. Apocalyptic theology will advocate for "the revolution of Life against the powers of death that surround it, the powers in which we ourselves are caught."[48] Faith in the reality of the resurrection of Jesus Christ warrants hope for a divinely wrought "future which negates the life-negating power of death."[49] This apocalyptic theological idiom may be adjudged uniquely adequate to discerning the realities of our age. Is anything less

---

46. Carl Braaten, *Christ and Counter-Christ* (Philadelphia: Fortress Press, 1972), 14. He continues, pointedly, "Theology still must decide whether Aristotle or Jesus is the teacher of God and how he relates or disrelates to the world."
47. Martyn, *Galatians*, 101.
48. Barth, "The Christian in Society (1919)," 47.
49. Carl Braaten, "The Significance of Apocalypticism for Systematic Theology," *Interpretation* 25, no. 4 (1971): 480–99, at 493.

fantastical to us than the autonomous, rationally transparent self of bourgeois modernity? A soteriological discourse that speaks of our captivity, complicity, and gracious liberation into the hands of another genuine and genuinely philanthropic Lord, is one able to illumine how it is that we are, in fact, played by powers, structures, and systems of all kinds (political, technological, etc.), subjected to effective discursive and disciplinary regimes (which, having been conjured by us as the outworking of sin, now prosecute us with a kind of "downward causation" all their own), and moved by unfathomable drives and obscure impulses, both psychological and social—all this as so many modes of repudiation of God's grace and freedom. Apocalyptic categories might be thought of as crucial tools of faith's historiography—or, if you rather, faith's bifocals—i.e., categories by which we give voice to a spiritual discernment of "what is going on" in what is taking place.[50]

(5) A Christian theology funded by a fresh hearing of New Testament apocalyptic will acknowledge that it is the world and not the church which is the object of divine salvation. It will thus conceive of the church as a provisional pilgrim community created by the effective announcement of the Gospel for the sake of the world. Both individually and corporately, the Christian life is chiefly to be understood as discipleship.

To hear the apocalyptic gospel is to see the cosmic scope of divine salvation in the recovery, liberation, and transformation of the whole of creation. It is in the service of the salvation of *this* world that the Christian community is an *ecclesia militans*. "Once we have become conscious of the Life in life, we can no longer bear living in the land of death, in an existence whose forms cause us most painfully to miss the meaning of life."[51] The congregation will ever be active and forthright

---

50. The trope of "bifocal vision" is taken over from J. Louis Martyn, "From Paul to Flannery O'Connor with the Power of Grace," in *Theological Issues in the Letters of Paul* (Edinburgh: T&T Clark, 1997), 284.
51. Barth, "The Christian in Society (1919)," 45.

in its public witness and service to attest the Life that is coming to the world and to seek to see God's reign justified, even now, before the world. Such discipleship involves an enactment of radical Christian freedom and love that actively denies and resists the false lordship of sin and death in open and courageous testimony to the truth of the lordship of Christ, even now in *this* or *that* place. Such a life of faith has Christ's own present exercise of his royal office and the ongoing empowerment of the Spirit as its basis, its media, and its hope. As Barth explains, those who hear the apocalyptic gospel "are not disinterested observers. We *are* moved by God. We do know God. The history of God is happening in us and toward us. The last word . . . our 'given' is the advancing rule of God."[52] All this could well be styled as a distinctively Christian witness, worship, and service, whose imagination is not unaffected by the "socially aggressive and politically aggravating" apocalyptic concepts and images in which the gospel comes to us from the first.[53]

(6) A Christian theology funded by a fresh hearing of New Testament apocalyptic will adopt a posture of prayerful expectation of an imminent future in which God will act decisively to vindicate publicly the victory of Life and Love over Sin and Death. The ordering of its tasks and concentration of its energies will befit the critical self-reflection of a community that prays, "Let grace come and let this world pass away."[54]

To hear the apocalyptic gospel is to receive the theological vocation as a call to serve the mission and service of the pilgrim church in the time that remains. In this, theology will cultivate Christian unease with the present world by calling to mind the advent of the Kingdom, lamenting its present contradiction, discerning and calling out its contemporary parables where they are to be found, and suspending all faith and hope from the knowledge of the God of Jesus Christ.[55] Apocalyptic

52. Ibid., 51.
53. Braaten, *Christ and Counter-Christ*, 17–18.
54. *Didache* 10:6.

theology will be a non-speculative, concrete, and practical form of knowing, committed to the work of discerning the signs of the times by Scripture and Spirit. It will itself be a militant discourse, always on the verge of proclamation, offering at most a kind of urgent and sufficient traveling instruction for pilgrims, and as such, will be impatient with more contemplative theological postures. Its primary service will always be to serve the clarification of the Christian witness to the present salutary agency of the crucified and risen One to whom faith owes allegiance and obedience.

Yet, one might ask at just this point whether such "apocalyptic theology" is possible at all, or whether, by its own accounting, there is really no time for such an undertaking. Does the very existence of the intellectual, institutional, and personal "space" to pursue such theology belie its seriousness and reality?[56] Or, is the writing of such theology a part of the faithful business of "waiting in action" required of Christians and their congregations in this time? If it is the latter, then theologians must labor under no illusions about the entirely transitory character of their work of fragile, mortal wisdom. For, if the apocalyptic hearing of the gospel is a true one, then in common with the Christian community—and indeed, with everything that is—the horizon of all theological endeavor lies,

> In the new Day's reversal of values, the decree
> That every mouth be stopped
> While grace invades, abases and destroys,
> And with each shoot of mortal skill and wisdom lopped
> In total loss,
> Christ holds the Sum of joys,
> No tree upon our land except his Cross.[57]

---

55. See Lowe, "Why we Need Apocalyptic," 52.
56. One might take such questions as echoes of the searching criticisms of modern Christian theology *as such* once ventured by Franz Overbeck. See his *On the Christianity of Theology*, ed. and trans. J. Wilson (San Jose, CA: Pickwick, 2002).
57. Jack Clemo, "The Awakening," in The Awakening: Poems *Newly Found*, eds. J. Hurst, A. M. Kent, and A. C. Symons (London: Francis Boutle, 2003), 68–69.

PART IV

11

Righteousness Revealed

The Death of Christ as the Definition of the
Righteousness of God in Romans 3:21–26

Jonathan A. Linebaugh

"He had his own strange way of judging things. I suspect he acquired it
from the Gospels."
—Victor Hugo, *Les Misérables*

Apocalyptic Backgrounds and/or a Christological Apocalypse?

"I had been captivated with a remarkable ardour for understanding
Paul in the epistle to the Romans . . . but a single saying in chapter
one [δικαιοσύνη θεοῦ] . . . stood in my way."[1] This autobiographical
reminiscence from Martin Luther describes the experience of
countless readers of Romans. When the phrase δικαιοσύνη θεοῦ first
appears in Romans (1:17), Paul's syntax—note the γάρ that links 1:16

---

1. M. Luther, *Preface to the Complete Edition of Luther's Latin Writings*, in *LW* 34, ed. L. W. Spitz
(Philadelphia: Muhlenberg, 1960), 336–37.

and 1:17—suggests that his reference to "the righteousness of God" is explanatory, but the spilt ink (and blood) in which the *Wirkungsgeschichte* of this Pauline phrase is written tells a different story: this part of Paul is "hard to understand" (2 Pet. 3:16).

But George Herbert can help:

Oh dreadful Justice, what a fright and terror
Wast thou of old,When sin and error
Did show and shape thy looks to me,
And through their glass discolor thee!

This poetic description, which resonates with Luther's recollection of "hat[ing] the phrase 'the righteousness of God'" because "according to use and custom," he understood it as "the active righteousness by which God is just and punishes unrighteous sinners," suggests that, at least for Herbert, the interpretative problem is not just grammatical; it has to do with what (or who) reveals the definition of righteousness. "When sin and error did show and shape" the "look" of God's justice, the result was "fright and terror." But something changes between stanzas two and three: "But now," Herbert says with a Pauline phrase (Rom. 3:21):

. . . that Christ's pure veil presents thy sight
I see no fears:
Thy hand is white,Thy scales like buckets, which attend
And interchangeably descend,
Lifting to heaven from this well of tears.

Where "sin and error" revealed a frightful justice, "Christ's pure veil presents" a righteousness that results in "no fear." Like Luther before him, who "mediated day and night" until the "connections of [Paul's] words" overcame "use and custom" with an exegetical entrance "into paradise itself," Herbert's transition from "fright" to "no fear" occurs at that Pauline point—"but now"—where Christ reveals the meaning of "the righteousness of God."

And this, I want to suggest, is an apocalyptic rendering of δικαιοσύνη θεοῦ in the most precise Pauline sense: It is in "the gospel . . . about

God's son . . . Jesus Christ" (Rom. 1:1–4 cf. 1:16–17), that "the righteousness of God" is "unveiled" (ἀποκαλύπτω, Rom. 1:17). For Luther, this meant a new definition: "the righteousness of God" is not the divine justice that punishes the unrighteous, but the gift of Jesus that justifies the ungodly.[2] For Herbert, a poem:

> God's promises have made thee mine;
> Why should I justice now decline?
> Against me there is none, but for me much.[3]

This, however, is not always what apocalyptic means when used as a description of Paul and his theology. Luther and Herbert are apocalyptic readers of Paul in the sense that they interpret God's gift of Jesus Christ as an apocalypse (cf. Gal. 1:12): "Christ's pure veil presents" the meaning of righteousness, sings Herbert, echoing Paul's insistence that "the righteousness of God is made visible" in "the redemption that is in Christ Jesus" (Rom. 3:21, 24). Here, apocalyptic names an interpretative movement, not from traditional "use and custom" to "the connection of [Paul's] words," but the other way around: from a revelatory event to the definition of God's righteousness it discloses. But apocalyptic, when used primarily to identify the history-of-religions background of Paul's theology, often serves to make the opposite point. Where apocalyptic names the "from whence" of Pauline concepts, this identification can invite a reading of Paul in which "use and custom" determine the definition of Paul's vocabulary, not least the phrase δικαιοσύνη θεοῦ.

Ernst Käsemann provides a representative and influential example. His interpretation of "'The Righteousness of God' in Paul," to quote the title of his 1961 address to the Oxford Congress,[4] is an instance of

---

2. Ibid. For Luther's christological understanding of "the righteousness of faith," see my "The Christo-Centrism of Faith in Christ: Martin Luther's Reading of Galatians 2:16, 19–20," NTS 59, no. 4 (2013): 535–44.

3. The above lines are all from a poem entitled "Justice II" that occurs in "The Church" section of Herbert's The Temple, Sacred Poem and Private Ejaculations (New York: Paulist, 1981), 265–66.

4. E. Käsemann, "'The Righteousness of God' in Paul," in New Testament Questions of Today, trans. W. J. Montague (London: SCM, 1969), 168–82. Käsemann's lecture-turned-essay crystalized the earlier work of A. Oepke ("Δικαιοσύνη Θεοῦ bei Paulus," TLZ 78 [1953]: cols. 257–63) and was subsequently expanded, defended, and adapted by C. Müller, Gottes Gerichtigkeit und Gottes Volk, FRLANT 86 (Göttingen: Vandenhoeck & Ruprecht, 1964); K. Kertelge, 'Rechtfertigung' bei Paulus (Münster:

a larger history-of-religions reconstruction. His celebrated thesis that "apocalyptic is the mother of all Christian theology" is, in the first instance, an historical rather than a theological claim.[5] It is a judgment about "Die Anfänge christlicher Theologie" and represents a shift from Käsemann's pre-1950 answer to the history-of-religions question in terms of Hellenistic and gnostic backgrounds.[6] From the start, the definition of "apocalyptic" proved elusive,[7] but for Käsemann, its use was necessary because the near equation in Germany of "eschatology" and a doctrine of history made it impossible to say "eschatology" and mean *"Endgeschichte."*[8] Apocalyptic, in Käsemann's use and context, thus refers to a specific kind of eschatology characterized by a constellation of features related to *Endgeschichte*: the expectation of an imminent parousia, a cosmic rather than individualistic orientation, the antithetical correspondence of *Urzeit* and *Endzeit*—all of which work together to pose an apocalyptic question: Who is the world's true Lord?[9]

Käsemann's interpretation of "the righteousness of God" in Paul is shaped by this *religionsgeschichtliche* thesis, especially in terms of method. Working in the tradition of Hermann Cremer's programmatic suggestion that Paul's expression, "the righteousness of God," is derived from and consonant with the Old Testament understanding of

Aschendorff, 1967); P. Stuhlmacher, *Gerechtigkeit Gottes bei Paulus*, FRLANT 87 (Göttingen: Vandenhoeck & Ruprecht, 1965).

5. E. Käsemann, "Die Anfänge christlicher Theologie," *ZTK* 57, no. 2 (1960): 162–85, at 180; ET, "The Beginnings of Christian Theology," in *New Testament Question of Today*, trans. W. J. Montague (London: SCM, 1969), 82–107.

6. On this shift, see D. V. Way, *The Lordship of Christ: Ernst Käsemann's Interpretation of Paul's Theology*, Oxford Theological Monographs (Oxford: Clarendon, 1991), 122–24.

7. See, for example G. Ebeling's call for a definition in "Der Grund christlicher Theologie," *ZThK* 58 (1961): 227–44, at 230. Cf. David Congdon's observation that Ebeling's search for the "Grund" of Christian theology, together with Fuchs's identification of its "Aufgabe," is the scholarly context for Käsemann's claim about the "Anfänge" of Christian theology ("Eschatologizing Apocalyptic: An Assessment of the Present Conversation on Pauline Apocalyptic," in *Apocalyptic and the Future of Theology: With and Beyond J. Louis Martyn*, eds. J. B. Davis and D. Harink [Eugene: Cascade, 2012], 118–36, at 119–20).

8. E. Käsemann, *Exegetische Versuche und Besinnungen*, ii (Göttingen: Vandenhoeck & Ruprecht, 1964), 105n1.

9. See, for instance, ibid., 94, 104n1. Because apocalyptic carries this constellation of features, Käsemann's history-of-religions claim is able to do theological work: apocalyptic is, for Käsemann, a "twofold 'correction'" to Bultmann's theology, emphasizing "the 'theology' pole of the theology-anthropology dialectic" and interpreting "both theology and anthropology in light of the lordship of Christ" (Way, *The Lordship of Christ*, 138).

righteousness as a "relational concept" (*Verhältnisbegriff*),[10] Käsemann's hermeneutic works to the Pauline definition of δικαιοσύνη θεοῦ from the pre-Pauline meaning of the phrase. In his words, "I begin my own attempt to interpret the facts by stating categorically that the expression δικαιοσύνη θεοῦ was not invented by Paul."[11] For Käsemann, δικαιοσύνη θεοῦ is a "formulation which Paul has taken over," a formulation stemming from Deut. 33:21 and mediated to Paul via apocalyptic Judaism, as evidenced by the use of the phrase in *T. Dan* 6:10; 1QS 10:25; 11:12; 1QM 4:6.[12] This means that, from where Paul stands in the history of his religion, δικαιοσύνη θεοῦ is a "feste Formel,"[13] a traditional phrase with a trajectory of use that pre-defines the phrase as used by Paul. Thus, while Käsemann can say, with reference to Phil. 3:9 and Rom. 3:22, that "whatever else God's eschatological righteousness may be, at any rate it is a gift,"[14] he insists on "der Machtcharakter der Gabe" because "the formulation which Paul has taken over [i.e., δικαιοσύνη θεοῦ] speaks primarily of God's saving activity, which is present in his gift."[15]

The hermeneutic, governed by the *religionsgeschichtliche* thesis, is that defining δικαιοσύνη θεοῦ in Paul requires finding δικαιοσύνη θεοῦ outside of and before Paul. Käsemann knows what Paul means when he writes "the righteousness of God"—"God's lordship over the world which reveals itself eschatologically in Jesus"[16]—because he knows that

10. H. Cremer, *Die paulinische Rechtfertigungslehre im Zusammenhange ihrer geschichtlichen Voraussetzungen* (Gütersloh: Bertelsmann, 1899).
11. Käsemann, "'The Righteousness of God,'" 172.
12. Ibid., 172–73. Several passages from the *Hodayoth* are also noted (1QH 4.37; 7.14, 19; 11.17–18, 30–31; 13.16–17; 15.14–15; 16.10), but none of them contain the precise phrase. Stuhlmacher's attempt to supplement this list could only cite *1 (Ethiopic) En.* 71.14; 99.10; 101.3; *4 Ezra* 8:36 as definitive (*Gerechtigkeit Gottes* 11, 98).
13. E. Käsemann, "Gottesgerechtigkeit bei Paulus," *ZThK* 58, no. 3 (1961): 367–78. The claim of Oepke, Käsemann, and (the earlier) Stuhlmacher that δικαιοσύνη θεοῦ is a *terminus technicus* is seriously problematized by the limited number of Old Testament and early Jewish texts that actually contain the formula and the linguistic flexibility with which Paul expresses the correlation of δικαιοσύνη and θεός (Rom. 1:17; 3:5, 21, 22, 25, 26; 10:3; 2 Cor. 5:21; Phil. 3:9); see especially, E. Güttgemanns, "'Gottesgerechtigkeit' und strukturale Semantik: Linguistische Analyse zu δικαιοσύνη θεοῦ," in *Studia linguistica Neotestamentica*, BEvTh 60 [München: Chr. Kaiser Verlag, 1971], 5–98).
14. E. Käsemann, *Commentary on Romans*, trans. G. W. Bromiley (Grand Rapids: Eerdmans, 1980), 94.
15. Käsemann, *Exegetische Versuche und Besinnungen* ii, 183, 185; ET from *New Testament Questions of Today* (London: SCM, 1969), 172.
16. This is a modified translation of Käsemann, *Exegetische Versuche und Besinnungen* ii, 192 provided

"in the field of the Old Testament and of Judaism in general," the same phase is used to describe God's saving action undertaken in faithfulness to those with whom he is in covenant relationship.[17] To borrow Luther's words to describe Käsemann's method, pre-Pauline "use and custom," what we might call the theological lexicon of the Old Testament and apocalyptic Judaism, interpret "the connection of [Paul's] words." Hence, David Way's suggestive observation: "although [Käsemann] pays a great deal of attention to the historical background of the theme . . . he does not treat the actual occurrences of [δικαιοσύνη θεοῦ] in Paul's letters in any detail."[18]

But that is not to say that Käsemann is necessarily wrong. Rather, what this juxtaposition with Luther and Herbert exposes is that the word "apocalyptic" can function in a variety of ways. This, perhaps, is both its peril and potential, but in this case, it is necessary "to call a thing what it is" (Luther).[19] For Käsemann, to say that "apocalyptic is the mother of [Paul's] theology" is to say that δικαιοσύνη θεοῦ is a "formulation which Paul has taken over," a "feste Formel" which he employs to interpret God's saving actions in Jesus Christ. By contrast, to call Luther and Herbert apocalyptic readers of Paul is to say that, for them, Jesus Christ is the apocalypse, the unveiling of God's righteousness, and thus the one who defines the phrase δικαιοσύνη θεοῦ. As an answer to the question concerning the religious and

by Way, *The Lordship of Christ*, 201. For a discussion of this theme, and Käsemann's reading of justification more generally, see especially, P. F. M. Zahl, *Die Rechtfertigungslehre Ernst Käsemann* (Stuttgart: Calwer, 1996).

17. The influence of Cremer on Käsemann's interpretation of the meaning of righteousness in the Old Testament and early Judaism is evident in his insistence that in this "field . . . righteousness does not convey primarily the sense of a personal, ethical quality, but of a relationship," ("'The Righteousness of God' in Paul," in *New Testament Questions of Today*, trans. W. J. Montague [London: SCM, 1969], 168–82, at 172). It is notable that Käsemann does see Paul expanding or editing the received definition of divine righteousness, interpreting it not as God's saving action in reference to the covenant with Israel, but as the creator coming on the scene of his creation in power to establish his right (see, e.g., Romans, 35, 56, 93, 123; *Exegetische Versuche und Besinnungen* ii, 100).

18. Way, *The Lordship of Christ*, 201. For recent examples of this methodological tendency, see M. F. Bird, *The Saving Righteousness of God: Studies on Paul, Justification and the New Perspective* (Milton Keynes: Paternoster, 2006), 15; G. Turner, "The Righteousness of God in Psalms and Romans," *SJT* 63, no. 3 (2010): 285–301, and N. T. Wright, "The Book of Romans," in *NIB*, vol. 10 (Nashville: Abingdon Press, 2002), 403. For review of research on δικαιοσύνη, especially but not only in Paul, see chapter one of C. L. Irons, *The Righteousness of God: A Lexical Examination of the Covenant-Faithfulness Interpretation*, WUNT 2/386 (Tübingen: Mohr Siebeck, 2015).

19. "The Heidelberg Disputation" (1518), LW 31, 35–70.

theological context for Paul's "righteousness of God" phrases, I regard Käsemann's identification of Jewish apocalyptic as both broadly correct and necessary. Paul's announcement of God's righteousness has eschatological judgment as its theological register, a prominent if not universal feature of the early Jewish apocalypses. Furthermore, an examination of righteousness language prior to and contemporaneous with Paul is an indispensable task in establishing what these lexemes have and can mean, and thus why they are apropos as an articulation of the Pauline gospel. The problem is not in the identification of Jewish apocalyptic as the history-of-religions background of Pauline theology; the problem occurs when this *religionsgeschichtliche* thesis morphs into a hermeneutic that defines Pauline terms by antecedent usage, and thereby, (ironically) fails to interpret the gift of Christ as itself the apocalypse that reveals the definition of "the righteousness of God."[20]

Written in Scripture, Revealed in Christ

Paul's use of the phrase δικαιοσύνη θεοῦ resists definition by an inherited, even canonical, lexicon. As Rom. 9:30–10:4 demonstrates, Paul's scriptural and theological heritage names δικαιοσύνη and incites Israel to pursue it (Rom. 9:31), but, for Paul, the content of God's righteousness cannot be dislocated from its unveiling in Christ (Rom. 1:17; 3:21-26; 10:4). In using the expression δικαιοσύνη θεοῦ, Paul is speaking the language of Deuteronomy, David, Deutero-Isaiah, and Daniel, but as Paul interprets the crisis of his present, it is precisely the readers of these scriptural texts who are "ignorant of the righteousness of God" (ἀγνοοῦντες τὴν τοῦ θεοῦ δικαιοσύνην, Rom. 10:3; cf. Phil. 3:4-9). Thus, while "the law and prophets witness to the righteousness of God," it is not in the law and the prophets that the righteousness of God is revealed. Rather, "the righteousness of God is revealed in the gospel" (Rom. 1:17).[21] To locate the definition of the specifically

20. For a critique of defining δικαιοσύνη θεοῦ on the basis of the concept's "prehistory," see H. Conzelmann, "Current Problems in Pauline Research," *Int* 22 (1968): 170-86, at 80; cf. S. K. Williams, "The 'Righteousness of God' in Romans," *JBL* 99, no. 2 (1980): 241-90, at 244.
21. Cf. the discussion of Paul's "localizing" reference to the "righteousness of God" that is revealed "in the gospel" in M. A. Seifrid, *Christ, Our Righteousness: Paul's Theology of Justification*, NSBT 9

Pauline use of the phrase δικαιοσύνη θεοῦ in the lexicon of the Old Testament and early Judaism is thus to find its meaning in a place Paul never put it. For Paul, "the righteousness of God" is not a conceptual *a priori* that enables him to gauge the soteriological significance of Jesus' history; "the righteousness of God" is that which "has been made visible" (φανερόω) in the event Paul calls "the redemption that is in Christ Jesus" (Rom. 3:21a, 24) and "continues to be unveiled" (ἀποκαλύπτω) in the proclamation of the same (Rom. 1:16–17). In the words of the first edition of Barth's *Römerbrief*, "Die Wirklichkeit der Gerechtigkeit Gottes im Christus ist das Neue im Evangelium."[22]

To suggest that Paul theologizes from an inherited notion of divine righteousness to an interpretation of the Christ-event is therefore to read Paul backwards, and to read him, in the most basic sense, un-apocalyptically. Paul does not employ δικαιοσύνη θεοῦ to make sense of what happens in Jesus; for Paul, δικαιοσύνη θεοῦ just is what happens in Jesus. The unveiling of the righteousness of God, for Paul, occurs, "in it"—that is, in "the gospel" (Rom. 1:16–17). And because, according to the opening lines of Romans, "God's son [Jesus Christ]" is the subject matter of "God's gospel" (εὐαγγέλιον θεοῦ . . . περὶ τοῦ υἱοῦ αὐτοῦ, 1:1, 3), Paul's evangelical definition of δικαιοσύνη θεοῦ is a christological definition.[23] Jesus Christ, in his comprehensive and constitutive history—"the one who was born of the seed of David" and "the one who was designated Son of God by resurrection" (1:3–4), the one "who was handed over for our trespasses and who was raised for our

---

(Leicester: Apollos, 2000), 46. A full discussion of "the righteousness of God" would include a consideration of "the law and the prophets" as witnesses to this righteousness, both in terms of Paul's explicit references to Hab. 2:4 and Gen. 15:6, and in the way Paul hears Scripture "promising beforehand" (Rom. 1:2) and "pre-preaching" (Gal. 3:8) the gospel in which the righteousness of God is revealed. For Christ and Scripture as mutually-interpreting, though with Christ as scripture's "now of legibility," see my *God, Grace, and Righteousness in Wisdom of Solomon and Paul's Letter to the Romans: Texts in Conversation*, NovTSup 152 (Leiden: Brill, 2013), 177–226; idem, "Not the End: The History and Hope of the Unfailing Word in Romans 9–11," in *Has God Rejected His People? Essays on Romans 9–11*, eds. B. R. Gaventa, T. Still, and B. Longenecker (Waco: Baylor University Press, forthcoming).

22. K. Barth, *Der Römerbrief (Erste Fassung) 1919* (Gesamtausgabe II: Akademische Werke; ed. Hermann Schmidt; Zürich: Theologischer Verlag, 1985), 23.

23. Richard Hays (*Echoes of Scripture in the Letters of Paul* [New Haven: Yale University Press, 1989], 85) suggests taking περὶ τοῦ υἱοῦ αὐτοῦ with γραφαῖς ἁγίαις rather than εὐαγγέλιον θεοῦ, but the christological focus of 1:3–4 indicates that περὶ τοῦ υἱοῦ αὐτοῦ identifies the subject matter of the gospel (so most commentators, e.g., Calvin, Cranfield, Dunn, Käsemann).

justification" (4:25)—is the content of the gospel, and as such, the one in whom "the righteousness of God is revealed."[24] As Luther might say, "omnia vocabula," or at least the phrase δικαιοσύνη θεοῦ, "in Christo novam significationem accipere."[25] To interpret "the righteousness of God" apocalyptically in this sense is to deduce its definition from the saving history of Jesus in which Paul sees God's righteousness "unveiled" (Rom. 1:17). Only if, in Eberhard Jüngel's words, we let Paul "decide on what a righteous God is like, not on the basis of the normal use of concepts, but only on the basis" of the event that "justifies the ungodly,"[26] can we sing George Herbert's song: "But now . . . Christ's veil presents thy sight."

The Death of Christ as the Apocalypse of God's Righteousness

Romans 3:21–26, at least in part, is Paul's attempt to define δικαιοσύνη θεοῦ by announcing the evangelical event that manifests, demonstrates, and constitutes it. As the three purpose clauses of Rom. 3:25–26 indicate, God's act of putting Jesus forward as a ἱλαστήριον is teleological: the cross of Jesus Christ intends the demonstration (ἔνδειξις, 3:25, 26a) and establishment (εἰς τὸ εἶναι, 3:26b) of God's righteousness. Earlier in Romans, Paul locates the "revelation of God's righteous judgment" (ἀποκαλύψεως δικαιοκρισίας τοῦ θεοῦ, 2:5) "in the day of wrath" (ἐν ἡμέρᾳ ὀργῆς), a time when "God will repay each one according to their deeds" (κατὰ τὰ ἔργα, 2:6). In this context, the initially generic "one who works the good" (2:7) is specified in Romans 2:13 as a "doer of the law." In this eschatological judgment, then, the law is the criterion, and therefore, because "all are under sin" (3:9) and "no one is righteous" (3:10), the revelation of God's righteousness in

---

24. See Origen's even stronger claim: "*Haec ergo iustitia Dei, quae est Christus*" (Migne, *Patrologia graeca* [*PG*] 14.944. Cf. Käsemann's observation that "Paul" "in [Rom.] 1:16f. interpreted the christological statement of 1:3f. soteriological" and that this also runs "conversely" (*Romans*, 95). This mutually interpreting christology-soteriology dialectic problematizes N. T. Wright's claim that the gospel is "Jesus Christ is Lord," and thus not "you can be saved" ("New Perspectives on Paul," in *Justification in Perspective: Historical Developments and Contemporary Challenges*, ed. B. L. McCormack [Grand Rapids: Baker Academic, 2006], 243–64, at 249).

25. M. Luther, *Disputatio de divinitate et humanitate Christi* (1540; WA 39/II, 94, 17f.).

26. E. Jüngel, *Justification: The Heart of Christian Faith*, trans. J. F. Cayzer (London: T&T Clark, 2001), 78.

accordance with this criterion can only mean wrath (3:5). Thus, when the eschatological judgment described in Rom. 2:5–16 is imagined in Romans 3:20, the confrontation of universal human unrighteousness and the forensic criterion of the law ends in universal condemnation: ἐξ ἔργων νόμου οὐ δικαιωθήσεται πᾶσα σὰρξ ἐνώπιον αὐτοῦ.

This is the rhetorical and theological prelude to Paul's announcement that "the righteousness of God is made visible" (3:21), a statement which in the forensic and nomological terms of Rom. 2:5–3:20 should mean an eschatological revelation of God's righteousness according to the law that results in the condemnation of the unrighteous. But Paul announces a "righteousness of God" that is "made visible apart from the law" (3:21) and that effects not the judgment, but the justification of sinners (3:23–24). One way to hear Paul's proclamation about God declaring the unrighteous righteous through the death of Christ as the demonstration rather than the disqualification of God's righteousness is to read Rom. 3:24–26 in conversation with Rom. 2:4–10. The universal non-justification of the unrighteous announced in Rom. 3:20 reads like the only and inevitable conclusion of the coming judgment. In its wake, Paul's location of God's righteousness in an event that calls the unrighteous righteous sounds like, to borrow Kant's characterization of the cross, a "moral outrage."[27] But for Paul, the righteousness of God is seen and instantiated in God's justifying act of putting Jesus forward as a ἱλαστήριον because, rather than circumventing the eschatological judgment envisioned earlier in the letter, Rom. 3:24–26 interprets the cross of Christ as the enactment of that eschatological judgment in the "now" (3:21, 26) of Jesus' death.

There is an oft-noted lexical connection between Rom. 2:4 and 3:26a (ἀνοχή), but it is seldom observed that this divine patience functions within parallel plotlines.[28] In both Rom. 2:4–10 and 3:24–26, ἀνοχή is used to characterize an era in contrast to a time defined by the disclosure of God's righteousness (δικαιοκρισίας τοῦ θεοῦ, 2:5; δικαιοσύνη αὐτοῦ, 3:26). As Bornkamm remarks, in Romans "the periods of

---

27. I. Kant, *Religion within the Limits of Reason Alone* (New York: Harper & Row, 1960), 164.
28. C. E. B. Cranfield, *A Critical and Exegetical Commentary on the Epistle to the Romans*, ICC (Edinburgh: T&T Clark, 1975), 1:211, is a partial exception.

salvation history" are "placed in contrast to each other as the time of patience and the time of the showing of righteousness."[29] This observation is offered by Bornkamm as an exegesis of Rom. 3:25–26, but as it stands, it is an equally apt description of the implicit plotline of Rom. 2:4–5: the present is the time of God's kindness and patience and concludes with the coming apocalypse of God's righteous judgment. Within this narrative sequence, the end of the era of divine patience is the arrival of the eschaton in the form of a future judgment (2:5–10).

Romans 3:24–26 tells a sequentially similar story, but with an all-important temporal twist. Romans 2:4–5 contrasts the *present* era of patience with the *future* enactment of justice in the form of a judgment κατὰ τὰ ἔργα. Romans 3:25–26, by contrast, presents the *past* as the time of the ἀνοχή τοῦ θεοῦ, the time in which God delayed the revelation of his righteous-judgment "by passing over former sins" (διὰ τὴν πάρεσιν τῶν προγεγονότων ἁμαρτημάτων).[30] And this era is juxtaposed, not with the *future* "day of wrath," but with the *present* demonstration of divine righteousness that is the cross of Jesus Christ. Thus, in narrative terms, God's act of putting Jesus forward as a ἱλαστήριον in Rom. 3:25–26 is functionally parallel to "the revelation of God's righteous-judgment" in Rom. 2:5.[31] In other words, the death of Jesus Christ is the demonstration of God's righteousness in that the "now" (νῦν) of Golgotha is the eschatological enactment of the final judgment.[32]

---

29. G. Bornkamm, "The Revelation of God's Wrath," in *Early Christian Experience* (New York: Harper & Row, 1966), 49.

30. The connection between Rom. 2:4–5 and 3:25–26 tells decisively against W. G. Kümmel's insistence that πάρεσις should be translated "forgiveness" rather than "passing over" ("Πάρεσις und ἔνδειξις. Ein Beitrag zum Verständis der paulinschen Rechtfertigungslehre," in *Heilsgeschehen und Geschichte: Gesammelte Aufsätze. 1933–1964*, ed. W. G. Kümmel [Marburg: Elwert Verlag, 1965], 260–70).

31. Paul's use of ἱλαστήριον in Rom. 3:25–26 operates within an interpretation of the cross as eschatological judgment, and therefore, together with the liberative (ἀπολύτρωσις) metaphor, the cultic evocations conjured by the use of ἱλαστήριον do not function as independent though complementary "lines of approximation" (Barth, *CD* IV/1, 274) to the ultimately non-metaphorical truth of God's salvific act. Rather, in Rom. 3:25–26, ἱλαστήριον and ἀπολύτρωσις are coordinated by, and thus contribute to, an interpretation of the cross as God's eschatological judgment.

32. See Hans Urs von Balthasar, *Mysterium Paschale*, trans. A. Nichols (Edinburgh: T&T Clark, 1990), 119: the cross is "the full achievement of the divine judgment." For a discussion of Paul's description of the death of Christ in relation to the final judgment imagined by an early Jewish apocalypse, see my "Debating Diagonal Δικαιοσύνη: The *Epistle of Enoch* and Paul in Theological Conversation," *Early Christianity* 1, no. 1 (2010): 107–28.

Expressed in terms of the parallel between Rom. 2:5 and 3:25–26a, the present "demonstration of divine righteousness" (ἔνδειξιν τῆς δικαιοσύνης αὐτοῦ, 3:25, 26a) is the occurrence of the promised "revelation of God's righteous judgment" (ἀποκαλύψεως δικαιοκρισίας τοῦ θεοῦ, 2:5).[33] The "now" of the cross is the "day of wrath" (2:5), the day God reveals his "righteous judgment" (2:5) and thereby, shows himself to be righteous (εἰς τὸ εἶναι αὐτὸν δίκαιον, 3:26; cf. 3:5).

As the καί that links the predicates "just" and "justifier" in Rom. 3:26b indicates, however, the cross is both the demonstration of God's righteousness and the declaration that those of Christ-faith are righteous. The death of Christ is the demonstration of God's righteousness as the proleptic enactment of God's eschatological judgment. But—and here, we approach what Jüngel calls "the deepest secret of God's righteousness"[34]—this carrying out of God's contention with sinful humanity effects, not as its counterpart but as its consequence, the "nevertheless" of justification.[35] In judging unrighteousness on the cross, God justifies the unrighteous. For Paul, "the righteousness of God" revealed in the gospel is this christological act of justifying judgment. Or, to anticipate my interpretation of Rom. 3:21–24, "the righteousness of God" is God's eschatological demonstration and declaration of righteousness enacted and spoken in the gift of Jesus Christ.

---

33. This does not mean, as Barth claims (*A Shorter Commentary on Romans*, trans. D. H. van Daalen [London: SCM Press, 1959], 24–26), that the "day" of Rom. 2:5 (cf. 1:18; 2:16) *refers* to the cross; but it does suggest, however paradoxically, that the future judgment referred to in 2:5–10 *occurs* on the cross. Thus, while Paul continues to affirm the futurity of judgment (Rom. 14:10–12; 1 Cor. 3:12–15; 4:4–5; 2 Cor. 5:10), his consideration of its soteriological shape in Rom. 8:31–34 is determined by God's prior and ongoing act in his Son (cf. the greater-to-lesser logic of Rom. 5:9). The relationship between present and future justification is thus the reverse of what Wright suggests: present justification is not an accurate "anticipation of the future verdict" ("The New Perspective on Paul," 260); the future word of justification is an echo and effect of the justifying judgment enacted in the cross.

34. Jüngel, *Justification*, 87.

35. It is therefore accurate to gloss "the righteousness of God" as *iustitia salutifera* (so, Cremer, *Die paulinische Rechtfertigungslehre*, 33), not because it is opposed to divine judgment, but because in the death of Jesus, as Seifrid comments, "the contention between the Creator and the fallen creature is decided in God's favor and yet savingly resolved" ("Paul's Use of Righteousness Language Against Its Hellenistic Background," in *Justification and Variegated Nomism: Volume II—The Paradoxes of Paul*, eds. D. A. Carson et al. [Tübingen: Mohr Siebeck, 2004], 39–74, at 59; cf. G. Theißen, *Erleben und Verhalten der ersten Christen: Eine Psychologie des Urchristentums* [Munich: Gütersloher, 2007], 315–16).

Defining Δικαιοσύνη θεοῦ as the Righteousness of God through Faith in Jesus Christ

In Rom. 2:1–3:20, eschatological judgment is not just the location of the revelation of God's righteous judgment (2:5), it is also the context in which God recognizes "the doers of the law" as righteous (2:13, 16; cf. 3:20). Both judgment and justification occur in this forensic future. And here, judgment is carried out "according to works" (κατὰ τὰ ἔργα)—that is, as Romans 2:13 specifies, God's pronouncement will correspond to one's nomistic observance: "the doers of the law will be declared righteous," or conversely, and, because "none are righteous" (3:10), inevitably, "by works of law no flesh will be declared righteous" (3:20). Because God's righteousness operates in accordance with the criterion of the law, it confronts sinners only with a word of condemnation.[36]

"But"—which is a very different word than "accordingly"—"the righteousness of God has been made visible apart from law" (χωρὶς νόμου, Rom. 3:21). Within the sphere of the law, divine and human justification are mutually exclusive: the justification of God (Rom. 3:4–5) entails the non-justification of sinners (3:19–20). But it is just this impossibility that Romans 3:21–26 proclaims: the divine act that is the cross of Christ establishes God as both "just" and "justifier" (3:26b). Here, as in Rom. 2:13 and 3:19–20, divine and human justification are located in the event of eschatological judgment, but in Rom. 3:21–26 the arrival of that eschaton in the "now" of Jesus' death rewrites God's future word of justification in the present tense (3:24; cf. 3:28 and the aorist in 5:1).[37] Justification is not a separate verdict from the one God will speak at final judgment, nor is it only "an anticipation of the future

---

36. See Philo's insistence that, as a matter of principle, δικαιοσύνη works κατ' ἀξίαν (*Leg.* 1.87; *Mos.* 2.9; *Sobr.* 40)—that is, in accordance with some criterion of "fit" or correspondence between human "worth" and divine action. For "correspondence" as the defining characteristic of God's righteousness in at least some early Jewish texts, see chapters two and seven in my *God, Grace, and Righteousness*.

37. Peter Stuhlmacher is therefore right to argue that "justification involves an act of judgment" and is "decidedly located in the final judgment," but he underemphasizes the Pauline stress on the "now-ness" of this justifying judgment (*Revisiting Paul's Doctrine of Justification: A Challenge to the New Perspective*, trans. D. P. Bailey [Downers Grove: IVP Academic, 2001], 14).

231

verdict."[38] Justification is the final verdict—a forensic word from the future spoken in the enactment of God's eschatological judgment that is the "now" of Jesus' death (and resurrection; cf. Rom. 4:25).[39]

Hence, the shock of Paul's announcement: those declared righteous in this judgment are not "the doers of the law," but "sinners." Whereas Rom. 2:5 describes a future judgment in which human action and juridical fate correspond (κατὰ τὰ ἔργα), Paul, in Rom. 3:21–26, locates the operations of God's righteousness in the contradiction between human unrighteousness and the somehow stronger word of justification: "All sinned . . . and are declared righteous" (Rom. 3:23–24). Grammatically, the objects of the divine saving action implied in the passive participle δικαιούμενοι (3:24) are the sinners of 3:23,[40] and thus as James Dunn construes this Pauline paradox, "it is precisely those who have sinned and fallen short of God's glory who are justified."[41] The "scandal and folly" of this "word of the cross" is not hard to hear: what Paul calls "the righteousness of God" appears to be (and, within the sphere of law described in Rom. 1:18–3:20, is) an instance of injustice in which God, with what looks like forensic schizophrenia, rightly diagnoses the unrighteous (Rom. 3:23; cf. 3:10) only to rename them *e contrario* with the word of justification (3:24).

For Paul, however, the declaration that sinners are righteous is not a groundless divine fiat; it is a pronouncement grounded in a gift. The adversative δέ that opens Rom. 3:21 serves what Jochen Flebbe describes as a "logisch-rhetorischen Funktion in der Opposition zu V.20."[42] In antithesis to the (excluded) possibility of justification before

---

38. Wright, "New Perspective on Paul," 260.
39. The term "forensic" indicates not just the legal connotations of the δικ- word group; it describes the enactment of final judgment in the arrival of the eschaton that is the death of Jesus Christ. The related phrase, "declare righteous," likewise indicates more than the verdict of an ordinary judge; it is the effective pronouncement of the creator that re-creates sinners as righteous.
40. Following Cranfield (*Romans*, 1.205), I take as the subject of 3:24 the "all" of 3:23 while recognizing that 3:24 continues the main theme from 3:21–22. Campbell is probably correct to see the anthropological statement of 3:23 as an elaboration of the "all the believing ones" of 3:22 such that the subject of the passive form of δικαιόω in 3:24 is doubly qualified by the "all of faith" and the "all sinned" (*The Rhetoric of Righteousness in Romans 3.21–22*, JSNTSup 65 [Sheffield: Sheffield Academic, 1992], 86–92).
41. J. D. G. Dunn, *Romans 1–8*, WBC 38a (Waco: Word, 1988), 168.
42. J. Flebbe, *Solus Deus: Untersuchungen zur Rede von Gott im Brief des Paulus an die Römer*, BZNW 158 (Berlin: de Gruyter, 2008), 68.

God by works of law (3:20), Rom. 3:21 announces a manifestation of the righteousness of God "apart from law." This logical contrast, however, is not between two abstract soteriological theses; it is between reality before and after the "now" of God's "gift" (χάρις) that is "the redemption which is in Christ Jesus" (3:24). The "now" of Romans 3:21 anticipates the ἐν τῷ νῦν καιρῷ of 3:26a, indicating that the manifestation of δικαιοσύνη θεοῦ (3:21) cannot be isolated from the demonstration of God's righteousness in the eschatological judgment that is the death of Christ (3:25–26). The contrast between Rom. 3:20 and 3:21 is thus properly eschatological: νυνὶ δέ signals the arrival of the eschaton in the event of grace that is the cross of Jesus Christ.[43]

It is in this new time, what Paul calls the "now-time" (3:26a), that "the righteousness of God is made visible," not according to the law—it is χωρὶς νόμου—but as the "righteousness of God through faith in Jesus Christ" (Rom. 3:21–22). As Simon Gathercole notes, "apart from law" and "through faith" are mutually interpreting, such "that χωρίς in verse 21 is clearly the opposite of διά in verse 22."[44] "Apart from law" is therefore a negative definition of the "righteousness of God through faith in Jesus Christ": "'by faith,'" writes Francis Watson, "*means 'apart from law.'*"[45] In Barth's words, "*sola fide*" is the "great negation"; it identifies the absence of law-defined righteousness, and thus names the nothingness from which God re-creates sinners as righteous.[46] This suggests that "the righteousness of God," as "the righteousness of faith," is not determined by the law-defined correspondence between human worth and God's judgment. Rather, as the incongruity between human worth ("sinners," Rom. 3:23) and God's word ("declared righteous," 3:24) indicates, "the righteousness of God" is characterized by creative contradiction. Just as Abraham's faith lived where his body and Sarah's womb were dead (νέκρωσις, Rom. 4:19) and so trusted "the one who gives life to the dead and calls into being that which does not

43. Cf. Käsemann, *Romans*, 93.
44. S. J. Gathercole, *Where is Boasting: Early Jewish Soteriology and Paul's Response in Romans 1–5* (Grand Rapids: Eerdmans, 2002), 224. He adds, "the 'righteousness of God revealed apart from the Law' in 3:21 is equivalent to "the righteousness of God through faith" in 3:22."
45. F. Watson, *Paul and the Hermeneutics of Faith* (London: T&T Clark, 2004), 72 (italics original).
46. Barth, *CD* IV/1, 621.

exist" (4:17), so Paul sets faith in the vacuum created by the absence of law (χωρὶς νόμου, 3:21) and works (ὁ μὴ ἐργαζόμενος, 4:5; χωρὶς ἔργων, 4:6) and identifies the God it trusts as "the one who justifies the ungodly" (4:5). Nothingness, death, and sin—for Paul, these are the site at which God utters a creative counter-statement: creation, life, righteousness.[47]

Faith, in the first instance, is this anthropological negation, the site of sin, death, and nothingness at which God operates out of the opposite. Defined by what it is not (i.e., law and works), faith "speaks," as Oswald Bayer puts it, "in the *via negationis.*"[48] Facing the human, faith says "no"; it hears God's impossible promise—"I will give you a son by Sarah" (Gen. 17:6)—looks at Abraham's age and Sarah's barrenness, and laughs (Gen. 17:7; Rom. 4:19). But faith's focus is not the believing human; it is the "God" who is "able to do as he promises" (Rom. 4:21). And looking here, faith laughs again: "the Lord did to Sarah as he promised . . . and Sarah said, 'the Lord has made laughter for me'" (Gen. 21:6). As Paul reads Genesis, Abraham's "faith was counted to him as righteousness" (Gen. 15:6; Rom. 4:3, 22) "because" (διό, 4:22) it is this double laughter: even as faith considers Abraham's age and Sarah's barrenness and says, "death" (Rom. 4:19), it hears the promise and "believes the God who gives life to the dead" (4:17; 4:20–21).[49]

This brings us back to Rom. 3:21-22. The "righteousness of God through faith," because it is defined by the absence of law, is first an anthropological negation. With Rom. 3:20, it says "no" to the possibility of righteousness before God by works of law. But as with Abraham, the laughter of faith's "yes" is louder than the laughter of its "no." And if "apart from law" identifies faith's "no," it is the name "Jesus Christ"

---

47. For the linking of the liturgical predictions of Romans 4:5 and 4:17 and the related claim that *creatio e contrario* describes a *modus operandi* that connects the divine acts of creation, resurrection, and justification, see my *God, Grace, and Righteousness*, 152–54; Käsemann, *Romans*, 123.

48. Bayer, *Martin Luther's Theology: A Contemporary Interpretation*, trans. Thomas H. Trapp (Grand Rapids: Eerdmans, 2008), 172.

49. Cf. Watson, *Hermeneutics*, 169: "Paul sets faith on the border between despair and hope and sees it facing in both directions. Faith is both despair of human capacity and hope in [the] saving act of God." The passive forms of ἐνδυναμόω and πληροφορέω in 4:20 and 4:21 suggest that even Abraham's believing is generated by God through the promise (cf. Rom. 10:17). It is suggestive that when Paul gives voices to "the righteousness of faith," he hears it saying an anthropological no—"Do not say in your heart who will ascend to heaven . . . or who will descend to the abyss?"—and a christological yes—"The word is near you" (Rom. 10:6-8).

that defines faith's "yes." In Rom. 3:21–22, the contrast between "law" and "faith" is asymmetrical. Whereas "law" is joined to a preposition (χωρίς), "faith" gets both a preposition (διά) and a name, Jesus Christ. The effect of this imbalance is to "christologize" faith. It is not faith in abstract antithesis to law that defines "the righteousness of God." Rather, "the righteousness of God" is the "righteousness of God through faith in Jesus Christ." Hence, Barth's question: "what is the *sola fide* but a faint yet necessary echo of the *solus Christus*?"[50] "Through faith in Christ" is the Pauline way of saying "Christ alone." Defined in antithesis to "works of law," it excludes law-defined worth as the grounds of justification; defined by the name Jesus Christ, it confesses Christ as the *one* by, in, and on the basis of whom God justifies the ungodly. "All sinned," says Paul, "and are justified . . . in Christ Jesus" (Rom. 3:23–24).

To say, then, that "the righteousness of God" is "the righteousness of God through faith in Jesus Christ" is to say that God's eschatological act of judgment and justification is irreducibly and exclusively singular—it is Jesus Christ. As Luther puts it, "faith justifies because it takes hold of and possesses this treasure, the present Christ," and therefore, "the true Christian righteousness" is not the human act of believing; it is "the Christ who is grasped by faith . . . and on account of whom God counts us righteous."[51] Rather than qualifying this christological singularity (*solus Christus*), *sola fide* is the apophatic affirmation of the "gift" that is "the redemption which is in Christ Jesus" (Rom. 3:24): διὰ τοῦτο ἐκ πίστεως, ἵνα κατὰ χάριν (Rom. 4:16).[52] To borrow Thomas

---

50. Barth, *CD* IV/1, 632.

51. *LW* 26:130 = *WA* 40/I:229, 22–30. Read with the hindsight of Romans 3 and 4, Paul's opening announcement that "the righteousness of God is revealed in the gospel" "just as it is written, 'the one who is righteous by faith will live" (Rom. 1:16–17, quoting Hab. 2:4) can be heard as an expression of the christological yes that positively defines "the righteousness of God through faith." Thus, to read Romans 1:17 as saying that God's righteousness is gifted to faith is, as filled out by Romans 3:22, to say that Christ, who is "our righteousness" (1 Cor. 1:30) is given to faith in the gospel.

52. Käsemann, *Romans*, 101: "Precision is given to *sola gratia* by *sola fide*." Cf. Jüngel, *Justification*, 149–226, 236–59, who demonstrates that the reformational *solas* are ordered in such a way as to preserve *solus Christus*. The common charge that the objective genitive reading of πίστις Χριστοῦ is anthropological rather than christological is simply false at the level of historical theological description. For this, see my "The Christo-Centrism of Faith in Christ." Once the theological objections are addressed, the strong semantic case for something like the objective genitive can

Cranmer's image, "faith" is the finger of "St John Baptist," pointing away from the self and to "the lamb of God that takes away the sins of the world."[53]

Paul's definition of "the righteousness of God" as "the righteousness of God through faith in Jesus Christ" is thus an instance of what Käsemann calls "applied Christology."[54] "The righteousness of God" is a description of the eschatological demonstration of righteousness and the eschatological declaration of righteousness that is God's gift of Jesus Christ. This means that Paul does not look in the lexicon of apocalyptic Judaism to define δικαιοσύνη θεοῦ; he deduces his definition from the gift of Christ that makes God's righteousness visible by demonstrating it in the enactment of eschatological judgment that both judges unrighteousness and justifies the unrighteous. For Paul, "the righteousness of God" is not a "feste Formel" that Paul "takes over" from apocalyptic Judaism. Rather, God's gift of Jesus Christ is the apocalypse—the event that unveils "the righteousness of God." Käsemann, in this sense, reads Paul backward: Paul does not employ a traditional concept to interpret what God has done in Christ; for Paul, "the righteousness of God" is what God has done in Christ. It is not "use and custom" that define the Pauline phrase δικαιοσύνη θεοῦ. Rather, "Christ's pure veil presents th[e] sight" of divine justice. As Origen put it, the "iustitia Dei . . . est Christus"—"the righteousness of God" is

---

be heard: 1) Paul's instrumental faith clauses are derived from the ἐκ πίστεως of Habakkuk 2:4, which does not (pace R. B. Hays, The Conversion of the Imagination: Paul as Interpreter of Israel's Scripture [Grand Rapids: Eerdmans, 2005], 119–42) employ ὁ δίκαιος as a christological title, but as a reference to the generic, believing human, a point confirmed by the appeal to Abraham in Romans 4 and Galatians 3 (Francis Watson, Paul, Judaism and the Gentiles: Beyond the New Perspective [Grand Rapids: Eerdmans, 2007], 240). 2) In Paul, Jesus is never the subject of the verb πιστεύω and Paul's habit of interpreting an instance of the verb in a citation with reference to the noun (e.g., Rom. 4:3, 5; 9:32–33 10:5–11, 16–17) indicates that the meaning of the noun and verb have not drifted apart (R. B. Matlock, "Detheologizing the ΠΙΣΤΙΣ ΧΡΙΣΤΟΥ Debate: Cautionary Remarks from a Lexical Semantic Perspective," NovT 42, no. 1 [2000]: 1–23, at 13–14; cf. Watson, Paul, Judaism and the Gentiles, 243). 3). The question of redundancy in Romans 3:22, Galatians 2:16, 3:22 and Philippians 3:9 points to "a much wider pattern of repetition of πίστις/πιστεύω in Galatians and Romans, rooted in Genesis 15:6 and Habakkuk 2:4" that functions to disambiguate the genitive phrase (R. B. Matlock, "Saving Faith: The Rhetoric and Semantics of πίστις in Paul," in The Faith of Jesus Christ: Exegetical, Biblical and Theological Studies, eds. M. F. Bird and P. M. Sprinkle [Peabody: Hendrickson, 2009], 73–89, at 89).

53. John Edmund Cox, Miscellaneous Writings and Letters of Thomas Cranmer (Cambridge: Parker Society, 1846; reproduced by Regent College Publishing), 132–33.

54. Käsemann, Romans, 96.

the gift of Jesus Christ in whom "we become the righteousness of God (2 Cor. 5:21) and who himself is "our righteousness (1 Cor. 1:30). For Paul, δικαιοσύνη θεοῦ is not just a concept from apocalyptic Judaism; δικαιοσύνη θεοῦ is what is apocalypsed in the gospel of Jesus Christ. An apocalyptic definition of "the righteousness of God" is, therefore, a christological definition: Jesus Christ, as both the eschatological demonstration and gift of God's righteousness, is the revelation of "the righteousness of God" and thus the one who defines δικαιοσύνη θεοῦ.

The Pauline definition of δικαιοσύνη θεοῦ is a christological redefinition—it is deduced from and descriptive of God's gift of Jesus Christ. Barth captures this:

> The Christian message does not at its heart express a concept or an idea . . . it recounts a history . . . in such a way that it declares a name. . . . This means that all the concepts and ideas used in this report [δικαιοσύνη θεοῦ, for example] can derive their significance only from the bearer of this name and from his history, and not the reverse. . . . They cannot say what has to be said with some meaning of their own or in some context of their own abstracted from this name. They can serve only to describe this name—the name of Jesus Christ.[55]

Victor Hugo's description of the merciful Monseigneur Bienvenu, however, seems the more fitting conclusion. "He had his own strange way of judging things," Hugo writes in *Les Misérables*, "I suspect he acquired it from the Gospels." For Paul, God has his own strange way of judging; he reveals it in the Gospel.

---

55. Barth, *CD* IV/1, 16–17. This does not, of course, mean that "the law and the prophets" do not "bear witness to" God's righteousness revealed in the gospel, but it does suggest they do so precisely as voices that "pre-preach" (Gal. 3:8) and "promise beforehand" the "gospel . . . about God's Son, Jesus Christ" (Rom. 1:1-4). The crucified and risen Christ is the definition of δικαιοσύνη θεοῦ both before and after the "now" of the gospel, but it is only in this "now" that the "mystery kept secret" in "the prophetic writings" is "disclosed" (Rom. 16:25-26, echoing the revelatory vocabulary—φανερόω—of Rom. 3:21).

12

Thinking from Christ to Israel

Romans 9–11 in Apocalyptic Context

Beverly Roberts Gaventa

"Therefore from now on we consider no one from a human point of view.
Even if we once considered Christ from a human point of view,
we no longer consider him in that way.
If anyone is in Christ: new creation!"
    —2 Corinthians 5:16–17

Sometime in the mid-to-late 50s of the Common Era, the Apostle Paul planned to travel from Corinth to Jerusalem, then Rome, and then Spain. In anticipation of this important venture, he wrote an extended letter to congregations of Christians[1] in Rome. The letter seeks Roman support, both for his encounter with those in Jerusalem who resist his understanding of the gospel and for his planned mission in Spain. Yet, the letter is also a proclamation of the gospel, as Paul fears or suspects that many Roman Christians (most, but not all of whom are gentiles)

---

1. The term "Christian" is admittedly anachronistic, but I find that preferable to the unwieldy character of some proposed alternatives.

have not heard the gospel in its fullness. What they comprehend is that God's Messiah has arrived in the person of Jesus of Nazareth and that this arrival means gentiles may be included among God's people without circumcision. Indeed, some of these gentile Christians even believe themselves to have displaced Jews as God's beloved.

Paul's letter strenuously affirms the inclusion of gentiles and rejects the false conclusion that gentiles have displaced Jews as God's beloved, but it does far more than that. As Paul presents the gospel in this letter, it is nothing less than God's powerful intervention on behalf of a humanity (both Jew and Gentile) enslaved by powers named Sin and Death. These powers have held in captivity all of humanity, all of the created order, to the extent that even the Law is employed by Sin and all of humanity is rendered hostile to God. In the death and resurrection of Jesus, God triumphs over Sin and Death, signaling God's imminent triumph over all anti-God powers and redeeming humanity (indeed, the whole of the cosmos) for new life. In other words, Romans belongs squarely under the heading of apocalyptic theology.[2]

Over the last decade or so, I have published a series of articles that contribute to the sketch above.[3] Most of those contributions focus on Romans 1–8, but what is to be said of Romans 9–11, which many scholars identify as the heart of the letter?[4] To put the question

---

2. For an explanation of my use of the term "apocalyptic theology" and a brief response to some of the objections to its use with regard to Paul, see *Our Mother Saint Paul* (Louisville: Westminster John Knox, 2007), 80–84.

3. In addition to *Our Mother Saint Paul*, 113–60, 194–205, see "Interpreting the Death of Jesus Apocalyptically: Reconsidering Romans 8:32," in *Jesus and Paul Reconnected: Fresh Pathways into an Old Debate*, ed. Todd Still (Grand Rapids: Eerdmans, 2007), 125–45; "From Toxic Speech to the Redemption of Doxology in Romans," in *The Word Leaps the Gap: Essays on Scripture and Theology in Honor of Richard B. Hays*, ed. J. Ross Wagner, C. Kavin Rowe, and A. Katherine Grieb (Grand Rapids: Eerdmans, 2008), 392–408; "'For the Glory of God': Theology and Experience in Paul's Letter to the Romans," in *Between Experience and Interpretation: Engaging the Writings of the New Testament*, ed. Mary F. Foskett and O. Wesley Allen Jr. (Nashville: Abingdon, 2008), 53–65; "'To Preach the Gospel': Romans 1, 15 and the Purposes of Romans," in *The Letter to the Romans*, BETL 226, ed. Udo Schnelle (Leuven: Peeters, 2009), 179–95; "Paul and the Roman Believers," in *Blackwell Companion to Paul*, ed. Stephen Westerholm (Oxford: Blackwell, 2011), 93–107; "'Neither Height nor Depth': Discerning the Cosmology of Romans," *SJT* 64, no. 3 (2011): 265–78; "The Shape of the 'I': The Psalter, the Gospel, and the Speaker in Romans 7," in *Apocalyptic Paul*, ed. Beverly Roberts Gaventa (Waco: Baylor University Press, 2013), 77–91; "The Rhetoric of Violence and the God of Peace in Paul's Letter to the Romans," in *Paul, John, and Apocalyptic Eschatology: Studies in Honour of Martinus C. de Boer*, NovTSup 149, eds. Jans Krans et al. (Leiden: Brill, 2013), 61–75; "The 'Glory of God' in Paul's Letter to the Romans," in *Interpretation and the Claims of the Text: Resourcing New Testament Theology*, eds. Jason A. Whitlark et al. (Waco: Baylor University Press, 2014), 29–40.

sharply, can an apocalyptic reading of Romans be extended beyond chapters 1-8 into 9-11, or does it fall apart at the white space that demarcates the chapters? Worse yet, does an apocalyptic reading of chapters 1-8 inevitably reduce the role of chapters 9-11, returning us to the time when scholars treated Paul's discussion of Israel as a mere "aside" or "appendix" to the main part of his argument?

In this chapter, I argue that Romans 9-11, far from being an "aside" or "appendix," extends the argument Paul has made from the beginning of the letter: in the death and resurrection of Christ Jesus, God has begun to reclaim the world that belongs to God alone. God's action in Christ Jesus reveals retrospectively the extent of human enslavement; the whole of humanity (indeed, the whole of creation) is, in effect, revealed in Christ Jesus. (In the familiar language of E. P. Sanders, "the solution precedes the problem."[5]) A similar argumentative logic is at work in Romans 9-11: the action of God in Christ Jesus reveals something about Israel. The argument here is not primarily about Israel's faith or lack thereof; it concerns Israel's past, present, and future, as Israel's very identity is revealed in light of Christ.

In addition, Christ is far from being sidelined in chapters 9-11, as it is Christ through whom Israel's identity is being revealed. In this sense, the shape of the argument in chapters 9-11 coheres with chapters 1-8 in that here also, the solution (in this case, the death and resurrection of Jesus Christ) reveals the problem (namely, the identity of Israel). What Paul does in these chapters is to think backward from the cross and resurrection, the event that inaugurates God's triumph. As he thinks backward, he sees Israel as God's adopted child, recipient of a number of gifts. Those gifts culminate with the Christ, who is from Israel physically, and yet, separated from Israel by his identity with God. In the argument that follows in Rom. 9:6-11:36, Israel is read

---

4. Although see "On the Calling-Into-Being of Israel: Rom. 9:6-29," in *Between Gospel and Election*, WUNT 257, ed. Florian Wilk and J. Ross Wagner (Tübingen: Mohr Siebeck, 2010), 255-69; *Our Mother Saint Paul*, 149-60, 202-5; "Questions about *Nomos*, Answers about *Christos*: Romans 10:4 in Context," forthcoming.

5. E. P. Sanders, *Paul and Palestinian Judaism* (Philadelphia: Fortress Press, 1977), 442-47.

through Jesus Christ, read through God's creative initiative, through God's staging of a race for righteousness, and through God's redemption. This story has far less to say about Israel's faithfulness or failings than it does about God's creation of and intervention in Israel for God's own purposes.

Because the preceding language about Israel's identity may be confused with the question of membership in Israel, it is important to be as clear as possible. When I say that God's action reveals Israel's identity, I do not mean that Israel is now identified with the (mostly gentile) church or that the notion of "Israel" refers only to those Jews who recognize Jesus of Nazareth as Israel's messiah (i.e., some faithful subset of Israel). I understand the membership of Israel to be coterminous with what is usually referred to as "ethnic" or "historic" or "biological" Israel. What I see at issue here is not the composition of Israel (the membership roster, to put it crudely), but how Israel is to be understood in relation to God; for Paul, the identity of Israel is known not by looking back to Abraham or Moses or David and reasoning forward, but through Christ and from Christ backward.[6] It is in that sense that the logic of chapters 9–11 resembles the logic of chapters 1–8. In both cases, the "solution precedes the problem," or better, the Christ event generates a new understanding. This is not a new Israel in terms of its human membership, but an Israel whose relationship to God is revealed in light of the apocalypse of the gospel (1:16–17).

Minding the Gap: Reading from 8:31–39 to 9:1–5

The white space that separates Rom. 9:1 from 8:39 in our Greek New Testaments may be helpful from the point of view of book designers, with their proper concerns for aesthetics and readability. Yet, the separation of Paul's comments at the outset of chapter 9 from what

---

6. Contrast N. T. Wright's repeated statement that Romans 9–11 is a great narrative of Abraham's family and its vocation (as in *Paul and the Faithfulness of God* [Minneapolis: Fortress Press, 2013], 499, 501, 503, 1158, 1172, and often elsewhere). What I am arguing is that, for Paul, Israel ("biological" Israel, not the church) is known through Jesus Christ, not the other way around. My further response to Wright's interpretation of Romans is available in "The Character of God's Faithfulness: A Response to N. T. Wright," *JSPL* 4, no. 2 (2014): 71–79.

precedes has severely misleading consequences, especially when it comes to the role played by Christ.[7] Paul's comments in 9:1-5 both connect Israel with what has been said earlier about the "we" of believers and simultaneously set Israel apart as a people with a particular relationship to God—a relationship that is now to be understood through Jesus Christ.

To begin with, in 8:31-39, Paul has succinctly identified Christ as God's "own son," not withheld but handed over on behalf of "us," the one who died, who was raised, who is at the right hand of God and intercedes on "our" behalf. It is because of God's action in this Christ that Paul can affirm with such conviction that nothing can separate "us" from the love of God in Christ Jesus (8:39). The assumption appears to be that there are, in fact, powers that want to separate humanity from its rightful Lord, but this separation is impossible because they have not the power (οὔτε . . . δυνήσεται). All of these comments assume that the risen Christ wields immense power (and see 1:4, 16).[8]

Bearing this same discourse of power in mind as we move into chapter 9 causes certain features of the text to leap off the page. In v. 1, as Paul repeatedly affirms the truthfulness of what he is about to say, he begins by insisting that "in Christ," he is speaking the truth. He speaks "in Christ," that is, as one who lives in the realm of the powerful Christ whose intervention and love have been so emphatically asserted in chapter 8.[9] And in v. 3, he swears that he would wish to be cut off from Christ because of his brothers and sisters. Paul's connection with and concern for fellow Jews cannot be overlooked or minimized here (or in 10:1), but the primary identity he asserts is his identification with Christ. In light of the end of chapter 8, the wish to be anathema from Christ is an absurdity: it cannot happen.[10] It is his location in Christ that

---

7. I disagree with Thomas Tobin's argument that Romans 8–11 is a single thematic and rhetorical unit, but he has rightly highlighted the connections between 8:31-39 and chapters 9–11 (*Paul's Rhetoric in Its Contexts: The Argument of Romans* [Peabody: Hendrickson, 2004], 251–72, 320–25).

8. Elsewhere in Paul's letters, that immense power is interpreted to be power in weakness, as in Rom. 3:24-25, 15:1-3, 7–9; 1 Cor. 1:22-25; 2 Cor. 8:9; 13:4; Gal. 2:20; 3:13-14; and Phil. 2:5-11, but here the emphasis lies on its redemptive character.

9. That is to say, ἐν Χριστῷ modifies λέγω rather than ἀλήθειαν. There are not two distinct standards of truth, Christ's and some other.

10. Wayne A. Meeks rightly labels this an "impossible vow" ("On Trusting an Unpredictable God: A

controls what he writes here and throughout 9–11 and not primarily his identity as a Jew.

That last statement may suggest an artificial distinction between Paul's identification with Christ and his identification with Israel. I am not suggesting that Paul has ceased to be a Jew or that he has ceased to think of himself as a Jew. What I want to show instead is that, for Paul, the priority lies with Christ: Paul reads Israel—past, present, and future—through God's action in Jesus Christ.[11]

After this strong introductory assertion of concern about his kinfolk, Paul identifies them as "the Israelites," and then clarifies that term with a list of descriptors. Theirs are "the adoption and the glory and the covenants and the giving of the law and the worship and the promises." The list continues with "theirs are the patriarchs and from them is the Christ, physically speaking."

Space precludes a full exploration of this list, but its beginning and ending are especially important. As Erin Heim has observed in her recent dissertation on the metaphor of adoption in Paul's letters, each of the other items in the list can be correlated with a specific historical moment (or moments), but "adoption" cannot.[12] Commentators routinely concede that the term υἱοθεσία does not appear in the LXX, but nonetheless, they also insist that, with this term, Paul is invoking the "concept" of Israel as God's "son" (as, e.g., in Exod. 4:22–23; Deut. 14:1–2; Hos. 11:1. Mal. 1:6; 2:10).[13] Paul does not, however, refer to Israel here as God's υἱοί or τέκνα, and his choice of terms may be particularly important in light of the discussion of 8:12–39.

In 8:15, Paul declares that "you received a spirit of adoption," and

Hermeneutical Meditation on Romans 9–11," in *In Search of the Early Christians: Selected Essays* [New Haven: Yale University Press, 2002], 214).

11. Re-thinking Israel "backward" from the present crisis seems to be a common feature of Jewish apocalyptic texts, especially *4 Ezra*.

12. "Light through a Prism: New Avenues of Inquiry for the Pauline Υἱοθεσία Metaphors" (D. Phil. Thesis, University of Otago, 2014), 247. Heim's entire discussion of 9:5 is instructive (pp. 241–312).

13. E.g., C. E. B. Cranfield, *A Critical and Exegetical Commentary on the Epistle to the Romans*, ICC (Edinburgh; T&T Clark, 1975), 2:459–60; Heinrich Schlier, *Der Römerbrief: Kommentar*, HThKNT 6 (Freiburg: Herder, 1977), 286; James D. G. Dunn, *Romans*, WBC 38 (Dallas: Word, 1988) 2:526; J. A. Fitzmyer, *Romans*, AB 33A (New York: Doubleday, 1993), 545–46; Douglas Moo, *The Epistle to the Romans*, NICNT (Grand Rapids: Eerdmans, 1996), 562; Klaus Haacker, *Der Brief des Paulus an die Römer*, THKNT (Leipzig: Evangelische Verlagsanstalt, 1999), 183–84; Robert Jewett, *Romans*, Hermeneia (Minneapolis: Fortress Press, 2007), 562–63.

he then proceeds to speak of "us" as God's τέκνα and of the longed-for apocalypse of God's υἱοί. In 8:29, he identifies Jesus as ὁ πρωτότοκος, the "first born" of many brothers and sisters. This is the only place in the undisputed Pauline letters where Christ is referred to as the firstborn (although see Col. 1:15, 18), and it undoubtedly signals Christ's priority. Christians (the "we" of this passage) are connected with Christ as their brother, but he is the first born (8:29). It is because of him that these brothers and sisters are chosen in advance, called, made right, and glorified.

Reading across the white space, then, suggests that identifying the Israelites as recipients of adoption is a complex matter. It does, to be sure, call to mind the historic relationship between God and Israel, especially in light of the remainder of 9:4-5. The people and events brought to mind in 9:4-5 tersely rehearse God's unilateral and unmerited action in the case of this particular people. God's adoption of Israel is crucial and, as will become clear at least in 11:29, it has no termination.

But the apocalypse of Jesus Christ prompts a rethinking of what that historic relationship means. Specifically, the argument of 8:18-39 implies that Israel is not the only child. The Israelites are not the only people whom God has adopted. Israel shares standing with the "we" of 8:15, the ones who have received the gift of the Spirit and who cry out to God as their father, the ones who are Christ's own heirs (8:17), Christ's own brothers and sisters (8:29). In addition, it is Christ who occupies the place of first born (8:29), so that all these children enter the family—metaphorically speaking—after Christ. That is to say: Christ interprets Israel rather than Israel interpreting Christ.

This primary role of Christ is reinforced at the end of v. 5, where the reference to Christ bookends the list of God's actions on behalf of Israel.[14] The symmetry of the list in v. 4 is disrupted when Paul resumes

---

14. The very fact that Paul refers to "Christ" or "Messiah" will suggest to some that he is thinking from an earlier conception of messiahship for Israel forward in order to interpret the gospel, especially in light of Matthew Novenson's recent argument that Χριστός is better understood in Paul as a title than as a proper name. However, among Novenson's important conclusions is that the term is used in a variety of ways and its usage does not come with prepackaged connotations

the ὤν that introduces the list and follows it with οἱ πατέρες καὶ ἐξ ὧν ὁ Χριστὸς τὸ κατὰ σάρκα. Setting apart "the fathers" and "the Christ" with separate phrases draws attention to them.[15] As he introduces "the Christ," however, the phrasing is distinctive. It is not ὧν ὁ Χριστός but ἐξ ὧν ὁ Χριστός and also ὁ Χριστὸς τὸ κατὰ σάρκα. Scholars often suggest that Paul is here polemicizing against those Jews who do not recognize Jesus as the Christ of Israel with his use of language that both separates (Christ is "from" the Israelites but not "of" them) and limits (the relationship is fleshly only).[16] However, the description here *both separates and connects*. Christ is (and remains) an Israelite in a bodily sense (as Paul affirms his own fleshly connection in v. 3).[17] Yet, Christ is not only an Israelite, a powerful successor to the fathers; he is also ὁ ὤν ἐπὶ πάντων.

Verse 5 is a notorious *crux interpretum*,[18] and the constraints of space preclude a review of the issues at stake. For the present, I simply stipulate the likelihood that ὁ ὤν ἐπὶ πάντων refers back to Christ.[19] Christ is simultaneously a descendent of Israel, separate from Israel, and is "over all." This interpretation of Christ is consistent with what Paul has said of him at 8:34–39 and what he will say in 14:9. To say that Christ is at God's right hand, and especially, to say that Christ is lord of the "dead and the living," is, in effect, to say that he is "over all." Even if the concluding ascription of praise to θεός does not refer to ὁ Χριστός, the language and ordering closely associate the two.

These opening verses, 9:1–5, are far more than an introduction to

---

(*Christ Among the Messiahs: Christ Language in Paul and Messiah Language in Ancient Judaism* [Oxford: Oxford University Press, 2012]).

15. So also Moo, *Romans*, 564; Jewett, *Romans*, 566. Paul has already referred to the patriarch Abraham and will refer to him and other patriarchs again in 9:6–13, and near the end of chapter 11, he will insist that Israel remains beloved "because of the fathers."

16. E.g., C. K. Barrett, *A Commentary on the Epistle to the Romans* (London: Adam & Charles Black, 1957), 178; Cranfield, *Romans*, 2:464; Moo, *Romans*, 565; Jewett, *Romans*, 566–67.

17. The insertion of the neuter article τό may limit this relationship (so BDF 266.2), but the parallel with Paul's highly charged expression of his own connection in v. 3 causes me to resist overemphasis on a "merely" fleshly connotation.

18. An instructive review of the treatment of this verse in early versions and in patristic texts is available in Bruce M. Metzger, "The Punctuation of Rom. 9:5," in *Christ and Spirit in the New Testament: In Honour of C. F. D. Moule*, ed. Barnabas Lindars and Stephen S. Smalley (Cambridge: Cambridge University Press, 1973), 95–112.

19. The most natural referent for the ὁ ὤν is the preceding ὁ Χριστός; so Cranfield, *Epistle to the Romans*, 2:464–70; Moo, *Romans*, 564–68; Jewett, *Romans*, 567–68.

a problem about which Paul has deep personal anguish. Indeed, the question of Israel's "faith" or "obedience" is nowhere mentioned and remains suppressed until chapter 10. Instead, Paul puts front and center the advent of Jesus Christ, and that arrival requires a rethinking of Israel.[20] Israel is God's adopted and gifted child, but that adoption has already been said to apply to "us" (gentile and Jewish Christians) as well. And Israel is the Christ's physical family of origin, yet Christ is the firstborn and the one "over all." As chapters 9–11 unfold, Paul continues this retelling of Israel's story. Although cast in the form of history, at least at the outset, and significant elements in Israel's history are at play throughout, this is not an account of Israel generated from Abraham forward. Instead, it is an account generated backward, beginning from the Christ-event.

What follows in 9:6–11:36 is an argument in three movements. First, Paul narrates God's creative justice in the case of Israel, culminating in the threat of destruction (9:6–29); second, in 9:30–10:21, he depicts God's tripping of Israel on the "rock" that proves to be, not the Law but Christ; and finally, in 11:1–36, he contends that God is acting through Israel's temporary division to redeem the entire cosmos. At every turning point, he shows God's action, holding God responsible.

The Creation of Israel and the Strange Justice of God: Romans 9:6–29

Implicit in 9:4–5 is God's unilateral, unmerited bestowal of gifts upon the people Israel, and that implicit claim comes to the foreground in 9:6a with the assertion that God's "word" has not failed.[21] Verse 6b explicates with the cryptic statement: οὐ γὰρ πάντες οἱ ἐξ Ἰσραὴλ οὗτοι Ἰσραήλ. Translations of this statement frequently (and wrongly) supply the word "truly" or "really" in order to distinguish those who are part of Israel "spiritually" from those who belong "merely" to physical

---

20. Elsewhere, Paul has claimed that the death and resurrection of Christ means that "we no longer know anyone from a human point of view" (2 Cor. 5:16). The epistemological implications of the apocalypse of Jesus Christ reverberate throughout Romans, but especially in 9–11.

21. This section draws heavily on my earlier essay, "On the Calling-Into-Being of Israel."

Israel.[22] Along similar lines, C. E. B. Cranfield explains that this is "the company of those who are willing, obedient, grateful witnesses to . . . grace and truth."[23]

Yet, the peculiar account of Israel that follows has nothing whatsoever to do with human willing or obedience or gratitude and everything to do with God's unilateral actions. To begin with, Paul insists that God brought Israel into being by providing Abraham and Sarah with a son.[24] Later still, God chose Jacob rather than his twin, Esau. Both Jewish and later Christian texts eagerly supply reasons for God's decisions.[25] Paul, however, is not simply silent on that question; he adamantly insists that the choice took place before they were born, before they could do anything at all, precisely so that decision (ἡ κατ'ἐκλογὴν πρόθεσις) would remain with God (vv. 11–13). What 9:6b means, therefore, is that Israel is constituted by God's creative action rather than by physical descent.

The same insistence on God's unilateral actions, albeit cast in negative terms, pertains to Pharaoh. To be sure, Scripture claims that God hardened Pharaoh's heart, but Scripture also says that Pharaoh hardened his own heart (Exod. 8:28; 9:34; 13:15; and see 1 Sam. 6:6). Paul recalls only the divine side of this action (anticipating 11:7-10). Pharaoh is as little responsible for his hardening as Isaac and Jacob are for their births and vocations.

This insistence on God's gracious action in the case of miraculous births and hardening in the case of the despised Pharaoh already recasts Israel's history in a peculiar way,[26] but things take an especially

22. See the NRSV and the translations of Barrett (*The Epistle to the Romans*, 179); and Fitzmyer (*Romans*, 558). And see the use of *wirklich* in Ernst Käsemann (*An die Römer*, HNT8a [Tübingen: J. C. B. Mohr (Paul Siebeck), 1974], 250); H. Schlier, (*Der Römerbrief*, 289); and Eduard Lohse (*Der Brief an die Römer*, MeyerK [Göttingen: Vandenhoeck & Ruprecht, 2003], 270).
23. *The Epistle to the Romans*, 2:474.
24. For the connection between "calling" and "creation," see 4:17 and my "On the Calling-Into-Being of Israel," 260–61.
25. See, for example, *Jub.* 19:13-14, 22:10-24; Philo, *Alleg. Interp.* 3.88–89; *Pelagius's Commentary on St. Paul's Epistle to the Romans*, OECS, ed. Th. De Bruyn (Oxford: Oxford University Press, 1993), 116; Chrysostom, *Homilies on Romans* 16. See also the discussions in N. Richardson, *Paul's Language about God*, JSNTSup 99 (Sheffield: Sheffield Academic, 1999), 26–94; and Martin Parmentier, "Greek Church Fathers on Romans 9: Part II," *Bijdragen: International Journal for Philosophy and Theology* 51 (1990): 2–20.
26. Note John M. G. Barclay's observation that, in 9:6-18, "It is hard to avoid the impression that

strange turn in 9:24–25 with the insistence that among those who are "called," who are "children of God," there are now gentiles.[27] Hosea's "not my people" now includes those who really are "not my people." And Isaiah's laments introduce the hopeful note of "remnant" and "seed," while simultaneously claiming the near extinction of Israel. In both cases, the action lies with God, who "works his decision" on the earth (v. 28) and who nonetheless "left for us a seed."

The question of v. 14, "Is there injustice/wrong-doing with God?" is answered with the emphatic μὴ γένοιτο, yet Paul's account of God's actions scarcely demonstrates a standard of justice that would be recognized in any human court. God's judgments here are based, not on impartiality (contrast 2:5–11[28]), but on God's prerogatives as creator. Just as the potter decides what to do with the pot, God decides what is to be the use of God's creations.

Within this peculiar history, not of a people but of God's actions with a people, there are several recollections of the account of God's apocalyptic action in chapters 1–8. First, as he draws on the LXX of Exod. 9:16, Paul (apparently? intentionally?) makes two slight modifications that are revealing. First, instead of the διατηρήθης in Exodus, Paul writes ἐξήγειρα, suggesting not simply that God has kept Pharaoh alive for a purpose, but that God brought Pharaoh into being for a specific reason. Paul also substitutes δύναμις for the LXX ἰσχύς, a slight change that has the effect of connecting the citation more closely with the discourse about divine power in the opening lines of Romans (1:4, 16–17) as well as the language about conflicting powers in 8:38–39. Second, vv. 22–23 not only re-introduce the language of divine power, but that of "wrath" and "glory" found earlier in 2:1–11. All these elements serve to connect Paul's argument back to the apocalyptic

Paul is out to scandalize his readers" ("Unnerving Grace: Approaching Romans 9-11 from the Wisdom of Solomon," in *Between Gospel and Election*, WUNT 257, ed. Florian Wilk and J. Ross Wagner [Tübingen: Mohr Siebeck, 2010], 91–109, quotation on 107).

27. On the Scriptural interpretation here, see especially J. Ross Wagner, *Heralds of the Good News: Isaiah and Paul in Context in the Letter to the Romans*, NovTSup 101 (Boston: Brill, 2002), 78–117.

28. I introduce 2:5–11 because the text is so often adduced as evidence of Paul's expectation about future judgment. My own view is that chapter 2 largely serves to undermine customary distinctions between Jew and gentile in order to drive the audience to the conclusion of 3:9.

account of God's deliverance of all humanity from Sin and Death in chapters 1–8.[29]

God Rigs a Race: Romans 9:30–10:21

Despite the fact that numerous discussions of Rom. 9:30–10:21 characterize it as addressing Israel's "failure" or "disbelief" or "rejection," here also, God's activity remains dominant.[30] The section opens by contrasting gentiles, who win a race they never entered, with Israel, which enters but is tripped before reaching the finish line. To be sure, the gentiles are said to arrive ἐκ πίστεως, which might suggest their own action of trust or belief, were it not for the assertion that these gentiles were not even registered for the race, as well as the emphatic claims immediately preceding which attribute gentile inclusion to God's calling (vv. 22–26).[31]

Unlike the gentiles, Israel did run, and Israel ran in pursuit of the "law under the power of rectification," that is, God's own rectification.[32] Although Israel ran a good race, Israel did not arrive at the finish line because, in the elliptical language of v. 32a: "not from faith but from works," not based on faith generated by God in Jesus Christ (as in v. 30), but based on "works." These are not "works of the law," a phrase which last appears in 3:28. Instead, these are the "works" referred to 9:10–12, namely, human effort in general. Israel undertakes the good race of arriving at divine rectification, but is tripped by none other than the God of Israel: ἰδοὺ τίθημι.[33] Further, the stumbling stone turns out to be none other than Christ (see 10:13), even if the identity of that stone remains unclear in 9:33. Israel's "problem," then, is christological and it is generated by God.

---

29. See also E. Elizabeth Johnson's survey of vocabulary in Romans 9–11 that "reflects attitudes common in apocalyptic contexts" both generally and specifically in Paul's writings in *The Function of Apocalyptic and Wisdom Traditions in Romans 9–11*, SBLDS 109 (Atlanta: Scholars, 1989), 127–29.
30. This discussion draws heavily on my forthcoming "Questions about *Nomos*."
31. This comment touches on the larger debate about πίστις Χριστοῦ in particular and Paul's understanding of faith in general. My own view is that ἐκ πίστεως here, as in 3:26, is a shorthand expression for those who have been grasped by the gospel of Jesus Christ (cf. Phil. 3:12).
32. This paragraph severely summarizes the discussion in "Questions about *Nomos*."
33. See especially, Ross Wagner's discussion of 9:33 in *Heralds*, 126–31.

With 10:2, Paul recasts his comment about Israel's race: Israel has zeal for God, but that zeal is uninformed. Verse 3 explains: they attempted to substitute their own δικαιοσύνη for that of God, because they did not know God's δικαιοσύνη. Israel does not understand what God has done. Paul thereby leaves open the possibility that will emerge in 11:7-10, namely, that it is God who has closed Israel's mind (at least temporarily). This is a significant thread in the remainder of chapter 10, where confession of the name of Christ depends on hearing, which in turn, depends on preaching, which in turn, depends on being sent, which in turn, depends on God's initiative. To be sure, 10:21 depicts Israel as disobedient, but that statement is preceded by the claim that God is the one who causes Israel to be jealous and angry: ἐγὼ παραζηλώσω ὑμᾶς . . . παροργιῶ ὑμᾶς.

This charge that Israel does not know what God has done reintroduces the important epistemological motif of 1:18-32. It also coheres with concerns about perception that appear in chapters 12–16 (e.g., 12:2, 3, 16; 13:11). And it recalls the important strand of epistemological concerns in the Corinthian correspondence (especially 1 Cor. 1:18-25; 2 Cor. 5:16-17).[34] In Paul's interpretation, particularly in 1 and 2 Corinthians, the epistemological divide—between those who see what God has done and those who do not—derives from the apocalyptic event of the cross. Only in light of God's apocalypse can the cross be understood as power and wisdom rather than scandal and foolishness, and that understanding comes only to those who are called (1 Cor. 1:23-24).

Space allows only the most cursory remark about the convoluted argument in 10:4-13. Whatever judgment is made about the statement in v. 4 that Christ is the law's τέλος, by the end of v. 13, Christ has, in effect, displaced the law. It is Christ who is near, Christ who is proclaimed and who is lord of all. In addition, this is the only part of

---

34. The classic articulation of Paul's apocalyptic epistemology appears in J. Louis Martyn, "Epistemology at the Turn of the Ages," in *Theological Issues in the Letters of Paul* (Nashville: Abingdon, 1997), 89–110. For an exploration of epistemology in 1 Corinthians, see Alexandra R. Brown, *The Cross and Human Transformation: Paul's Apocalyptic Word in 1 Corinthians* (Minneapolis: Fortress Press, 1995).

chapters 9–11 that takes up the Mosaic law, suggesting that, whatever Paul is saying about Israel, Israel is not understood in light of the law. Confirming the observations above about 9:1–5, Israel's identity is discussed in relationship to the God who raised Jesus Christ from the dead—not in relationship to the law.[35]

"All Israel Will Be Saved": Romans 11:1–36

The rhetorical question that opens chapter 11 may represent the attitude of some gentile Christians, as is suggested by the strong language of 11:18. Elements of the preceding argument would seem to reinforce that conclusion, and both 9:27–29 and 10:21 would seem to align Paul with such a view. That impression appears to be confirmed by the way 9:30–10:21 speaks of Israel as a whole, as if all of Israel were among the disobedient. Yet, Paul immediately rejects the question with another μὴ γένοιτο. Indeed, Paul's disposition betrays itself when he asks in 11:1: "Has God rejected his people?" rather than "this" people or "that people" or "disobedient Israel." With "his people," the relationship between God and Israel that is emphatically asserted in 11:25–32 already comes into view.

Before taking up the eschatological future, however, there is more to say about the present, specifically, about what God is doing in the present. God has introduced a fissure into Israel. There is a remnant, consisting of the part of Israel that is ἡ ἐκλογή as a result of divine grace (11:2–7). And there are οἱ λοιποί, those who have been hardened (11:7). The passive ἐπωρώθησαν suggests divine agency at work (as earlier with the hardening of Pharaoh), and that divine agency comes to explicit expression in v. 8: It is God who gave them a "spirit of stupefaction, eyes that do not see and ears that do not hear" (cf. 9:16–18). Here again, the epistemological factor comes into play. The remainder do not respond to the gospel because God has, at present, rendered them unable to do so.

---

35. See further the important observations regarding the role of Christology in Romans 10 in Jonathan A. Linebaugh, *God, Grace, and Righteousness in Wisdom of Solomon and Paul's Letter to the Romans: Texts in Conversation*, NovTSup 152 (Leiden: Brill, 2013), 198–209.

This division is not the last word, however. To such a conclusion, Paul responds again with μὴ γένοιτο. The division has as its purpose nothing less than the salvation of the gentiles and the jealousy of "my flesh." Romans 11:15 contrasts the present and future state of οἱ λοιποί in cosmic terms. Since their present rejection means reconciliation of the cosmos, their future acceptance is nothing less than life out of death. The stumble of the remainder is not something that can be repaired by human repentance.[36] Instead, Paul reverts to the language of reconciliation from 5:1-11, where it implies reconciliation between warring parties. What Israel's οἱ λοιποί need is more than reconciliation; it is "life from the dead," which is resurrection if not re-creation. Linebaugh rightly draws attention to the christological implications: this reading of Israel's story is only possible in the light of the Christ-event.[37]

What is anticipated with "life from the dead" Paul announces directly in 11:25-32, the salvation of "all Israel." The divinely created division between "the elect" and "the rest" will be divinely healed. Paul identifies this assertion as τὸ μυστήριον τοῦτο, using technical terminology for the disclosure of divinely revealed information.[38] With the remainder of vv. 25-32, Paul explains what he understands about the mystery. Israel's double-standing at present is part of God's action. Israel's rescue is meant for the world's deliverance: God has confined all to disobedience that God might have mercy on all.

The use of the term "mystery" suggests that we are in the realm of apocalyptic thinking, but its function is far more than simply revealing to us Paul's apocalyptic proclivities. With "mystery," Paul fully assigns Israel's future to God, just as he has argued throughout that Israel has always belonged to God. He can no more claim to understand this mystery in full than he can encourage the Romans to be wise among

---

36. Even in 11:23, it is God who is said to be powerful to re-graft οἱ λοιποί. The conditional statements of vv. 22-23 are both prior and subordinate to the eschatological claims off 11:25-32.

37. *God, Grace, and Righteousness*, 217-18.

38. Michael Wolter, "Apokalyptik als Reform im Neuen Testament," *NTS* 51, no. 2 (2005): 171-91, especially pp. 183-84; R. E. Brown, *The Semitic Background of the Term "Mystery" in the New Testament* (Philadelphia: Fortress Press, 1968); Markus Bockmuehl, *Revelation and Mystery in Ancient Judaism and Pauline Christianity* (Grand Rapids: Eerdmans, 1990), 170-74.

themselves. Not only is it part and parcel of mystery that it cannot be fully disclosed,[39] but the conclusion of the chapter eloquently limns the divine prerogatives that make human comprehension of the mystery impossible.

From Christ to Israel: Concluding Reflections

The goal here has not been to offer a reading of the whole of Romans 9–11, but to ask what relationship there is between the cosmic apocalyptic conflict reflected in chapters 1–8 and the discussion of God's dealings with Israel (and the Gentiles) in chapters 9–11. To begin with, certain apocalyptic motifs recur here, including especially divine power and wrath, epistemology, and the revelation of mystery.

The larger claim is that, just as chapters 1–8 concern the way God's intervention in Jesus Christ has revealed the situation of all humanity, so 9–11 concerns what God's intervention has revealed about Israel in particular. We know what the enslavement of (all of) humanity looks like only from the cross and resurrection; we also know what Israel is—Israel's creation and vocation and salvation—only from the cross and resurrection.[40]

Reading back across the editors' white space, we see what has happened at the end of chapter 8. Paul has led his readers to the brink of the parousia, with his affirmations of the glory that awaits "us," the anticipation of the freedom of creation, the heightened declaration of God's love and identification of "us" as "supervictors." The triumphant return of Christ Jesus seems only a half-step away (rhetorically speaking), and Paul has such language available to him (as in 1 Thessalonians 4 and 1 Corinthians 15). He does not take that step,

---

39. As Samuel I. Thomas puts it, "The term 'mystery' itself entails a denial of access to its meanings; it often denotes things not understandable by human imagination, things—in Elliot Wolfson's words—that are beyond 'the spot where intellect falters before its own limit'" (in The "Mysteries" of Qumran: Mystery, Secrecy, and Esotericism in the Dead Sea Scrolls, SBLEJL [Leiden: Brill, 2009], 1). This feature of mystery stands in considerable tension with the exegetical industry devoted to parsing precisely the manner and means of "all Israel's" salvation.

40. This statement also applies to Paul's discussion of Abraham in Romans 4; see especially the statement that Abraham is "father of those who believe while uncircumcised" (4:11) and that Abraham trusted the "God who makes the dead live and who calls into being that which does not exist" (4:17).

however, as the triumph over God's enemies is not complete without the salvation of all Israel.[41]

41. A second "conclusion" to 8:31–39 comes in 15:7–13, with the unified praise of God, but defense of that point will need to wait for another occasion.

13

Apocalyptic Allegiance and Disinvestment in the World

A Reading of 1 Corinthians 7:25–35

John M. G. Barclay

The label "apocalyptic" is a scholarly construct, even when applied to texts that contain the matching Greek vocabulary. It is a term *we* use to describe a cluster of texts, or a constellation of ideas, as defined by our own selections and configurations of the material.[1] For this reason, what counts as "apocalyptic" is constantly negotiable and inherently malleable, influenced by ideological preferences and theological trends.[2] It is a sign of health that New Testament scholarship

---

1. At the SBL session which inaugurated this volume, I sensed the term "apocalyptic" being used in at least six ways: i) for the revelation of mysteries; ii) for a strong sense of newness (compatible with "new covenant"), perhaps accompanied by shock or surprise; iii) for eschatology of a particular kind; iv) for the expectation of an imminent end; v) for an epistemological stance, whereby truth is ascertained, first and foremost, through the Christ-event; vi) for a three-actor drama (involving God, humanity, and evil forces), in which God saves by invading the world. I am grateful to all those who gave me feedback at and after that session, and to Troels Engberg-Pedersen for a careful and penetrating written response soon after.

undergoes periodic convulsions of self-questioning on the deployment of this term, and in the present, as on previous occasions, it seems best to re-ground our discourse in the textual evidence of Jewish "apocalyptic" literature. Here too, of course, the label is a scholarly construct, encompassing a changing literary tradition of considerable inner variety and extremely fuzzy edges. But we can trace Paul's deployment of themes, motifs, and patterns of thought that are characteristic of such literature, without needing to make strong claims that their notions of revealed knowledge, oppressive powers, determinate times, or future cosmic change constitute a single package, or are taken over unchanged into Pauline theology.

First Corinthians is shot through with motifs whose closest literary parallels lie in this Jewish "apocalyptic" tradition. The clash of cosmic powers narrated in 1 Cor. 15:20–28 is replete with constructs of time, power, and resurrection that echo that tradition, while Paul's celebration of a selectively revealed wisdom which confounds the truth-claims of "this age" or "this world" (1 Cor. 1:18–3:21) can be readily shown to match motifs familiar from "apocalyptic" literature.[3] Sandwiched between these significant expositions of the meaning of Christ in cosmic time and reality is a passage that has often struck scholars as an "apocalyptic" moment in Pauline reasoning. In 1 Cor. 7:25–31, Paul refers to "the present constraint" (διὰ τὴν ἐνεστῶσαν ἀνάγκην, 7:26) and "suffering in the flesh" (θλῖψιν τῇ σαρκί, 7:28) in terms that remind many of eschatological expectations of crisis and woe. He also refers to the compression of time (ὁ καιρὸς συνεσταλμένος ἐστίν, 7:29) and the passing of "the form of this world" (παράγει τὸ σχῆμα τοῦ κόσμου τούτου, 7:31) in language that evokes "apocalyptic" configurations of time, urgency, and cosmic change. Significant parallels can be drawn between Paul's policy of detachment ("as not")

---

2. The same could be said, of course, for other scholarly labels, not least the terms "covenant" and "covenantal."

3. See, e.g., M. C. de Boer, *The Defeat of Death: Apocalyptic Eschatology in 1 Corinthians 15 and Romans 5*, JSNTSup 22 (Sheffield: Sheffield Academic, 1988); A. R. Brown, *The Cross and Human Transformation: Paul's Apocalyptic Word in 1 Corinthians* (Minneapolis: Fortress Press, 1989). See further E. Adams, *Constructing the World: A Study in Paul's Cosmological Language*, SNTW (Edinburgh: T&T Clark, 2000), 105–49.

in 7:29–31 and the calls for disinvestment found in some "apocalyptic" texts,[4] and it is frequently argued that Paul's expectation of an imminent end here decisively influences his preference for singleness over marriage.

I wish to argue here for a new reading of ἡ ἐνεστῶσα ἀνάγκη (7:26) and to suggest: a) that the deep structure of Paul's reasoning in this chapter is shaped by an "apocalyptic" understanding of the Christ-event; b) that the alteration to the structures of the cosmos effected by the resurrection has reconfigured human allegiances, establishing a new order of priorities; and c) that this re-prioritization (rather than simply the imminence of the end) so downgrades normal investment in the routine structures of life that singleness is found preferable to the divided loyalties of marriage. Without that edge, scandalous as it is to our modern sensibilities, the Pauline policy of disinvestment is in danger of collapsing into inner detachment (as in Stoicism) or into an existentialist, individualized freedom of decision (Bultmann).

The Present Constraint (ἡ ἐνεστῶσα ἀνάγκη) and Life Mid-Apocalypse

Paul lives in a very special time. On the one hand, he awaits the "revelation" (ἀποκάλυψις) of Christ (1 Cor. 1:7), the "day of the Lord" (4:1–5; 5:5) that will "reveal" the value of each person's work (3:11–15) and on which the world, including the angels, will be judged by the saints (6:2). On the other hand, the decisive event that has altered the structures of time and existence has already taken place. Christ has been installed, since the resurrection, as the Lord of the cosmos, and his reign is already battling with every rule, authority, and power (15:20–28). The cross has already made foolish the wisdom of this world (1:18–25) and revealed a wisdom hitherto hidden, but now

---

4. For a classic treatment, see W. Schrage, "Die Stellung zur Welt bei Paulus, Epiktet und in der Apokalyptik: Ein Beitrag zu 1Kor 7,29-31," *ZTK* 61, no. 2 (1964): 125–54, drawing heavily on a parallel passage in *6 Ezra* (2 Esdras) 16:35–50. The apocalyptic features of 1 Cor. 7:25–31 are widely recognized, but the paragraph is sometimes treated as a piece of pre-formed tradition that sits awkwardly in its present context; see, e.g., V. Wimbush, *Paul, The Worldly Ascetic: Response to the World and Self-Understanding according to 1 Corinthians 7* (Macon, GA: Mercer University Press, 1987).

disseminated by the Spirit (2:6–16). The resurrection of Christ is the "first-fruits" of the harvest (15:23), the beginning of an event whose completion is now inevitable in a timeframe that Paul does not expect to last long ("we shall not all sleep"; "the dead shall be raised and we shall be changed," 15:51, 52). In an important sense, Paul lives mid-apocalypse. The death and resurrection of Jesus have sealed the destiny of all things: the "rulers of this age" are being rendered ineffective (καταργούμενοι, 2:6); a distinction is being created between those who are "perishing" (condemned along with the world, 11:32) and those who are being saved (1:18); and it is certain that every present power and authority will be put out of operation (καταργέω), including, finally, death (15:24–26).

This special bracket of time is what Paul calls the καιρὸς συνεσταλμένος (7:29), an unparalleled expression which appears to suggest not that a longer period of time has been "cut short" by subtraction, but that time (or opportunity) has been compressed or contracted.[5] This is the "acceptable time, the day of salvation" (2 Cor. 6:2), a window of time in which the reign of Christ has been inaugurated but remains incomplete, a time when the ages meet and overlap (1 Cor. 10:11). Believers are already distinguished from "this age" or "this world" (1 Cor. 1:20; 2:6; 3:18–21; 5:9–13), not spatially (5:10) but "politically," in the sense that they have adopted a different orientation and a more pressing loyalty. They bear allegiance to a κύριος (12:3) whose service takes precedence in every condition of life, for both slave and free (7:20–23). The whole of their lives revolves around the recognition of this "Lord of glory" (2:8), whose death and resurrection they remember in "the Lord's supper" and whose coming they await (11:20, 26; 16:22: μαράνα θά).

In the present, they are acutely conscious of, and frustrated by, "the present constraint" (ἡ ἐνεστῶσα ἀνάγκη, 7:26). The participle ἐνεστῶσα is variously here translated as "present" or "impending," while the noun is commonly taken to mean "crisis" or "distress." In fact,

---

5. See W. Deming, *Paul on Marriage and Celibacy: The Hellenistic Background of 1 Corinthians 7*, 2nd ed. (Grand Rapids: Eerdmans, 2004), 179–80.

ἐνεστῶσα cannot mean anything other than "present" (cf. Gal. 1:4; Rom. 8:38; 1 Cor. 3:22: the latter two in contrast to "the future").[6] And what about the noun? Does ἀνάγκη mean "distress" or "crisis," or something else? It is commonly asserted that this is a technical term for a time of eschatological distress, the woes that beset the world at or just before its end ("messianic woes" or "messianic birth-pangs").[7] But the linguistic basis for that assertion is extremely weak. The only texts that use this term in relation to eschatological woes are LXX Zeph. 1:15 (where ἀνάγκη is one of several terms for anguish or difficulty on the day of the Lord) and Luke 21:23, where pregnant women and nursing mothers are warned that "in those days . . . there will be ἀνάγκη μεγάλη on the earth and wrath on this people." But even here, "distress" or "crisis" is hardly the most obvious translation. The term ἀνάγκη commonly has the meaning "necessity," "compulsion," or "fate": it expresses a force of compulsion or constraint. This is how Paul uses the term on several occasions, contrasting ἀνάγκη with freedom of choice.[8] By extension, it can mean circumstances that bring one under constraint or dire necessity, such as imprisonment or captivity, the acute necessities created by famine, or torture.[9] Hence, Paul uses the term (in the plural, or in the phrase πᾶσα ἡ ἀνάγκη) to refer to physical constrictions, necessities, punishments, and (perhaps) tortures (2 Cor. 6:4–5; 12:10; 1 Thess. 3:7). This is the sense in which Luke uses the term in the verse cited above (Luke 21:23): in those days, people will be in dire straits regarding the physical needs of life, and this will be

---

6. It is remarkable how often commentators retain the meaning "imminent" without, it appears, any persuasive philological support. See, e.g., H. Conzelmann, *1 Corinthians*, Hermeneia (Philadelphia: Fortress Press, 1975), 132; A. C. Thiselton, *The First Epistle to the Corinthians*, NIGTC (Grand Rapids: Eerdmans, 2000), 572.

7. Conzelmann, *1 Corinthians*, 132; C. K. Barrett, *A Commentary on the First Epistle to the Corinthians*, BNTC, 2nd ed. (London: A&C Black, 1971), 175–76; W. Schrage, *Der Erste Brief an die Korinther* (1Kor 6,12–11,16), EKK VII/2 (Solothurn: Benzier; Neukirchen-Vluyn: Neukirchener, 1995), 156, with others in his n. 600.

8. Later in this chapter, 1 Cor. 7:37; later in this letter, 1 Cor. 9:16; elsewhere, 2 Cor. 9:7; Philem. 14; cf. Rom. 13:5.

9. See, e.g., Josephus, *Ant.* 2.67 (confinement in prison); *Bell.* 5.571 (famine in Jerusalem under siege led εἰς τοσοῦτον ἀνάγκης); *Ant.* 16.253 (torture). Cf. *LSJ* s.v. which lists the meanings as 1. force, constraint, necessity; 2. natural want or desire; fate, destiny; philosophical necessity; 3. actual force, violence, punishment; 4. bodily pain, anguish, suffering, distress. Note that this last is found only in poetic texts.

particularly bad for women who are pregnant or nursing a baby. There is no reason to consider this word a *terminus technicus* for eschatological distress; we should expect the term to mean necessity or circumstances that cause constraint.[10] But what does Paul consider to be the present "necessity" or "circumstance of constraint"?

Two recent proposals seem to me speculative or weakly supported. Winter finds here reference to a present or impending famine in Corinth, but it is not clear why Paul would allude to this so obliquely or why famine should affect the question of marriage and not other topics in this letter (e.g., food).[11] Hays appeals to 1 Cor. 9:16 (Paul's ἀνάγκη to preach), and considers the "present necessity" to refer to "the urgent imperative of proclaiming the gospel and doing the work of the Lord in the short time that remains."[12] But Paul's "necessity" in 1 Cor. 9:16 seems very specific to him, and is not applied there, or elsewhere, to other believers. And if these specific interpretations do not convince, we should not resort to the common opinion that Paul here evokes the messianic tribulations. Ἀνάγκη is *not* a technical term for eschatological calamity, and, despite a line of interpretation stretching back to Schweitzer, there is no indication that Paul saw his present as a time of "messianic woes" or "the birth-pangs" of the new age.[13] So, what is there about the present that can be described in the language of necessity or constraint?

"The present constraint" (ἡ ἐνεστῶσα ἀνάγκη) refers, I suggest, to

---

10. BAGD's category "distress, calamity" seems to me unfounded, and its reference to "the distress in the last days" is based only on Luke 21:23 and 1 Cor. 7:26. All the texts referred to under this heading (2) refer not to distress in general, but to circumstances of dire necessity or constraint. And this Greek term can hardly be accorded a technical meaning by reference to apocalyptic texts written in a different language (*pace* Conzelmann's appeal to *4 Ezra* and *Jubilees*, *1 Corinthians*, 132n13).

11. B. Winter, "Secular and Christian Responses to Corinthian Famines," *TynBul* 40, no. 1 (1989): 86–106, followed by, among others, Thiselton, *First Epistle*, 573.

12. R. B. Hays, *First Corinthians*, Interpretation (Louisville: Westminster John Knox, 1997), 129.

13. If there are "birth-pangs" they are future (1 Thess. 5:3), the immediate prelude to the *parousia*. Cf. A. Schweitzer, *The Mysticism of Paul the Apostle* (New York: Seabury, 1968), 142–45; D. Allison, *The End of the Ages has Come: An Early Interpretation of the Passion and Resurrection of Jesus* (Philadelphia: Fortress Press, 1985), 62–69 (putting considerable weight on an uncertain reading of Col. 1:24). If 2 Thessalonians is by Paul (which I doubt), the eschatological scenario of lawlessness is emphatically future, not present. For a recent full treatment of eschatological "tribulation" in the early Jewish tradition, see B. Pitre, *Jesus, the Tribulation, and the End of the Exile*, WUNT 2/204 (Tübingen: Mohr Siebeck, 2005). He does not appeal to our verse as evidence.

a feature of "the present evil age" (ὁ αἰὼν ὁ ἐνεστώς, Gal. 1:4), the "constraint" being the inevitable mortality and decay of all things in "this age." Life in "this world" is lived under the hegemony of "powers" and "authorities," of which death is the final and most potent (1 Cor. 15:24-26). This power currently holds sway over all humans, and even over the bodies of believers, which are limited and vulnerable because of their weakness and corruptibility (1 Cor. 15:42-44; cf. Phil. 3:21). As Paul explains in Romans 8, this liability to corruption and death is a mark of creation's subjugation to futility (Rom. 8:20-21)—an unwilling subjugation (οὐχ ἑκοῦσα) that is tantamount to being under constraint (for ἀνάγκη as the opposite of what is willed, see 1 Cor. 7:37; 9:16; 2 Cor. 9:7; Philem. 14).[14] This slavery to decay (δουλεία τῆς φθορᾶς) is an indelible feature of the present age, to be escaped only in the "freedom" of the future (Rom. 8:21). Meanwhile, the creation groans and writhes in pain "up to the present" (ἄχρι τοῦ νῦν, Rom. 8:22; cf. 8:18: τὰ παθήματα τοῦ νῦν καιροῦ). In other words, the present is marked by the limitation and constraint of decay.

It would make excellent sense for Paul to refer to "the present constraint" of life under the hegemony of death and decay in our context in 1 Corinthians 7. Because of this constraint, life is vulnerable to disease, pain, and death, and it would be wise to reduce that vulnerability wherever possible. The reference to "present constraint" is connected to the statement that "it is good for people to remain as they are" (7:26). This is applied to both the married and the unmarried (7:27), but the context indicates that Paul's particular concern here is with the question whether the unmarried should marry (7:25, 28; cf. 7:32-38). "The present constraint" seems connected to Paul's concern about "affliction in the flesh" (7:28), which is evoked to persuade the

---

14. At this point, Paul stands very close to the visions of present reality in apocalyptic texts such as 4 Ezra and 2 Baruch. According to 4 Ezra, this age is full of sadness and infirmities (4 Ezra 4:27); the entrances of this world are narrow, sorrowful, toilsome, few, evil, full of dangers, and liable to great hardship (7:12); an evil heart has brought about corruption and death (7:48); we live in sorrow, knowing we are doomed to perish (7:64, 117). According to 2 Baruch, this world is a struggle (2 Bar. 15:8) and the present years are few and evil (16:1); the world is full of corruption, and the present time is polluted by evils (44:9-10). For an eloquent account of the tendency of all things towards decay and degradation, see 2 Baruch 83.

unmarried that it is better if they remain as they are. To be married is to make oneself vulnerable to an additional set of dangers, those that threaten one's spouse, and those entailed in childbirth (with its enormous rate of mortality), and in the care of highly vulnerable children.[15] Under the present constraints of this mortal existence, those who marry will certainly have "physical affliction" (θλῖψις τῇ σαρκί), "and I would spare you that" (7:28).[16]

"The present constraint," then, is the tendency towards decay characteristic of this present world, whose power and cruelty have become openly apparent, in all their hostile intent, in the wake of the counter-power of the resurrection. People have always died, in Paul's perception, since Adam (1 Cor. 15:22), and in this sense, "the present constraint," like "the present evil age," is as old as humanity. What has changed since the resurrection is that this can now be seen as a temporary and transient phenomenon—it is a *present* constraint, but it will not hold sway in the *future*. The new reign of Christ is set *against* the rule of death. A struggle has broken out in the cosmos, and the believer is entitled to chafe against death in a way that was neither possible nor imaginable before. Believers here groan, knowing how much better is the future yet to come (Rom. 8:23), and Paul's sage advice is that they should not increase those occasions for groaning beyond what is unavoidably necessary.[17] In the newly established force-field of conflicting powers, suffering for the gospel is inevitable,

---

15. See Schrage, *Erste Brief*, 165–66, for the early history of reception, which understood Paul along such lines. We do not need to imagine here specifically eschatological difficulties, nor the persecutions that attended faithfulness to Christ (1 Thess. 3:3–4; 2 Cor. 6:4–10).

16. Could this phrase be read along the lines of "but I spare you censure for getting married" (with reference to 7:28a)? That has been suggested to me by Troels Engberg-Pedersen (in a private communication), though I am not quite persuaded. Where Paul speaks of sparing the Corinthians from grief or reproach (2 Cor. 1:23; 13:2), the context makes clear that this is the case, whereas in 1 Corinthians 7, Paul never makes explicit that he would otherwise ban them altogether from getting married. However, he does take pains to insist that he is not placing them under restraint (7:35), so conceivably, the meaning could be, "But I spare you from imposing my preference on you" (cf. 7:6–7). However, the sequence of the clauses in 7:28 probably supports the normal interpretation, and the present tense may be conative: "and I am trying to spare you that (affliction)" (so Barrett, *First Epistle*, 176).

17. *2 Baruch* offers a partially parallel scenario, where an event (in that case the destruction of Jerusalem) renders marriage and child-bearing joyless and pointless. In such a context, the seer urges brides and bridegrooms not to marry, and wives not to bear children. "Those who have no children will be glad, and those who have children will be sad. For why do they bear in pain only to bury in grief?" (*2 Bar.* 10:13–15).

and the outer person is decaying while the inner self is being renewed (2 Cor. 4:16). In such frustrating circumstances, while marriage is no sin, its greater exposure to the forces of decay makes it an undesirable option for those who are currently unmarried.

If this reading is right, Paul's reasoning at this point is thoroughly "apocalyptic," but not in the manner usually imagined. He is not referring to a special period of eschatological (or messianic) woes, as the immediate prelude to the end of the cosmos: the ἀνάγκη and θλῖψις are not a particular final-era phenomenon, but the reality of all mortal existence, newly exposed in its thwarting, hostile power. Nor, as we shall see, is Paul's appeal for singleness founded only on the shortness of time that remains. Rather, the theological basis of his reasoning is "apocalyptic" in the sense that the believers' life is oriented to a new reality, begun in the cross and resurrection of Christ, which is at odds with the conditions of the current passing age. In this peculiar cosmic phase, the life-decisions of a believer are governed by a loyalty that will seem counter-intuitive by the standards of "this age." In "compressed time," these alternatives are rendered more urgent and stark, but their basis lies as much in the transience of the old world as in the imminence of its end. In this overlap of the ages, whether long or short, the believers' investments are newly prioritized. In the light of the resurrection, they know that "the form of this world is passing away" (7:31); the present tense (παράγει) indicates that its passing has already begun.[18] The decisive change of circumstances is not to be awaited or prepared for by emergency measures, but is already in existence. Paul calls for adjustment to a present "apocalyptic" reality, in whose light marriage seems an unnecessary form of exposure to the death-soaked conditions of the present evil age.[19]

A Superior Allegiance: The Lordship of Jesus in a Passing World

Paul addresses the married, the unmarried, and the widowed in

---

18. Not that the condition Paul describes is somehow "perennial" (pace Wimbush, Worldly Ascetic, 34).
19. Thus much more is at stake here than the "difficult circumstances" that might make Stoics hesitate to commit to marriage, pace Deming, Paul on Marriage and Celibacy, 174–93.

different sections of 1 Corinthians 7, and the paragraphs in 7:25-38 are unified by their focus on the παρθένοι (7:25). The term apparently refers to young *women* who have never been married (7:25, 36, 37, 38),[20] although the discussion broadens to include the advisability of marriage for both women and men (7:28, 32-34). For our purposes, it is significant that this section encompasses *both* the paragraph about "compressed time," with its ὡς μή statements (7:29-31) *and* the paragraph about the divided loyalties of the married (7:32-35). Each of these offers a theological frame in which to understand marriage and singleness, but we should clearly take them together and not in isolation from each other or from their context.

The famous ὡς μή clauses are placed between the reference to "compressed time" (7:29) and the statement about the passing of the σχῆμα of this world (7:31). They grow from the former via the adverbial phrase τὸ λοιπόν ("henceforth," 7:29), as an indication that this mode of disinvestment is related to the situation of believers mid-apocalypse. Similarly, the γάρ in 7:31 indicates that the passing of the σχῆμα of this world is foundational to the ὡς μή policy outlined in the five clauses of 7:29-31. The first concerns marriage. The three that follow might refer in particular to the emotional and financial commitments of marriage, but they might also apply more widely. In any case, the final clause is general enough to embrace all dealings with "the world"—including, but not limited to, those already listed.

Τὸ λοιπόν, ἵνα καὶ οἱ ἔχοντες γυναῖκας ὡς μὴ ἔχοντες ὦσιν
καὶ οἱ κλαίοντες ὡς μὴ κλαίοντες
καὶ οἱ χαίροντες ὡς μὴ χαίροντες
καὶ οἱ ἀγοράζοντες ὡς μὴ κατέχοντες,
καὶ οἱ χρώμενοι τὸν κόσμον ὡς μὴ καταχρώμενοι

The "as not" statements do not cancel out what precedes in the sense

---

20. The difficulties of interpretation in 7:36-38 have led to suggestions that the issue is particularly a) the duty of fathers to give their daughters in marriage; or b) the practice of "spiritual marriage" between men and women; or c) the pressure on young people who are already betrothed to go ahead and marry. See the discussion in the commentaries, e.g., G. Fee, *The First Epistle to the Corinthians*, NICNT (Grand Rapids: Eerdmans, 1987), 325-27. Schrage insists that the whole of 7:25-38 is about girls who are already betrothed (*Erste Brief*, 152-53), but most other commentators disagree. Fortunately, it is not necessary to resolve this issue here.

that they command those who do something to desist from doing it: the married are not here instructed to divorce (cf. 7:10–11) any more than purchasers are told to stop making purchases. It is presumed that such activities will continue, but in an unusual mode, with a detachment or disinvestment that reduces believers' involvement in such activities in quality or in degree. One either buys or does not buy, but "as not owning" suggests a minimal quality of investment, an attitude to what one has acquired that hollows out the normal purposes of buying (which are precisely to own, and thus to have legal power over, one's possessions). Similarly, one either has a wife or one does not, but varying qualities of investment are possible in such a relationship. The final clause, which summarizes and generalizes the others, distinguishes between χρώμενοι and καταχρώμενοι, between "using" and "using to the full." In all cases, what seems to be addressed is the level of investment in activities in which believers may participate, but without the normal practical and/or emotional attachments. And the reason for this disinvestment is that these activities belong, in one form or another, to the κόσμος. That is the key term picked up in the final explanatory statement: παράγει γὰρ τὸ σχῆμα τοῦ κόσμου τούτου.[21]

The logic for this disinvestment is sometimes felt to lie in the fact that there is no point investing in something that is soon to pass away. Hence, the appeal to an apparently parallel passage such as 6 Ezra (2 Esdras) 16.40–50, which prepares people for the coming "apocalyptic" turmoil by instructing: "let him who sells be like one who will flee; let him who buys be like one who will lose . . . ; let one who builds a house be like one who will not live in it . . . ; those who marry like those who will have no children," and so on.[22] But the focus in 1 Corinthians 7 is not quite the same. Paul is not declaring that the structures of society are about to collapse, and he is not predicting a future frustration of

---

21. The superficially similar phrase used by Philostratus (*Vit. Apoll.* 8.7: καὶ τί τὸ σχῆμα τοῦ κόσμου τούτου;), cited by Conzelmann, *1 Corinthians*, 134n28) has a very different sense: it refers to the universe of wayward people dependent on the wisdom of the wise. For further linguistic parallels, see G. van Kooten, "How Greek was Paul's Eschatology?," *NTS* 61, no. 2 (2015): 239–53, at 242n5.

22. For an exposition of the parallels, see esp. Schrage, "Stellung zur Welt," slightly modified in his *Erste Brief*, 168–69.

hopes ("will flee," "will lose" etc.). The world's passing is described, rather, in the present tense (παράγει), because Paul is speaking of a disinvestment in *one* world *while another is already emerging*. The logic is not "don't invest in this world because another is about to begin," but "don't invest in this world because an alternative and more important investment is already required." What is already passing away is τὸ σχῆμα τοῦ κόσμου τούτου, a difficult phrase which probably means something like "this world in its present form" (or "as presently constituted"); σχῆμα (as in Phil. 2:7) signals not some outward phenomenon, but the configuration of reality which constitutes what is meant by "this world" (cf. Rom. 12:2: μὴ συσχηματίζεσθε τῷ αἰῶνι τούτῳ).[23] Paul does not mean that they should invest in *nothing* in the present (because nothing will last), but that they should not invest in what belongs to "this world" in its present configuration. There is something, meanwhile, that they should invest in, and that is what belongs directly to the Lord. There are some things that are wood, hay, and stubble (and to be destroyed) and some things that are gold that will last (1 Cor. 3:11-15); knowledge and tongues will not last, but love remains (1 Cor. 13:8-13); there is some work that is fruitless, but "the work of the Lord" will not be in vain (1 Cor. 15:58; cf. 16:10). Thus, the deepest reason for disinvestment in the affairs of this world is that they are overshadowed by commitments of greater significance and higher priority.[24] There is service to do *for the Lord* who has established his authority over the lives of believers and whose reign already grates against the present constitution of the world.

For this reason, Paul's policy of disinvestment in dealings with "the world" is only partially similar to the Stoic policy of "indifference." The Stoic cannot let outer affairs, over which he has no control, affect the equilibrium of his inner self (the one thing he *can* control). Thus, he treats all external conditions as *adiaphora*, matters of no ultimate

---

23. For the different uses of the term κόσμος in 1 Corinthians and Romans, see Adams, *Constructing the World*. It is Paul's hope for the future liberation of creation (Romans 8) that saves his negative comments about "this world" from turning into a Gnostic dualism.

24. Cf. Schrage, *Erste Brief*, 183: "Der eigentliche Grund der christlichen Freiheit von der Welt ist aber nicht die in der Zukunft oder auch schon in der Gegenwart vergehende Welt, sondern der gegenwärtige und wiederkommende Herr, dem die Christen schon gehören."

significance, even if some might be preferable for the exercise of reason.[25] Paul is *not* indifferent to what goes on in his churches, and he certainly lets things "get to him" where they concern the progress of the gospel. His is not the detachment of the inner self from outward circumstances, but the disinvestment of the believer from what belongs to the world in its present constitution because of a simultaneous investment in what belongs to the "new creation" arising from the current cosmic Lordship of Christ. The "weeping" and "rejoicing" referred to in our passage are emotional reactions to events or conditions of this currently configured world; they do not refer to *every* kind of emotional reaction. It is fine to "weep with those who weep and rejoice with those who rejoice" concerning things that matter for Christ or for the church (1 Cor. 12:26; Rom. 12:15). Paul is not advocating a blanket emotional disinvestment (to preserve the serenity of the inner self), but a selective investment of emotional energy, and a limitation of emotional (and practical) investment in things now superseded by the already unfolding "apocalypse." The "compression of time" makes this choice of investment urgent and immediate, but this world is already overshadowed by the "apocalyptic" transformation of reality that has begun in the cross and resurrection of Jesus.

This sense of choice is immediately clarified in 7:32-35. "I want you to be free of anxieties (ἀμέριμνοι)," says Paul, but what looks like a blanket statement turns out to be carefully differentiated. The unmarried person is, quite rightly, "anxious" about the business of the Lord (μεριμνᾷ τὰ τοῦ κυρίου). He/she is concerned with how to please the Lord (7:32), a concern that is unambiguously proper (cf. 1 Thess. 4:1; Rom. 8:8). The married person, on the contrary, is anxious about the business of the world (μεριμνᾷ τὰ τοῦ κόσμου), that is, how to please his/her spouse (7:33, 34). As a result they are "divided" (μεμέρισται, 7:34), whereas Paul advises well-ordered and undistracted attendance on the Lord (7:35). At this point, there are well-known parallels in

---

25. See, e.g., Diogenes of Laertius 7.101-3. For comparison with Paul, see J. L. Jaquette, *Discerning What Counts: The Function of the Adiaphora Topos in Paul's Letters*, SBLDS 146 (Atlanta: Scholars, 1995).

the radical Stoic or Cynic attitude to marriage, as liable to distract the philosopher from the more urgent business of leading people to a better manner of life (e.g., Epictetus, *Diss.* 3.22).[26] For Paul, what counts is allegiance to the newly installed κύριος: to declare, at baptism, κύριος Ἰησοῦς (12:3) is to commit oneself unreservedly to the service of the present and future cosmic ruler, and he is best served with both hands, not with one effectively tied behind one's back.

What is striking about this passage, and grossly offensive to Protestant Christians in the modern era, is the way it places concern for one's spouse in the category of τὰ τοῦ κόσμου, a category which is juxtaposed with, and non-identical to, τὰ τοῦ κυρίου. The two spheres are clearly differentiated such that attention to both makes one "divided." They are not opposed in the sense that one is wholly incompatible with the other. Belonging to a prostitute and belonging to the Lord *are* incompatible (1 Cor. 6:15–16), but belonging to, and attending to, one's spouse does not exclude one from belonging to the Lord. But neither are these two relations simply harmonized, such that pleasing one's spouse could be construed as a way of pleasing the Lord. To please one's spouse would not be to destroy one's devotion to the Lord, but it would weaken it. Single-hearted, undivided attention to the Lord would be preferable, and to combine these two allegiances threatens to limit one's attention to the Lord. Hence, while Paul does not insist on singleness, which carries some risks (7:9), he clearly thinks it is the preferable state (7:35).

The fact that to attend to one's spouse is to be concerned with τὰ τοῦ κόσμου is of a piece with the detachment Paul advocated for the married in 7:29 ("those who have wives as not having them"); that, as we saw, was a disinvestment not in relationships *per se*, but in relationships that "use the world." It is notable that Paul does not categorize pleasing one's spouse as a form of *love*, and that would surely have changed the picture: loving others and serving the Lord certainly *can* be placed in synthesis (Gal. 6:2). Perhaps Paul is conscious that

---

26. For an excellent analysis of the Stoic and Cynic debates on marriage, see Deming, *Paul on Marriage and Celibacy.*

many marriages were mixed (1 Cor. 7:12–16), or that marriage was often undertaken for familial or civic purposes that bore no positive relation to love or to any aspect of "the business of the Lord."[27] Later in this letter, Paul draws a distinction between what goes on ἐν οἴκῳ and what happens ἐν ἐκκλησίᾳ (11:18, 22, 33; cf. 14:34–35).[28] Even when the church met in a household (as it often, but not always, did),[29] Paul seems to have drawn a distinction between the ordinary affairs of the household and the business of the Lord (e.g., the "Lord's meal") that takes place when believers met as a church. The many demands of marriage (emotional, social, and financial) are summed up in Paul's language about being "bound" to a spouse (7:27). Paul seems to have regarded such demands and activities as τὰ τοῦ κόσμου in distinction from τὰ τοῦ κυρίου, much as he elsewhere refers to money as σαρκικά in distinction from the πνευματικά given in the gospel (1 Cor. 9:11; Rom. 15:27), and in parallel to the way that he applies the adjective σαρκικός to ordinary everyday wisdom (2 Cor. 1:12) or ordinary human weapons (2 Cor. 10:4). This suggests that there is a wide sphere of social relations that have no direct relation to the inaugurated Lordship of Jesus. They are not necessarily opposed to that Lordship, but they do not bear allegiance to Christ, as does the social sphere of the church. A believer may certainly seek to honor Christ *in* such a sphere, but the sphere of relations itself (e.g., the household, work-relations, the sphere of economic activity, or the activities of the state) are not themselves "Christianized" by being brought into direct relation to Christ. In the undisputed letters, one can be a Christian slave (1 Cor. 7:21–24; Philemon), but slavery itself is not "Christianized," such that owning and ruling a slave becomes a way of serving Christ. Onesimus is to be a beloved brother both in the sphere of ordinary household relations (καὶ ἐν σαρκί) and in the sphere of relations that are directly aligned to Christ (καὶ ἐν κυρίῳ, Philemon 16). The believer is responsible to the

27. Even in the household codes, love is named in relation to husbands, but not to wives (Col. 3:19–20; Eph. 5:21–33).
28. See J. Økland, *Women in their Place: Paul and the Corinthian Discourse of Gender and Sanctuary Space*, JSNTSup 269 (London: T&T Clark, 2004).
29. E. Adams, *Early Christian Meeting Places: Almost Exclusively Houses?*, LNTS 450 (London: T&T Clark, 2013).

Lord *in* both spheres, but they are not one and the same, and "the business of the world" in slavery (buying and selling slaves; organizing them, allocating their duties, dealing with the recalcitrant), like "the business of the world" in marriage (acquiring and maintaining a home; running household affairs; earning enough to maintain a family; dealing with the resultant sickness and sorrow) can distract one's attention and lessen one's devotion to the Lord.[30]

Inasmuch as the sphere of the world, as presently constituted, is not part of that "new creation" which has emerged with the resurrection of Christ, it is not itself amenable to redemption or Christian reform, even if the believer seeks to live in it with as much faithfulness as possible. One lives within it, but without full investment, because "the form of this world" [= this world as presently constituted] "is passing away" (7:31). On these terms, marriage is not itself a sin, but the married believer has no investment in the "goods" that marriage is thought to bring (financial security; social honor; the generation of children; the continuance of one's name; the maintenance of one's property-line), and thus lives in marriage "as not" having a spouse. Better, in fact, to be single, and without the worldly distractions that impede the believer from giving full attention to the business of the Lord. This is not because sex is polluting,[31] or because the body is to be despised. In fact, it is precisely because the body is "for the Lord" that it is awkward for ownership of the body to be shared between the spouse (7:4) and the Lord (6:19–20).[32]

---

30. The household codes, of course, *do* move towards "Christianizing" the household, and thereby leave an ambiguous legacy: the organization of the household becomes a matter of direct relationship to Christ, but its hierarchical relations, including the ownership of slaves, thereby becomes normalized, even idealized, as the direct expression of allegiance to Christ. For reflections on this matter, see my "Ordinary but Different: Colossians and Hidden Moral Identity," in J. M. G. Barclay, *Pauline Churches and Diaspora Jews*, WUNT 275 (Tübingen: Mohr Siebeck, 2011), 237–55.

31. That the single woman seeks to be "holy in body and spirit" (7:34) *could* be interpreted that way, and quickly was in the history of reception: see, e.g., *The Acts of Paul and Thecla*.

32. See the fine analysis by A. S. May, *The Body for the Lord: Sex and Identity in 1 Corinthians 5–7*, JSNTSup 278 (Sheffield: Sheffield Academic, 2004), who, to my mind, rightly argues that it is not the Corinthians who advocate singleness ("it is better for a man not to touch a woman," 7:1), but Paul.

Conclusions: "Apocalyptic" Ethics

First Corinthians 7 opens a fascinating window onto the original "apocalyptic" mindset that was "the mother of Christian theology" (Käsemann), and onto its practical, ethical implications. Bultmann was correct to insist (against Schweitzer) that the early Christian "apocalyptic" ethic was not fundamentally an emergency, interim ethic, a special set of conditions imaginable only when believers awaited the imminent new dawn. Paul (like other early Christians of his generation) *did* believe in the imminence of the end, but this was not the only reason why they disinvested in "the world." In his view, believers lived in the midst of the "apocalypse" itself, and their newly aligned allegiance to the risen, reigning, but embattled, Lord reset their priorities and encouraged a critical distance from all that was not directly aligned to Christ—a form of disinvestment that limited the quality and/or the quantity of engagements with worldly activities. Bultmann's existentialist reading of this phenomenon was one of the defining characteristics of his theology.[33] What is eschatological about the Christ-event is, for Bultmann, the way it tears us from our past, and sets before us the possibility of living from and for the future—in a radical dependence on God's grace that is simultaneously our freedom from our sinful self-reliance, from captivity to the illusion that the world is at our disposal. In the address of God's word to each person "as an isolated individual being,"[34] the eschaton is not an objectifiable event in history but the ever-renewed impact of the gospel, which repeatedly calls forth a decision of obedience and faith. As Käsemann insisted, this collapse of eschatology into a repeatable present, and its restriction to the inner life of the individual, risks obscuring the purchase of the gospel on the real-life world of social allegiance and social conflict, in which the Lordship of Christ requires to be expressed

---

33. See esp. R. Bultmann, "The Understanding of Man and the World in the New Testament and in the Greek World," in *Essays Philosophical and Theological* (London: SCM, 1955), 67–89, and "Man Between the Times according to the New Testament," in *Existence and Faith* (London: Hodder and Stoughton, 1961), 248–66. For comment on this motif in Bultmann, see the introduction to the latter volume by S. Ogden.
34. Bultmann, "Understanding of Man," 78.

in practical, physical, ways.[35] Paul did not call for an inner freedom from all circumstances: he called for discrimination between the business of the Lord and the business of the world, on the grounds that the one was the harbinger of the coming rule of God, and the other the residue of the past, in the limited time before its end. In this bracket of time, believers look in two directions—both back, to the "apocalyptic" intrusion of God into "the present evil age," and forward to the moment when death, which rules by its current "constraint," is swallowed up in the victory of Christ. If that chronological frame is lost or demythologized, Christian disengagement becomes a purely internal and psychological phenomenon.[36] Where it is retained, it calls forth hard and highly practical decisions about the places where believers, both individually and collectively, invest or disinvest their energy and attention. Even if we do not draw the line between "the business of the world" and "the business of the Lord" in exactly the same place as Paul, the question he poses remains highly pertinent. And the decision of many early Christians, shaped by "apocalyptic" convictions, to choose singleness over marriage, poverty over wealth, and martyrdom over life, remains a challenge which modern Western Christians are all too eager to forget.

35. Against common misperceptions, it is important to note that "apocalyptic" meant far more to Käsemann than the imminence of the end. Its critical question was "to whom does the world belong?," and in pointing to the coming Lord, the early Christians declared that the answer had already been given in Jesus' enthronement over the powers that threaten and enslave the cosmos. See, e.g., E. Käsemann, "On the Subject of Primitive Christian Apocalyptic," in *New Testament Questions of Today*, trans. W. J. Montague (Philadelphia: Fortress Press, 1969), 108–37, at 135.

36. This is the direction in which Agamben's reading seems to tend, collapsing the future into an aesthetic transformation of the present and "the time of the end" into "the time that time takes to come to an end." See G. Agamben, *The Time that Remains: A Commentary on the Letter to the Romans* (Stanford: Stanford University Press, 2005), 19–43, 62–87.

14

After Destroying Every Rule, Authority, and Power

Paul, Apocalyptic, and Politics in 1 Corinthians

John K. Goodrich

Apocalyptic is the disquieting question which not only moves the apostle but apparently faces every Christian, a question bound up with his task and his existence: who owns the earth?[1]

At the beginning of his now famous essay "On the Subject of Primitive Christian Apocalyptic," Ernst Käsemann referred to apocalyptic as an "unfashionable theme" (unzeitgemäßes Thema).[2] Such cannot be maintained today. Following recent efforts to reconcile biblical and theological studies as interdependent disciplines, apocalyptic readings of the NT have come to abound in modern scholarship, and Pauline

---

1. Ernst Käsemann, "On Paul's Anthropology," in *Perspectives on Paul* (Philadelphia: Fortress Press, 1971), 1–31, at 24–25; cf. idem, "Zur paulinischen Anthropologie," in *Paulinische Perspektiven* (Tübingen: J. C. B. Mohr [Paul Siebeck], 1969), 9–60, at 48.
2. Idem, "On the Subject of Primitive Christian Apocalyptic," in *New Testament Questions of Today* (Philadelphia: Fortress Press, 1969), 108–37, at 108; cf. idem, "Zum Thema der urchristlichen Apokalyptik," *ZTK* 59, no. 3 (1962): 267–84.

theology is unquestionably one of the primary fields in which fascination with apocalyptic has reached new heights.

In the wake of this frenzy, biblical scholars have highlighted numerous themes they consider to be fundamental to the genre and worldview of early Jewish apocalyptic. Perhaps the single most stimulating insight emphasized afresh in recent years is the notion that apocalyptic, for all its fascination with *otherworldly* conflicts, originated as political discourse and is thus routinely concerned with promoting various modes of resistance to *terrestrial* empires. Richard Horsley, for example, discounting the notion of a hard cosmic dualism perpetuated in some older scholarship, contends that the clashes within the angelic arena narrated by Jewish seers had direct correlations to events occurring on the earthly political stage. By portraying God's heavenly armies as defeating those evil powers standing behind human political and military agents, these visions imparted hope to, and incited active resistance among, faithful Israelites who suffered under the oppressive hand of foreign rule.[3] "The Second Temple Judean texts that have been classified as apocalyptic," Horsley asserts, "are the expressions of their struggles to affirm that God was still in control of history and to resist Hellenistic or Roman rule that had become overly oppressive."[4] Put differently: "Unless it is simply a historical accident, it is surely significant that no Second Temple Judean text classified as 'apocalyptic' has survived that does *not* focus on imperial rule and the opposition to it."[5]

For Horsley, this inherent relationship between political resistance and apocalyptic modes of thinking extends also to the letters of Paul. As he maintains, "It is precisely against the [apocalyptic] background of . . . God's (plan for the) overcoming of imperial rule that Paul's anti-Roman imperial stance and anti-Roman imperial rhetoric [in 1

---

3. Richard A. Horsley, *Revolt of the Scribes: Resistance and Apocalyptic Origins* (Minneapolis: Fortress Press, 2010), 6 and 199–203. Cf. Idem, *Jesus and the Spiral of Violence: Popular Jewish Resistance in Roman Palestine* (Minneapolis: Fortress Press, 1993); idem, ed., *Scribes, Visionaries, and the Politics of Second Temple Judea* (Louisville: Westminster John Knox 2007); idem, *Jesus and the Powers: Conflict, Covenant, and the Hope of the Poor* (Minneapolis: Fortress Press, 2011).

4. Horsley, *Revolt of the Scribes*, 3–4.

5. Ibid., 3 (original emphasis).

Corinthians] can be understood."[6] Many of Horsley's conclusions are embraced by others, including N. T. Wright, who likewise insists that "we should really see 'apocalyptic,' in both its Jewish and Pauline contexts, as all about the fresh revelation of Israel's God and particularly the exposé of the folly and blasphemy of pagan power."[7]

There remains disagreement, however, over the extent to which all such apocalyptic writings sought to advocate resistance. Although Anathea Portier-Young endorses Horsley's basic premise about the relationship between empire and apocalyptic and affirms the function of the early apocalypses as resistance literature, she distinguishes between the genre's earlier and later functions.[8] "The genre pattern of the historical apocalypse emerged," she explains, "in response to a situational pattern. But this bond was not indissoluble. Later Jewish apocalyptic literature would reuse and adapt the forms and conventions of this genre to respond to different kinds of situations, and in different ways."[9] Such later apocalyptic writings, she continues, could "embody discursive resistance as well as aim to motivate and sustain a program of resistance to domination and hegemony. But this was not a necessary function of the genre apocalypse. Resistance literature proves to be an apt category for some apocalyptic literature, but by no means all."[10] For Portier-Young, an individual apocalyptic work must not be forced to convey the same message and apply it in the same manner as its generic or theological antecedents. Readers, rather, must remain sensitive to a text's historical setting and original voice. As she concludes, "The crucial link between resistance literature and the situations in which it arises means that we cannot make a general claim about the function of Jewish apocalyptic literature as

---

6. Richard A. Horsley, "Rhetoric and Empire—and 1 Corinthians," in *Paul and Politics: Ekklesia, Israel, Imperium, Interpretation. Essays in Honor of Krister Stendahl*, ed. R. A. Horsley (Harrisburg: Trinity Press International, 2000), 72–102, at 96.

7. N. T. Wright, *Paul and the Faithfulness of God* (Minneapolis: Fortress Press, 2013), 2:1309–10.

8. Anathea Portier-Young, *Apocalypse against Empire: Theologies of Resistance in Early Judaism* (Grand Rapids: Eerdmans, 2011), 383; idem, "Jewish Apocalyptic Literature as Resistance Literature," in *The Oxford Handbook of Apocalyptic Literature*, ed. J. J. Collins (Oxford: Oxford University Press, 2014), 145–62, at 149.

9. Ibid., 160.

10. Ibid., 146. Cf. Portier-Young, *Apocalypse against Empire*, 45; John J. Collins, "Apocalypse and Empire," *SEÅ* 76, no. 1 (2011): 1–19.

resistance literature. Genre matters, but genre is fluid, and times change. If we wish to articulate what kinds of cultural work a text performed we must also be able to articulate when and where, for whom, and under what circumstances."[11]

These concessions are instructive for the study of Paul. Although the apostle's letters can be—and have been—read as resistance literature (insofar as they can serve to "limit, oppose, reject, or transform hegemonic institutions"), it is not always clear that this is what his letters *aim* to do—the *intention*, and not just *implication*, of a particular work being an important component of Portier-Young's definition of resistance literature.[12] Nor is there widespread agreement about precisely *how* and *to what extent* Paul's letters function to resist imperialism when they do. For while it is incorrect to maintain that Paul's writings pose *no* challenge to political authorities,[13] the counter-imperial sentiment of some apocalyptic literature has led many NT interpreters to conclude that Paul's letters, infused as they are with apocalyptic themes, insist on a degree of separation from and opposition to Roman rule that goes too far beyond what they, at least on the surface, seem to promote.[14]

Due to these currents within recent scholarship, it is the goal of

---

11. Portier-Young, "Jewish Apocalyptic Literature," 160.

12. Portier-Young, *Apocalypse against Empire*, 11 and 44. She defines resistance literature as that which "*aims* to limit, oppose, reject, or transform hegemonic institutions and cosmologies and systems, strategies, and acts of domination" (44, emphasis added). While I recognize the importance of incorporating inexplicit statements about government in the construction of a Pauline political theology (see Douglas A. Campbell, "Paul's Apocalyptic Politics," *ProEccl* 22, no. 2 [2013]: 129–52), I prioritize the explicit here in order to meet Portier-Young's definition of resistance literature.

13. For important, recent contributions to the counter-imperial Paul project, see, e.g., Joseph D. Fantin, *Lord of the Entire World: Lord Jesus, a Challenge to Lord Caesar?*, NTM 31 (Sheffield: Sheffield Phoenix, 2011); James R. Harrison, *Paul and the Imperial Authorities at Thessalonica and Rome: A Study in the Conflict of Ideology*, WUNT 173 (Tübingen, Germany: Mohr Siebeck, 2011); Wright, *Paul and the Faithfulness of God*, 2:1271–1319; Christoph Heilig, *Hidden Criticism? The Methodology and Plausibility of the Search for a Counter-Imperial Subtext in Paul*, WUNT 2/392 (Tübingen: Mohr Siebeck, 2015). See also select volumes in Fortress Press's *Paul in Critical Contexts* series.

14. For recent critical evaluations of the counter-imperial approach to Paul, see, e.g., Seyoon Kim, *Christ and Caesar: The Gospel and the Roman Empire in the Writings of Paul and Luke* (Grand Rapids: Eerdmans, 2008); John M. G. Barclay, "Why the Roman Empire Was Insignificant to Paul," in *Pauline Churches and Diaspora Jews*, WUNT 275 (Tübingen: Mohr Siebeck, 2011), 363–87; J. Albert Harrill, *Paul the Apostle: His Life and Legacy in Their Roman Context* (Cambridge: Cambridge University Press, 2012), 76–94; Matthew V. Novenson, "What the Apostles Did Not See," in *Reactions to Empire: Sacred Texts in Their Socio-Political Contexts*, eds. J. A. Dunne and D. Batovici, WUNT 2/372 (Tübingen: Mohr Siebeck, 2014), 55–72.

this chapter to investigate how and to what extent apocalyptic and politics intersect within Paul's thinking, as well as how and to what extent Paul's apocalyptic discourses promote resistance to political authorities.[15] Our focus here will be limited to three passages in 1 Corinthians where apocalyptic and politics undoubtedly converge: 1 Cor. 2:6–8; 6:1–11; and 15:20–28. My thesis is quite simple: these three passages function as what Portier-Young calls *discursive resistance*, asserting God's supremacy over empires by forecasting the certain, future, and final demise of all inimical powers, including all governing authorities who remain unsubmissive to Christ. Nevertheless, Paul's letter neither advocates *active resistance* to empire nor insists upon a wholesale opposition to Rome. In fact, within Paul's rhetorical polemic, these rulers remain nameless, faceless, and generally less "significant" than the named ontological powers of sin and death (cf. 1 Cor. 15:26, 54–56).[16]

As we treat these passages in sequence, I will, in each case, seek to establish that: (1) Paul had political authorities in view; (2) Paul considered these authorities to be asserting power and hegemony warranting resistance; and (3) Paul's discourse serves to resist the power assertions and power claims of those in political authority by exposing the transience of their power and by turning his readership's attention to God's future redemptive work, not by promoting rebellion. Finally, I will briefly assess the extent to which Rome as a specific political entity figures into Paul's apocalyptic discourse.

Resisting the Rulers of this Age
(1 Corinthians 2:6–8)

The first explicit mention of earthly political authorities in 1

---

15. I am using "politics" quite broadly, to encompass the organization and governance of community life. By "political authorities," I mean those agents "who manage to get hold of and to make use of means of temporal power such as making laws, commanding instruments of physical coercion and being able to extract and use funds from a certain community" (Dorothea H. Bertschmann, *Bowing before Christ—Nodding to the State? Reading Paul Politically with Oliver O'Donovan and John Howard Yoder*, LNTS 502 [London: Bloomsbury T&T Clark, 2014], 72).

16. For an exchange on the relative "significance" of the Roman empire in Paul, see Barclay, "Why the Roman Empire Was Insignificant to Paul," and Wright, *Paul and the Faithfulness of God*, 2:1271–1319.

Corinthians occurs in 2:6-8. Seeking to censure the Corinthians for their spiritual immaturity (esp. in 3:1-4),[17] Paul in 2:6-3:4 turns his attention first to the recipients of the divine wisdom he has been commissioned to impart. This wisdom, he explains, is spoken among the mature, and it is a wisdom neither "of this age" nor "of the rulers of this age, who are passing away" (τῶν ἀρχόντων τοῦ αἰῶνος τούτου τῶν καταργουμένων, 2:6). But how can we be sure about the identity of "the rulers" in this hotly contested passage?

Although ἄρχων occasionally refers to celestial beings in apocalyptic literature,[18] and such a reading of 1 Cor. 2:6-8 has been vigorously defended throughout the history of biblical scholarship,[19] Paul's only other use of the plural ἄρχοντες (Rom. 13:3), together with the progression of thought in the immediate context of our passage, suggests that οἱ ἄρχοντες τοῦ αἰῶνος τούτου in 1 Cor. 2:6-8 refer only to human political authorities.[20] Indeed, the primary topic of 2:6-3:4

17. For the rhetorical divisions and aims of 1 Corinthians 1-4, see Joop F. M. Smit, "'What Is Apollos? What Is Paul?': In Search for the Coherence of First Corinthians 1:10-4:21," *NovT* 44, no. 3 (2002): 231-51.

18. Cf. Dan. (Theod.) 10:13, 20-21; 11:5, 18; 12:1; *1 En.* 6:2-3, 7; John 12:31; 14:30; 16:11; Eph. 2:2; *Ep. Barn.* 4:13; 18:2; *T. Sol.* 2:7.

19. See, e.g., Otto Everling, *Die paulinische Angelologie und Dämonologie: Ein biblisch-theologischer Versuch* (Göttingen: Vandenhoeck & Ruprecht, 1888), 11-14; Martin Dibelius, *Die Geisterwelt im Glauben des Paulus* (Göttingen: Vandenhoeck & Ruprecht, 1909), 88-99; Julius Schniewind, "Die Archonten dieses Äons: I. Kor. 2,6-8," in *Nachgelassene Reden und Aufsätze* (Berlin: Töpelmann, 1952), 104-9; Gerhard Delling, "ἄρχων," in TDNT (Vol. 1), ed. G. Kittel (Grand Rapids: Eerdmans, 1964), 488-89, at 489n7; C. K. Barrett, *A Commentary on the First Epistle to the Corinthians*, HNTC (New York: Harper & Row, 1968), 70; Hans Conzelmann, *1 Corinthians*, Hermeneia (Philadelphia: Fortress Press, 1975), 61-63; Judith L. Kovacs, "The Archons, the Spirit and the Death of Christ: Do We Need the Hypothesis of Gnostic Opponents to Explain 1 Cor. 2.6-16?," in *Apocalyptic and the New Testament*, eds. J. Marcus and M. L. Soards, JSNTSup 24 (Sheffield: JSOT, 1989), 217-36; Wolfgang Schrage, *Der erste Brief an die Korinther (1 Kor 1,1-6,11)*, EKK VII/1 (Zurich: Benziger/Neukirchen Vluyn, 1991), 250-54; Clinton E. Arnold, *Powers of Darkness: Principalities and Powers in Paul's Letters* (Downers Grove: InterVarsity, 1992), 100-104; Raymond F. Collins, *First Corinthians*, Sacra Pagina 7 (Collegeville: Liturgical, 1999), 129; Guy Williams, *The Spirit World in the Letters of Paul the Apostle: A Critical Examination of the Role of Spiritual Beings in the Authentic Pauline Epistles*, FRLANT 231 (Göttingen: Vandenhoeck & Ruprecht, 2009), 136-37; Robert Ewusie Moses, *Practices of Power: Revisiting the Principalities and Powers in the Pauline Letters*, Emerging Scholars (Minneapolis: Fortress Press, 2014), 84-94.

20. Gene Miller, "ἀρχόντων τοῦ αἰῶνος τούτου—a New Look at 1 Corinthians 2:6-8," *JBL* 91, no. 4 (1972): 522-28; Wesley Carr, "The Rulers of This Age—1 Corinthians 2.6-8," *NTS* 23, no. 1 (1976/77): 20-35; Mauro Pesce, *Paolo e gli arconti a Corinto: Storia della ricerca (1888-1975) ed esegesi di I Cor. 2,6.8*, Testi e ricerche di Scienze religiose 13 (Brescia: Oaedeia Editrice, 1977); Gordon D. Fee, *The First Epistle to the Corinthians*, NICNT (Grand Rapids: Eerdmans, 1987), 103-4; Neil Elliott, *Liberating Paul: The Justice of God and the Politics of the Apostle* (Sheffield: Sheffield Academic, 1995), 43; Ben Witherington, *Conflict and Community in Corinth: A Socio-Rhetorical Commentary on 1 and 2 Corinthians* (Grand Rapids: Eerdmans, 1995), 127; Richard B. Hays, *First Corinthians*, Interpretation (Louisville:

concerns the means for understanding divine wisdom. God's previously hidden wisdom, Paul shows, has now been revealed to believers "through the Spirit" (2:10), such that it is only through the Spirit's agency that a mere human (ἄνθρωπος) is capable of comprehending and accepting the gospel (2:11–16). This line of thought is apparent through the repeated contrast between human and divine/Spirit agency in both the previous and present sections (see Figure 1).

Figure 1: Key Contrasts between Human and Divine/Spirit Agency in 1 Corinthians 2–3

	Human	**Divine/Spirit**
2:4	οὐκ ἐν πειθοῖς σοφίας λόγοις	ἀλλ' ἐν ἀποδείξει πνεύματος καὶ δυνάμεως
2:5	μὴ ᾖ ἐν σοφίᾳ ἀνθρώπων	ἀλλ' ἐν δυνάμει θεοῦ
2:13	οὐκ ἐν διδακτοῖς ἀνθρωπίνης σοφίας λόγοις	ἀλλ' ἐν διδακτοῖς πνεύματος
2:14–15	ψυχικὸς ἄνθρωπος οὐ δέχεται	τὰ τοῦ πνεύματος τοῦ θεοῦ
3:1–4	οὐχὶ σαρκικοί ἐστε καὶ κατὰ ἄνθρωπον περιπατεῖτε; . . . οὐκ ἄνθρωποί ἐστε;	πνευματικοί

In the light of our passage's consistent anthropolemical discourse, it is right to conclude, as one recent monograph explains, that "the wisdom of God identified with the message of the cross is perceived only by the 'mature' and 'spiritual' as a result of the revelation of God's Spirit *and not as a result of human wisdom*, and much less of the teachers' eloquence."[21] That being the case, it would make little sense for Paul in 2:6–8 to fault *angelic* beings for failing to understand wisdom comprehensible only through the assistance of the Holy Spirit. A polemic against *human* governing authorities, on the contrary, would do well to advance his argument.

John Knox, 1997), 43; David E. Garland, *1 Corinthians*, BECNT (Grand Rapids: Baker, 2003), 93; Joseph A. Fitzmyer, *First Corinthians: A New Translation with Introduction and Commentary*, AYB 32 (New Haven: Yale University Press, 2008), 175.

21. Corin Mihaila, *The Paul-Apollos Relationship and Paul's Stance toward Greco-Roman Rhetoric: An Exegetical and Socio-Historical Study of 1 Corinthians 1-4*, LNTS 402 (London T&T Clark, 2009), 26 (emphasis added).

In fact, given Paul's abundant use of contrast in both 1:18–2:5 and 2:6–3:4, it should be clear that when Paul juxtaposes "the rulers of this age who are being destroyed" with "the mature" (2:6; cf. 14:20; Phil. 3:15) who are destined "for glory" (εἰς δόξαν, 2:7), he does so to create an anthropological distinction between believers and unbelievers. This becomes clearer as the passage progresses. For it is this reference to "our glory" (δόξαν ἡμῶν, 2:7) that leads Paul to contrast "the rulers of this age" (2:8)—"who *crucified* the Lord *of glory* [τῆς δόξης]" and have never seen, heard, or comprehended the eschatological blessings "God has prepared" (2:9)—with "us" (2:10)—believers "who *love* [God]" (2:9) and have been "revealed" divine mysteries (2:10). In view of these elaborate contrasts, it is quite doubtful that οἱ ἄρχοντες τοῦ αἰῶνος τούτου in 2:6–8 is a reference to angelic beings, or even a double-reference to human *and* angelic beings.[22] Rather, Paul here has terrestrial powers and the wisdom they propound exclusively in view; otherwise, his denunciation of human wisdom (ἀνθρωπίνη σοφία) and the natural person (ψυχικὸς ἄνθρωπος) in 2:13–3:4 is a non sequitur.[23]

---

22. For the latter, see, e.g., G. H. C. MacGregor, "Principalities and Powers: The Cosmic Background of St Paul's Thought," *NTS* 1, no. 1 (1954/55): 17–28, at 22–24; G. B. Caird, *Principalities and Powers: A Study in Pauline Theology* (Oxford: Clarendon, 1956), 82–101; Walter Wink, *Naming the Powers: The Language of Power in the New Testament* (Philadelphia: Fortress Press, 1984), 40–45 and 106; Roy E. Ciampa and Brian S. Rosner, *The First Letter to the Corinthians*, PNTC (Grand Rapids: Eerdmans, 2010), 125.

23. Scholars continue to dispute this reading. Williams (*Spirit World*, 137) defends the celestial view by pointing to: (a) the history of interpretation (Ignatius [*Eph.* 18–19]; Marcion [Tertullian, *Marc.* 5.6.5]; *Ascen. Isa.* [11.24; cf. v. 19]); (b) the "highly suggestive parallel" of ἀρχή in 1 Cor. 15:24; (c) God's decree of wisdom πρὸ τῶν αἰώνων—"a point of some relevance to immortal angels, but meaningless in connection with humans"; (d) the rulers' *present* destruction, which would exclude Herod and Pilate; (e) the cosmic/demonic significance of τοῦ αἰῶνος τούτου (cf. Gal. 1:4; 2 Cor. 4:4; Eph. 2:2; *Ascen. Isa.* 2:4). Yet, each of these arguments is problematic. For (a), not only is exegesis based in the first place on *Auslegungsgeschichte* quite tenuous, but the earliest interpretations of 1 Cor. 2:8 were followed shortly thereafter by the political readings of Tertullian (*Marc.* 5.6.5) and John Chrysostom (*Hom. 1 Cor.*, 7.1); cf. Anthony C. Thiselton, *The First Epistle to the Corinthians*, NIGTC (Grand Rapids: Eerdmans, 2000), 236–37. For (b), the referent of ἀρχή in 1 Cor. 15:24 is probably ontologically inclusive, as suggested by the repetition of πᾶς and other contextual clues. For (c), it remains unclear how God's decree of wisdom *before the ages* is any more relevant for one reading than another; the rulers plainly belong to "*this age*," not before it, so God's wisdom would have remained inaccessible even to angels until it was climactically revealed in Christ. For (d), the present tense participle οἱ καταργούμενοι (2:6) probably has a future rather than present implicature (cf. 1:28; 15:24). This is suggested in 1:18, where Paul uses the near synonym οἱ ἀπολλύμενοι and likewise emphasizes crucifixion, *future* destruction, and epistemological inability; the rulers, then, are to be understood collectively, rather than as a specific reference to Herod and Pilate. For (e), ὁ αἰὼν οὗτος relates to humans in 1:20 and 3:18, suggesting its similar deployment in-between.

Having, then, identified οἱ ἄρχοντες τοῦ αἰῶνος τούτου as human authorities, we are now in a position to ask how Paul's apocalyptic discourse in 1 Cor. 2:6–8 advocates resistance to political authorities. In order to answer this question, we must inquire about how these rulers established the conditions for resistance through domination and hegemony, as well as how Paul here aims to subvert these conditions.

Although the rulers Paul has in view undoubtedly exercised power in a variety of ways, according to our passage, they do so principally by obtaining and exercising a monopoly on intellectual, socio-economic, and executive power. These rulers prided themselves for belonging to the world's wise, powerful, and well-born elite (σοφοί, δυνατοί/ἰσχυρά, εὐγενεῖς, τὰ ὄντα, 1:26–29; cf. 2:6), and Paul attributes to them a contemptuous outlook upon those comprising the church: God chose foolish, weak, lowly-born, and despised nobodies (τὰ μωρά, τὰ ἀσθενῆ, τὰ ἀγενῆ, τὰ ἐξουθενημένα, τὰ μὴ ὄντα, 1:27–28).[24] This attitude, far from harmless, not only manifested in the rulers' disregard for the divine wisdom revealed in Jesus Christ, but climaxed in his crucifixion (2:8). Indeed, the very wisdom and power that distinguished these aristocrats from those whom they governed were ironically leveraged in the murder of the one who embodies God's true wisdom and power (1:24, 30).

Paul, however, challenges the dominion of the world's rulers, first, by exposing their lack of true and lasting resources. While the rulers assume they possess the lion's share of the world's intellectual and social capital, Paul perceives them to be intellectually and spiritually bankrupt for failing to grasp God's transcendent wisdom. It is in this way that the revelation of mysteries is inherently polemical, demonstrating the insufficiency of mundane knowledge and the superiority of those with access to the knowledge only God can unveil. Just as Daniel's revealed mysteries served to subvert the wise men of Nebuchadnezzar's court (Dan. 2:13, 27–28), so Paul's revealed

---

24. While Paul does not attribute a pejorative outlook specifically to political authorities, he attributes to them "wisdom of this age" and the epistemology consistent with the world (1:18–28).

mysteries, indebted as they are to the Danielic concept, analogously serve to undermine the pretension of the σοφοί and ἄρχοντες of this age (1:19–20; 2:6–8).[25]

More to the point, God subverted the wisdom and power of the world (1:19-20) by equipping believers, through the Spirit, with new epistemological lenses (2:10–16), enabling them to understand and appreciate God's norm-defying criteria for distributing his eschatological resources.[26] The rulers, to be sure, see things κατὰ σάρκα (1:26), and from their distorted vantage point, they do, in fact, appear to possess one form of wisdom and power. Paul, however, would have believers view their existence ἐν Χριστῷ Ἰησοῦ (1:30), and it is from within that epistemological location that one learns those concepts anew—that "[Christ] *became* wisdom for us from God [ὃς ἐγενήθη σοφία ἡμῖν ἀπὸ θεοῦ], righteousness and sanctification and redemption" (1:30; cf. 1:24). The much sought after wisdom and power of this world, then, while prized by the rulers of this age, have become obsolete for those who belong to the age to come. What truly matters is God's *revealed* wisdom, *spiritual* discernment, and the mind *of Christ* (2:10–16), manifesting in power through weakness (2:1–5; cf. 2 Cor. 12:9–10; Phil. 2:5–11).

Paul, then, destabilizes the rulers' dominance by forecasting their certain, future destruction (1 Cor. 2:6; cf. 1:28). The rulers of this age and the authority they possess are passing away (2:6), a perceived impossibility to those with executive power (2:8), but an inevitable reality to the God who decrees the end from before the ages (2:7). God's supremacy over the rulers is, for believers, apparent in his ironic exploitation of the cross: rather than eliminating Jesus and thereby prolonging the status quo, the cross redefines wisdom and power as Christ crucified (1:18–25) and serves to redeem the very outcasts over whom the rulers exercise control (1:26–31). While those who embrace the folly of the cross are being saved, the world and its rulers are

25. Benjamin L. Gladd, *Revealing the Mysterion: The Use of Mystery in Daniel and Second Temple Judaism with Its Bearing on First Corinthians*, BZNT 160 (Berlin: de Gruyter, 2008), 159–63.
26. Alexandra R. Brown, *The Cross and Human Transformation: Paul's Apocalyptic Word in 1 Corinthians* (Minneapolis: Fortress Press, 1995), 157–67.

naively perishing as they relentlessly boast in their autonomy (1:18, 29; 2:6). The cross, then, symbolizes, for those with eyes to see, the transient nature of this world and the eventual demise of all who belong to it.

In sum, Paul's apocalyptic discourse in 1 Cor. 2:6–8 (and adjacent texts) functions as *discursive* resistance, seeking in a way similar to Daniel's apocalyptic message to expose the folly of the rulers of this age and the transience of their power. Nothing said here, however, advocates *active* resistance to the governing authorities. Rebellion would be at odds with the cross, and the shaming and neutralization of the aristocracy will occur at the final judgment (ἐνώπιον τοῦ θεοῦ, 1:27–29). Meanwhile, believers are to remain as they were called (cf. 7:20, 24), which, for most, means at the margins of society (1:26). All, however, should seek to embody the crucified Lord of glory as they await their own glorious redemption (2:7–9).

Resisting Unrighteous Judges
(1 Corinthians 6:1–11)

Following on his call to judge and discipline community members participating in sin (5:11–13), Paul turns his attention in 6:1–11 to those believers engaging one another in civil litigation. These cases, likely issuing from financial disputes,[27] were symptomatic of at least two greater spiritual shortcomings. First, the church was divided. Indeed, Paul's principal complaint here is that there exist internal conflicts at all: "That you have lawsuits with one another is already a complete defeat for you" (6:7). Such fractures, Paul insists, should not occur between brothers in Christ (6:8). Second, the church was relying on outsiders (ἄδικοι, 6:1; ἄπιστοι, 6:6) to resolve their disputes. Rather than turning to the public courts, Paul instructs the community to handle its conflicts internally (6:4).

The adjudication of legal proceedings in the public court system is an obvious way in which rulers asserted their hegemony over their

---

27. Michael Peppard, "Brother against Brother: *Controversiae* About Inheritance Disputes and 1 Corinthians 6:1–11," *JBL* 133, no. 1 (2014): 179–92, at 189.

subjects. Judges were appointed by local magistrates, and injustices proliferated within the system as favorable verdicts were often awarded on the basis of social status and bribery.[28] Paul seems to acknowledge such injustices when he censures those believers who "dare . . . to be judged before the *unrighteous*" (τολμᾷ τις ὑμῶν . . . κρίνεσθαι ἐπὶ τῶν ἀδίκων, 6:1; cf. 6:9). To involve oneself in the public courts, then, is to place oneself under the authority of judges who represent the governing authorities and whose rulings tended to perpetuate inequity.

Paul, however, employs apocalyptic discourse to resist the power of these judges in at least two ways. First, Paul calls into question the supposed superior qualifications of local court justices by reminding the church of its own role in the future judgment of both the world and angels: οὐκ οἴδατε ὅτι οἱ ἅγιοι τὸν κόσμον κρινοῦσιν; . . . οὐκ οἴδατε ὅτι ἀγγέλους κρινοῦμεν; (6:2-3). Due to the rhetorical nature of these questions, Paul probably assumes the church is familiar with Dan. 7:22 (τὴν κρίσιν ἔδωκε τοῖς ἁγίοις τοῦ ὑψίστου, LXX) or a tradition influenced by it.[29] In any case, Paul's point is clear: for the church to take its disputes before unbelieving judges is for believers not only to exaggerate the significance of their petty grievances; it is also to fail to recognize and put to use their own judicial competence in the resolution of these conflicts (6:2-5). For those properly oriented to the end, these are "trivial cases" (κριτηρίων ἐλαχίστων, 6:2) pertaining to mere "life issues" (βιωτικά, 6:3-4). Moreover, as those who have been washed, sanctified, justified, and given the Holy Spirit (6:11), the Corinthians are more than worthy (ἀνάξιος), wise (σοφός), and capable (δυνήσεται) enough to adjudicate their own disputes (6:2, 5), and therefore, they themselves should appoint as judges (καθίζετε) even

---

28. Bruce W. Winter, "Civil Litigation in Secular Corinth and the Church: The Forensic Background to 1 Corinthians 6.1-8," *NTS* 37, no. 4 (1991): 559–72; Alan C. Mitchell, "Rich and Poor in the Courts of Corinth: Litigiousness and Status in 1 Corinthians 6.1-11," *NTS* 39, no. 4 (1993): 562–86.

29. Note also the shared use of κριτήριον, καθίζω, and βασιλεία in 1 Cor. 6:2–10 and LXX Dan. 7:26–27; cf. κρίμα, 1 Cor. 6:7; Dan. (Theod.) 7:22. Cf. Brian S. Rosner, *Paul, Scripture, and Ethics: A Study of 1 Corinthians 5-7*, AGJU 22 (Leiden: Brill, 1994), 111. See, however, Paul M. Hoskins, "The Use of Biblical and Extrabiblical Parallels in the Interpretation of First Corinthians 6:2-3," *CBQ* 63, no. 2 (2001): 287–97.

"the despised in the church" (τοὺς ἐξουθενημένους ἐν τῇ ἐκκλησίᾳ, 6:4).[30] Appointing a private arbiter was indeed permitted in Greco-Roman antiquity, and thus would not have been viewed as active resistance, especially within a familial context.[31] By stressing, then, the judicial competence of the Corinthians in this way, Paul diminishes the significance and exceptionality of the "unrighteous" who preside over public courts. And having relativized the importance of ordinary lawsuits, Paul curtails the power these judges possess. They indeed have authority, but only over the mundane.

Furthermore, Paul challenges the authority of local judges by forecasting their certain, future demise. By highlighting the believer's role in the judgment of the world (κόσμος), Paul anticipates a time when all political agents, including court justices, will cease to exercise authority. Furthermore, it is judges such as these who belong to the community of the "unrighteous" and will fail to inherit the kingdom of God (6:1, 9). The end of their tenure is approaching, and at that time their judicial authority will be seized and transferred to the saints (cf. Dan. 7:22, 27).

In sum, Paul's apocalyptic discourse in 1 Cor. 6:1–11, again, functions as *discursive* resistance, but not *active* resistance. Paul urges the church to reevaluate the subject matter of their disputes and to reconsider the relative authority, competence, and permanence of local judges. But we must be careful not to assume that Paul sought to repudiate the authority of the public courts over believers entirely, as Horsley maintains.[32] Paul continues to recognize the role and rights of governing authorities (Rom. 13:1–7), and he would have probably expected that a dispute between a believer and an unbeliever, if requiring arbitration, would be settled through the public courts—for what has the church to do with judging outsiders (5:12)? The only

30. For καθίζετε (6:4) as an imperative, see Brent Kinman, "'Appoint the Despised as Judges!' (1 Corinthians 6:4)," *TynBul* 48, no. 2 (1997): 345–54.

31. Winter, "Civil Litigation," 568-69; Peppard, "Brother against Brother," 190.

32. Horsley repeatedly overstates the degree of separation Paul demands between the church and non-Christian society; cf. Richard A. Horsley, *1 Corinthians*, ANTC (Nashville: Abingdon, 1998), 88; idem, "1 Corinthians: A Case Study of Paul's Assembly as an Alternative Society," in *Paul and Empire: Religion and Power in Roman Imperial Society*, ed. R. A. Horsley (Harrisburg: Trinity Press International, 1997), 242–52, esp. 245–46; idem, "Rhetoric and Empire—and 1 Corinthians," 100.

proscription he gives here is for believers not to litigate against one another; when grievances do arise within the church, they should be settled internally. Paul, then, maintains the place for external systems of judicial authority, but he believes they are inappropriate channels for dealing with conflicts between those within the family of God.

Resisting Every Rule, Authority, and Power
(1 Corinthians 15:20–28)

First Corinthians 15 contains numerous apocalyptic themes, though explicit political terms and images are all but absent from the chapter's earliest verses. Having begun his argument by reminding the church about the gospel he preached to them—a gospel founded on Jesus' resurrection from the dead (15:1-11)—Paul then expresses concerns about those Corinthians who do not believe Christ's followers will be bodily resurrected (15:12). Seeking to problematize their erroneous eschatology, Paul exposes the theological incoherence (15:13-19) and practical absurdities (15:30-34) that surface as a result of them doubting the resurrection of the dead.[33]

Sandwiched between these two arguments is a third proof based on administrative order (15:20-24a) and cosmic control (15:24b-28). That is, in his demonstration of the certain, future resurrection of all believers, Paul goes beyond projecting a basic sequence of eschatological events, by narrating Christ's final defeat of all evil powers and God's subjugation of all things to himself. The last opponent to be subdued is death (15:26), though prior to that climactic statement Paul refers also to God's enemies as πᾶσαν ἀρχὴν καὶ πᾶσαν ἐξουσίαν καὶ δύναμιν (15:24). But who or what are these powers?

Although a few scholars consider the rules, authorities, and powers in 1 Cor. 15:24 to be exclusively human agents,[34] this view is untenable

---

33. Paul J. Brown, *Bodily Resurrection and Ethics in 1 Cor. 15: Connecting Faith and Morality in the Context of Greco-Roman Mythology*, WUNT 2/360 (Tübingen: Mohr Siebeck, 2014), 97–102.

34. Wesley Carr, *Angels and Principalities: The Background, Meaning, and Development of the Pauline Phrase hai archai kai hai exousiai*, SNTSMS 42 (Cambridge: Cambridge University Press, 1981), 91. Horsley ("1 Corinthians," 244) divides the terms between spiritual and Roman political authorities (δύναμις = death, etc.; ἀρχή/ἐξουσία = "the rulers of the Roman imperial system"). Cf. Horsley, "Rhetoric and Empire—and 1 Corinthians," 99; Witherington, *Conflict and Community in Corinth*, 304–5.

since, as the γάρ in 15:25 suggests, πᾶσαν ἀρχὴν καὶ πᾶσαν ἐξουσίαν καὶ δύναμιν is coextensive with πάντας τοὺς ἐχθρούς (15:25), the last enemy being death (15:26). For this reason, many have concluded that Paul here has suprahuman powers—both demonic and ontological—exclusively in view.[35] This position is largely defended by demonstrating the currency of ἀρχή/ἄρχων, ἐξουσία, δύναμις, and related language for celestial beings within early Jewish literature,[36] as well as similar uses in Pauline and other early Christian texts.[37]

Despite these parallels, a more compelling case can be made for these powers encompassing *all* evil authorities, *both* human *and* suprahuman.[38] This inclusive sense is supported in several ways. First, the repetition of πᾶς in 15:24 could easily broaden the referents of ἀρχή, ἐξουσία, and δύναμις to include every evil power irrespective of ontology.[39] Second, Paul's mention of ἀρχή, appearing as it does at the end of the letter, would seem especially to include the human

35. See, e.g., Everling, *Angelologie* 44–45; Dibelius, *Die Geisterwelt*, 99–103; MacGregor, "Principalities and Powers," 18; Caird, *Principalities and Powers*, 1–17; Delling, "ἀρχή," 483–84; Barrett, *First Epistle to the Corinthians*, 357–58; Conzelmann, *1 Corinthians*, 271–72; Matthew Black, "Πᾶσαι ἐξουσίαι αὐτῷ ὑποταγήσονται," in *Paul and Paulinism: Essays in Honour of C. K. Barrett*, eds. M. D. Hooker and S. G. Wilson (London: SPCK, 1982), 74–82; Fee, *The First Epistle to the Corinthians*, 754n41; Martinus C. de Boer, *The Defeat of Death: Apocalyptic Eschatology in 1 Corinthians 15 and Romans 5*, JSNTSup 22 (Sheffield: JSOT, 1988), 136; Arnold, *Powers of Darkness*, 101–4; Scott M. Lewis, *So That God May Be All in All: The Apocalyptic Message of 1 Corinthians 15,12–34*, TGST 42 (Rome: Pontifical Gregorian University, 1998), 56; Collins, *First Corinthians*, 553; Garland, *1 Corinthians*, 710; Fitzmyer, *First Corinthians*, 572; Williams, *Spirit World*, 127–40; Moses, *Practices of Power*, 84–94. For impersonal structures of power, see Hendrik Berkhof, *Christ and the Powers*, trans. J. H. Yoder (Scottdale, PA: Herald, 1977), 39–43.
36. For δύναμις, see how the LXX translates צבאות יהוה (Yahweh of Hosts) with some variation of κύριε/-ος (ὁ θεὸς) τῶν δυνάμεων (2 Kgdms. 6:2, 18; 3 Kgdms. 17:1; 18:15; 4 Kgdms. 3:14; 19:20, 31; Ps. 23:10; 45:8, 12; 47:9; 58:6; 68:7; 79:5, 8, 20; 83:2, 4, 9, 13; 88:9; 148:2; Isa. 42:13; Jer. 40:12; Zeph. 2:9; Zech. 7:4; cf. LXX Ps. 32:6; 67:35; 102:21). See also *1 En.* 20:1; *3 Bar.* 1:8; Philo, *Con.* 171–72; *Spec. leg.* 2.45; *Plant.* 14; *T. Levi* 3:3. For ἐξουσία, see 2 Macc. 3:24; *T. Levi* 3:8. For ἀρχή/ἄρχων, see *1 En.* 6:2–3, 7–8; cf. ἄρχειν, 9:7.
37. The juxtaposition of ἀρχαί (and perhaps δυνάμεις) with ἄγγελοι in Rom. 8:38 probably suggests all those entities are celestial beings. Cf. Eph. 1:21; 2:2; 3:10; 6:12; Col. 1:16; 2:10, 15. The probably-early-Christian *Testament of Solomon* makes mention of ἄρχων τῶν δαιμόνων (2:9; 3:5; 6:1; 16:5) and includes a striking reference to "the rules, authority, and powers" who "fly above" (αἱ γὰρ ἀρχαὶ καὶ ἐξουσία καὶ δυνάμεις ἄνω ἵππανται, 20:15) and are identified as δαίμονες (20:14, 16).
38. Archibald Robertson and Alfred Plummer, *The First Epistle of St Paul to the Corinthians*, ICC (Edinburgh: T&T Clark, 1911), 355; Hays, *First Corinthians*, 265; Ciampa and Rosner, *The First Letter to the Corinthians*, 769–70. Wink (*Naming the Powers*, 50–51) and Thiselton (*The First Epistle to the Corinthians*, 1232) believe these personal powers include impersonal structures as well.
39. This may even be how πᾶς functions in Eph. 1:21, where Christ is said to be seated ὑπεράνω πάσης ἀρχῆς καὶ ἐξουσίας καὶ δυνάμεως καὶ κυριότητος. While these and related terms refer to spiritual powers in Eph. 3:10 and 6:12, this is clear mainly because of τὰ πνευματικά and the modifier ἐν τοῖς ἐπουρανίοις, which are not appended to πάσης ἀρχῆς καὶ ἐξουσίας καὶ δυνάμεως in Eph. 1:21. Cf.

ἄρχοντες mentioned earlier in 2:6–8. This is strongly suggested by the shared use of καταργέω in both passages in forecasting the eventual destruction of God's enemies. Moreover, as we saw in 6:1–11, Paul includes unrighteous human judges as those who "will not inherit the kingdom of God" (6:9-10), a statement echoed in 15:50 and probably implied in 15:24-28 as well. Finally, similar eschatological scenarios appear in other apocalyptic and eschatologically oriented literature. For example, both Daniel 7 and *Psalms of Solomon* 17 refer, in ways quite similar to 1 Cor. 15:20–28, to a human eschatological agent who will establish his reign (Dan. 7:27; *Ps. Sol.* 17:21, 30-36) after permanently destroying enemy political rulers (τὴν ἐξουσίαν ἀπολοῦσι, LXX Dan. 7:26; τοῦ θραῦσαι ἄρχοντας ἀδίκους, *Ps. Sol.* 17:22). In fact, the shared use of βασιλεία, ἀρχή, ἐξουσία, and τέλος in 1 Cor. 15:24 and the Greek versions of Dan. 7:26-27—terms not originating from the other scriptural passages alluded to in 1 Cor. 15:25-27 (LXX Ps. 8:7; 109:1)—strongly suggests that the book of Daniel and the resistance to earthly kingdoms it embodied lurk in the background of Paul's discourse in 1 Cor. 15:24-28.[40] Given these evidences, Paul probably has in view *both* human *and* suprahuman powers in 15:24 when he forecasts their future and final destruction.

Paul does very little in this passage to establish the circumstances for resistance to specifically political authorities. He probably assumes his readers will recall the pretension and domination of the rulers and judges critiqued in 1:18–31, 2:6–8, and 6:1–11. Moreover, it is probably the case that Paul introduces these abstract powers in 15:24 not as a *novum*, but as a means of establishing familiar ground before his climactic revelation concerning the defeat of death in 15:26. Thus, while the offenses of these rules and authorities are ambiguous, their identity as "enemies" (ἐχθροί) who have failed to submit to Christ remains clear (15:25).

Nijay K. Gupta and Fredrick J. Long, "The Politics of Ephesians and the Empire: Accommodation or Resistance?," *JGRChJ* 7 (2010): 112–36.

40. See, e.g., Black, "Πᾶσαι ἐξουσίαι αὐτῷ ὑποταγήσονται," 74; Martin Hengel, "'Sit at My Right Hand!,'" in *Studies in Early Christology* (Edinburgh: T&T Clark, 1995), 119–226, at 164; Ciampa and Rosner, *The First Letter to the Corinthians*, 768–69. This does not, however, preclude the influence of other texts or communal traditions, such as those suggested by de Boer, *Defeat of Death*, 114–20.

In the light of the foregoing discussion, we conclude that Paul's apocalyptic discourse subverts the rules, authorities, and powers mainly by forecasting their certain, future demise as a result of the expansion of Christ's reign over the world. Paul's eschatological narrative envisions what Scott Lewis calls "God's reconquest of the cosmos,"[41] and even resembles the "revolt and reconquest" model Portier-Young observes enacted by the Hellenistic kings.[42] "[T]he repression of revolt through the reenactment of conquest," Portier-Young explains, "functioned to integrate the empire, providing kings with opportunities to consolidate power and assert a unifying system of order."[43] This model of "revolt and reconquest" is a fitting way of conceptualizing God's redemptive work in 1 Corinthians 15. To the degree that ancient rulers utilized local revolts as opportunities to re-conquer and re-create occupied territories, the eschatological defeat of God's enemies in Paul's apocalyptic discourse should also be read as envisioning God's own re-conquest and re-creation of his contested possession—the cosmos.

The revolt Paul narrates begins with the invasion of death into the cosmos through Adam's sin, followed by their shared occupation of the world (15:21–22, 55–56; cf. Rom. 5:12, 14, 17; 6:6–23).[44] Sin and death are not alone in their opposition to God; they have allied themselves with God's other enemies to comprise those forces referred to as "every rule, every authority, and power" (1 Cor. 15:24). God's enemies are involved in a variety of malevolent activity, but this cosmic revolt is most apparent in our passage in its somatic effects on the world's inhabitants. The tyranny of sin and death has impacted the world such that all people in Adam have come to possess natural ($\psi\upsilon\chi\iota\kappa\acute{o}\nu$), feeble ($\grave{\alpha}\sigma\theta\acute{\epsilon}\nu\epsilon\iota\alpha$), perishable ($\phi\theta\alpha\rho\tau\acute{o}\nu$) bodies and eventually die (15:42–54). Without God's intervention on behalf of his people, all creation would

---

41. Lewis, *So That God May Be All in All*, 217.
42. Portier-Young's model is indebted to Vincent Gabrielsen, "Provincial Challenges to the Imperial Centre in Achaemenid and Seleucid Asia Minor," in *The Province Strikes Back: Imperial Dynamics in the Eastern Mediterranean*, eds. Björn Forsén and Giovanni Salmeri (Helsinki: Foundation of the Finnish Institute at Athens, 2008), 15–44.
43. Portier-Young, *Apocalypse against Empire*, 192.
44. I am aware that the invasive nature of death's reign (i.e., that it emerges from without) departs from the analogy. Still, I believe the similarities are instructive.

remain indefinitely in subjugation to death's destructive power (Rom. 7:24; 8:19–23).

God, however, has indeed responded, and done so decisively. By sending his son Jesus Christ not only to die, but to raise from the dead, God has begun to reconquer the cosmos, defeating the powers of sin and death and sharing that victory (νῖκος) with his subjects (1 Cor. 15:54–57). God's rescue operation, however, remains in progress. Rather than abolishing death permanently through a single invasion, Jesus through his resurrection deposed death's reign over himself and established his own rule over the world, though he has postponed the bodily resurrection of his subjects until the Parousia (15:23; cf. Rom. 8:18–23). Nor does Christ currently exercise his rule by immediately subjecting all people and every power to his own authority. Instead, Christ re-conquers and re-creates the world progressively as his followers proclaim and believe the good news that God has both forgiven sins (1 Cor. 15:3) and regained custody of creation.[45] Indeed, Christ "must reign until he has placed all his enemies under his feet" (15:25, citing LXX Ps. 8:7). Once death is finally and permanently defeated at Christ's return (15:26), God will have "placed all things under his feet" (15:27, citing LXX Ps. 109:1) and Christ will both deliver his kingdom to God and be subjected to the Father (15:24, 28). Only at that time will the Father's eschatological reign be actualized and his reconquest of the world be completed. The primary enemies to be defeated in this narrative are sin and death. But Paul also underscores the transient rule of human political authorities, who will be displaced by Christ as his reign overtakes the world.

In sum, Paul's apocalyptic discourse once again functions as *discursive* resistance. Despite the momentary uprising of the forces of evil, Paul undermines their power by exposing their transiency and God's supreme governance over the world, even as hostile powers remain in play. The tenure of all God's enemies, including human

---

45. "[T]he new creation emerges from the old world through the Christian proclamation. Spirits, powers and dominions part eschatologically at the crossroads of the gospel." Ernst Käsemann, "Justification and Salvation History in the Epistle to the Romans," in *Perspectives on Paul* (Philadelphia: Fortress Press, 1971), 60–78, at 67.

political rulers, will indeed expire and be subjected to Christ, who will establish his reign in their place. Our passage, then, meets its rhetorical end by demonstrating, in Käsemann's words, "who owns the earth" (Wem gehört die Erde).[46] Nothing in the passage, however, advocates *active* resistance to governing authorities, nor is it suggested that political and hierarchical structures are to be repudiated altogether. Even as Paul anticipates the removal of all rules, authorities, and powers, he envisions their replacement by the supreme governance of the Son, and then that of the Father. Whether or not Paul here participates in a kind of ideological *mimicry* (to borrow a term from postcolonialism), it would seem that his concern, like that of the other NT authors, is about *which* kingdom people belong to, not about *whether* they in fact belong to one.[47]

Conclusion—Paul and Politics in 1 Corinthians

In the light of this investigation, we conclude that, as one might expect, apocalyptic and politics do in fact intersect in 1 Corinthians, and they do so repeatedly. As this study has shown, on no less than three occasions in the letter, Paul not only makes mention of governing authorities, but he does so while incorporating into the discourse several apocalyptic themes, including the existence of suprahuman powers, the revelation of mysteries, the periodization of history, resurrection, eschatological judgment, the messianic reign, and the kingdom of God—all of which, in 1 Corinthians, appear to have been heavily resourced by the book of Daniel (among other OT texts). In each instance, moreover, Paul's apocalyptic discourse functions as *discursive* resistance—Paul issues criticisms against political authorities and forecasts their eventual demise (2:6; 6:1–2, 9; 15:24) while anticipating the eschatological blessing of believers (2:7, 9; 6:2–3, 9–11; 15:22–23).

In none of these texts, however, does Paul advocate *active* resistance to empire. In fact, while apocalyptic has certain social functions and

---

46. Käsemann, "On Paul's Anthropology," 25.
47. Cf. Stephen D. Moore, *Empire and Apocalypse: Postcolonialism and the New Testament*, The Bible in the Modern World 12 (Sheffield: Sheffield Phoenix, 2006), 122–23; Harrill, *Paul the Apostle*, 90.

implications, it is far from clear that the church, as Horsley maintains, stands diametrically opposed to non-Christian society. Believers will often be marginalized and despised by those in power (cf. οἱ ἐξουθενημένοι, 1:28; 6:4), but there is no indication that the church, though it should handle in-house disputes internally, must remain completely independent from the state (cf. Rom. 13:1–7).

Moreover, despite Paul's repeated stress on the transiency of political authorities, it is questionable on the basis of these passages to assume that Paul grants any special place to *Rome* in the pecking order of God's enemies. Rome is singled out by Paul neither for killing Jesus, nor for establishing social injustice, nor for persecuting believers, all about which Paul has (equally) sharp words for the Jewish authorities (cf. 1 Thess. 2:14–15). Paul experiences "hourly dangers" and "daily deaths" (1 Cor. 15:30–32; cf. 16:9), but he never suggests these sufferings took place at the hands of political agents, Roman or otherwise. Neither do the Corinthians appear to be suffering due to such rulers; in fact, they seem to be experiencing a high degree of privilege as a result of being too heavily integrated into non-Christian society. To be sure, one of Paul's rhetorical purposes for the apocalyptic motif in the early parts of 1 Corinthians is to re-incorporate cruciformity as a critical feature of life in Christ, but he nowhere suggests that the Corinthians should be experiencing such Christ-like suffering specifically from the hands of Roman authorities.[48] Paul desires the church to stand opposed to "this age" and "this world," but there is no evidence, as Horsley supposes, that Paul considered "this world" to be coextensive with the "Roman imperial order."[49]

Admittedly, it could be that Paul, in step with many of his Jewish contemporaries, identified Daniel's fourth beast with the Roman empire.[50] There is, however, no explicit reference to the fourth beast

---

48. No doubt Paul suffered as a result of his imprisonments (Phil. 1:18–26; 3:10; perhaps 1 Thess. 2:2), but it is striking that he focuses not on the inflictions he faces as a result of Roman rulers and guards, but on those coming from false teachers (Phil. 1:17).

49. Richard A. Horsley, "General Introduction," in *Paul and Empire: Religion and Power in Roman Imperial Society*, ed. R. A. Horsley (Harrisburg: Trinity Press International, 1997), 1–8, at 7. Cf. Edward Adams, *Constructing the World: A Study in Paul's Cosmological Language*, SNTW (Edinburgh: T&T Clark, 2000), 241.

50. Wright, *Paul and the Faithfulness of God*, 2:1311: "when Paul looked at the Roman empire he

anywhere in 1 Corinthians, and it seems quite clear that Paul has a plurality of political entities in view when he forecasts their defeat in each of the three passages we have examined. Daniel likewise envisioned the destruction of *multiple* systems of governance in both the middle and final verses of his vision of the four beasts (τέσσαρες βασιλεῖαι αἳ ἀπολοῦνται ἀπὸ τῆς γῆς, LXX 7:17; πᾶσαι αἱ ἐξουσίαι ὑποταγήσονται αὐτῷ, LXX 7:27), and even while Daniel envisions the saints being commissioned with the judgment of the fourth beast (7:22), Paul broadens the scope of this judgment to encompass the whole world as well as angels (1 Cor. 6:2-3). It seems to be the case, then, that as Paul evokes the Danielic visions to support his message, he gives prominence to no *single* political power, but rather refers only generally to all hostile rulers and governments on his way toward narrating the downfall of the principal forces that possess dominion over humanity—sin and death (15:54-57).

Thus, Wright may be correct to say, in reply to Barclay, that Rome was not "insignificant" to Paul, but neither can we affirm as confidently as Wright that Paul "saw [the suprahuman] powers coming together and doing their worst precisely in and through Rome itself."[51] Paul nowhere unambiguously makes such critical claims about the Roman authorities or the empire. Nor are human rulers afforded the textual attention required to claim with Horsley that the apostle stood opposed to them in any absolute sense. Paul, to be sure, expects judgment to befall Caesar and his delegates,[52] but Rome is simply one ἔθνος among many, all of which "the root of Jesse . . . will arise to rule" (Rom. 15:12, citing Isa. 11:10).[53]

---

glimpsed the face of the Monster." Wright is more confident about the influence of Daniel 7 on 1 Cor. 15:20-28 in idem, *The Resurrection of the Son of God* (Minneapolis: Fortress Press, 2003), 335-36, than in *Paul and the Faithfulness of God*, 1063-65, 1293n63. See also Joel White, "Anti-Imperial Subtexts in Paul: An Attempt at Building a Firmer Foundation," *Biblica* 90, no. 3 (2009): 305-33, at 326-27. Christoph Heilig critiques this reading, arguing that Paul interpreted the fourth beast as the power of death, the "last" of God's enemies (*Hidden Criticism*, 114-21).

51. Wright, *Paul and the Faithfulness of God*, 2:1311.

52. Judgment of course will not extend, however, to believing rulers and magistrates (e.g., Erastus, Rom. 16:23).

53. "'Who Hopes for What is Seen?': Political Theology through Romans," in *The Unrelenting God: Essays on God's Action in Scripture in Honor of Beverly Roberts Gaventa*, eds. D. J. Downs and M. Skinner (Grand Rapids: Eerdmans, 2013), 150-71, at 156.

15

Plight and Solution in Paul's Apocalyptic Perspective

A Study of 2 Corinthians 5:18–21

Jason Maston

As many scholars recognize, 2 Cor. 5:11–21 is teeming with apocalyptic elements.[1] The passage is eschatologically driven: the death of Christ has initiated a new era, a new creation that is set over against the old creation (v.17). One key way in which these two eras are different is the epistemological criterion. The old age viewed things according to the flesh, while the new creation sees all things in Christ (v.16). The soteriological aspect centers on union with Christ, particularly in his death (v.15). Paul stresses in a variety of ways that God has initiated this new salvation.

Yet, vv.18–21 have received little attention in the formation of apocalyptic readings. J. L. Martyn's important essay, "Epistemology at

1. The research for this study was supported by a British Academy/Leverhulme Trust Small Research Grant.

the Turn of the Ages," makes no mention of them, and in his book *The Deliverance of God*, Douglas Campbell devotes a mere page to this passage when he discusses the meaning of the righteousness of God in v.21.[2] Similarly, J. Christiaan Beker cites these verses a handful of times as cross-references, but has no discussion of them.[3] Why these verses have not received much attention is unclear, but one may venture a guess: their central theological claims sit in tension with the central ideas of what many consider to be an apocalyptic reading of Paul.[4] This, at least, was Käsemann's conclusion.

According to Käsemann, 2 Cor. 5:18–21 is a pre-Pauline tradition that Paul incorporates, but does not fully embrace. For example, he asserts that the idea that God does not reckon transgression (v.19), which he claims "makes the saving event evident in the forgiveness of the accumulated guilt of sin," is foreign to Paul. He contends instead that Paul "lays the entire emphasis on liberation from the *power* of sin."[5] Käsemann also questions whether Paul could have written that Christ "became sin": "We must give careful thought to the question of whether on the basis of his conception of sin as a power he could say that Jesus was made sin for us, i.e., made the bearer of all earthly guilt."[6] These reasons, among others, lead Käsemann to downplay the value of this text for formulating Paul's theology.

These reasons point to a particular understanding of the human plight that has become ubiquitous in the convention of reading Paul "apocalyptically." According to this stream, the human plight is particularly enslavement to the cosmic powers of Sin, the Flesh, and Death. The corresponding solution, then, is not forgiveness, but a shift

---

2. J. Louis Martyn, "Epistemology at the Turn of the Ages," in *Theological Issues in the Letters of Paul* (Nashville: Abingdon, 1997), 89–110; Douglas A. Campbell, *The Deliverance of God: An Apocalyptic Rereading of Justification in Paul* (Grand Rapids: Eerdmans, 2009), 912–13.

3. J. Christiaan Beker, *Paul the Apostle: The Triumph of God in Life and Thought* (Philadelphia: Fortress, 1984).

4. It is worth noting as well that N. T. Wright does not mention these verses in his discussion of the human plight; see *Paul and the Faithfulness of God*, 2 vols. (London: SPCK, 2013), 2:747–772.

5. Ernst Käsemann, "Some Thoughts on the Theme 'The Doctrine of Reconciliation in the New Testament,'" in *The Future of Our Religious Past: Essays in Honour of Rudolf Bultmann*, ed. James M. Robinson, trans. Charles E. Carlston and Robert P. Scharlemann (London: SCM Press, 1971), 49–64, at 52 (emphasis original).

6. Ibid., 53.

in lordship and the destruction of the Powers through God's act in Christ. As Käsemann explains elsewhere, "for Paul, salvation does not primarily mean the end of past disaster and the forgiving cancellation of former guilt. It is, according to Rom. 5.9f.; 8.2, freedom from the power of sin, death and the divine wrath; that is to say, it is the possibility of new life."[7] Importantly, for Käsemann, this account of the plight and solution (i.e., enslavement to and liberation from the Powers) is set *against* alternative configurations wherein the plight is linked closely with guilt and disobedience, and the solution is forgiveness.

In more recent scholarship, this account of the plight has been developed most consistently and strongly by Martyn. Simply put, Martyn writes, "The human plight consists fundamentally of enslavement to supra-human powers; and God's redemptive act is his deed of liberation."[8] Like Käsemann, Martyn's account of the plight is set in direct contrast with alternative claims that the plight is guilt and disobedience. He writes,

> God has invaded the world in order to bring it under his liberating control. From that deed of God a conclusion is to be drawn, and the conclusion is decidedly apocalyptic: God would not have to carry out an invasion in order merely to forgive erring human beings. The root trouble lies deeper than human guilt, and it is more sinister. The whole of humanity—indeed, the whole of creation ([Gal.] 3:22)—is, in fact, trapped, enslaved under the power of the present evil age.[9]

This view can be seen clearly in Martyn's interpretation of Gal. 1:4. Martyn contends that Paul takes up a traditional expression of Christ's death ("[Christ] 'who gave up his very life for our sins'"), but significantly modifies it with the explanatory gloss "so that he might snatch us out of the grasp of the present evil age."[10] The tradition

7. Ernst Käsemann, "The Saving Significance of the Death of Jesus in Paul," in *Perspectives on Paul*, trans. Margaret Kohl (London: SCM Press, 1971), 32–59, at 44. Similarly, in his portrayal of Pauline anthropology, Käsemann focuses on the cosmological place of humanity as enslaved (see his "On Paul's Anthropology," in *Perspectives on Paul*, 1–31).

8. J. Louis Martyn, *Galatians: A New Translation with Introduction and Commentary*, AB 33A (New York: Doubleday, 1997), 97.

9. Ibid., 105.

10. Martyn's translation (*Galatians*, 81). Martinus de Boer develops an almost identical reading of this

"identifies discrete sins as humanity's (in the first instances Israel's) fundamental liability; and it sees forgiveness of sins as the remedy provided by God."[11] These ideas are "to a significant degree foreign to Paul's own theology," thus the significance of Paul's gloss.[12] Here, Paul introduces a different plight, which is expressed succinctly in the phrase "present evil age." "The present evil age" is this world ruled by the power of Sin. For Martyn, "sin" is not a reference to wrongdoing; rather, as Paul uses the term in the singular, it "is precisely a powerful, cosmic enemy of God, and an enemy of every human being."[13] As a cosmic power, Sin wreaks havoc in its destructive reign over humanity and reduces humanity to enslaved victims.[14]

The resolution to this problem of enslavement is not a renewed attempt by humans to live more morally acceptable lives. As enslaved victims/captives, they are incapable of enacting their own escape. Thus, similarly to Käsemann, Martyn insists that God initiates the liberation of humanity from the enslaving Powers when he invades the world in the event of the cross and the sending of the Spirit.[15]

This vision of the plight as enslavement—and its corresponding opposition to the idea that the plight is directly about guilt and disobedience—has been powerfully defended by Douglas Campbell in his *The Deliverance of God*. Like Martyn, Campbell maintains that humans are enslaved to Sin and Death, which reveals itself in "an oppressed and somewhat agonized condition."[16] This condition

passage in his *Galatians*, NTL (Louisville: Westminster John Knox Press, 2011), 30. Mention should also be made of his claim that apocalyptic Judaism consisted of two tracks, "cosmological" and "forensic," that conceived of plight and solution differently (see his contribution to this volume and ibid., 31–35).

11. Martyn, *Galatians*, 90 (emphasis original).

12. Ibid.

13. J. Louis Martyn, "World Without End or Twice-Invaded World?," in *Shaking Heaven and Earth: Essays in Honor of Walter Brueggemann and Charles B. Cousar*, eds. Christine Roy Yoder et al. (Louisville: Westminster John Knox, 2005), 117–32, at 121. Martyn is building on the grammatical use of "sin" in the singular to indicate the power of Sin.

14. It is worth noting in passing the common way in which assumed tradition is treated by Käsemann, Martyn, and de Boer in their analyses of these verses. All maintain that Paul cites a tradition with which he largely disagrees and he must modify or reinterpret. While not addressed here, more consideration of how Paul relates to and uses traditional views may present additional problems for their interpretations.

15. Martyn, *Galatians*, 99; idem, "Epilogue: An Essay in Pauline Meta-Ethics," in *Divine and Human Agency in Paul and His Cultural Environment*, eds. John M. G. Barclay and Simon J. Gathercole, LNTS 335 (London: T&T Clark, 2006), 173–83, at 180.

prevents humanity from being able both to act appropriately and even to diagnose its own condition, which then invalidates the suggestion that the plight is fundamentally about guilt and disobedience.[17] Rather, Campbell maintains, God takes the initiative to redeem humanity through an act of deliverance.[18] Campbell writes, "Having grasped both the incapacity of the human condition in Adam and the basis for that claim in the event of salvation (i.e., that it is a retrospective claim), we can recognize that the only appropriate solution to this sort of problem is one of deliverance, or rescue."[19] The solution to his plight is, as for Käsemann and Martyn, not an act of divine forgiveness, but rather, an act of deliverance.

Despite exegetical differences and points of emphasis, there is a consistency in the presentation of plight and solution across these accounts. All three authors make the following points:

1. The human plight is fundamentally enslavement to the Powers. Guilt and disobedience are given, at best, secondary roles in the conception of the plight.
2. Because of humanity's enslaved condition, humans are incompetent agents incapable of securing their own deliverance. God, therefore, must (and does) take the initiative to redeem humanity (and the world).
3. Salvation consists, then, in deliverance from the Powers, not in forgiveness of individual acts of disobedience.

On the surface, then, Käsemann's contention that 2 Cor. 5:18–21 does not fit Paul's soteriological outlook (as perceived in this tradition) seems accurate. Yet, given how in the previous verses, Paul has utilized so many apocalyptic features and how he does not offer any explicit corrective to the tradition, the question I pose for this chapter is how

16. Campbell, *The Deliverance of God*, 63.
17. The epistemological element is crucial to Campbell, who is drawing most directly on Barth. See his contribution to this volume. Epistemology is also important to Martyn (see his "Epistemology at the Turn of the Ages"; and *Galatians*, 95n43; 266n163).
18. Campbell, *The Deliverance of God*, 63.
19. Ibid., 65.

an apocalyptic reading can accommodate them. That is, rather than sidelining them as a piece of pre-Pauline tradition (as Käsemann did), I contend that they express an account of the plight and its solution that not only fits well within Paul's soteriological structure, but it does so while accommodating (most of) the main concerns of this apocalyptic reading of Paul. These verses exhibit a stress on divine initiative and human inability—two features that are crucial to the apocalyptic reading. Moreover, when read from the light of Paul's claim in v.16 about the epistemological change, one sees that his account of the plight and its solution is indeed altered by the Christ-event.

Paul's New Way of Knowing

Throughout the opening chapters of 2 Corinthians, Paul articulates a vision of the world seen from his position in Christ. Reality as it is perceived from the vantage point of the flesh is presented as a false alternative to how Paul sees it and wants his readers to see it. He, for example, contrasts Moses' glory with that of the gospel and its messengers so that the gospel, although built on the *death* of Christ, is viewed as more glorious (3:1–18). Similarly, he insists that his sufferings are not indications of a *failed* mission, but paradoxically, expressions of the *success* of his work (2:12–17; 4:7–18; 6:3–10). The same for the body: although the present body is wasting away, and it appears then that Paul's gospel cannot bring life, it is actually through wasting away that the glorious promises of resurrection are already being made evident (5:1–10). On what basis, though, does Paul make these claims for a re-envisioned world?

At the heart of this new outlook lies a shift in time. As Martyn has shown, "Paul's statements establish an inextricable connexion between eschatology and epistemology."[20] Because of the Christ-event, the times have shifted, and with the change of time arises a new and different way to understand. Second Corinthians 5:16 provides the

---

20. Martyn, "Epistemology at the Turn of the Ages," 92.

foundation for this alternative claim about how to understand. There are two ways to know. The first is "according to the flesh" and is associated with the old age that has now passed away. The second way is not spelled out precisely by Paul, but given how Paul's portrayal of the new way of viewing has centered on the Christ-event, it is probably best characterized as "according to the Christ-event."[21]

This alternative way of seeing causes Paul to re-envision everything around him, and his previous comments have given examples of this. But in what way has it caused him to rethink the plight of humanity and God's solution?

Reconciliation according to the Old Way of Knowing

Paul's account of divine deliverance in 2 Cor. 5:18-21 centers on the concept of reconciliation. Although not extremely common in Jewish circles, the idea of divine reconciliation was known and there was a fairly consistent way of formulating it. Second Maccabees functions well as a representative text.[22]

As is repeated on several occasions, the breakdown in the divine-human relationship is a result of the people's sins. The people suffer and the temple can be desecrated "because of the sins of those who live in the city" (2 Macc. 5:17). The resolution to this problem is an action performed by humans. In his opening greeting, the writer expresses his hope that God "may hear your prayers and be reconciled to you (καταλλαγείη ὑμῖν) and not abandon you in the time of evil" (1:5). In these verses, there seems to be a sequential progression and a causal relationship between the prayers heard and God's decision to be

---

21. Martyn argues that the new way is best expressed as "*kata stauron*" (ibid., 108). There is some truth to Martyn's point that the cross is the most obvious point at which the shift in times can be seen. However, his separation of resurrection, the role of the Spirit, and indeed, the life of Jesus is unnecessary. Of course, the import of these only makes sense from the perspective of the cross, but without them, the cross does not make sense.

22. For additional Jewish texts, see, e.g., Jos. *Ant.* 3.315; 7.153, 295; *J. W.* 5.415. For brief discussions of these and other texts, see I. Howard Marshall, "The Meaning of 'Reconciliation,'" in *Unity and Diversity in New Testament Theology: Essays in Honor of George E. Ladd*, ed. Robert A. Guelich (Grand Rapids: Eerdmans, 1978), 117–32, at 118–21; and Reimund Bieringer, "'Reconcile Yourselves to God': An Unusual Interpretation of 2 Corinthians 5:20 in Its Context," in *Jesus, Paul, and Early Christianity: Studies in Honour of Henk Jan De Jonge*, eds. Rieuwerd Buitenwerf, Harm W. Hollander, and Johannes Tromp (Leiden: Brill, 2008), 11–38, at 18–28.

reconciled to his people. This idea that prayer is linked with reconciliation comes out also in 8:29, where the people implore God "to be wholly reconciled" (εἰς τέλος καταλλαγῆναι). In the account of the seven martyred sons, the final son defies the king by announcing that while "we are suffering for our sins," God's anger will not last forever and "he will again be reconciled to his servants" (πάλιν καταλλαγήσεται τοῖς ἑαυτοῦ δούλοις, 7:32–33). It is precisely through the action of the brothers that God's wrath will come to an end (ἐν ἐμοὶ δὲ καὶ τοῖς ἀδελφοῖς μου στῆσαι τὴν τοῦ παντοκράτορος ὀργὴν τὴν ἐπὶ τὸ σύμπαν ἡμῶν γένος δικαίως ἐπηγμένην, 7:38). Indeed, their martyrdom has an atoning affect and removes the cause of God's wrath against the people. It is because of acts such as this and the prayers of the people that the author can remark, "what was forsaken in the wrath of the Almighty was restored again in all its glory when the great Lord became reconciled" (5:20). Moreover, in these texts, it is the human who initiates the process of reconciliation, and God responds accordingly. While the author acknowledges the disobedience of the people, this in itself presents no significant problem. He conceives of the people as morally competent agents who are able through acts of prayer or martyrdom to secure God's favor.

Reconciliation according to the New Way of Knowing

Whether Paul held this precise view of reconciliation prior to his conversion is difficult to know. The consistency of the view among the Jewish sources suggests, at a minimum, that it is possible, and perhaps even likely, that he would have held something like this prior to his conversion. As Paul takes up the theological language of reconciliation in 2 Corinthians 5, though, he offers an alternative account that turns the main features around. Like his contemporaries, he identifies disobedience as the issue that causes the disruption in the relationship between God and humanity. Yet, unlike his contemporaries, he claims that the solution originates from God.

Divine Initiative in Reconciliation

Since Paul's new way of evaluating everything is according to Christ, the starting point for this investigation should be how he presents the divine solution. First, then, one should note that, at the outset, Paul stresses that God has taken the initiative. The opening statement of this section, "All this is from God who reconciles us" (v.18), places firmly before the reader a picture of an active and initiating God. Aside from the imperative in v.20, the active agent throughout the whole section is God. The structure of the section indicates that the imperative has its basis in the prior act of God. In v.18 and v.19, Paul recounts twice that God has established reconciliation, and it is on this basis that the appeal of v.20 is made.

Furthermore, Marshall has shown that Paul's use of the active voice καταλλάξαντος to describe God removing the reason for his anger against humanity is unusual, if not unique.[23] In other texts, the verb is used in four ways: (1) in the active for a third party persuading two people to give up their anger against one another; (2) in the active for a person persuading another to give up his or her anger; (3) in the passive or middle in the same manner as (2); and (4) in the passive for a person giving up his anger toward another. Paul's use of the active voice does not fit any of these usages. His unusual grammar suggests that he is making a distinctive theological point—namely, that reconciliation is initiated by God. God does not wait for humanity to turn to him. Rather, he initiates the process of reconciliation by setting aside his enmity. Furnish captures the sense nicely: "Here the reconciliation is not of God but *from* and *to* God."[24]

The Method of God's Reconciliation

The divine decision to set aside hostility takes place in the work of

---

23. Marshall, "The Meaning of 'Reconciliation.'" Marshall's study has been extended by Stanley E. Porter. See particularly idem, *Καταλλάσσω in Ancient Greek Literature: With Reference to the Pauline Writings*, EFN 5 (Cordoba: Ediciones el Almendro, 1994); and idem, "Reconciliation and 2 Cor. 5,18-21," in *The Corinthian Correspondence*, ed. Reimund Bieringer, BETL 125 (Leuven: Leuven University Press, 1996), 693–705.

24. Victor P. Furnish, *II Corinthians*, AB 32A (New York: Doubleday, 1984), 335 (emphasis original).

Christ. This is noted from the outset with "through Christ" in v.18 and the phrase θεὸς ἦν ἐν Χριστῷ κόσμον καταλλάσσων ἑαυτῷ in v.19.[25] Neither statement, however, gives much specification to how God has acted in Christ. This lack of detail is filled out in vv.14–15 and v.21.

Although Paul does not name Jesus Christ in vv.14–15, it is beyond doubt that he is describing him as the one who dies for all humanity and the one to whom the living are to orientate their lives.[26] At a minimum, the statement presumes that the "one" represents the rest of humanity. The preposition ὑπέρ may also indicate substitution: Christ stood in the place of humanity.[27] The preposition alone is insufficient to carry the weight of any understanding of the atonement, and it is in v.21 particularly that Paul fills out the meaning of vv.14–15.

Verse 21 is soteriologically rich and stands apart in the context as a declarative announcement of how God has worked reconciliation.[28] Its richness is masked in its terseness, and the meaning of almost every word is widely disputed. The primary concern now is to see how Paul's new way of knowing according to Christ is expressed in his account of how God has worked in Jesus by making him "sin."

Although he committed no sin, Christ is "made ἁμαρτία" (ἁμαρτίαν ἐποίησεν). Two issues arise from this statement: what does ἁμαρτία mean, and when was Jesus "made" sin? Many argue that ἁμαρτία refers to the "sin offering" (חטאת; Leviticus 4).[29] However, this does not seem to be the best interpretation since ἁμαρτία is not normally used for

---

25. The exact meaning of this phrase in v.19 is debated. Many understand ἦν . . . καταλλάσσων as an imperfect periphrastic; see, e.g., Porter, "Reconciliation and 2 Cor. 5,18-21," 698–99; and Margaret Thrall, *A Critical and Exegetical Commentary on the Second Epistle to the Corinthians*, 2 vols., ICC 34 (Edinburgh: T&T Clark, 1994), 433–34. Another common view posits that θεὸς ἦν ἐν Χριστῷ is a self-contained clause meaning "God-in-Christ;" see, e.g., Richard H. Bell, "Sacrifice and Christology in Paul," *JTS* 53, no. 1 (2002): 1–27, at 11–12; and Murray J. Harris, *The Second Epistle to the Corinthians: A Commentary on the Greek Text*, NIGTC (Grand Rapids: Eerdmans, 2005), 440–43.

26. In the background may be the Adam-Christ antithesis (cf. 1 Cor. 15:21–22, 45–49; Rom. 5:12–20).

27. M. J. Harris, "Prepositions and Theology in the Greek New Testament," in *New International Dictionary of New Testament Theology*, ed. Colin Brown, 3 vols. (Grand Rapids: Zondervan, 1978), 3:1171–1215, at 1197.

28. Grammatically the statement is not linked with the previous or following verse.

29. This view is summarized well by Linda Belleville in "Gospel and Kerygma in 2 Corinthians," in *Gospel in Paul: Studies on Corinthians, Galatians and Romans for Richard N. Longenecker*, eds. L. Ann Jervis and Peter Richardson, JSNTSup 108 (Sheffield: Sheffield Academic Press, 1994), 110–33.

the sin offering and there are no cultic references in the immediate context.[30] More likely, Paul's statement indicates that Jesus came into a profound relationship with sin itself. It may indicate "that Paul is thinking in a general way of Christ's identification with sinful humanity."[31] This general level, however, does not account for the contrast that Paul creates between Christ and "we." A better option is presented by Bultmann: "this clause intends to express the paradoxical fact that God made the (ethically) sinless Christ to be a sinner (in the forensic sense)—viz. by letting him die on the cross as one accursed (*cf.* Gal. 3:13)."[32] In this position, Christ identifies with sinful humanity because "he came to stand in that relation with God which normally is the result of sin, estranged from God and the object of his wrath."[33]

The next issue to decide is when Christ came to be recognized as a sinner. Most scholars understand this as a reference to Jesus' crucifixion because of the earlier statement about Jesus' death (vv.14–15).[34] However, Hooker rightly cautions, "we should again be wary of driving a wedge between incarnation and crucifixion."[35] Although, for Paul, the cross is the high point of God's salvific work in Jesus, this event cannot be isolated from the totality of Jesus' human existence. The phrase τὸν μὴ γνόντα ἁμαρτίαν probably refers to Jesus as a human and means that he committed no actual sins during his life.[36]

---

30. In the LXX, ἁμαρτία is occasionally used for חטאת, although the more common and precise phrases are τὸ περὶ τῆς ἁμαρτίας and περὶ ἁμαρτίας (see Leviticus 4). When ἁμαρτία indicates the sin offering, the context always contains other cultic terms which provide the indication that the word is a reference to the specific sacrifice. Commentators who argue for sin offering in 2 Cor. 5:21 also often draw a parallel with Rom. 8:3, where the phrase περὶ ἁμαρτίας is understood as a reference to the sin offering. These commentators also suggest that Paul is dependent on Isa. 53:10, where the servant is put forth περὶ ἁμαρτίας. The cross-references to Rom. 8:3 and Isa. 53:10 fail to acknowledge that the meaning of both texts is disputed. Indeed, there is an element of circularity in the arguments of those who defend references to "sin offering" in these three texts since they often appeal to the other verses to support their argument.

31. Furnish, *II Corinthians*, 340.

32. Rudolf Bultmann, *Theology of the New Testament*, Repr. (Waco: Baylor University Press, 2007), 277.

33. C. K. Barrett, *The Second Epistle to the Corinthians*, BNTC (London: A&C Black, 1993), 180; cf. Thrall, *Second Corinthians*, 441–42.

34. Thrall, *Second Corinthians*, 439; Paul Barnett, *The Second Epistle to the Corinthians*, NICNT (Grand Rapids: Eerdmans, 1997), 314n62; Harris, *The Second Epistle to the Corinthians*, 451–52; Ben C. Blackwell, *Christosis: Pauline Soteriology in Light of Deification in Irenaeus and Cyril of Alexandria*, WUNT 2.314 (Tübingen: Mohr Siebeck, 2011), 226, 230.

35. Morna D. Hooker, *From Adam to Christ: Essays on Paul* (Cambridge: CUP, 1990), 17.

36. So most commentators. For the argument that the phrase refers to Christ's pre-existent condition, see Bell, "Sacrifice and Christology in Paul," 14–16.

It is by becoming human that the Son of God participates in the human realm, identifying with other humans in their sin and being identified by his Father as a sinner.[37] In his death, he suffers the judgment due all sinners because his whole life has been one marked by the reality that he was "made sin."[38]

Paul's portrayal of God becoming human is the trigger that led him to a new understanding of the world, humanity, and God (v.16). Out of his new way of knowing arises Paul's claim that Jesus "became sin." Just as his paradoxical claim that his sufferings are proof of his ministry success arose from his new way of knowing, so here, Paul extends the idea of God becoming human to the paradox that he became a sinner.[39] In developing this understanding of God's action, Paul has not entirely abandoned the tradition that reconciliation required a human action. He presents Jesus here as a human—indeed, a human caught up in the very depths of the human plight. He even presents Jesus as something of a martyr, not unlike the brothers of 2 Maccabees. Yet, the crucial and vital difference for Paul is that the act of Jesus is not that of a mere human. Rather, God is at work in Jesus. The act of reconciliation, then, is both a divine and human act: a divinely initiated action in which God becomes human.

The Reconfigured Human Plight

In his act in Christ, God establishes a means by which the hostility between himself and humanity can be resolved, and this raises the question of what caused the rupture in the relationship. From Paul's presentation of Christ as "the sinless one made sin" arises his view of the plight. The expression "for us" in v.21, which reconnects with vv.14–15, indicates that this divine act is for the benefit of humanity. These expressions are imprecise and raise the question of how Christ's life and death are "for us." It is in v.19 that more precision is given.

---

37. Cf. ibid., 14.
38. Cf. the Heidelberg Catechism, Question 37: "What do you understand by the word 'suffered'? Answer: That during his whole life on earth, but especially at the end, Christ sustained in body and soul the wrath of God against the sin of the whole human race."
39. Cf. Rom. 8:3.

Here, Paul claims that the rupture between God and humans was caused by "transgressions."[40] This comment disrupts the repetition between v.18 and v.19 and functions to clarify both why reconciliation is needed (human disobedience) and how God will resolve it ("not counting their trespasses [παραπτώματα] against them").[41] Importantly, this view of the plight matches Paul's vision of Christ as "made sin."

The description of Christ as "not knowing sin [ἁμαρτίαν]" and "being made sin [ἁμαρτίαν]" suggests that Paul is here using the terms ἁμαρτία and παράπτωμα as equivalents. While the term παράπτωμα is not widely used by Paul (or the rest of the NT), it is a particularly Pauline term and the idea to which it points is widespread.[42] It has the basic denotation of "a violation of moral standards,"[43] and belongs with other words that indicate disobedience. In the immediate context, disobedience may primarily convey the notion of living for one's self (5:15). More widely, Paul spends much of his letters to the Corinthians exposing the variety of ways in which their lives fail to match God's expectations.

Whereas Paul's Jewish contemporaries thought that their sinfulness presented no real problem for their ability to act, Paul's account of reconciliation makes the exact opposite point. For Paul, transgressions are not merely a human problem of disobedience that can be resolved by a renewed attempt at obedience. Instead, the disobedience of humanity has radically disrupted and distorted the divine-human relationship, and it is impossible for the human alone to restore it. This vision of the problem is one consequence of Paul's new way of knowing according to Christ. God's decisive action in Christ reveals to Paul a

---

40. The ease with which Paul shifts from "transgression" to "for us" suggests that, whatever differences may exist, one should not hold these two expressions too far apart.

41. Although some argue for a cosmic interpretation of "world" (κόσμος), the meaning is specified by the "us" in v.18 and "them" and "theirs" in v.19—all of which clearly denote human beings.

42. The word appears 16x in the Pauline corpus while only 3x (possibly 6x) outside it: Rom. 4:25; 5:15 (2x), 16, 17, 18, 20; 11:11, 12; Gal. 6:1; Eph. 1:7; 2:1, 5; Col. 2:13 (2x); Matt. 6:14, 15; 18:35 (v.l.); Mark 11:25, 26 (v.l.); Jam 5:16 (v.l.). Many scholars consider vv.18–21 in part or whole as a traditional statement, and this word is a support for this idea. See Thrall, *Second Corinthians*, 445–49, for a review and critique. Even if this is a traditional statement, there is no indication here that Paul objects to the tradition. In fact, the methodological starting point should be that Paul agrees with traditions he cites unless otherwise made clear.

43. BDAG, s.v. παράπτωμα.

deeper understanding of the human plight than can be grasped before and outside of knowing in light of Christ. As Käsemann comments, "The cross also shows us that from the aspect of the question of salvation, true man is always the sinner who is fundamentally unable to help himself, who cannot by his own action bridge the endless distance to God, and who is hence a member of the lost, chaotic, futile world, which at best waits for the resurrection of the dead."[44]

Paul's account of God's action in Christ coheres well with Martyn's description of God's action as one of invasion. That is, the claim Paul makes is that God has entered into the human realm in a profound and drastic manner to free humans. Although the account is not that of freedom from the Powers, it is nonetheless a liberation: humans are freed from their destructive selves. This perception of liberation, though, includes an element of a forensic understanding of the atonement. For in God's act of making Christ sin, he removes the problem of human transgression that led to his enmity with humanity by "not reckoning their transgressions to them" (5:19). This action, as Käsemann remarked, "makes the saving event evident in the forgiveness of the accumulated guilt of sin."[45] It is precisely in this act of "non-imputation," which is attained by virtue of Christ becoming sin, that God removes the enmity that existed between himself and humanity.[46]

---

44. Käsemann, "Saving Significance," 40. Cilliers Breytenbach argues that Paul differs from other Jewish ideas of reconciliation because in the latter it is God who is reconciled to humanity by setting aside his wrath. In Paul, though, God is not angry with humanity and he reconciles humanity to himself ("Salvation of the Reconciled [with a Note on the Background of Paul's Metaphor of Reconciliation]," in *Salvation in the New Testament: Perspectives on Soteriology*, ed. J. G. Van der Watt, NovTSup 121 [Leiden: Brill, 2005], 271–86, at 277–78). This interpretation misses on two accounts. First, it fails to realize that Paul and the tradition differ on who is the primary agent. In the Jewish sources, the initiative is taken by the human and God is the responding actor. Second, it does not take sufficient account of the human plight as disobedience.

45. Käsemann, "Some Thoughts," 52. Cf. de Boer, *Galatians*, 30n42.

46. The best manner in which to describe the atonement theory of these verses is not obvious. The theory of "interchange" popularized by Morna Hooker has great explanatory power for vv.14–15 and 21 (see her essays collected in *From Adam to Christ*). However, this theory need not be opposed to forensic or substitutionary categories. See Blackwell, *Christosis*, 227, 231–32; and more broadly, Simon Gathercole, *Defending Substitution: An Essay on Atonement in Paul* (Grand Rapids: Baker Academic, 2015).

The Recreated Human

Before concluding this study, one final element should be addressed. An important feature of Martyn's interpretation of Paul is his contention that humans are recreated as competent agents. For Martyn, this recreation happens when God meets humanity in the word of the cross. In this encounter, God abolishes the old age account of the human, who was incompetent and enslaved, and recreates the human agent as *"the corporate, newly competent and newly addressable agent"* who is being shaped into the image of the Son.[47] This important element of Martyn's account is also evident in these verses.

Emphasized throughout 2 Cor. 5.11–21 is that the divine act was "for us." This divine act has the purpose and result (ἵνα) that "we might become the righteousness of God in him" (v.21). According to Käsemann, the phrase "the righteousness of God" denotes God's salvific activity.[48] While Käsemann built his view on Paul's statements in Romans, Hooker and Campbell have argued that a similar understanding can also be found in this verse.[49] Differently, Wright reads this phrase as a statement of God's covenantal faithfulness, which is being displayed through Paul's ministry. That is, Paul as a minister of the gospel embodies God's covenant faithfulness.[50] At the risk of sidestepping the extensive debate about the phrase "the righteousness of God," several observations can be made about the statement here.[51]

First, one must give due attention to the verb "become."[52] The verb parallels "made" in the previous clause and indicates a change from one category to another. This suggests that the phrase "righteousness of God" denotes a characteristic of God. In the same manner that Christ

---

47. Martyn, "Epilogue," 180 (emphasis original).
48. Ernst Käsemann, "'The Righteousness of God' in Paul," in *New Testament Questions of Today* (Philadelphia: Fortress, 1969), 168–82.
49. Morna D. Hooker, "On Becoming the Righteousness of God: Another Look at 2 Cor. 5:21," *NovT* 50, no. 4 (2008): 358–75; Campbell, *The Deliverance of God*, 912–13, and his fuller discussion of the phrase on pp. 677–704.
50. N. T. Wright, *Pauline Perspectives: Essays on Paul, 1978-2013* (London: SPCK, 2013), 68–76; Wright, *Paul and the Faithfulness of God*, 2:879–85.
51. See Linebaugh's essay in this volume.
52. Cf. Harris, *The Second Epistle to the Corinthians*, 454–55.

is perceived as having the identity of a sinner when he is made sin, believers take on a new identity when they are transformed into God's righteous character. Both verbs may recall the "new creation" language of v.17. Certainly, the process being described in v.17 and v.21 is the same: a change from one position (old person and transgressor) to a new position (new creation and "righteousness of God"). The two ideas may be brought together in this manner: the believer is identified not by one's old status as a transgressor, but rather, by the new creation as "the righteousness of God."

Giving due attention to the verb "become" calls into question Käsemann's and others' interpretation. It makes little sense to claim that believers "become" the saving activity of God, a statement that is fundamentally about divine activity. By contrast, while Wright's interpretation can better account for the verb "become," his interpretation fails to maintain the parallelism in the verse.[53] The parallelism suggests something related to the natures of Christ and of believers, an idea that is lost in Wright's interpretation of "righteousness of God" as Paul's missionary work.

Second, the prepositional clause "in him" is crucial. It indicates that this statement is an expression of participation or union. Far from opposing forensic and participatory categories, this statement unites them together. By being united to Christ, believers become the righteousness of God. Drawing upon the description of Christ's story in 2 Corinthians, Aernie contends that "to *become* the righteousness of God is an explicit statement about the reality that Christians are defined by their participation in Christ's story or narrative, that they are defined by their participation in this new creation."[54] And this participation in the new creation is identified as a change from a transgressor to being righteous.

This change in status and condition brings with it a change in

---

53. The strength of Wright's interpretation lies in his claim that v.21 is the fourth in which Paul has adopted a dual pattern that speaks first of God's salvific act and then of Paul's ministry (see vv.15, 18, 19). He, though, has over-read verse 15. Moreover, the grammatical disconnection of v.21 suggests that it is intended not as a repeat but something new.
54. Jeffrey W. Aernie, "Participation in Christ: An Analysis of Pauline Soteriology," *HBT* 37 (2015): 50–68, at 61.

agency. After summarizing God's act of reconciliation in 5:18–19, Paul highlights that he and his co-workers are God's ambassadors who appeal to all καταλλάγητε τῷ θεῷ (v.20). Regardless of how one understands the voice (passive or middle) of the imperative, the key point is that those who hear the divine call are viewed as active participants.[55] This action, though, is not that of an autonomous human. Rather, the call must be viewed in light of God's action in Christ to bring forgiveness for transgressions. It was the human outside of Christ who was bound up in transgression. Now, united to Christ, the reconciled human hears the gospel message that God has reconciled the world to himself and responds.[56] By giving himself in Christ, God draws humanity into union with himself (through the Son) and this union forms the basis on which believers act. Their action is thus predicated upon union with Christ and the new identity of being God's righteousness. The believer's task, then, is not to placate God nor to perform some action by which reconciliation can be attained (in a manner similar to the martyred sons of 2 Maccabees 7).[57] The appeal is probably not even for the human to set aside his or her own opposition toward God. Rather, the call here is for the human to recognize that God has accomplished reconciliation and recreated the human into a new being who is capable now to follow God.[58]

In the immediate context, this conception of human action takes two primary forms. There is, first, the task of making known God's act of reconciliation. In vv.18–19, the act of God to establish reconciliation is matched by Paul's apostolic task to deliver that message: the reconciled becomes the ambassador for the divine reconciler (v.20).

---

55. Most scholars opt for a passive; see, e.g., Marshall, "The Meaning of 'Reconciliation,'" 123–24; Porter, *Katallassō in Ancient Greek Literature*, 140–41, 143. For a middle, reflexive meaning, see Bieringer, "Reconcile Yourselves to God," 33–35.
56. Cf. Joseph A. Fitzmyer, "Reconciliation in Pauline Theology," in *To Advance the Gospel: New Testament Studies*, 2nd ed. (Grand Rapids: Eerdmans, 1998), 162–85, at 168: "True, Paul invites human beings to be reconciled to God (2 Cor. 5:20), but that is an invitation to appropriate or apprehend the effect of the Christ-event for themselves (the aspect of subjective redemption)."
57. Marshall ("The Meaning of 'Reconciliation,'" 123) comments, "It is no doubt significant that the active sense of the verb is not used for this human action, because there is no need to reconcile a God who has reconciled the world to himself."
58. Cf. ibid., 128; Rudolf Bultmann, *The Second Letter to the Corinthians*, trans. Roy A. Harrisville (Minneapolis: Augsburg Publishing House, 1985), 159, 164.

Second, the newly created human agents are called to live "no longer for themselves but for the one who died for them and was raised" (v.15). Rather than selfish lives that produce transgressions, those united to Christ devote themselves to him. Paul's vision of the newly created moral agent arises from his new way of knowing. Because God took such drastic measures in sending his Son, this shows to Paul that humanity was bankrupt. Now, after the incarnation, Paul sees that God has made it possible for humans to hear again the call to live moral lives—lives that are shaped and determined by the incarnation.

Conclusion

As outlined at the beginning of this chapter, one version of the apocalyptic Paul has maintained that the human plight, according to Paul, is fundamentally about enslavement to the Powers and not guilt and disobedience. Second Corinthians 5:18-21 is a thorn for this interpretation because it clearly identifies the plight as transgressions. In this chapter, though, I have attempted to show how this passage is actually infused with the premises of this interpretive tradition. God's action in Christ has led Paul to a new way of knowing and evaluating everything around him. He contends that God has worked through Christ by identifying him as a sinner. This understanding of the Christ-event leads Paul to the idea that the human problem was transgressions. Over against other claims that humans are transgressors, though, Paul maintains that the plight cannot be resolved by virtue of a renewed attempt at obedience. He knows this because God has acted so decisively in Christ. Because God took the initiative, this reveals to Paul that the human was incapable of restoring the relationship. As well, Paul's new understanding of the plight and the solution is accompanied by a new understanding of human agency. As transgressors, humans were rendered incompetent, but now, as the righteousness of God, they are fully enabled to respond to the divine word. The solution has given insight to the problem.

If this reading has any merit, then it follows that the dichotomy between a plight of enslavement to the Powers and one of human disobedience and guilt must be rejected. There is, to be sure, much to be said for the contention that in Galatians and Romans, Paul describes the human plight as (primarily) enslavement to hostile Powers.[59] Nevertheless, a full apocalyptic interpretation of Paul must account not only for his description of humans as enslaved, but also his insight into the human will as deeply sinful.

In addition, the dichotomy between a solution in terms of liberation and one that is forensic must be rejected. The act of God described in 2 Cor. 5:18–21 matches well Martyn's notion that the solution is one of in-breaking or invasion. Yet, restricting this to a theory of liberation only captures one aspect of God's manifold work in Christ. The in-breaking of God in the Son is precisely to address the forensic problem of human disobedience and guilt. Such a plight necessitated such a profound solution, but it is only because of the profoundness of the solution that the depth of the plight becomes known. Moreover, a wider lens on the divine solution allows us to incorporate a fully incarnational account.[60] The incarnation is precisely the solution to human transgression, but in a paradoxical way. Christ is identified and treated by his Father as a transgressor. This vision of the totality of Jesus' human existence sees in him the defeat of the very sinful nature of humans. God confronts the anthropological problem by becoming an *anthropos*, and thus restores the anthropological condition.

59. The apocalyptic reading of Martyn was crucial to my interpretation of Romans 7 in *Divine and Human Agency in Second Temple Judaism and Paul: A Comparative Study*, WUNT 2.297 (Tübingen: Mohr Siebeck, 2010), 127–52. Nothing argued in this essay leads me to rethink the way I employed Martyn's perspectives there. My contention is that this version of the apocalyptic Paul simply needs to be wider and not operate with such an either-or perspective.
60. Campbell's incarnational reading is a welcome expansion to the narrow focus on the death of Jesus. See also Susan Grove Eastman, "Apocalypse and Incarnation: The Participatory Logic of Paul's Gospel," in *Apocalyptic and the Future of Theology: With and Beyond J. Louis Martyn*, eds. Joshua B. Davis and Douglas Harink (Eugene: Cascade Books, 2012), 165–82.

16

The Apocalyptic New Covenant and the Shape of Life in the Spirit according to Galatians

Michael J. Gorman

There is more than one sense to the term *apocalyptic*, and more than one way in which Paul was an apocalyptic figure. I have no doubt that he viewed the coming, death, and resurrection of Jesus as a disruptive, divine, liberating "invasion" or "incursion," and that the term *apocalyptic* can be appropriately used to characterize that saving event. But Christopher Rowland has rightly drawn our attention to Paul's apocalyptic autobiographical statements in Galatians 1:

> . . . for I did not receive it [the gospel] from a human source, nor was I taught it, but I received it through a revelation of Jesus Christ [ἀλλὰ δι᾽ ἀποκαλύψεως Ἰησοῦ Χριστοῦ] (Gal. 1:12).[1]

God . . . was pleased to reveal his Son to me [ἀποκαλύψαι τὸν υἱὸν αὐτοῦ ἐν ἐμοί; or "in me" (so NET, NIV, NJB)] so that I might proclaim him among the Gentiles (Gal. 1:15–16a).

Rowland argues that Paul was an apocalyptic figure because he received a revelation, an *apokalypsis*, and not because of a particular theological perspective or agenda that could be called "apocalyptic."[2]

I want to develop, but also nuance, Rowland's view, the nuance being the rejection of the possible implications in his statement that (1) experience and theology should be pitted against each other and (2) Paul is only, or at least primarily, apocalyptic experientially. We should resist this kind of unnecessary and ultimately unhelpful dichotomy.[3] Paul's apocalyptic experience shaped his apocalyptic theology (including his "politics"), and his apocalyptic theology helped him to interpret, and likely also shaped, his apocalyptic experience.

Focusing on Galatians, I wish to make four main points about Paul as an apocalyptic figure under the general rubric of "the apocalyptic new covenant and the shape of life in the Spirit"—an attempt to hold together Paul's apocalyptic experience and his apocalyptic theology as well as his apocalyptic and his new-covenant perspectives.

1. With Tom Wright and others, I contend that Paul is both an *apocalyptic* theologian and a *covenant* theologian—and specifically, a *new*-covenant theologian. What is revealed is the radically unexpected and new way in which the new covenant has come to fruition.[4]

---

1. Scripture translations are from the NRSV unless otherwise indicated.
2. See, e.g., Christopher Rowland, "Paul and the Apocalypse of Jesus Christ," in *The Mystery of God: Early Jewish Mysticism and the New Testament*, Compendium rerum Iudaicarum ad Novum Testamentum 12, eds. Christopher Rowland and Christopher R. A. Morray-Jones (Leiden: Brill, 2009), 137–65.
3. I do not mean that Rowland himself is necessarily guilty of such a dichotomy.
4. See esp. N. T. Wright, *Paul and the Faithfulness of God* (Minneapolis: Fortress Press, 2013), e.g., 2:1013, 1025, 1038, 1071–72, 1262–63, 1513. Wright appears to concur (e.g., 2:725, 984) that Paul is speaking of what I am calling the apocalyptic new covenant. See also David A. Shaw, "Apocalyptic and Covenant: Perspectives on Paul or Antinomies at War?" *JSNT* 36, no. 2 (2013): 155–71. Shaw argues that recent "apocalyptic" interpreters actually unknowingly espouse new-covenant themes. Shaw erroneously maintains, however, that apocalyptic interpreters need to admit "a greater place for forensic categories in Paul's thought" in order to acknowledge his new-covenant framework (168). Rather, this essay argues that full recognition of a claim made by J. Louis Martyn, which Shaw cites approvingly (160n9), is closer to what is needed: recognizing an analogy

2. Borrowing Wright's language, we need to recognize how Paul has reworked his theology of the new covenant in light of God's apocalyptic incursion into human history and life in the Messiah and the Spirit—and specifically, Paul's *experience* of the Messiah and the Spirit.

3. A critical aspect of the content of Paul's revelation is that the gracious "invasion" of God's Spirit (Ezekiel) and Law (Jeremiah) into the hearts of God's people that was associated with the promised new covenant has, in fact, occurred, but in a shocking, cruciform mode. This fulfillment is expressed in the language of the faithful and loving Messiah who now indwells Paul (and, implicitly, all believers; Gal. 2:19–20), the presence of the Spirit of the Son in believers' hearts (Gal. 4:6), and believers' fulfilling the "Law of the Messiah" (Gal. 6:2).[5]

4. Thus, to return to the conjunction of Gal. 1:12 and 1:16, the revelation *to* Paul and the revelation *in* Paul are inseparable—a claim that is developed most fully in 2 Corinthians, but also in Galatians itself. By means of the invading and indwelling Messiah/Spirit/Law of the Messiah, Paul becomes his gospel, and he expects others to do so similarly—to live out the new covenant of faithfulness and love, the beginning of the new creation.

That is to say, the in-breaking of God into human history in Jesus' new-covenant-inaugurating death and in the gift of the Spirit contains inseparably with it a divine in-breaking into the lives of individual human beings to create a community of the new covenant that embodies the character of that divine invasion. The result is both shockingly new and surprisingly continuous with the prophetic promises in Scripture.[6]

between divine invasion and the prophetic promise of a new heart and spirit (J. Louis Martyn, "Afterword: The Human Moral Drama," in *Apocalyptic Paul: Cosmos and Anthropos in Romans 5–8*, ed. Beverly Roberts Gaventa [Waco: Baylor University Press, 2013], 157–66, at 164n13).

5. I have deliberately used an uppercase initial letter for most occurrences of the words "Law" and "Spirit" (altering English translations where necessary) throughout this essay in order to indicate that they are proper nouns, having specific referents and functioning essentially as technical terms. This is true even for translations of νόμος in Paul, even if there is debate about whether a specific occurrence should be rendered "Torah," "Jewish Law," or something else.

The Promise of the New Covenant

Promises of a renewed or new covenant are associated with the prophets Jeremiah and Ezekiel as well as Deuteronomy. Jeremiah and Ezekiel addressed similar situations with similar, though not identical, promises. Both employ the idiom of the covenant: YHWH being the people's God, and the people being YHWH's people. Yet Jeremiah actually uses the term "new covenant" and speaks of the *Law* being put within God's people, specifically in their hearts, while Ezekiel does not use the term "new covenant" (though he does speak of a "covenant of peace" and "an everlasting covenant"[7]) and talks about God's own *Spirit* being put within the people.[8]

Moreover, both prophets speak metaphorically but realistically of something happening to the people's heart(s), though precisely what that is varies: the inscription of God's Law (Jer. 31:33)[9]; a transplant (Jer. 24:7; Ezek. 18:31; 36:26), involving a softening or "fleshification" (Ezek. 11:19; 36:26); circumcision (Jer. 4:4; cf. Ezek. 44:7, 9)[10]; and unification (Jer. 32:39; Ezek. 11:19). For both Jeremiah and Ezekiel, then, the heart is the heart of the problem.[11] The purpose of the divine activity on and in the people's hearts is clearly indicated by Ezekiel: "so that they may follow my statutes and keep my ordinances and obey them," and thus "they shall be my people, and I will be their God" (Ezek. 11:20; cf. 36:27). This is the language of both covenant fulfillment and the covenant "formula"—the idiom of a unified people in proper relation to God.[12]

---

6. See also my *The Death of the Messiah and the Birth of the New Covenant: A (Not So) New Model of the Atonement* (Eugene: Cascade, 2014), esp. (for Paul) 51–68, 89–94, 109–11, 118–27, 135–36, 141–61, 186–95.

7. E.g. Ezek. 16:60; 34:25; 37:26.

8. See Ezek. 36:26–27: "A new heart I will give you, and a new spirit I will put within you (LXX ἐν ὑμῖν); and I will remove from your body the heart of stone and give you a heart of flesh. I will put my Spirit within you (LXX ἐν ὑμῖν), and make you follow my statutes and be careful to observe my ordinances." Cf. Ezek. 11:19, "I will give them one heart, and put a new spirit within them (LXX ἐν αὐτοῖς)."

9. "I will put my Law within them (LXX 38:33 εἰς τὴν διάνοιαν αὐτῶν), and I will write it on their hearts."

10. Ezekiel describes the foreigner as "uncircumcised in heart and flesh" (Ezek. 44:7, 9), implying the need for circumcision of the heart to be part of the covenant people. Thus, as we will see below, internalization and obedience to the Law are not antithetical; the latter results from the former, as Paul also says in, e.g., Rom. 8:3–4.

11. E.g. Ezek. 3:7; 14:3–7; 16:30; 28:5, 17; Jer. 5:23; 9:14; 12:2; 17:1; 32:40.

Similarly, Deut. 30:6–10 promises a covenant renewal that will consist of heart-circumcision followed by love of God and observation of the commandments (cf. 10:16–22).

Jeremiah's "I will write it [my Law] on their hearts; and I will be their God, and they shall be my people" (Jer. 31:33) is more or less equivalent to Ezekiel's "I will remove the heart of stone from their flesh and give them a heart of flesh, so that they may follow my statutes and keep my ordinances and obey them" (Ezek. 11:19–20). Furthermore, Ezekiel's parallel phrases "A new heart I will give you" and "a new spirit I will put within you" (Ezek. 36:26; cf. 11:19; 18:31), which is in fact "my [God's] Spirit" (Ezek. 36:27), suggest that his understanding of what God will do to the heart with the Spirit is fundamentally synonymous with Jeremiah's vision of the inscription of the Law on the people's hearts. The new covenant will be a powerful act of divine grace entailing the people's receipt of the Law or the Spirit within, their inner transformation, and their consequent faithfulness to the covenant. Clearly, for both Jeremiah and Ezekiel, as well as Deuteronomy, there is no disjunction between internalization of the covenant and external adherence to its stipulations, between the heart and obedience. Taking the two prophets together, we must also deny any disjunction between the Spirit and the Law—a subject to which we will have to return in considering Paul.

Indeed, it is likely that Paul, like certain other scriptural interpreters of his era, read these key texts from Jeremiah, Ezekiel, and Deuteronomy together, as a collective witness to God's anticipated activity among and within the people of God.[13] Moreover, this coming divine action was envisioned not only as a new (or renewed) covenant, but also as the restoration of Israel and as a new creation—and more.[14] This merger of metaphors is especially potent in Ezekiel 36–37, where

---

12. The prophetic promises of land restoration (e.g., Ezek. 36:24, 28) also stress the re-creation of such a covenant community and carry through into Paul in terms of community, if not in terms of land itself.

13. See Kyle B. Wells, *Grace and Agency in Paul and Second Temple Judaism: Interpreting the Transformation of the Heart*, NovTSup 157 (Leiden: Brill, 2014), esp. the summaries on 221 (including n. 52) and 275. Cf. also, e.g., 12–13, 24, 134–39, 255–69.

14. On eschatological restoration (including new exodus), see Wells, *Grace and Agency*; Rodrigo J. Morales, *The Spirit and the Restoration of Israel*, WUNT 2/282 (Tübingen: Mohr Siebeck, 2010). On

images of forgiveness and cleansing, a new heart, a new spirit (the indwelling of God's Spirit), restoration to the land, and abundant living (Ezek. 36:25ff) are then graphically displayed as resurrection, as new creation, in the famous vision of dry bones in Ezekiel 37.

It is difficult, then, not to think about this promised new-covenant activity of divine heart surgery as a sort of divine incursion—in other words, as an apocalyptic event. Paul appears to have been thinking similarly. As J. Louis Martyn said, Paul's "divine *invasion* . . . has a highly illuminating theological analogue in Ezek. 11:19."[15] If Ezekiel is any indication, Paul himself could also blend images of covenant renewal and new creation, resulting in what we are calling an "apocalyptic new covenant." We find the phrases "new covenant" and "new creation" (the latter generally understood in an apocalyptic sense), of course, in 2 Corinthians (3:6; 5:17), but only "new creation" in Galatians (6:15). Yet Martyn's insightful observation, together with the merger of metaphors in both Ezekiel and 2 Corinthians, suggests that we should anticipate both apocalyptic and new-covenant language in Galatians.

The Apocalypse "in" Paul

In Gal. 1:15–16a, Paul claims that God was pleased "to reveal his Son to me [ἀποκαλύψαι τὸν υἱὸν αὐτοῦ ἐν ἐμοί]," as many translations render it.[16] But what does Paul mean when he states that God was pleased to reveal the Son ἐν ἐμοί? To consider this question, we turn to the recent work of one of the self-identified apocalyptic interpreters of Paul, Martin de Boer. De Boer summarizes the scholarly debate about ἐν ἐμοί in 1:16 as offering three main interpretations, to which he adds his own (no. 4):[17]

1. "to me" (equivalent to a simple dative);
2. "through me" (through Paul's preaching);

---

new creation specifically, see John W. Yates, *The Spirit and Creation in Paul*, WUNT 2/251 (Tübingen: Mohr Siebeck, 2008), with special attention to Ezekiel 36–37 in Paul's theology.

15. Martyn, "Afterword," 164n13, in a discussion of agency in Paul (emphasis his).

16. Though not all: "to" is found in, e.g., CEB, NAB, NRSV, RSV; "in" is used in, e.g., NASB, NET, NIV, NJB.

17. Martinus C. de Boer, *Galatians: A Commentary*, NTL (Louisville: Westminster John Knox, 2012), 93.

THE APOCALYPTIC NEW COVENANT

3. "within me" (an inner, subjective experience); and

4. "in my former manner of life."

While each of the first two interpretations is possible, the strength of the last two is that each recognizes the "locative" semantic value of ἐν, implying that Paul would have used a simple dative or a preposition such as διά had he intended to signify either mere receipt of the revelation (1) or kerygmatic instrumentality (2). The translation "within me" (3), referring primarily to an inner, subjective experience, does not, however, correspond to the way Paul elsewhere narrates his encounter with the risen Christ as the Lord's appearing to him (cf. 1 Cor. 9:1; 15:8).

De Boer's proposal (4) is therefore helpful because it retains the locative sense of the subjective interpretation (3) while foregrounding the apocalyptic and public character of the experience. That is, "God entered into the life of Paul, the persecutor of God's church . . . in order to bring that manner of life to a complete and irrevocable end."[18] In other words, "Paul personifies the radical discontinuity between the two ages (this one and the one to come) of all apocalyptic eschatology."[19] What God has done apocalyptically in Christ to and for the world, God has also done apocalyptically to and for Paul.

What Paul is referring to in Gal. 1:16, therefore, according to de Boer, is Paul's "conversion" (de Boer's term).[20] Moreover, argues de Boer, Paul continues this apocalyptic interpretation of his conversion and its after-effects in Gal. 2:15–21, especially in 2:19–20, where (de Boer contends) Paul re-narrates the "Damascus road" experience in which he was crucified with Christ and died to the Law as his nomistically determined self was ended and a new life begun.[21] The crucifixion of the old self, says de Boer, is another way of interpreting the death of Paul's old, Pharisaical self. Not only Paul, however, but everyone who believes in Christ (2:16) "participates in, is joined to or taken up into,

18. Ibid.
19. Ibid.
20. Ibid., 89. By "conversion" de Boer means God's conversion of Paul "from his manner of life in Judaism to Christ" (89n143; cf. 77n120).
21. Ibid., 159–63. "Damascus road" is again his term (160).

this all-embracing, cosmic, apocalyptic event that spells the end of the old age."[22]

De Boer rightly notes Paul's re-use of the phrase ἐν ἐμοί from 1:16 in 2:20—Christ lives ἐν ἐμοί. The difference between the uses of the two phrases, he avers, is that the earlier one refers to Paul's *former* life and the later one to Paul's *apostolic* life.[23] Although de Boer does not "exclude the notion of Christ's dwelling inside Paul (or the believer) in some sense"—he points to Gal. 4:6—Paul's emphasis, according to de Boer, is on the public domain of human affairs and interpersonal relationships.[24]

Although de Boer moves us in the right direction by interpreting the revelation "in" Paul as a reference to a public reality and connecting it (strongly) to Gal. 2:15–21 and (less strongly) to Gal. 4:6, de Boer also unnecessarily limits the referent of ἐν ἐμοί to Paul's conversion and misses Paul's allusions to the new covenant. What I propose, then, is that Paul's self-portrayal as the apocalyptically "invaded" persecutor, crucified (and raised) with the Messiah, is simultaneously a self-portrayal as the recipient of the surprising Spirit of the new covenant that enables him, and all believers, to embody the cruciform pattern of the Messiah's self-giving love: the "Law of the Messiah" (Gal. 6:2, my translation). This is the case, I suggest, even though the term *new covenant* does not appear in Galatians and the Spirit is explicitly associated with the fulfillment of the "old" (that is, the original) covenant with Abraham.[25]

---

22. Ibid., 161.
23. Ibid., 161–62. We will offer a different interpretation below.
24. Ibid., 162n242.
25. Even Richard Hays, in arguing for a similar understanding of "the law of Christ," does not mention the phrase "new covenant." See Richard B. Hays, "Christology and Ethics in Galatians: The Law of Christ," *CBQ* 49, no. 2 (1987): 268–90. His thesis is that a "careful reading of the evidence will suggest that 'the law of Christ' is a formulation coined (or employed) by Paul" as a reference to "the paradigmatic self-giving of Jesus Christ" as the "definitive expression" of ἀγάπη (274–75).

Rereading Galatians as Witness
to the Apocalyptic New Covenant

De Boer rightly sees three key passages in Galatians as interconnected texts: 1:15–16; 2:20; and 4:4–6. We will consider them in reverse order.

Galatians 4:4–6

The first thing to note about Gal. 4:4–6 is its apocalyptic flavor. The phrase about "the fullness of time" is, among other things, "an apocalyptic assertion."[26] But this apocalyptic event of benign invasion, of liberation and redemption, occurs in two steps: (1) the sending forth of the Son followed by (2) the sending forth of the Spirit. The cosmic divine event in Christ becomes existentially real for human beings through the work of the Spirit. What takes place "out there" must, and does, also take place "in here," in the intimate space of knowledge and imagination (the heart) that issues in corresponding activity in the world. Paul will later speak about this activity as walking "by," or better "in," the Spirit (πνεύματι; 5:16) and being led by the Spirit (5:18) in order to bear the fruit of the Spirit (5:22–23).[27]

The next thing to note about Gal. 4:4–6, then, is the phrase "God has sent the Spirit of his Son into our hearts [ἐξαπέστειλεν ὁ θεὸς τὸ πνεῦμα τοῦ υἱοῦ αὐτοῦ εἰς τὰς καρδίας ἡμῶν]" (4:6). The divine action is described, by its use of "Spirit" and "hearts" (cf. Rom. 5:5), in language echoing the prophetic promises of a new covenant in Jeremiah and Ezekiel, though it is not a direct quote from either prophet. The focus on the heart as the object of divine action appears also in Rom. 2:25–29, where the image of heart-circumcision is reminiscent of both prophets as well as Deuteronomy. Paul sees the prophetic promise of a new covenant fulfilled in the gift of the Spirit's being sent into people's hearts. Curiously, although de Boer correctly notes the echo of Ezek. 36:26 and Jer. 31:33–34 in Gal. 4:4–6, he does not mention the phrase

---

26. de Boer, *Galatians*, 262.

27. "In" the Spirit is to be preferred for πνεύματι in 5:16 because it indicates the sphere in which the community of believers exists and moves forward. The location of the Spirit in believers, and vice versa, may be called mutual indwelling or reciprocal residence; it is discussed below.

"new covenant."[28] Similarly, in his commentary, Martyn notes the allusion to Jeremiah and Ezekiel, and he speaks vividly and apocalyptically of the divine "invasion" of the heart/the human being, but he does not call this the inauguration of the new covenant.[29]

It seems clear, however, if we put our first two observations about this passage together, that what Paul is talking about is an apocalyptic new covenant. There are elements of both continuity and discontinuity with the specific prophetic promises. We should not be surprised if there is something unexpected about the fulfillment of these promises, especially since the promised Spirit arrives with a significant qualifier—as the *messianic* Spirit.

The third thing to note about Gal. 4:4-6, then, is that this Spirit is specifically the Spirit of the Son.[30] The identity of the *promised* Spirit, now the *present* Spirit, has been reconfigured in terms of God's Son, the Messiah Jesus. In other words, this is the apocalyptic Spirit, and that in two senses: the Spirit of the Jesus who has been apocalypsed, and the Spirit who participates in the divine apocalyptic activity of liberating people from this age and giving them a share in the life of the age to come that was inaugurated by God's action in Christ. Thus, Paul is continuing here (cf. 3:1-5) to forge an inseparable bond between the Spirit and the Messiah Jesus, which of course means the *crucified* Messiah, now raised by the Father.

Although Paul's main point in using the language of sonship and adoption is the connection between Jesus' sonship and ours, the language of knowing God as "Abba, Father" also continues the new-covenant theme. In Jeremiah's promise of a new covenant and similar texts, we see the covenant formula about the intimate bond between God and the people: "I will be their God, and they shall be my people" (Jer. 31:33).[31] The "Abba, Father" relationship described in Gal. 4:4-6 (cf. Rom. 8:15-16) is, in part, the restatement of that covenant formula

---

28. de Boer, *Galatians*, 265.

29. J. Louis Martyn, *Galatians: A New Translation with Introduction and Commentary*, AB 33A (New York: Doubleday, 1997), 391–92. In fairness to de Boer and Martyn, I note that most commentators do not mention the new covenant.

30. Cf. Rom. 8:9; Phil. 1:19.

31. Cf. Jer. 24:7; 30:22; 32:38; Ezek. 11:20; 14:11; 36:28; 37:23, 27.

in light of the apocalypse of Jesus as God's Son, and the corollary reconfiguration of the Spirit as the one who relates people covenantally to both God the Father and Jesus the Son. This covenantal, Father-Son relationship now extends, surprisingly, beyond Israel to include the gentiles. In the giving of the Messiah and the Spirit of the Messiah, God is speaking the language of (new) covenant, saying, "I am your Father, and you are my children."[32] God's people/children, both Jew and gentile, respond, "Abba."

So what we have, finally, is an apocalyptic new covenant in which, at the initiative of God the Father, Christ effects humanity's liberation and redemption, and the Spirit establishes and maintains a residential, new-covenant relationship between God the Father and God's adopted children. It is nearly impossible to resist a Trinitarian conclusion regarding Paul's theology and spirituality. His explicit language elsewhere, in one breath, of the Spirit being the Spirit of both the Son and the Father (Rom. 8:9) makes this conclusion even more inevitable. In any case, the identification of the indwelling Spirit as the Spirit of the Son drives us back to Gal. 2:15–21.

Galatians 2:15–21

I have argued elsewhere that the one and only subject of Gal. 2:15–21 is justification.[33] Co-crucifixion with Christ and being inhabited by Christ are not separate or additional topics, but key elements in Paul's reconfiguration of justification around a crucified and resurrected Messiah. Justification is both participatory and transformative. It is transformative as an experience of death and resurrection, of co-crucifixion and new life. It is participatory as an event that occurs "in Christ" (δικαιωθῆναι ἐν Χριστῷ; 2:17) and results in having Christ within (ζῇ δὲ ἐν ἐμοὶ Χριστός; 2:20). The phrase ἐν ἐμοί in 2:20 is of particular interest.

Galatians 2:20 can be translated "And I no longer live; rather, the

---

32. Cf. Rev. 21:7.
33. *Inhabiting the Cruciform God: Kenosis, Justification, and Theosis in Paul's Narrative Soteriology* (Grand Rapids: Eerdmans, 2009), 63–72.

Messiah lives in me. But the life I do live in the flesh I live by the faithfulness of the Son of God, who loved me by giving himself for me" (my translation).[34] I contend that Paul is also here speaking about the apocalyptic new covenant, and specifically, of the existential impact of God's incursion into Paul's life, and indeed, the life of all believers. Paul's first-person language is meant to be representative.

Although explicit covenant or new-covenant language does not appear in this passage, it has been widely and rightly advocated by the "new perspective" on Paul that justification is about membership in the covenant, even if the new perspective occasionally over-emphasized ecclesiology (or, more precisely the corporate dimension of justification) at the expense of the individual. What has completely reshaped the terms of justification for Paul, and thus also of covenant membership, is the apocalyptic event of Jesus' death and resurrection. Covenant membership, or the right relations with God that effect or demonstrate covenant membership, is by death and resurrection with the Messiah. The crucified person, whether Jew or gentile, rises to new life, a new life characterized most fundamentally by the presence of the indwelling Messiah/Son of God. This means, according to most interpreters, that the Spirit inhabits believers. As suggested above, this interpretation is implicitly confirmed by the following passage, 3:1–5, in which Paul associates the coming of the Spirit with the preaching of the crucified Messiah, and it is explicitly confirmed in 4:6 when Paul writes about God's sending "the Spirit of his son into our hearts."[35]

It is thus absolutely critical for Paul that Christ (or, better, the Messiah) is the indwelling one, that this Spirit is specifically the Spirit *of the Son* (4:6). The apocalyptic event that has made justification, liberation, and redemption a reality is the concrete faithful and loving activity of the Son in his death. Galatians 2:20 picks up from Gal. 1:4 that the death of Jesus was his self-sacrificial activity, telling us now

---

34. It is beyond the scope of this chapter to defend in any detail the translation and interpretation offered of the critical texts in this passage. See *Inhabiting*, 63–72, 76–85.

35. Richard Longenecker calls the phrase "into our hearts" from 4:6 a "collective synonym" for the phrase "in me" in 2:20 (Richard N. Longenecker, *Galatians*, WBC 41 [Waco: Word, 1990], 174). It may be better to say that 2:20 individualizes the more corporate, prophetic perspective of 4:6.

not only that it was apocalyptically liberating ("who gave himself for our sins to set us free from the present evil age," 1:4), but also covenantally faithful to God and loving toward us: "I live by the faithfulness of the Son of God, who loved me by giving himself for me" (my translation). Paul is describing the Son's apocalyptic death as the fulfillment of the covenantal requirements of love for God (meaning faithfulness to God) and love for others. It is the crucified and now resurrected Son who embodies, indeed who *is*, this apocalyptic-covenantal reality that "invades" human beings. The implication is that to be inhabited by *this* Messiah, to receive the Spirit of *this* Son in fulfillment of the prophetic promises about the new-covenant gift of the Spirit within, is to die and rise to a new self, to a new, apocalyptically shaped form of covenant existence characterized by cruciform faithfulness and love. The identity marker of covenant membership is now the presence of the (lovingly) invading, indwelling Messiah/Son of God, i.e., the Spirit of the Son, who enables covenant-fulfillment.[36]

An immediate objection to this line of thinking would be simply to quote 2:19a: "For I, through the Law, died in relation to the Law so that I might live in relation to God [ἐγὼ γὰρ διὰ νόμου νόμῳ ἀπέθανον, ἵνα θεῷ ζήσω]" (my translation). The antithesis of the Law and God would seem to rule out any implicit reference to the new covenant, which is said to re-inscribe the Law on people's hearts. But if, as Paul later says, the fundamental issue about the Law has to do with relying on it once the Messiah and faith (or faithfulness) have arrived and the written Law's function has ceased (3:23–24), then it is not impossible to think that Paul would allow for the existence of a reconfigured Law that is not the *basis* of justification, but the *expression* of it, Law summarized in the words "faithfulness" issuing in "love" (5:6)—what we might call the "Law [νόμος] of the Messiah" (as Paul does in 6:2) associated with the presence of the Spirit. We, of course, struggle with how to translate the νόμος of 6:2 into English, but Paul is not engaged in dealing with a source and a target language. Rather, his use of νόμος in

---

36. Cf. Rom. 8:3–4.

6:2 indicates that there is continuity with his overall argument about νόμος in Galatians, but his specific usage of the word—in connection with the Messiah and in the context of discussing the work of the Spirit—implies as well a certain discontinuity with previous understandings of νόμος. Paul is singing νόμος in a new key.

Accordingly, when Paul speaks of "the Law of the Messiah, he is likely once again speaking about the indwelling of Christ, not in terms of the internalized *Spirit* promised by Ezekiel, as in 4:6, but in terms of the internalized *Law* promised by Jeremiah. Yet, for Paul, I would argue, these two promises and their fulfillments are one and the same. Richard Hays rightly suggested that we understand this "Law" as the "pattern" of Christ, a normative pattern (or "life-pattern") of self-giving love that gave expression to the faith, or faithfulness, of Christ.[37] It is important to stress that this is the pattern of both the dying and the indwelling Messiah, the latter continuous with the former. The primary point is that the presence of the living crucified Son of God, the presence of "the Spirit of the Son," will shape people into Christ-like faithful and loving individuals and communities (5:6). This is clearly for Paul the work of the Spirit, as the context of 5:6 makes plain (5:16–6:8).[38]

I suggest, then, that Paul has interpreted the complementary prophetic promises that God would place "my" πνεῦμα and "my" νόμος (i.e., the Spirit and the Law of God) within the people of God as having been fulfilled in the indwelling presence of the πνεῦμα τοῦ υἱοῦ αὐτοῦ (4:6) and the νόμος τοῦ Χριστοῦ (6:2)—the Spirit and the Law of the Messiah Jesus. To be sure, Paul only explicitly says that the *Spirit* of the Son—not the *Law* of the Son—has been sent "into our hearts" (4:6). Nonetheless, there is an implicit theological link between the indwelling Spirit and the indwelling Law: love.

The fruit of the Spirit's presence is love (5:22), which can only mean Christ-like, cruciform love (2:20). But love is also connected to Law in Galatians. Those who, by the Spirit, practice Christlike servant-love

---

37. Hays, "Christology and Ethics," esp. 273, 278, 280–83, 286–90.
38. The Spirit is mentioned ten times in these verses.

(5:13) are, ironically, embodying the very νόμος that could not justify them (3:11) because the whole Law is "fulfilled" in the love command (5:14). Furthermore, since the syntactically and semantically similar phrases about serving one another in love (διὰ τῆς ἀγάπης δουλεύετε ἀλλήλοις; 5:13) and bearing one another's burdens (Ἀλλήλων τὰ βάρη βαστάζετε; 6:2) have to do with the fulfillment of νόμος—either "the" νόμος (5:13) or "the Messiah's" νόμος (6:2)—it also stands to reason that, in some fundamental sense, the presence of the love-enabling *Spirit* of the Messiah implies the presence of the *Law* of the Messiah. Thus, Paul makes a tight connection between those who "have received the Spirit" (οἱ πνευματικοί; 6:1) and those who practice the Law of the Messiah (6:2). Moreover, although Paul does not say that this νόμος of the Messiah is inscribed on the Galatians' hearts, such a claim may be implied, for Paul can clearly conceive of a textually indwelt heart. In Romans, for instance, he will quote and interpret Deuteronomy 30 (which refers to heart-circumcision): "'The word is near you, on your lips and in your heart' (that is, the word of faith that we proclaim)" (Rom. 10:8). Kyle Wells has argued convincingly that this "eschatological Torah" written on people's hearts means, for Paul, the "presence and agency" of Christ that comes with union with him, to which Gal. 2:20 bears witness.[39] The Messiah and his νόμος are, for Paul, inseparable.

With respect to 2:20, then, de Boer is partly right to say that ἐν ἐμοί means "in Paul's current apostolic ministry," which is public and visible.[40] But because Paul is not merely speaking autobiographically, this life of faithfulness and love is also meant for *all* who are inhabited by the Messiah (i.e., by the Spirit and the Law of the Messiah) and who live in him.[41] The *cosmic*, apocalyptic, new-world-creating and new-covenant-creating event must and does become an *intimate*, apocalyptic, and new-person-creating event. The knowledge that

---

39. Wells, *Grace and Agency*, 269–75, esp. 273–74. Wells (255–69) also finds connections between the promised Law-inscription in the heart, love, and moral transformation in Romans 6; Rom. 8:3ff; and 1 Thess. 4:8–9.
40. de Boer, *Galatians*, 161–62.
41. As de Boer himself implies (*Galatians*, 161).

Christ gave himself for our sins to liberate us from the present evil age (Gal. 1:4) must also become the personal knowledge that he loved me by giving himself for me (Gal. 2:20).[42]

Moreover, the death of Paul and of all believers has a starting point, but no ending point in this life. The perfect verb συνεσταύρωμαι ("I have been crucified") suggests an ongoing reality. The paradox is that the resurrected self is always also the crucified self, just as the resurrected Jesus remains the crucified Jesus. This ongoing crucifixion is not, however, something that kills but something that gives life, for it is nothing other than a life of Messiah-like faithfulness and love. It is a death that brings about life for both self and others, as Paul will say especially in 2 Cor. 4:10: "always carrying in our body the dying of Jesus so that the life of Jesus may also be made visible [φανερωθῇ] in our bodies" (my translation). That is, Paul, speaking with and for others, has become the apocalypse that has claimed his life and set him free. Christ is being revealed in his body, his life. Paul likely implies the same thing in Galatians itself: in his ministry, "Jesus Christ was publicly exhibited as crucified" (3:1; Ἰησοῦς Χριστὸς προεγράφη ἐσταυρωμένος), and he "carr[ies] the marks of Jesus branded on [his] body" (6:17; τὰ στίγματα τοῦ Ἰησοῦ ἐν τῷ σώματί μου βαστάζω).

This discussion now points us back to Gal. 1:16 and Paul's claim that God was pleased to reveal his son ἐν ἐμοί.

Galatians 1:16, in Conversation with 2 Corinthians

As noted earlier, there is significant debate about what Paul means when he speaks of God's pleasure in revealing his Son "in me." It seems clear, however, from our study of later texts in Galatians, that Paul was convinced that whatever precisely happened at that moment of revelation to or in him, its immediate impact could be narrated as an experience of death and resurrection, indeed a co-crucifixion and co-

---

42. At the same time, because the Messiah's death is for "our" sins (1:4), in 2:20 Paul is implicitly speaking not just about himself or about individuals, but also about communities, in whom the Messiah corporately dwells and who corporately live in the Messiah (cf. the more explicit formulation of this claim in Rom. 8:3-4). See the comment in n. 27 above about the close connection between the Spirit and community in Galatians 5 and 6.

resurrection, and its long-term effect on him could be described in terms of ongoing Christ-like dying and rising to new life enabled by the Spirit of Christ and shaped by the Law/pattern of Christ. This sort of language appears not only in Galatians, but also in Romans 6 and 8.

Moreover, similar language appears as well in 2 Corinthians, and not far from the occurrence of the important terms "new covenant" (2 Cor. 3:6) and "new creation" (5:17). As we saw in 2 Cor. 4:10, the ministry of the new covenant/new creation is a ministry of paradoxical, Christlike, life-giving dying, enabled by the Spirit ("the Spirit gives life"; 3:6), but conveyed through the agency of weak apostles such as Paul. They are powerless in themselves (4:7), and their difficult, deathlike existence is the manifestation of Jesus' life (φανερωθῇ, 4:11), and thus the means of life for others (4:12), only by God's power.

This is the paradoxical modus operandi of the apocalyptic new covenant: the power of God is revealed in the weakness of the cross (cf. 1 Cor. 1:18–25) and of those who enslave themselves to others for Jesus' sake (2 Cor. 4:5) and in the mode of Jesus (cf. Phil. 2:1–11). The glorious ministry of life comes through suffering and death—Christ's death on the cross, and the ongoing suffering and even dying of Paul and his team that are an ongoing revelation of the death of Jesus himself (2 Cor. 4:10; cf. Phil. 3:17). What we find developed at length in 2 Corinthians, we see also in Galatians: Paul's "crucifixion" and suffering are part of his participation in the new creation and evidence of it (Gal. 6:12–17; cf. 5:11). At the same time, if, as it seems, the Galatian believers also suffered (Gal. 3:5, ἐπάθετε; cf. 4:29), it was because of their apocalyptic participation in the new-covenant gifts of Messiah and Spirit (3:1–5).[43]

According to Paul, therefore, life in the Messiah, and specifically ministry, is a kind of revelation, or apocalypse. He does not use ἀποκαλύπτω and ἀποκάλυψις to describe that ministry in 2 Corinthians, however, but φανερόω and φανέρωσις (esp. 2:14; 4:10–11; cf. 4:2; 7:12; 11:6). Paul explains and defends the peculiar narrative shape of his ministry to the Corinthians as one means by which the gospel is made

---

43. See John Anthony Dunne, "Suffering and Covenantal Hope in Galatians: A Critique of the 'Apocalyptic Reading' and its Proponents," *SJT* 68, no. 1 (2015): 1–15; idem, "Suffering in Vain: A Study of the Interpretation of ΠΑΣΧΩ in Galatians 3.4," *JSNT* 36, no. 1 (2013): 3–16.

visible or manifest to the world. Without such a revelation, the gospel cannot be known, for it must be proclaimed not only in word as *audition,* but in life as *vision.*

This is not to say that ἀποκαλύπτω and ἀποκάλυψις are necessarily precise overlapping synonyms with φανερόω and φανέρωσις. Contrary to the general thrust of scholarship on this question, Dominika Kurek-Chomycz has recently argued that they are not.[44] Rather, she contends, φανερόω and φανέρωσις refer to *mediated* rather than unmediated revelation.[45] Paul uses this word-family to represent himself as "the medium of divine revelation."[46] We might say that Paul is the necessary public face of his revelations, both initial (such as mentioned in Gal. 1:16) and ongoing (such as narrated in 2 Cor. 12:1–10), to which ἀποκαλύπτω and ἀποκάλυψις refer.[47] *Revelation* becomes *manifestation.*[48]

If Kurek-Chomycz is right about the vocabulary of revelation, then that which occurred ἐν ἐμοί according to Gal. 1:16 should be understood as a direct, and perhaps even private, revelation *to* Paul, not *in* (or *through*) him in any public way. I am not convinced, however, that the verb alone should determine the force of ἐν ἐμοί. Paul's use of the same phrase in 2:20 suggests that the initial revelation of the Son "in" Paul was, or at least organically became, an ongoing mode of existence shaped by the Son/Messiah "in" him.[49] However, even if the revelation of 1:16 is not a specifically public event (because it is not described in terms of φανερόω or φανέρωσις), my main contention remains intact: Paul's apocalypse is complete only when it is embodied, when it has a public ("mediated") manifestation. Rowland agrees: no matter the interpretation of 1:16, "there is other evidence in Paul's

---

44. Dominika A. Kurek-Chomycz, "The Scent of (Mediated) Revelation? Some Remarks on φανερόω with a Particular Focus on 2 Corinthians," in *Theologizing in the Corinthian Conflict: Studies in the Theology and Exegesis of 2 Corinthians,* eds. Reimund Bieringer et al. (Leuven: Peeters, 2013), 69–108.

45. Ibid., 70.

46. Ibid.

47. See the word ἀποκάλυψις, in the plural, in 2 Cor. 12:1, 7.

48. Kurek-Chomycz suggests that "reveal" and "manifest" may sometimes best capture the distinction in the two semantic domains ("The Scent," 106). She argues persuasively (90–100) that in 2 Corinthians, Paul maintains a clear distinction between the two-word families (ἀποκαλύπτω/ἀποκάλυψις and φανερόω/φανέρωσις).

49. Ben Witherington similarly interprets 1:16 in connection with 2:20 (*Grace in Galatia* [Grand Rapids: Eerdmans, 1998], 106).

letters of an intimate link between the human medium (the apostle) and the message about, and even the person of, Christ."[50]

The medium, however, is greater than the apostle himself, even if (at times) he and his colleagues constitute the focal point of the Christ-medium for rhetorical purposes.[51] The apocalyptically revealed new covenant is, and must be, revealed for what it is by being made visible in human lives and communities that are being transformed by the Spirit to bear testimony to the paradoxical reality of the nature of God's apocalypse and new creation in the crucified Christ. To put it in new-covenant language, new covenant, reception of the Spirit, and Spirit-enabled obedience are inseparable.

Our consideration of Gal. 1:16 in connection with parts of 2 Corinthians means that the divine apocalypse is that which inaugurates the new covenant, and the evidence of the presence of the new covenant is life and ministry that correspond to the apocalypse—to the death and resurrection of Jesus. The common factor in each (the apocalypse and the new covenant) is the activity of the Father and the Son by the Spirit. Our inquiry into 2 Corinthians reinforces precisely what we see, in less developed form, in Galatians itself. The apocalypse of the apocalypse, according to Galatians, means the crucified Messiah alive and active (2:20); it consists of both the apostle who exhibits Christ crucified, bearing the marks of Jesus the crucified, and the community that shares in the faithfulness and love of the crucified and in all the "fruit" his Spirit produces. Of course, Paul also exemplifies faithfulness and love, and the community also, more than likely, suffers. Each manifestation of the new covenant/new creation is due to the activity of God in sending the Son and the Spirit (4:4–6).

"In the Spirit"

We have seen that it is absolutely critical for Paul that the Spirit of God that is sent into human hearts is the Spirit of the Son. This essay's

50. Rowland, "Paul and the Apocalypse of Jesus Christ," 145.
51. Even Rowland (ibid.) notes that the medium is not limited to apostles. See, e.g., 2 Cor. 3:3, 18.

title, however, refers to the shape of life *in the Spirit*,[52] yet our focus has been on the *Spirit within*. These two ways of looking at the "location" of the Spirit are not contradictory. It is significant for Paul that the Spirit is both internal and external to believers, reflecting, I would suggest, the "Spirit in" language (indwelling, internal) and the "Spirit on" language (anointing, external) of the biblical tradition, as well as the prophetic eschatological expectation that the Spirit would be both put *within* God's people and poured out *on* them.[53]

The result for Paul is the mutual indwelling, or reciprocal residence, of: (a) both the Spirit and the Messiah, and (b) the community of believers (as Rom. 8:1–17 makes most clear)—by which, Paul means the Messiah's dwelling by means of, or in the person of, the Spirit. This intricate understanding of the Spirit is another aspect of the surprising newness of the new covenant. It is a development from the prophetic expectation, especially in the notion of the Spirit *of* the Messiah. Paul's use of the idiom of being "in" the Spirit may well be modeled on his language of being "in" the Messiah.[54] It is perhaps his way of saying that it is in fact the surprising messianic Spirit, the Spirit associated with anointing, and thus with the anointed one (cf. 2 Cor. 1:21[55]), that is revealed and given in the new covenant. In any event, to be in Christ is to be in the Spirit, and to be in the Spirit is simultaneously to have the Spirit within (individuals) and among (the community). This is the result of God's all-encompassing new-covenant incursion.

Conclusion

As noted earlier, it was Lou Martyn who wrote that God's apocalyptic

---

52. In the undisputed letters, there are more than twenty occurrences of the phrase ἐν πνεύματι (or a similar phrase, including πνεύματι alone) in which location "in" the Spirit is at least a plausible interpretation. For the apocalyptic/revelatory significance of the phrase ἐν πνεύματι, see also Rev. 1:10.

53. E.g. Ezek. 11:9; 36:26–27; 37:14 (put within); Isa. 32:15; 44:3; Ezek. 39:29; Joel 2:28–29 (poured out on).

54. I am not claiming that Paul invented the language of being in the Spirit but suggesting (part of) the reason for his attraction to it. The Spirit is of course "upon" the figure(s) in Isaiah (Isa. 11:2; 42:1; 61:1).

55. ὁ δὲ ... χρίσας ἡμᾶς θεός. It is also likely that the gospel tradition about Jesus' mission of baptizing in/with the Holy Spirit (Mark 1:8 par; cf. 1 Cor. 12:13) is known to Paul.

divine invasion in Christ is analogous to the prophetic promise of a new, divinely given heart and spirit.[56] The argument of this essay suggests that Martyn was absolutely right. We have encountered evidence from Paul's letters for the inseparability of apocalypse and new covenant, and have therefore contended that Paul should be described as a proponent of the apocalyptic new covenant, the coming of which is an event of disruptive continuity. Moreover, we have seen that inherent in this apocalyptic new covenant is the need for apostles and all believers to embody, and thus also to manifest, the revelation. By means of the Spirit, the church is to be an apocalypse of the apocalypse, a living manifestation and exegesis of the surprising new covenant.[57] Life in the Spirit of the crucified Messiah will therefore reflect the counterintuitive and countercultural ways of God revealed in that messianic apocalypse. Paul's own life is an attempt to bear witness to that apocalypse, empowered by the Spirit, and to encourage those who encounter him, whether in person or via his letters, to do the same.[58]

---

56. Martyn, "Afterword," 164n13.

57. See further my *Becoming the Gospel: Paul, Participation, and Mission* (Grand Rapids: Eerdmans, 2015).

58. I am grateful to my research assistant, Gary Staszak, and to the editors for their feedback on versions of this chapter.

17

The Two Ages and Salvation History in Paul's Apocalyptic Imagination

A Comparison of 4 Ezra and Galatians

J. P. Davies

Introduction

In 1970, Klaus Koch published a short but polemical book on what he saw as a neglected area in biblical studies, entitled *Ratlos vor der Apokalyptik*.[1] A generation later, this area is far from neglected, as the present volume demonstrates. But the question remains: are we still "clueless about apocalyptic"?

Faced with the cloud of methodological confusion that surrounds it, some have considered abandoning the term "apocalyptic" altogether.[2]

---

1. K. Koch, *Ratlos vor der Apokalyptik* (Gütersloh: Gütersloher Verlaghaus Gerd Mohn, 1970), translated by Margaret Kohl and published as *The Rediscovery of Apocalyptic* (London: SCM, 1972). This rather bloodless English title loses the polemic of the original German.
2. See, e.g., the discussion in R. E. Sturm, "Defining the Word 'apocalyptic': A Problem in Biblical Criticism," in *Apocalyptic and the New Testament: Essays in Honour of J. Louis Martyn* (Sheffield: Sheffield University, 1989), 17–48, at 17. T. F. Glasson considered it "a useless word which no

As tempting as this may seem, such drastic measures are unnecessary, especially as the current state of apocalyptic study is promising. While the seminal work of John Collins and Christopher Rowland continues to be the basis of discussion for many, recent work by the members of the *Enoch Seminar* has also taken us further in our understanding of the texts, and in particular Loren Stuckenbruck's recent work has connected this study of the apocalypses to the question of Pauline apocalyptic.[3]

When it comes to the "apocalyptic Paul," however, some have expressed concern that this connection has been severed, as in this recent discussion by N. T. Wright:

> Whatever else the word "apocalyptic" does in western scholarship, it always appeals implicitly to a *historical context* within the so-called 'history of religions' of the time. . . . If the word "apocalyptic," as a label for a mode or type of thought, is intended to carry any implication in terms of the religio-historical context to which appeal is being made, it must be to these books [i.e., Daniel, Ezekiel, 1 Enoch, 4 Ezra, Revelation], and the many others like them, that the writer is appealing. Otherwise the word has been cut loose from any recognisable historical moorings. . . . That, I think, has happened on a massive scale in recent discussions.[4]

Is Wright's bleak assessment on target? It may well be the case that some recent discussions of apocalyptic in Paul have floated free from

---

one can define and which produces nothing but confusion and acres of verbiage" ("What Is Apocalyptic?," *NTS* 27, no. 1 [1980]: 98–105, at 99).

3. J. J. Collins, *Apocalyptic Imagination: An Introduction to Jewish Apocalyptic Literature* (Grand Rapids: Eerdmans, 1998). Collins's definition of the apocalyptic genre is for many, though not all, the basis for discussion: "'Apocalypse' is a genre of revelatory literature with a narrative framework, in which a revelation is mediated by an otherworldly being to a human recipient, disclosing a transcendent reality which is both temporal, insofar as it envisages eschatological salvation, and spatial insofar as it involves another, supernatural world" (J. J. Collins, "Towards the Morphology of a Genre," *Semeia* 14, no. 1 [1979]: 1–20, at 9). For Rowland, see *The Open Heaven* (London: SPCK, 1982); C. Rowland and C. R. A. Morray-Jones, *The Mystery of God: Early Jewish Mysticism and the New Testament* (Leiden: Brill, 2009). Among recent studies from the Enoch Seminar see, e.g., M. Henze, *Jewish Apocalypticism in Late First Century Israel: Reading Second Baruch in Context* (Tübingen: Mohr Siebeck: 2011); M. Henze and Boccaccini, eds., *Fourth Ezra and Second Baruch: Reconstruction After the Fall* (Leiden: Brill, 2013); K. M. Hogan, *Theologies in Conflict in 4 Ezra: Wisdom Debate and Apocalyptic Solution* (Leiden: Brill, 2008); and L. Stuckenbruck, *1 Enoch 91-108* (Berlin: de Gruyter, 2007). For Stuckenbruck's work on Paul, see L. Stuckenbruck, "Overlapping Ages at Qumran and 'Apocalyptic' in Pauline Theology," in *The Dead Sea Scrolls and Pauline Literature*, ed. Jean-Sébastien Rey (Leiden: Brill, 2013), 309–26; "Posturing 'Apocalyptic' in Pauline Theology: How Much Contrast with Jewish Tradition?," in *The Myth of Rebellious Angels: Studies in Second Temple Judaism and New Testament Texts* (Tübingen: Mohr Siebeck, 2014), 240–56.

4. N. T. Wright, *Paul and His Recent Interpreters* (London: SPCK, 2015), 138.

the apocalypses, at least functionally. But, in principle at least, most scholars agree that to use the word "apocalyptic" in reference to Paul is to make an historical and literary connection between his epistles and a body of second Temple Jewish and Christian literature, and the worldview that literature expresses. J. Louis Martyn's approach to apocalyptic in Paul, which is enormously influential in the contemporary debate, appeals to exegesis of the apocalyptic literature. For example, his emphasis on the doctrine of the two ages in Galatians as a "scheme fundamental to apocalyptic thought" was argued on the basis that such a frame of reference can be discerned "from writings and traditions of Paul's time."[5] Martyn does not say here which writings and traditions he has in mind, but it seems safe to assume that they include the Second Temple Jewish apocalypses. Martinus de Boer is more explicit when he insists that defining apocalyptic is "partly a matter of defining what apocalyptic eschatology is apart from Paul,"[6] and that his definition "is based, as it ought to be, upon the data of the available sources, namely, such books as Revelation, Daniel, 1 Enoch, 2 Baruch, and 4 Ezra."[7] On this matter at least, de Boer is in broad agreement with another vocal critic, Barry Matlock, who insists that "[t]he abstraction 'apocalyptic' (or whatever else it may fittingly be called) must, if terminology is to signify anything other than confusion, be made on the basis of the apocalypses."[8] Matlock subsequently complains that "recent discussion has fluctuated oddly between being claimed to be free of the apocalyptic literature and yet still being claimed to be tied to the literature somehow," something which he attributes to a desire "to preserve the concept from attempts to make it accountable to the literature."[9] Responding to these criticisms, Beverly

---

5. J. L. Martyn, *Galatians: A New Translation with Introduction and Commentary*, ABC 33a (New York: Doubleday, 1997), 98. Martyn died in June 2015, as this volume was in preparation, and New Testament scholarship, particularly on the subject of apocalyptic, lost one of its most important and stimulating voices.

6. M. C. de Boer, *The Defeat of Death: Apocalyptic Eschatology in 1 Corinthians 15 and Romans 5*, JSNTSup 22 (Sheffield: JSOT, 1988), 19, cf. 181–82.

7. M. C. de Boer, "Paul and Apocalyptic Eschatology," in *The Encyclopedia of Apocalypticism*, eds. John J. Collins and Bernard McGinn (New York: Continuum, 2000), 345–83, at 353.

8. R. B. Matlock, *Unveiling the Apocalyptic Paul: Paul's Interpreters and the Rhetoric of Criticism*, JSNTSup 127 (Sheffield: Sheffield University, 1996), 261.

9. Ibid., 291–92.

Gaventa has pointed to the exegesis done on the apocalypses in de Boer's early work,[10] and in so doing, she implies agreement on at least the basic methodological point being made, that "when 'apocalyptic Paul' is being discussed, it should sound as if something historical is being discussed."[11] There does, therefore, seem to be sufficient methodological agreement to provide cause for optimism.[12] We may disagree about the exegesis of the apocalypses, but it is about these texts and the worldview they express that we are disagreeing—or at least it should be.

The more difficult methodological question is how we are to move from the historical and literary phenomenon of the apocalypses to the examination of apocalyptic thought in texts that do not belong to that genre. How do we talk about "apocalyptic" *beyond* the apocalypses, about, for example, Paul's "apocalyptic imagination"?

The Genre Apocalypse and the Apocalyptic Mode

To this end, a useful framework is available in contemporary literary criticism—specifically, the notion of "modes" of thinking and writing, described in detail by Alasdair Fowler.[13] To illustrate the concept of "mode," Fowler uses the example of the noun "comedy" and the related adjective "comic." In literary criticism at least, "comedy" is a

10. B. R. Gaventa, *Our Mother Saint Paul* (Louisville: Westminster John Knox, 2007), 83, directing Matlock to de Boer, *Defeat of Death*, 39–91. Whether or not one finds de Boer's treatment of the texts satisfactory, he is at least attempting to anchor his definition of "apocalyptic" in those texts, despite Matlock's protestations.

11. Matlock, *Unveiling the Apocalyptic Paul*, 292. Cf. Gaventa's statement that, apocalyptic means "not simply that Paul's metaphors of maternity have some parallels in apocalyptic literature or that they come to Paul from the sphere of apocalyptic thought" (*Our Mother Saint Paul*, 79). What I understand Gaventa to be saying is that "apocalyptic" is not *simply* this historical connection, but it is as *at least* this.

12. The position of Douglas Campbell seems to be something of an outlier. While acknowledging that, for some interpreters "[apocalyptic] denotes certain positions within the more diverse, Jewish apocalyptic corpus and worldview," he prefers to use the word "at an introductory level of discussion when broad loyalties and orientations are being sketched in relation to different basic approaches to Paul" which, for Campbell, means "that an approach to Paul is being pursued that ultimately aligns with the concerns and readings of—in this context in particular—Lou Martyn" (D. A. Campbell, *The Deliverance of God: An Apocalyptic Rereading of Justification in Paul* [Grand Rapids: Eerdmans, 2009], 191). That Martyn himself, as we have just seen, insisted on a connection with the apocalyptic texts seems to go unnoticed in Campbell's summary (189–90).

13. A. Fowler, *Kinds of Literature: An Introduction to the Theory of Genres and Modes* (Cambridge, MA: Harvard University Press, 1982), esp. 106–11.

specific generic label designating a kind of literature—namely, a play with certain distinguishing features. But the related adjective "comic" can also be applied to other forms of writing, such as the description of Jane Austen's *Emma* as a "comic novel." "Then," Fowler says, "we mean that *Emma* is by kind a novel, by mode comic."[14] This all seems quite straightforward, but the extrapolation from the concrete and contingent embodiment of the comedies to the more broad modal application "comic" is by no means a simple process, as many have found in the case of the kind "apocalypse" and the mode "apocalyptic." Fowler thus concedes, with perhaps a touch of understatement, that "the adjectival use of generic terms is a little complicated."[15] He rejects the conclusion, however, that this means that such usage is inherently vague—limits can and must be applied to the modal adjectives on the basis of an examination of the nonstructural features of that mode's repertoire and the application of those features to another kind of literature. Fowler speaks of modes as "distillations" of the most valuable features from its embodiment in the contingent texts of any given genre. It is only by keeping the implied connection with this textual repertoire in mind that modal usage can avoid vagueness.[16]

This literary-critical tool may be useful in providing methodological clarity in the discussion of Paul and apocalyptic. For an evaluation of the hypothesis that Paul was a theologian in the "apocalyptic mode," it is vital that we examine the apocalypses, discerning and distilling important non-structural features, and then discuss the presence of such features (including their Christological adaptation) in Paul.

The Doctrine of the Two Ages: A Litmus Test for Apocalyptic?

Such modal distillations involve making judgments as to which "nonstructural features" of the texts are most important, mapping what Richard Hays has recently called Paul's "apocalyptic DNA."[17] One frequently invoked contender for the genetic essence of apocalyptic

---

14. Ibid., 106.
15. Ibid.
16. Ibid., 111. Fowler's framework has been used to good effect by Eibert Tigchelaar, cf. esp. *Prophets of Old and the Day of the End: Zechariah, the Book of Watchers, and Apocalyptic* (Leiden: Brill, 1996), 5–8.

is the dualistic eschatological doctrine of the two ages. In this connection, some scholars examining Paul's apocalyptic thought have cited the following programmatic statement of Philipp Vielhauer:

> The essential feature of Apocalyptic is its dualism which, in various expressions, dominates its thought-world. Above all, in the doctrine of the Two Ages, in the dualistic time-scheme of world eras (ὁ αἰὼν οὗτος and ὁ αἰὼν μέλλων), the entire course of the world is comprehended. . . . The dualism of the Two-Ages doctrine recognizes no continuity between the time of this world and that which is to come. . . . This eschatological dualism is the essential characteristic of Apocalyptic so far as its contents are concerned.[18]

In support of this basic definition are the contentions of Paul Hanson and D. S. Russell that this kind of dualistic eschatology is the "basic perspective" of the apocalyptic "symbolic universe"[19] and that its expression in the doctrine of the two ages is "characteristic of apocalyptic eschatology."[20]

When it comes to examining apocalyptic thought outside the apocalypses, it is asserted that the doctrine of the two ages is the *sine qua non.* Indications of this eschatological framework in Paul are thus interpreted as the sign that the apostle is thinking in the apocalyptic mode. The most influential proponent of this approach is Martyn, who cites Paul's use of the "distinctly apocalyptic expression 'the present evil age,'" as decisive evidence of the two-ages framework, "a scheme fundamental to apocalyptic thought."[21] Likewise, de Boer is clear that, for him, the two ages motif is "the fundamental characteristic of all apocalyptic eschatology," including that of Paul.[22]

At first glance, all this seems promising. However, scholars of the apocalyptic literature have noted a number of problems associated

---

17. R. B. Hays, "Apocalyptic Poiesis in Galatians," in *Galatians and Christian Theology*, eds. M. W. Elliott et al. (Grand Rapids: Baker, 2014), 200–219, at 203.
18. P. Vielhauer, "Apocalypses and Related Literature: Introduction," in *New Testament Apocrypha*, ed. W. Schneemelcher, 2 vols. (Philadelphia: Westminster, 1964), 581–607, at 588–89.
19. Paul D. Hanson, *The Dawn of Apocalyptic: The Historical and Sociological Roots of Jewish Apocalyptic Eschatology* (Philadelphia: Fortress Press, 1979), 432–33.
20. D. S. Russell, *The Method and Message of Jewish Apocalyptic* (London: SCM, 1964), 266.
21. Martyn, *Galatians*, 97–98.
22. de Boer, *Defeat of Death*, 7. Cf. Also his discussion in de Boer, "Paul and Apocalyptic Eschatology," 347–49. See also his contribution to the present volume.

with this simple definition and its employment as a "litmus test" for apocalyptic. I will note three briefly and then concentrate on a fourth.

First, the two-ages scheme it is not a *sufficient* definition. Apocalyptic is about much more than eschatology, involving the revelation of, among other things, cosmological and soteriological mysteries. In short, as Rowland has argued, eschatology in the apocalypses is "not their most distinctive feature, nor does it deserve to become the focus of attention in the study of apocalyptic to the exclusion of the other secrets which the apocalypses claim to reveal."[23]

Second, the two-ages scheme is not an *exclusive* defining characteristic. It is, after all, a doctrine found throughout the Old Testament, Second Temple Jewish literature, and the Rabbinic writings. This is a simple but important point, which has been argued by many. As Rowland and Morray-Jones have put it, "evidence from the apocalypses themselves indicates that, apart from a handful of passages, their doctrine of the future hope seems to be pretty much the same as that found in other Jewish sources."[24]

Third, the characterization of the two-ages scheme as radically "dualistic" is problematic.[25] This assertion, it appears, owes less to an examination of the literature itself and more to Vielhauer's assertion that "the dualism of the Two-Ages doctrine recognizes no continuity between the time of this world and of that which is to come."[26] This has been variously challenged, not least by Collins, who has argued that the "two age" eschatologies of some Jewish apocalypses are characterized by "significant continuity from this world to the next."[27]

Fourth, and finally, the two-ages scheme, which is certainly *a* characteristic of apocalyptic eschatology is by no means the *only* one.

---

23. Rowland, *Open Heaven*, 26.
24. Rowland and Morray-Jones, *Mystery of God*, 15. Another example is N. T. Wright, who has made this point repeatedly: see N. T. Wright, *The New Testament and the People of God* (London: SPCK, 1992), 254; 299–300; idem. *Paul and the Faithfulness of God* (London: SPCK, 2013), 1059–60; idem. *Interpreters*, 157–58. (cf. esp. the list of references at 158n12.)
25. I have argued this more fully in chapter 3 of J. P. Davies, *Paul Among the Apocalypses? An Evaluation of the 'Apocalyptic Paul' in the Context of Jewish and Christian Apocalyptic Literature*, LNTS 562 (London: Bloomsbury T&T Clark, 2016).
26. Vielhauer, "Apocalypses and Related Literature: Introduction," 588; cf. e.g., de Boer, "Paul and Apocalyptic Eschatology," 348.
27. Collins, *Apocalyptic Imagination*, 222. I will return to this point below.

Eschatology in the apocalypses should not be reduced to this motif: there are other eschatological metaphors that are woven together in ways that are complex and mutually enriching. Stuckenbruck considers the exclusive focus on the two ages offered by Vielhauer (with Hanson and Russell) as demonstrably flawed and says that "construals of time in Second Temple Jewish literature cannot be simplified into such a scheme," citing as evidence the presence of the periodization of history, cyclical understandings of time, and the framework of *Endzeit/Urzeit*.[28]

In stating this fourth point, I have already anticipated some of what follows. Part of the problem here is that Vielhauer and Russell, in making their arguments for the two ages as the *sine qua non* of apocalyptic, have almost exclusively emphasized its expression in 4 *Ezra* 7:47–50, while bracketing out temporal and eschatological themes found elsewhere in that book and in the rest of the apocalyptic literature. These conclusions have subsequently been taken up by some Pauline interpreters, who have placed all the weight on the two ages as the essence of apocalyptic. Other eschatological themes, such as the periodization of history, are then relegated to the status of "optional feature[s]."[29]

But this approach risks question-begging. The two-ages scheme is certainly important, but should not be employed as a reductionist litmus test for apocalyptic thought. Whether it is the *Animal Apocalypse* of *1 Enoch* 85–90, the cloud vision of *2 Baruch* 53–74, or the statue and beasts of Daniel 2 and 7, what we find in apocalyptic literature (woven together with the doctrine of the two ages) is an eschatological concern with telling the story of Israel through periods of history—the very thing that some contemporary approaches to apocalyptic in Paul seek to downplay or rule out. But, as Stuckenbruck has argued, "beyond contrasting present and future reality, some writers of

---

28. Stuckenbruck, "Overlapping Ages," 312. See also idem, "Posturing 'Apocalyptic' in Pauline Theology: How Much Contrast with Jewish Tradition?" Cf. J. J. Collins, "Apocalyptic Eschatology as the Transcendence of Death," *CBQ* 36, no. 1 (1974): 21–43, and Stuckenbruck's contribution to the present volume.

29. M. C. de Boer, *Galatians: A Commentary*, NTL (Louisville: Westminster John Knox, 2011), 261n389.

apocalyptic texts demonstrated a concern with divine activity as a constant that shaped the unfolding story of Israel as a way of understanding and posing questions about the present."[30] What is needed, then, is an approach to eschatology in the apocalyptic mode that distils its essential features from the literature in their rich variety, without oversimplification into any one scheme.

In the rest of this chapter, I will attempt to provide a case study for such an approach by offering a comparison of temporal metaphors in one apocalyptic text, 4 Ezra, and would-be apocalyptic interpretations of time in Paul's letter to the Galatians.

Multiple Eschatological Themes in 4 Ezra

"Not one world but two": 4 Ezra 7

Any discussion of apocalyptic eschatology must deal with 4 Ezra 7:47–50, where, as Stone comments, "the author sees a clear separation of two ages."[31] The passage involves Ezra's response to a vision of coming judgment:

> I answered and said, "O sovereign Lord, I said then and I say now: Blessed are those who are alive and keep your commandments! But what of those for whom I prayed? For who among the living is there that has not sinned, or who among men that has not transgressed your covenant? And now I see that the world to come will bring delight to few, but torments to many. For an evil heart has grown up in us, which has alienated us from God, and has brought us into corruption and the ways of death, and has shown us the paths of perdition and removed us far from life—and that not just a few of us but almost all who have been created!"
>
> He answered me and said, "Listen to me, Ezra, and I will instruct you, and will admonish you yet again. For this reason the Most High has made not one world but two."[32]

I have already commented on the (almost exclusive) importance of this

---

30. Stuckenbruck, "Overlapping Ages," 322.

31. M. E. Stone, Fourth Ezra, Hermeneia (Minneapolis: Fortress Press, 1990), 93.

32. 4 Ezra 7:45–50. Translations of 4 Ezra are those of Metzger in J. H. Charlesworth, The Old Testament Pseudepigrapha. I. Apocalyptic Literature and Testaments (Peabody: Hendrickson, 2009), 525–59, though I will also refer to the more recent work of Stone, M. E. and Henze, M., 4 Ezra and 2 Baruch: Translations, Introductions, and Notes (Minneapolis: Fortress Press, 2013).

text for Vielhauer and Russell. Bruce Longenecker likewise observes that 7:50 is "most often cited as the centrepiece of Uriel's two-age scheme"[33] and cites Koch, who says that "Der Satz 7,50 . . . gilt weithin als der 'Grundsatz,' mit dem die Argumentationen des Verfassers stehen und fallen."[34] Appeals to the doctrine of two ages, when they cite the apocalyptic literature, generally hold up *4 Ezra* 7:47–50 as the parade example, and rightly so. But it is by no means the only statement of this theme in the book.[35] It is clear that the duality of "two world-ages" is a crucial aspect of the eschatology of *4 Ezra*. So far, this is uncontroversial and readily cited by scholars in regard to Paul. But it is by no means the only feature of *4 Ezra*'s eschatology. I turn now to a second important theme, expressed in two interrelated metaphors.

History and Harvest, Maternity and Maturation: Salvation History in *4 Ezra* 4

4 Ezra 7:50 may be the clearest example of the two-ages scheme in the book, but it is not the first. It is a theme that is introduced earlier, in chapter 4, where it is woven together with other eschatological images:[36]

> He answered me and said, "If you are alive, you will see, and if you live long, you will often marvel, because the age is hastening swiftly to its end. For it will not be able to bring the things that have been promised to the righteous in their appointed times, because this age is full of sadness and infirmities. For the evil about which you ask me has been sown, but the harvest of it has not yet come. If therefore that which has been sown is not reaped, and if the place where the evil has been sown does not pass away, the field where the good has been sown will not come. For

---

33. B. W. Longenecker, *Eschatology and the Covenant: A Comparison of 4 Ezra and Romans 1–11*, JSNTSup 57 (Sheffield: Sheffield Academic, 1991), 81n3.
34. K. Koch, "Esras erste Vision: Weltzeiten und Weg des Höchste," *BZ* 22 (1978): 46–75, at 46.
35. In 7:112–14, for example, Ezra is told that "the day of judgement will be the end of this age and the beginning of the immortal age to come, in which corruption has passed away.' Again, statements such as that found in 8:46 indicate the continuing importance of an eschatological duality for *4 Ezra*: "things that are present [or 'in this world'] are for those who live now, and things that are future [or 'in that world'] are for those who will live hereafter" (see the notes in Stone, M. E. and Henze, M., *4 Ezra and 2 Baruch*, 56.)
36. Longenecker observes that "if Uriel ever gives Ezra an answer in explanation of the ways of God it is imbedded in the two-age scheme which he propagates for the first time (*in nuce*) at this point" (Longenecker, *Eschatology and the Covenant*, 61).

a grain of evil seed was sown in Adam's heart from the beginning, and how much ungodliness it has produced until now, and will produce until the time of threshing comes! Consider now for yourself how much fruit of ungodliness a grain of evil seed has produced. When heads of grain without number are sown, how great a threshing floor they will fill!"[37]

The point being made by the use of this agricultural metaphor is that the relationship between the two ages is more complex than a simple binary scheme allows. Certainly, there is a duality of the time before and the time after the day of harvest, but the division of times does not result in the irrelevance of what came before. Far from it—the period of maturation before the day of threshing is of vital and continuing importance. The point is made all the clearer as the passage continues with Ezra's next question (the characteristically apocalyptic "how long?"), and Uriel's response:

Then I answered and said "How long and when will these things be? Why are our years few and evil?" He answered me and said, "You do not hasten faster than the Most High, for your haste is for yourself, but the Highest hastens on behalf of many. Did not the souls of the righteous in their chambers ask about these matters, saying "How long are we to remain here? And when will come the harvest of our reward?" And Jeremiel the archangel answered them and said, "When the number of those like yourselves is completed; for *he has weighed the age in the balance, and measured the times by measure, and numbered the times by number; and he will not move or arouse them until that measure is fulfilled.*"[38]

Uriel is clear about the role of history in relation to the two ages. The times must be first "measured" by God until their number is "fulfilled" (36–37), and only then will God move to act and bring about the time of reaping and threshing. Crucially, this is not portrayed as smooth developmental progress that can be discerned by the human eye: it is a time of fullness known to God alone. But the day of reaping, imperceptible to human reason, is nevertheless the long-promised, long-awaited, and (retrospectively) appropriate and logical climax of the time of maturation.

---

37. *4 Ezra* 4:26–32.

38. *4 Ezra* 4:33–37 (emphasis mine). Cf. also *4 Ezra* 11:44: "the Most High has looked upon his times, and behold, they are ended, and *his ages are completed!*"

The dialogue continues with Ezra's suggestion that it is because of the sins of humanity that the time of threshing has been delayed. To explain further the relationship between this age and the age to come, and the delay of the judgment of God, the angel switches the metaphor:

> He answered me and said, "Go and ask a woman who is with child if, when her nine months have been completed, her womb can keep the child within her any longer.""No, my lord," I said, "it cannot."
> He said to me, "In Hades the chambers of the souls are like the womb. For just as a woman who is in travail makes haste to escape the pangs of birth, so also do these places hasten to give back those things that were committed to them from the beginning. Then the things that you desire to see will be disclosed to you."[39]

The point being made by the childbirth imagery is similar to the one made by the harvest metaphor: labor pains are a signal of the arrival of an end of an appointed span of time (a maturation of nine months, in the case of human gestation), which leads up to and anticipates (but *does not condition*) the birth event. There is, importantly, no radical separation between the pangs of birth and the arrival of the child, even though the birth event may be dramatic or even, in a sense, unexpected.[40] There is thus a continuity of this expectation while also surprising discontinuity in the manner of its fulfillment.

How do these apocalyptic eschatological images of harvest and childbirth work together with the two-ages scheme? Answering this question is important for any distillation of apocalyptic eschatology in *4 Ezra*. Yes, there is a binary in these images—there is a qualitative difference between the time before and the time after the threshing/birth—but that should not obscure the importance of the motif of the "fullness of the times." These redemptive-historical

---

39. *4 Ezra* 4:40–43.
40. I say "in a sense" because the point subsequently made in, for example, 5:6 is not that a coming reign was unanticipated, but that the one who exercises that reign does not meet expectations. The most influential study of apocalyptic and maternal imagery in Paul is, of course, Gaventa, *Our Mother Saint Paul*. However, Gaventa's approach to apocalyptic, which follows Martyn closely, leads her to emphasize "God's unilateral action of intervention in the cross and resurrection of Jesus Christ" (14) and to downplay the importance of "maturation" and continuity (cf. 122). I have discussed these issues in more detail in J. P. Davies, "What to Expect when you're Expecting: Maternity, Salvation History, and the 'Apocalyptic Paul'" *JSNT* 38, no. 3 (March 2016), 301–15.

metaphors work together with the two ages motif in a complex whole, and so, we should resist overly simplistic schemes that employ the latter to the exclusion of the former.

With these two apocalyptic eschatological motifs in mind we come to Paul, and in particular to the letter that has become the storm center of the debate about his apocalyptic theology, the epistle to the Galatians.

Apocalyptic and Salvation History in Galatians?

In the continuing discussion of apocalyptic in Paul, the present focus on Galatians is a surprising turn. J. C. Beker, for whom "only a consistent apocalyptic interpretation of Paul's thought is able to demonstrate its fundamental coherence"[41] nevertheless considered Galatians a contingent exception to this overall scheme. Its lack of concern with future eschatology, among other things, caused Beker to view Galatians as a letter whose "situational demands suppress the apocalyptic theme of the gospel."[42] For Beker, apocalyptic in Paul must be explored on the basis of other letters. Reviewing his *Paul the Apostle* shortly after its publication, Martyn asked the following pointed questions:

> Is the apocalyptic theme of the gospel suppressed in that letter in which Paul says with unmistakable emphasis that the truth of the gospel is a matter of apocalypse (Gal 1:12, 16; 2:2, 5, 14)? One is driven to ask whether it is not Paul's voice in Galatians that is being suppressed, perhaps because that letter is felt to be offensive on two counts: it contains very few references to God's future triumph, that is, to what Beker views as the core of the coherent apocalyptic core, and it can be read as revealing a conscious avoidance of the continuum of salvation history.... Could Galatians perhaps be allowed to play its own role in showing us precisely what the nature of Paul's apocalyptic was? If one should answer that question in the affirmative, one would be driven back to the issue of the relationship between apocalyptic and salvation history.[43]

41. J. C. Beker, *Paul the Apostle: The Triumph of God in Life and Thought* (Philadelphia: Fortress Press, 1980), 143.

42. Ibid., x.

43. J. L. Martyn, "Review of Paul the Apostle: The Triumph of God in Life and Thought, by J. Christiaan Beker," *Word & World* 2, no. 2 (1982): 194–98, at 196–97.

And driven back we are, for it is this relationship between apocalyptic and salvation history that concerns us here. Martyn's concerns are those of Käsemann, namely that we should guard carefully against any view of history as a *smooth evolutionary development*. But this is a concern that Beker shares while still affirming the importance of salvation history.[44] For Beker, apocalyptic in Paul was characterized by an intimate and dynamic relationship between the two eschatological motifs of the two ages and salvation history

> because the history of Israel is for him not simply the old age of darkness. Israel's past contains the footprints of the promises of God, and these promises are taken up into the new age rather than cast aside. . . . The dualism between the old age and the new age, then, is *tempered* in the first place by Paul's stress on continuity in the midst of discontinuity with respect to God's continuing faithfulness to Israel. In the second place, the incursion of the new age occurs in the midst of the old because of the new life brought about by Christ's death and resurrection.[45]

For Martyn, one of the major problems with Beker's approach to Pauline apocalyptic was what he saw as a methodology which "play[ed] down the disjunctive dualism of the two ages, accenting instead the linear matter of God's victorious faithfulness as it is directed toward the future consummation of his gracious plan." This Martyn saw as "a brand of apocalyptic primarily focused not on dualistic patterns of thought, but rather on the continuum of history that God is directing toward his final triumph."[46] Martyn's antithetical assessment indicates a dichotomy that lies at the heart of his own approach to apocalyptic in Paul, as the following statement reveals: "Beker is able to discover a kind of marriage between apocalyptic (as core) and salvation history (as structure?). My own opinion is that the marriage . . . is rather more arranged by Beker than discovered in Paul."[47]

Martyn's critique of Beker highlights the importance of determining

---

44. E.g. J. C. Beker, *Paul's Apocalyptic Gospel: The Coming Triumph of God* (Philadelphia: Fortress Press, 1982), 50, where he says that "with the apocalyptic authors, Paul expects the future to entail a definitive closure/completion-event in time and space, rather than simply a continuous, open-ended process."
45. Ibid., 40.
46. Martyn, "Review of Beker," 196.
47. Ibid.

the relationship between salvation history and apocalyptic in Galatians—a topic that continues to draw attention.[48] In the hope of making a contribution to this debate, I now turn to a sharper focus on two verses that have borne considerable weight in this discussion of apocalyptic eschatology in Paul, namely, Gal. 1:4 and 4:4.

"The present evil age": Galatians 1:4

The theme of the two ages is suggested right at the very start of the letter:

χάρις ὑμῖν καὶ εἰρήνη ἀπὸ θεοῦ πατρὸς ἡμῶν καὶ κυρίου Ἰησοῦ Χριστοῦ, τοῦ δόντος ἑαυτὸν ὑπὲρ τῶν ἁμαρτιῶν ἡμῶν ὅπως ἐξέληται ἡμᾶς ἐκ τοῦ αἰῶνος τοῦ ἐνεστῶτος πονηροῦ κατὰ τὸ θέλημα τοῦ θεοῦ καὶ πατρὸς ἡμῶν

Grace to you and peace from God our Father and the Lord Jesus Christ, who gave himself for our sins to set us free from the present evil age, according to the will of our God and Father.[49]

Martyn is in no doubt about the significance of Paul's language: the phrase τοῦ αἰῶνος τοῦ ἐνεστῶτος πονηροῦ is a "distinctly apocalyptic expression . . . the first of numerous apocalyptic expressions in the letter."[50] De Boer follows Martyn in seeing 1:4b as a clear indication that Paul is "indebted to Jewish apocalyptic eschatology," and in particular its "classic expression in the apocalypse of *4 Ezra* [2 Esd.] 7:50."[51] Of course, Martyn and de Boer are by no means alone in seeing a connection between Paul's use of the expression "the present evil age" and the Jewish apocalyptic literature.[52] But Paul has not simply lifted

---

48. See, for example, three recent contributions to the *Journal for the Study of Paul and His Letters*: B. W. Longenecker, "Salvation History in Galatians and the Making of a Pauline Discourse," *JSPL* 2, no. 2 (2012): 65–87; J. Maston, "The Nature of Salvation History in Galatians," *JSPL* 2, no. 2 (2012): 89–103; T. D. Still, "'Once upon a Time': Galatians as an Apocalyptic Story," *JSPL* 2, no. 2 (2012): 133–41.

49. Gal. 1:3-4 (NRSV).

50. Martyn, *Galatians*, 97.

51. de Boer, *Galatians*, 30. De Boer's list of additional references is very useful, and demonstrates that the "two ages" is not simply "apocalyptic" but is something found across a wide range of Jewish and Christian texts.

52. E.g. H. D. Betz, *Galatians: A Commentary on Paul's Letter to the Churches in Galatia*, Hermeneia (Philadelphia: Fortress Press, 1979), 42n58; J. D. G. Dunn, *A Commentary on the Epistle to the Galatians*, BNTC (London: A&C Black, 1993), 36; R. N. Longenecker, *Galatians*, WBC 41 (Dallas: Word, 1990),

this theme from his tradition and used it uncritically, but has subjected it to modification in the light of the revelation of Jesus Christ.

The most obvious difference in Paul's use of this eschatological duality is that he does not speak straightforwardly about "the age to come." What are we to make of this? For Martyn, the recognition that Paul does not mention "the age to come" is no impediment to identifying the two ages doctrine in Galatians and elsewhere in Paul.

> To speak of the present age is obviously to imply that there is another age (or something like another age). . . . Although Paul himself never speaks literally of "the coming age," his numerous references to "the present age" (in addition to Gal. 1:4, see Rom. 12:2; 1 Cor. 1:2; 2:6; 2:8; 3:18; 2 Cor. 4:4) reflect this assumption of eschatological dualism.[53]

For Martyn, the distinction between the two ages in Galatians is not between "this age" and "the age to come," but between "this age" and "the new creation" (6:15). This adaptation of the two ages reflects, for Martyn, the development of the doctrine in the exilic period.[54] But it is also a variation on the two-ages theme that can be found in Jewish apocalyptic literature. De Boer also notes this connection, commenting that "the concept of a 'new creation' is at home in Jewish apocalyptic eschatology" citing, among other texts, 4 Ezra 7. There, in 7:75, Ezra voices his conviction that the Lord will "renew the creation." This statement is found sandwiched between the classic statements of the two ages in 7:50 and 7:112-14. As such, there is support from Paul's context for reading the "[re]new[ed] creation" as roughly equivalent to the "age to come" in the dualistic eschatological scheme. When the whole passage is read, however, it becomes clear that 4 Ezra weaves this eschatological duality, together with other eschatological motifs, such as the notion of "the last days/times" (7:73, 77) and a belief in the divinely foreordained periodization of history (7:74). Returning to Galatians, this observation tempers Martyn's assertion that the "new creation" is a motif "in which the accent lies on the motif of radical,

8; T. R. Schreiner, *Galatians*, ZECNT (Grand Rapids: Zondervan, 2010), 77; S. K. Williams, *Galatians*, ANTC (Nashville: Abingdon, 1997), 35; Wright, *PFG*, 1068–69.

53. Martyn, *Galatians*, 98.

54. E.g. Isa. 43:18–19; cf. Hanson, *Dawn of Apocalyptic*, 127.

uncompromising newness" and the resulting conclusion that "far from repairing the old cosmos, God is in the process of replacing it."[55] Galatians 1:4 and 6:15 are certainly indications of the two-ages doctrine and that Paul is writing his letter in an apocalyptic mode. But the relationship in 4 Ezra between that dualistic eschatological scheme and other temporal motifs leads us to ask whether, for Paul, a similar interweaving of eschatological metaphors might be in play.

"The fullness of time": Galatians 4:4

Thus, we come to a passage that lies, for many, at the heart of the question of Paul's eschatology in Galatians, 3:15–4:7, and to one verse in particular, 4:4, dubbed by Martyn "the theological center of the entire letter."[56] Here it is, with its following context:

ὅτε δὲ ἦλθεν τὸ πλήρωμα τοῦ χρόνου, ἐξαπέστειλεν ὁ θεὸς τὸν υἱὸν αὐτοῦ, γενόμενον ἐκ γυναικός, γενόμενον ὑπὸ νόμον, ἵνα τοὺς ὑπὸ νόμον ἐξαγοράσῃ, ἵνα τὴν υἱοθεσίαν ἀπολάβωμεν.

But when the fullness of time had come, God sent his Son, born of a woman, born under the law, in order to redeem those who were under the law, so that we might receive adoption as children.

The phrase τὸ πλήρωμα τοῦ χρόνου, translated by the NRSV as "the fullness of time," arguably invokes a redemptive-historical metaphor that is potentially at odds with the "two age" scheme of 1:4 and 6:15. Martyn and de Boer are aware of this tension in their own discussions of the verse. Martyn, for example, asks whether the phrase τὸ πλήρωμα τοῦ χρόνου indicates "a point that lies at the end of a line" and whether "after rejecting the Teachers' view of redemptive history . . . Paul finally embraces in 4.4 his own way of affirming that view."[57] Martyn

---

55. Martyn, *Galatians*, 565. A questionable dichotomy is invoked here: there are other options besides "repair" and "replacement" as creation's "renewal" in 4 Ezra 7:75 suggests and the bodily resurrection of Jesus demonstrates. A useful study of apocalyptic, the "two ages" and resurrection is D. M. Moffitt, *Atonement and the Logic of Resurrection in the Epistle to the Hebrews*, NovTSup 141 (Leiden: Brill, 2011), esp. 96–104, on 4 Ezra. This is not the only false dichotomy involved in Martyn's approach (see below).

56. Martyn, *Galatians*, 388; cf. 406–8.

57. Ibid., 389.

emphatically rejects this option, concluding that "throughout this passage, Paul does not think of a gradual maturation, but rather of a punctiliar liberation, enacted by God in his own sovereign time."[58] This is an interpretation reflected clearly in his rendering of τὸ πλήρωμα τοῦ χρόνου as "at a time selected by [God]."[59] Thus, Martyn employs a dichotomy, central to his approach to apocalyptic, between a "gradual maturation" and a "punctiliar liberation." It is questionable, however, whether the notion of a "gradual maturation" is something that accurately describes salvation history, and whether these extremes are really the only two options.

For de Boer, 4:4 is also "the central theological announcement of the letter."[60] He offers a similar discussion, rejecting any smooth redemptive-historical readings of τὸ πλήρωμα τοῦ χρόνου, arguing that

> it would be wrong, however, to conclude that God's action is somehow dependent on time, on the course of human history. That approach would lead to a futile endeavor to study the history of the Greco-Roman period, or of Israel, around the time of Jesus in order to establish the marks of that fullness.[61]

His conclusion is that τὸ πλήρωμα τοῦ χρόνου "signifies a clean break with the past and may be regarded as an apocalyptic assertion on Paul's part: it announces the end of 'the present evil age' (1:4) and the beginning of the 'new creation' (6:15)."[62]

The same problematic dichotomy which drives Martyn's critique of salvation history can be seen here. For de Boer, the two-ages scheme is the controlling eschatological metaphor to the exclusion of any redemptive-historical themes. It is significant that it is precisely here that de Boer makes his comment, noted earlier, that the "periodization of history in certain strands of Jewish and Christian apocalyptic eschatology" is "an optional feature."[63] The above discussion of *4 Ezra*

58. Ibid.
59. Ibid., 388.
60. de Boer, *Galatians*, 261.
61. Ibid.
62. Ibid., 262.
63. Ibid., 261n389.

has attempted to demonstrate that this stance is problematic, and that, while the two ages motif is important, it is a theme woven together with other eschatological themes, among them a focus on redemptive history. There is no need to dismiss this as an "optional feature" or to treat it as alien to Pauline apocalyptic. Rather, Paul's use of τὸ πλήρωμα τοῦ χρόνου "bespeaks a conviction about God's control of history that is at home in Jewish and early Christian apocalyptic thought."[64] There is thus no reason to avoid, on the basis of Paul's apocalyptic theology, the redemptive-historical translation of the phrase as "the fullness of time." Indeed, there is every reason why we should expect an "apocalyptic Paul" to weave the two eschatological themes together.

The way in which the two ages doctrine is employed by de Boer to exclude redemptive history, resulting in the interpretation of τὸ πλήρωμα τοῦ χρόνου as "a clean break with the past," thus appears rather more like an exercise in *Sachkritik* than an interpretation informed by the complex eschatological patterns of the apocalyptic literature. Martyn's approach is more nuanced, since he rightly rules out such a "clean break" interpretation, observing that "the picture . . . is not so simple."[65] But his solution, employing the motif of "invasion" and interpreting τὸ πλήρωμα τοῦ χρόνου as "a time selected by God" has much the same result. For both de Boer and Martyn, Paul's use of that phrase is a problem to be solved, and their solutions demonstrate that a dualistic two-ages scheme is being employed as an apocalyptic *sine qua non* over against any redemptive-historical framework, caricatured as "gradual maturation."

What our earlier analysis of *4 Ezra* suggests, however, is that there is, in these interpretations, a false antithesis between the "punctiliar" and the "linear," between the two ages and redemptive history, that does not do justice to the way in which the multiple eschatological metaphors interrelate in the apocalypses. As Wright has argued concerning Galatians 4:4, "we cannot, then, invoke something called 'apocalyptic' to rule out the idea of a continuous flow of history,

64. Williams, *Galatians*, 111.
65. Martyn, *Galatians*, 99.

looking back to Abraham and trusting in the promises God made to him, and eventually reaching a point of 'fullness.' . . . The radical newness of this moment does not constitute a denial of all that has gone before."[66] Martyn's approach to Galatians 4:4 constitutes an interpretation which "unravel[s] the controlling metaphor of the chapter."[67] There is a real danger here of taking the two-ages scheme, absolutizing it and applying it to Paul univocally, and thus failing to account for the complex but coherent character of the apostle's use of multiple eschatological metaphors.

The Two Ages and Salvation History in Paul's Apocalyptic Imagination

Thirty years ago, Richard Hays issued a warning against one-dimensional approaches to Paul's language in Galatians:

> Perhaps Paul's language is less univocal and more "poetic" than the Western theological tradition has usually supposed. In the quest for clarity and accuracy, NT exegetes have tended to strive for *the* single right interpretation of Paul's theological expressions. . . . I am not proposing that NT exegesis should abandon the quest for *clarity* in interpreting Paul. I am advocating only that the presupposition of *univocity* be discarded. The texts and symbols which grasp and move us most profoundly are almost always polyvalent.[68]

To be sure, it is not always clear how the apocalypses hold together themes which modern minds find incompatible—this requires careful attention to the complex metaphorical logic.[69] Hays has more recently repeated his call for this sort of attention to poetics, and now particularly, in evaluating the nature of Paul's apocalyptic imagination:

> to understand "apocalyptic" in Paul, we must attend to the gospel's imaginative remaking of the world. To interpret the apocalyptic rhetoric

---

66. Wright, *PFG*, 877.
67. Ibid., 876n286. Cf. Martyn, *Galatians*, 389.
68. Richard B. Hays, *The Faith of Jesus Christ: The Narrative Substructure of Galatians 3:1–4:11*, 2nd ed. (Grand Rapids: Eerdmans, 2002), 227–28.
69. Here, the important work of George Lakoff and Mark Johnson is instructive (see *Metaphors We Live By* [Chicago: University of Chicago Press, 1981], esp. chapter 17 (pp. 97–105) on "Complex Coherences Across Metaphors").

and theology of Galatians we must reflect on the poetics of the letter, the way in which Paul deploys language and imagery to reshape the symbolic world in which his readers live and move.[70]

In Galatians, the complex, polyvalent, but coherent interweaving of the eschatological themes of two ages (1:4) and redemptive history (4:4) is just such a poetic endeavor, and one which is attested, *mutatis mutandis*, elsewhere in the apocalyptic literature, as the present discussion of *4 Ezra* has exemplified. Evaluating Paul as a thinker in the apocalyptic mode should not be oversimplified into the presence of one feature, such as the two ages, but requires attention to this complex eschatology. In Galatians, Paul asks the apocalyptic question "what time is it?"[71] and answers in the apocalyptic mode. But in exploring his answer, we must resist a false dichotomy between the "linear" and the "punctiliar," between the *equally apocalyptic* eschatological doctrines of the two ages and salvation history.

---

70. Hays, "Apocalyptic Poiesis in Galatians," 205.
71. Cf. Martyn, *Galatians*, 104; and also N. T. Wright, *Jesus and the Victory of God* (London: SPCK, 1996), 467–72; Wright, *PFG*, 550–62.

Index of Names

Index of Ancient Writings